FLORA OF CHESHIRE

FLORA OF CHESHIRE

by

Alan Newton, M.A.(Oxon.)

Edited by James Cullen, B.Sc., Ph.D.

CHESHIRE COMMUNITY COUNCIL
Publications Trust Limited
CHESTER

Made and printed in England by

Dean & Co. (Stpt) Ltd., Cheadle Heath, Stockport, SK3 0PR

To my wife

PREFACE

Though many eminent botanists, both amateur and professional, have collected in Cheshire, only one Flora, that of Lord de Tabley, has previously been published. The date on the title page is 1899, but it is a posthumous work, and most of the observations on which it was based are a hundred years old. Thus the time is ripe for this new Flora which Mr. Newton has provided.

All the records in the Flora have been made during the period 1964 to 1969, and the older data are not given, except in special circumstances. What we have now is the flora as we see it today, recorded carefully and accurately, largely by Mr. Newton himself but also by a number of enthusiastic helpers, who have given willingly of their time and labour to make the records as complete as possible. The habitat data, as well as the localities, are given and this is most valuable. It is sad to know that some of the interesting species of former times, such as the wintergreens (*Pyrola* spp.) are now extinct; but it is encouraging to see that decorative invaders from abroad, such as the Indian balsam, *Impatiens glandulifera*, which is not even mentioned in de Tabley's Flora, are now well established.

Two features of the Flora are of special interest to me. The first is the treatment of the genus *Rubus* (the blackberries) on which Mr. Newton, with the help of Mr. Edees, has spent much time. This continues the valuable tradition of the previous Flora, in which the Rubi were also thoroughly treated, and it is interesting to compare the accounts. The second is the production of the maps of geographical distribution within the county. These, together with the comments which Mr. Newton has made on them, are of the greatest value. Although Perring & Walters' Atlas gives maps for all British flowering plants, there is still a need for mapping on a finer scale, to show how plant distribution is affected by local factors of climate and soil. Information of this kind about species also gives information about habitats; and this makes it much easier for those who are concerned with nature conservation to compare and evaluate habitats, and thus to make a case for conservation and a plan for management.

I commend this Flora not only to local naturalists but to all those in the British Isles who are interested in plants.

D. H. Valentine,
Manchester, 26th August, 1970

5

LIST OF ABBREVIATIONS

agg.	aggregate species.
B.E.C. Rep.	Botanical Exchange Club – Reports.
BM	British Museum (herbarium).
BSBI	Botanical Society of the British Isles.
CGE	Cambridge University (herbarium).
coll.	collected by.
conf.	confirmed by.
Critical Atlas	Perring, F. H. & Sell, P.D., *Critical Supplement to the Atlas of the British Flora* (1968).
De Tabley	Warren, J. L. (Lord de Tabley), *Flora of Cheshire* (1899).
det.	determined by.
Hb.	Herbarium.
J. Bot.	Journal of Botany (London).
J. Ecol.	Journal of Ecology.
L. & C. Nat.	Lancashire and Cheshire Naturalist.
L.B.S.	Liverpool Botanical Society.
Lancs. Nat.	Lancashire Naturalist.
L.N.F.C. Proc.	Liverpool Naturalists' Field Club Proceedings.
Merseyside Nats. Assoc.	Merseyside Naturalists' Association.
MS. Flora	Owen, G., *MS. Flora of Mid-Cheshire*.
Mus.	Museum.
N.W. Nat.	North Western Naturalist.
p.p.	*pro parte* (in part).
Proc. Manch. Lit & Phil. Soc.	Proceedings of the Manchester Literary & Philosophical Society.
s.l.	*sensu lato* (in the broad sense).
spec.	specimen.
s.s.	*sensu stricto* (in the strict sense).

6

ACKNOWLEDGMENTS

Without the devoted support of many Cheshire botanists in making field records of species observed over the survey period and supplying freely the information obtained, it would have been quite impossible to prepare this account over the time scale involved. My sincere thanks for their sustained efforts and invaluable assistance in bringing the project to fruition are extended to all who contributed and particularly to those who undertook to survey specific areas and submitted field records over a prolonged period.

A tremendous amount of indoor work such as typing, map drawing, and other assistance with the preparation of the manuscript has been most generously afforded by P. Newton, Mrs. G. Mackie, Miss K. Simpson, Mrs. C. Ashburn to whose efforts the production itself must be the tribute.

A number of specimens in critical groups were submitted to taxonomic experts for confirmation or determination; their advice and comments are gratefully acknowledged and due mention of their conclusions is made under the relevant species.

Other individuals and organisations who have helped in innumerable ways include the many Cheshire landowners who allowed access to their land, the Leverhulme Trust who made a grant towards field work, the Nature Conservancy and its officers in the Midlands area and at Monk's Wood, John Rylands library, the Department of Botany at Manchester University, and Mr. A. G. Hodgkiss, who drew the map on p.229.

List of Principal Contributors

K. G. Allenby, Haslington, nr. Crewe
Mrs. A. Blacklay, Nantwich
T. Edmondson, Chester and Helsby
A. Gibson, Cheadle Hulme
Miss V. Gordon, Liverpool
Mrs. E. Hall, Greasby
J. G. & Mrs. N. Kelcey,
    Northwich and Partington

Mrs. N. F. McMillan, Bromborough
Mrs. G. Mackie, Cheadle Heath
G. Meredith, Audlem
P. Newton, Timperley
Miss K. Simpson, Wilmslow
Dr. F. Tyrer, Rochdale
Dr. R. E. Thomas, Northwich

The Directors of the Cheshire Community Council Publications Trust Ltd., acknowledge, with gratitude, the very generous financial assistance received from:

The Cheshire County Council and its Countryside Committee.
The Royal Society.
Mr. A. Bowker.
Mr. & Mrs. Desmond Parish,
The North of England Zoological Society.
The John Spedan Lewis Trust.
The Educational Foundation of Dr. Robert Oldfield,
without whose support this publication would not have proved possible.

CONTENTS

LIST OF ILLUSTRATIONS

Plates 5–12 are in colour; 1–4 and 13–16 are in black and white; photographs are by the author unless otherwise noted.

10

INTRODUCTION

The object of this work is to present a snapshot picture of Cheshire vegetation as it was observed on the ground over the period 1964-9. To this end the county has been surveyed in detail on a 5 × 5 km. square basis (i.e ¼ of a National Grid 10 km. square). Each square within the political county as at 1964, including "Wythenshawe", viz. the portion of the Manchester C. B. lying south of the river Mersey, is treated as one recording unit, with the following exceptions:—

1. The whole of each of the following 10 km. squares lying within the county is treated as a single recording unit:—SJ 27, 38, 44, 74, 85.

2. Fragmentary portions of 5 × 5 km. squares lying within the county have in some cases been included with neighbouring units within the same 10 km. square:—

SJ	28NW	with	28SW	SJ	58NE	with	58SE
„	29SW	„	29SE	„	96NW	„	96SW
„	36SW	„	36SE	„	96NE	„	96SE
„	54NW	„	54SW	SE	00SW	„	00SE
„	54NE	„	54SE	SK	09NW	„	09NE & 09SW

3. The following very small outliers of 10 km. squares lying within the county boundary have not been mapped separately due to their insignificant areas; only where stated are species present which are not found in a neighbouring 5 km. unit:—

SD 90
SJ 18 (*Cerastium arvense, Limonium binervosum*)
„   35 (*Stratiotes aloides*)
„   39, 48, 63, 69, 89.
SK 06 (*Rubus chamaemorus*)
    07, 08, 19.

The total number of recording units thus amounts to 110.

The early history of the Cheshire Flora is fully documented in Lord de Tabley's excellent Flora which was published in 1899, though largely based on observations made up to 1875. It is felt that a link between the two accounts will be useful for an appreciation of the floristic changes which have taken place in the intervening years, and this is attempted in the chapter on "Gains and losses, 1875-1969". Wherever possible, the literature and herbaria have been searched for dates when species recorded by De Tabley but not observed during the survey were last recorded; these are included after each family in the species list and a bibliography of the more important published literature is appended: since about 1930, the period of greatest change due to increasing urbanisation and changed agricultural practices, the amount of published material is small and it is therefore difficult to account for some of the

11

disappearances; continuous observations of sensitive areas are totally lacking. It can only be said that despite intensive search, no trace of these species has been found.

Method of Survey

1. Territorial assessment.

BSBI cards were used in the first place to record observations made. At the end of each season these were transferred to a master card for each square which provided a basic check list on which to base a programme of visits for the following year. Repeated visits were made until the additions noted decreased to a minimal percentage of the total observations made. A map showing the number of species recorded for each unit, on which the distribution comment is based, is given on page 227.

2. Species assessment.

A map of each species was compiled showing date and recorder of the first record accepted for each 5 × 5 km. square. Frequency of each species was assessed by a count of records each year and lists were made of those for which more intensive search seemed likely to be productive. Most records of the scarcer species were verified *in situ*; specimens of critical groups where necessary were sent to referees for their comments. As a general rule recorders' names are given for the scarcer plants, and authorities are quoted for critical and unusual species.

3. Habitat assessment.

After preliminary observations had been made to determine the main ecological distinctions apparent on the ground, habitat lists were made out for completion on field visits. The information collected forms the basis for the chapters on "plant habitats" and the associated tables.

GEOLOGICAL AND PHYSICAL FEATURES AND
THEIR INFLUENCE ON PLANT DISTRIBUTION

The greater part of the county consists of a plain in which post-glacial deposits overlie Triassic rocks at varying depths. Protruding from this cover the fault scarps of Bunter pebble beds and Keuper waterstones (e.g. the ridge Runcorn-Helsby-Tarporley-Bickerton and Alderley Edge) provide well-marked physical features. In Wirral similar fault scarps provide low ridges between Bidston and Storeton and Grange to Burton. Extensive tracts of indigenous heathland still persist in these areas though encroachment from housing development in Wirral and reclamation for farming or commercial forestry elsewhere reduces the area annually.

The nature and texture of the post-glacial deposits in the plain have great influence on the floristic facies. Where sandy deposits prevail, as in the Rudheath, Delamere and Congleton areas the podsolised soils formerly gave rise to lightly wooded heathland similar to that visible on the Triassic sandstone outcrops. Unattractive to agricultural operators these districts have been extensively afforested and more recently are increasingly worked for sand and gravel. In general, the lowering of the water table due to underground pumping has resulted in the loss of the damp heath habitat which formerly provided *Lepidotis inundata, Pilularia globulifera, Hypericum elodes* and *Gentiana pneumonanthe,* and has led to a widespread invasion of Birch scrub.

The Boulder clay portions of the plain are farmed as improved grassland and provide few traces of an indigenous flora apart from vestiges in hedgerows and copses, and, in poorer drained spots, the commoner hygrophilous species. On the better drained areas in the north and mid-west of the county an increasing tendency towards mechanised arable farming is noticeable, resulting in a large acreage of botanical monotony.

The major rivers, Bollin, Dane, Weaver and their tributaries, have incised through glacial deposits and terraces into the underlying strata at numerous places exposing steep banks which being unsuitable for agriculture form a valuable reservoir of what must formerly have been a more extensive grassland scrubland and woodland flora. At the eastern and western limits of the plain, the Mottled Sandstone series is exposed which produces on weathering a loamy brown earth soil, whereas in the centre and south the two lower Keuper marls with their intercalated calcareous and saliferous beds provide a similar but more species rich habitat. An outlier of these rocks is exposed also along the Bollin between Wilmslow and Altrincham and was well-known as a locality for notable plants to the 19th century botanists. Deposits of the highest Keuper marls and lower Lias are poorly exposed in the extreme south near Audlem and have few distinctive species. The flushed grassland, marsh, scrub and woodland communities to be found along these valley slopes provide some of the most rewarding botanising in the county and are the source of many of the records of the scarcer plants in the plain.

Where particularly along the southern and eastern fringes of the plain the Glacial Drift cover is hummocky morraine, several characteristic patches of sandy grassland still survive. Where the water table is locally high, meres such as Rostherne, Oakmere, Redesmere, and a group of small meres in the south-west of the county remain in the hollows. Typically these shelve steeply and are narrowly fringed with reedswamp and alder carr. Other shallower waters are now silting up and exhibit fen characteristics where the inflow water is moderately base rich (e.g. Bagmere, Hatchmere). A third range of aquatic habitats consists of sphagnum filled hollows (e.g. Flaxmere, Abbott's Moss, Wybunbury Moss). The number of these small mosslands was formerly large but most have been drained and converted into agricultural land, now only distinguishable by "moss" names and black peaty soil when ploughed; others on drying out have been colonised by birch, alder and sallows and allowed to remain in this state as game coverts. Remnants of a group of more extensive raised bogs, mostly sited on post-glacial terraces (e.g. Carrington, Lindow and Danes Mosses) are still visible though in a degenerate condition due to drainage and peat cutting. These mosses presented the 19th century botanists with the sight of such species as *Osmunda regalis, Drosera anglica, Rhynchospora alba, Carex limosa, Narthecium ossifragum* in such profusion that individual localities were sometimes not enumerated; these species are almost if not entirely extinct in these places to-day.

The portion of the county lying east of the Red Rock fault (roughly following a line from Hyde-Macclesfield-Congleton-Alsager) consists largely of Carboniferous age grits and shales exposed at surface. This much faulted area is deeply cut by the headwaters of Goyt, Etherow, Tame and Dane giving rise to grassland on the better drained shale slopes, moorland and degenerate oak woodland on the rocky gritstone hillsides, and mixed oak woodland on damper sheer ravines cut into friable shales. In places the floristic appearance of the grassland has also been radically changed by drainage, reseeding and application of fertiliser but in general is used as rough grazing or hay meadow and reveals least interference of any habitat in the county over the past century.

The gritstone plateaux of the Longdendale and Staffordshire frontier moors consist largely of closed communities of ericaceous species or cotton grass (*Eriophorum vaginatum*) based on inactive peat. Rarely flushes occur on the moorland slopes which retain rare species such as *Myosotis repens, Scutellaria minor, Wahlenbergia hederacea* and *Carex laevigata*.

The area to the west of the Delamere ridge contains important if greatly altered alluvial flats with brackish marshes at the mouths of the Weaver and Gowy merging along the Mersey littoral to form Frodsham marshes. This district together with a part of the Dee marshes below Burton has been embanked and ditched and while almost all the wet meadow communities have disappeared, an interesting aquatic flora survives in some ditches due to the admixture of saline seepage: gradually, however, the petrochemical complex based on Ellesmere Port spreads eastwards along the Manchester Ship Canal and future survival is doubtful. Outside the Dee and Ship Canal embankments large tracts of salt marsh are present, particularly between Parkgate and West Kirby much of which is dominated by Cord grass

14

(*Spartina anglica*) and the native salt marsh plants are confined largely to a narrow strip along the shore.

An extensive area of consolidated sand dunes now mostly converted into golf courses survives along the Irish Sea frontage between Hoylake and Wallasey, and smaller fragments near Gayton still support characteristic species such as *Thymus drucei, Geranium sanguineum, Trifolium striatum* which are not now to be found elsewhere in the county. The golf courses provide a refuge for plants such as *Arabis hirsuta, Saxifraga tridactylites*, and *Thalictrum minus*. The formerly extensive areas of damp slack have suffered severely from encroachment for allotments, house building and refuse disposal and this important habitat has all but disappeared completely. With the almost total exclusion of fresh supplies of blown sand due to the building of sea walls, the species typical of unstable dunes are much diminished, formerly common plants such as *Salsola kali, Cynoglossum officinale, Vulpia membrancea* being apparently extinct. Curiously however *Rhynchosinapis monensis* still flourishes in quantity exactly where De Tabley described it though admittedly this plant appears to prefer the zone immediately behind mobile dune.

The practice of "marl spreading" was prevalent in the 18th and 19th centuries throughout those parts of Cheshire where deposits of Keuper marl, Boulder clay derived from this series, or the mildly calcareous drift of the Dee valley and south Wirral were at or near the surface: by this process thousands of ponds were created. Examination of the Ordnance Survey maps shows large tracts of the county, particularly south Wirral, the area south of Northwich-Knutsford, and that between Nantwich and Audlem to be honeycombed with these pits, which a century ago were relatively fresh and in process of colonisation by a rich variety of species as witnessed by Lord de Tabley and his contemporaries. With changes in agricultural practice whereby artificial fertilisers have replaced "marl spreading" and an increasing emphasis on mechanisation these pits have become an embarrassment to many farmers. Quite apart from the natural tendency to silt up and become shaded by sallows, alder and other trees, large numbers have been filled in by spoil from earth-moving operations (such sites are eagerly sought by motorway constructors and housing developers) and many others have been partially drained at least, or by connection to field drains have become repositories for highly saturated run-off. Even a comparison with recent studies (viz: J. P. Savidge in L.N.F.C. Proceedings approx. 15 years ago) shows a decreasing variety in pond flora, a process which is bound to accelerate as increasing pressure to fill in or drain mounts. The number of pits where sufficient aeration is available from circulation of uncontaminated water and which still provide open habitats for mixed communities of aquatic and marsh plants diminishes annually. It is only the difficulties of remote access or chance inhibition of factors conducive to more intensive land use which enable patches of rich and varied flora to survive.

GAINS AND LOSSES, 1875-1969

As might be expected, the species which show least change in status over the century are those characteristic of habitats which for a variety of reasons have suffered least interference. These include woodland, grassland, scrub and marsh. While the total area of each may perhaps be less, while e.g. grassland of "native" character may represent relatively a fraction of its former extent confined to slopes unsuitable for the plough, and some former marshes affected by drainage silting or overgrowth, sufficient remains to enable the main constituent communities to be described as widespread.

There is strong evidence that woodland species were severely under-recorded in de Tabley's Flora since the following are now found to be much commoner than is there suggested:—

Adoxa moschatellina	Galium odoratum
Agropyron caninum	Holcus mollis
Allium ursinum	Lamiastrum galeobdolon
Arum maculatum	Milium effusum
Carex pendula	Myosotis sylvatica
Dipsacus pilosus	Phyllitis scolopendrium
Equisetum sylvaticum	Veronica montana
Equisetum telmateia	

The amount of woodland in the county has not increased and the explanation lies on Flora p.330 "the woods are so rigorously preserved that many sylvestral plants escape notice." Thanks to more liberal contemporary attitudes, it has been possible to redress the balance. We can reasonably assume from the evidence that woodland species exhibit a distribution pattern very similar to that of a century ago, and that a certain stability is evident.

Analysis of the species which have apparently become extinct shows a close correspondence between communities which even then were local and rare and sensitive habitats where change in environment has rendered the terrain inhospitable, or where it has been severely mutilated if not totally destroyed. These include (1) plants of mobile sand and shingle, e.g. *Calystegia soldanella, Salsola kali, Cynoglossum officinale*—affected by embankment and therefore cut-off of wind blown sand; (2) plants of coastal grassland and slacks e.g. *Gentianella campestris, Lithospermum officinale, Spiranthes spiralis, Selaginella selaginoides*—affected by drainage and interference; (3) plants of open sandy heathland e.g. *Filago vulgaris, F. minima, Hypochoeris glabra, Moenchia erecta, Radiola linoides*—affected by afforestation, reclamation and overgrowth, perhaps at least partly attributable to the demise of rabbits which formerly assisted in the maintenance of open ground; (4) plants of wet heathland e.g. *Genista anglica, Hypericum elodes, Lepidotis inundata, Mentha pulegium, Pilularia globulifera*—affected by lowering of the ground water table as a result of pumping or drainage, and reclamation; (5) plants of bogs and bog margins e.g. *Carex lasiocarpa, Drosera anglica, Dryopteris*

16

cristata, Hammarbya paludosa, Rhynchospora alba, Schoenus nigricans, Scheuchzeria palustris—affected by the same considerations as the last group. There are two further categories of species where the factors affecting disappearance appear to apply regionally or even nationally; in the first case, arable weeds, e.g. *Agrostemma githago, Descurainia sophia, Ranunculus arvensis, Scandix pecten-veneris,* improved screening methods and perhaps increasing use of artificial fertilisers are responsible. Even a century ago, the annual decrease of *Agrostemma* was remarked upon, and there is little doubt of the casual status of some of this group even then, e.g. *Acinos arvensis, Cuscuta spp., Galeopsis angustifolium, Misopates orontium* etc.

The final group of species now apparently extinct includes those which reference to the Atlas of the British Flora shows to be in eclipse—though the pattern of diminution varies; *Orobanche rapum-genistae* and *Coeloglossum viride* exhibiting overall decline, others such as *Carex dioica, Pseudorchis albida, Listera cordata,* certain *Lycopodium spp., Thelypteris phegopteris, Gymnocarpium dryopteris* a northerly retreat.

Consideration of apparently extinct species should not be allowed to disguise a reduction in the numbers of precariously placed species. Most of these, now of very rare occurrence, linger in isolated spots where continued existence depends on the survival of a relict micro-habitat. There is a lengthy list of these:—

Arabis hirsuta
*Carex diandra
*C. elongata
*C. hostiana
C. limosa
C. serotina
Cerastium arvense
*Cirsium dissectum
*C. heterophyllum
Circaea intermedia
Drosera intermedia
Eleocharis multicaulis
E. quinqueflora
Gentiana pneumonanthe
*Gentianella amarella

Gnaphalium sylvaticum
*Myriophyllum verticillatum
Orchis morio
*Paris quadrifolia
*Parnassia palustris
*Pedicularis palustris
*Pinguicula vulgaris
*Scutellaria minor
*Serratula tinctoria
Sparganium minimum
Teesdalia nudicaulis
Trifolium striatum
*Wahlenbergia hederacea
Utricularia minor

More important if less spectacular are those species which, formerly abundant or widespread, are now much less frequent, e.g.

Andromeda polifolia
Baldellia ranunculoides
Botrychium lunaria
Carex vesicaria
Drosera rotundifolia
Leontodon taraxacoides
Odontites verna
Orchis mascula

Platanthera chlorantha
Potamogeton alpinus
P. polygonifolius
Senecio erucifolius
Silaum silaus
Sison amomum
Narthecium ossifragum

17

and those which form the general matrix of communities which have been under pressure:

Agrostis canina	Molinia caerulea
Erica cinerea	Myrica gale
E. tetralix	Scirpus caespitosus
Festuca ovina	Sieglingia decumbens

Doubtless during the next century some of the very rare species will disappear completely, while the distribution spectrum of the other two groups will shrink until their maps take on a "relict" appearance.

In view of this melancholy saga it is perhaps heartening to notice a group of species which, rare and local a century ago, inhabit more or less the same localities to-day without apparent increase or decrease. This can only be explained on the basis that they favour a particular ecological niche which survives unscathed:

Artemisia maritima	Limonium binervosum
Asplenium marinum	Onopordum acanthium
Geranium sanguineum	Picris echioides
Hippuris vulgaris	Rhynchosinapis monensis
Hypericum hirsutum	Rubus chamaemorus
Lathyrus sylvestris	Thalictrum minus

Similar remarks apply to the commoner but still sporadically occurring arable weeds *Cichorium intybus, Papaver rhoeas* and *Thlaspi arvense.*

It is worth noting that many of the "very rare and local" species have been discovered in "new" localities (those marked with *). In most cases they must have been present a century ago but went undetected or unrecorded by De Tabley and his contributors—the only new county record however for an indigenous species in a stable habitat is *Cirsium dissectum* (ignoring critical groups).

Turning to the credit side of the account, it is interesting to note the colonisation by certain rare and local species of habitats which have been formed during the century as the result of human activity. Major instances are *Alopecurus aequalis* and *Eleocharis acicularis* at Langley reservoirs near Macclesfield, *Carex vesicaria, Limosella aquatica* and *Myriophyllum alterniflorum* at Bosley reservoirs, and the orchid species on the lime waste beds of central Cheshire. *Lycopodium clavatum* in a damp sandpit near Congleton is a further example. The provenance of the colonising stocks poses some interesting speculations—were the strand-loving plants brought by water fowl from the Cheshire localities Oakmere and Mere Mere before they became extinct there? Was the *Anacamptis pyramidalis* at Northwich derived from an isolated colony in Wirral, or was seed blown from Anglesey or the Lancashire dunes? Without answers to questions such as these, it makes little sense to assign "status" labels to species which in default of clear evidence can be no more than assumptions.

18

As far as additions to the flora are concerned, some of these originated with ballast and a few have become locally established in Wirral, but not on the scale envisaged by the writers of a century ago. These include *Melilotus alba, Coronopus didymus* and *Conyza canadensis, Sisymbrium orientale* and *Diplotaxis muralis*. Much more widespread are species of garden origin, notably *Polygonum cuspidatum, Impatiens glandulifera, Symphoricarpos rivularis, Aster novi-belgii, Solidago altissima*, all inhabitants of railway embankments, river banks and roadsides and *Rhododendron ponticum* which spreads rapidly from original plantings in woodland on sandy and peaty soils. More locally *Veronica filiformis, Arenaria balearica* and *Lysimachia punctata* are established, while *Cymbalaria muralis* has greatly increased on shady walls. Another fifty or so species of garden origin are sporadically naturalised.

Armoracia rusticana and *Symphytum officinale* agg. have spread extensively to roadsides from cottage gardens, and *Tanacetum parthenium* to a lesser degree; *Tragopogon pratense* (subsp. *minor*) inhabits similar terrain but with more obscure origins. *Trifolium hybridum* and *Lolium multiflorum* have spilled over from agricultural leys to open roadsides, field margins and temporarily waste places.

Railway ballast is favoured particularly by *Chaenorrhinum minus* and *Senecio viscosus* and abandoned track beds provide suitable ground for the inland spread of such species as *Cerastium diffusum, Cochlearia danica* and others such as *Aira caryophyllea* and *Sagina apetala* which require dry, open ground to thrive. Increasing industrialisation and the associated open waste habitats—sandpits, quarry heaps, cinder and spoil banks have encouraged *Reseda lutea, R. luteola, Linaria repens, Hieracium* and *Oenothera spp., Senecio squalidus, Rubus dumetorum* agg., *Festuca arundinacea* and *Hordeum murinum. Geranium pyrenaicum*, while well established in parts of S.W. Wirral has not lived up to the expectations of a century ago, and *Cardaria draba*, while maintaining a presence, is not the aggressive colonist it is in parts of southern England; *Erysimum cheiranthoides* and *Mercurialis annua* are still rare casuals, now as then.

Some aquatics have undoubtedly expanded their range due to the obsolescence of canals as transport routes when they were regularly cleared of encroaching vegetation: *Sagittaria sagittifolia, Potamogeton perfoliatus* and *P. pectinatus* are much more widespread, while *Luronium natans*, first recorded in the Macclesfield Canal in 1916 is now found throughout its length in the county. Increases are noticeable in *Acorus calamus, Bidens cernua, Callitriche hermaphroditica, Ceratophyllum demersum, Glyceria maxima, Mimulus guttatus, Myosotis caespitosa* and *M. palustris*, and *Scutellaria galericulata* as well as other marsh loving species which were already common. *Butomus umbellatus* has also found them congenial, although reduced in its other habitats. Of the more exotic plants, *Angelica archangelica* forms a conspicuous fringe along parts of the Manchester Ship Canal and *Heracleum mantegazzianum* along the lower Bollin, while *Impatiens capensis* is well entrenched in an old loop of the Mersey.

The most striking invaders however are the two species *Epilobium angustifolium* and *Matricaria matricarioides*, both of which are currently present in all 110 recording areas; the spread of the first dates from about the first World War, the second was first recorded by Wheldon at Birkenhead in 1900 and by Druce in 1905—significantly not far from Crewe station. Species now establishing a bridgehead are *Galinsoga ciliata* and particularly the rayed forms of *Senecio vulgaris*, first noticed at Northwich in 1910, which are now spreading in urbanised parts of the county.

Not quite so obviously expansive but impressive from their infiltration into indigenous communities are *Juncus tenuis* (1st record 1912), *Claytonia sibirica* and *Calystegia silvatica. C. pulchra* may be about to follow the rampant march of the last.

To summarise the situation—due to a deterioration in the number and variety of habitats, the more sensitive indigenous species have diminished or become extinct; some scarce species continue to exist against expectation in the very places in which they were recorded a century or more ago, others are present in small quantity in areas from which they have not previously been recorded, and a further group has been saved from extinction, or has become established from outside the county, at sites which unwitting human activity has provided. As far as gains are concerned, many of the species for which an expanding future was forecast have disappointed expectation but others, following widespread changes to the character of the land surface, have filled the vacuum, and in the most successful instances compete with the indigenous vegetation as if their antecedents were equally respectable.

THE BUCKLOW HUNDRED—THEN AND NOW

Lord de Tabley's "Flora of Cheshire", in which the Hundreds of the county were adopted as botanical divisions, contains short accounts of two, Bucklow and Wirral, which were not only the best known areas botanically in the county at that time, but have also suffered most change in the intervening period. There is little doubt that this is largely ascribable to their proximity to the conurbations of Manchester and Liverpool. Whereas in the remaining Hundreds, despite the revolution in agricultural practices due to mechanisation and drainage, the majority of the localities mentioned in the Flora are recognisable, in Bucklow and Wirral certain sites have either disappeared completely, or if still open ground are so changed in character as to create incredulity that the species recorded could ever have thrived as stated. In Wirral, even a century ago, the literature was already reflecting the growth of Birkenhead, as F. M. Webb often states "no longer to be found in these localities", or similar words, when reviewing records for some species, e.g., *Cerastium arvense* (Flora of Cheshire, p.47), in the older Floras. A century ago Hale Moss (p. lxvii) was "fast disappearing"; perusal of "Old botanising haunts of Birkenhead"—written by Miss A. Lee in 1917 (Lancs. & Ches. Nat., 11 p.214) reveals that nostalgia for lost delights is not the prerogative of the present day.

Bucklow is the Hundred which Lord de Tabley himself knew best, and it is instructive in forming a view of the extent of environmental change wrought during the last hundred years, to compare the situation he described with that of the present day.

1. "It is pasture country . . . In that portion . . . which lies north of the River Bollin . . . horticulture or market-gardening supplants the agriculture of the centre." The market-gardening district is now all but submerged under bricks and mortar, and while the south of the Hundred is still largely under pasture, the northern and westerly portions are predominantly arable.

2. "A strip of circling shore extends from Weston Point to Norbury Wood", While a small piece of salt marsh still remains in the political county of Cheshire, the construction of the Manchester Ship Canal has radically altered both the boundary of the county and the character of the marshy flats formerly fringing the River Mersey.

3. "The horticultural region has *Barbarea intermedia*." This is not now to be found in the district.

4. "The mosses of Bucklow are characterised notably by *Andromeda* and *Drosera anglica*; more locally by *Carex curta, elongata* and *limosa*." With the exception of *Carex curta* which survives in sphagnum-filled pits, all these species are extinct in the Hundred. Other species, e.g., *Osmunda regalis* and *Drosera rotundifolia,* not mentioned on account of their former frequency are also extinct.

21

5. The fields of root crops still support *Galeopsis speciosa* and *Fumaria muralis* subsp. *boraei*; cereal crops have a very limited weed flora, poppies are still a rarity; *Malva sylvestris* and *Hordeum murinum* occur but only as scarce roadside weeds. *Rubus ulmifolius* is virtually absent.

6. The following list of "pit-side" species met with in Bucklow is annotated with its current status:—

Oenanthe aquatica	— rare	Carex paniculata	— common
Oenanthe fistulosa	— absent	Cicuta virosa	— frequent
Potentilla palustris	— frequent	Ranunculus lingua	— very rare
Carex pseudocyperus	— common	Potamogeton alpinus	— rare
rostrata	— occasional	obtusifolius	— rare
vesicaria	— absent	Elodea canadensis	— frequent

7. The chief botanical stations in the Hundred were given as follows. Comment on current status is appended.

1875	1968
Seamans Moss Pits	— disappeared
Hale Moss	— disappeared
Baguley Moor	— disappeared
Carrington Moss	— drained and dry—now arable farmland or industrial development
Ashley Meadows	— ploughed up for nursery, now reverting to pasture
Woods near Castle Mill	— still of notable botanical interest
Cotterill Clough	— overshaded by mature canopy
Burleyhurst Wood	— overshaded by mature canopy
Mere Mere	— *Littorella uniflora* of the species mentioned is the only apparent survivor
Rostherne Mere	— *Carex elata* still persists, but *Cladium mariscus* appears to be extinct
Holford Mill Dam	— *Acorus calamus* still present
Holford Mill Wood	— now grown into mature carr; *Carex elongata* and *Carex rostrata* have not been found
Peover Brook	— the banks are now mostly dry and no longer skirted with *Geum rivale*
Pickmere Moss	— dense scrub of *Rubus fruticosus* agg.; *Paris quadrifolia* not found
Pickmere	— *Sagina nodosa* and *Parnassia palustris* no longer found
Knutsford Lower Moor	— now drained; *Carex limosa*, *Thelypteris palustris* and *Gymnadenia conopsea* extinct.

It is sad to note that of the sixteen locations given, only five (the woodlands and the meres) are still noteworthy, and that even at these places some of the outstanding plants have disappeared. While particularly noticeable in this Hundred, the same survival quality of woodland and meres is evident throughout the county; heathland, damp meadows and sandy areas are more easily converted to other uses, or their plant communities more susceptible to interference.

CHESHIRE PLANT HABITATS.
WOODLAND

1. Woodland on Keuper marl and marl-derived boulder clays

Forest dominated by *Quercus robur, Quercus petraea* or intermediates between the two doubtless originally covered the whole of the land surface of Cheshire except for small areas occupied by sphagnum bog, open water, salt marsh or dunes. Remnants of indigenous mixed oak forest are indeed very scarce in the County today, but there are many instances of sites which must have been more or less wooded throughout their post-glacial history. Although these may have been cleared and in some cases partly replanted several times, the ground flora and scrub flora have persisted. While woodland has been relatively little exploited commercially, and the practice of coppicing has never been widespread, it has been the policy of the large estates to retain and occasionally to create woodland as game coverts, shelter belts and ornamental amenities. The many examples on the flat leached soils of the Cheshire plain are of no great interest floristically. On the other hand, on the incised banks of the Weaver, Bollin and Dane valleys a large acreage of interesting "semi-natural" wood has survived, perhaps chiefly because of the difficulty of making any alternative use of the steep slopes—subject as they are to sporadic erosion, and too steep or too expensive to drain or cultivate for pasture or arable use. In each of these valleys there are lengthy reaches where the river has cut down into the pre-glacial surface; in places into the more friable siltstones and mudstones, and in the centre of the County particularly, into Keuper marls and their associated saliferous beds. The valley slopes are frequently very steep and the humus layer consequently shallow, enabling a rich ground flora to develop. By contrast, on the higher portions of the banks, where glacial drift or river terrace sands and gravels are present, the soils are leached and the humus frequently thick, giving rise to a less distinguished flora in which the major constituents are *Pteridium aquilinum, Holcus mollis* and *Endymion non-scriptus,* or *Rubus spp.*

Examination of the ground flora of mixed oakwood in Cheshire reveals a complex situation in which, however, two major associations can be distinguished, (1) with species-rich ground layer—on underlying Keuper marls, Carboniferous shales at lower levels in the Pennines, and the more calcareous drift clays, (2) with species-poor ground layer—on neutral or leached boulder clays, sandy drift soils, Triassic sandstones, and carboniferous grits up to approximately 1,200 feet. In fact,a whole series of gradations can be observed, ranging through (1) the heathy *Quercus petraea* remnants of Congleton Edge with *Vaccinium myrtillus, Deschampsia flexuosa, Galium saxatile* and *Melampyrum pratense,* (2) the fern-rich communities of the Upper Dane with *Luzula sylvatica* and *Thelypteris limbosperma,* (3) the intermediate shale woods of the lower slopes characterised by *Equisetum sylvaticum, Crepis paludosa* and *Prunus padus,* but containing also some of the species present in the plain, notably *Galium odoratum,* (4) the characteristic Keuper marl facies with *Campanula latifolia, Primula vulgaris* and *Lamiastrum galeobdolon,* to (5) the most herb-rich examples, usually on gypsiferous marls, with *Myosotis sylvatica*, *Orchis mascula* and *Vicia sylvatica*.

Woods with species-rich ground layer, perhaps the most typical Cheshire oakwood, certainly of the plain, have been surveyed to provide a profile of the predominant plant communities. The sample consists of thirty-two stands along the valleys of the Bollin, Weaver and Dee and their tributaries, and a constancy factor of 40 per cent has been adopted as a qualification for inclusion:—

	Constancy (No. of stands, Max. 32)
Upper Canopy	
Acer pseudoplatanus	17
Fraxinus excelsior	16
Prunus avium	14
Quercus robur	20
Ulmus glabra	18
Lower Canopy	
Corylus avellana	23
Crataegus monogyna	27
Ilex aquifolium	22
Lonicera periclymenum	23
Malus sylvestris subsp. sylvestris	13
Prunus spinosa	15
Rosa arvensis	22
Rosa canina agg.	13
Rubus fruticosus agg. (mostly R. vestitus)	27
Sambucus nigra	27
Viburnum opulus	13
Tall Herb Ground Layer	
Angelica sylvestris	14
Anthriscus sylvestris	24
Campanula latifolia	13
Deschampsia caespitosa	30
Digitalis purpurea	14
Dryopteris dilatata	26
Dryopteris filix-mas	24
Festuca gigantea	23
Galium aparine	26
Heracleum sphondylium	27
Milium effusum	13
Pteridium aquilinum	23

	Constancy (No. of stands, Max. 32)
Tall Herb Ground Layer—contd.	
Silene dioica	30
Stachys sylvatica	24
Urtica dioica	25
Lower Herb Ground Layer	
Adoxa moschatellina	25
Allium ursinum	26
Anemone nemorosa	29
Arum maculatum	26
Brachypodium sylvaticum	19
Cardamine flexuosa	21
Carex sylvatica	13
Chrysosplenium oppositifolium	27
Circaea lutetiana	20
Conopodium majus	24
Endymion non-scriptus	30
Galium odoratum	18
Geranium robertianum	30
Geum urbanum	24
Glechoma hederacea	22
Hedera helix	25
Lamiastrum galeobdolon	28
Luzula pilosa	18
Melica uniflora	20
Mercurialis perennis	29
Moehringia trinervia	15
Oxalis acetosella	29
Potentilla sterilis	14
Primula vulgaris	23
Ranunculus ficaria	29
Stellaria holostea	22
Veronica montana	28
Vicia sepium	13
Viola riviniana	21

In fact, these species should be regarded as representative in total of the mosaic of microhabitats present in these woodlands, which include variations from light to dense canopy, steep to shallow slope, humus-rich to mineral soils, well-drained to impeded drainage, low to high nutrient status. The striking feature is the homogeneity of the community taken as a whole, given the potentially wide range of topographical variation.

Associated species (1)

The following list of species were found in a significant proportion of the survey stands, but are equally (if not more) characteristic of other habitats:

	No. of Stands	Habitat Preferences
Agropyron caninum	11	Shaded river and stream banks
Ajuga reptans	8	Scrub and wood borders
Alnus glutinosa	8	Swampy woods, shaded river and stream banks
Arctium minus s.l.	11	Wood borders, disturbed ground
Athyrium filix-femina	11	Woods on sandstone and gritstone strata
Bromus ramosus	9	Wood borders, hedge banks
Caltha palustris	10	Marshes
Cardamine amara	10	Shaded alluvial flats
Carex pendula	4	Shaded spring lines on clay or shale
Carex remota	4	Shaded pools, canal banks
Equisetum telmateia	8	Damp shaded places in general
Filipendula ulmaria	11	Ditch and stream sides, mere fringes
Fragaria vesca	7	Scrub and wood borders
Lapsana communis	9	Wood borders, disturbed ground
Lysimachia nemorum	10	Damp flushes, marshes
Mycelis muralis	5	Walls, rock faces
Narcissus pseudo-narcissus	3	Open woods on light soils
Petasites hybridus	5	Alluvial flats, river banks
Phyllitis scolopendrium	7	Walls, rock faces
Ribes rubrum	10	Swampy woods
Ribes uva-crispa	6	Scrub and wood borders, stream banks
Rubus idaeus	9	Wood borders, open woods on peat or sand
Rumex sanguineus	7	Woods on light or neutral soils
Scrophularia nodosa	5	Shady stream banks, ditches
Sorbus aucuparia	7	Heathy woods, upland woods
Stellaria neglecta	10	Shady stream banks
Valeriana officinalis	6	Stream and river banks, ditches

Associated species (2)

The following species, rare in woods on marl and clay, are more frequently found in rocky woods on sandstone or gritstone:—

	No. of Stands		No. of Stands
Blechnum spicant	2	Stellaria nemorum	1
Dryopteris pseudo-mas	1	Teucrium scorodonia	2
Luzula sylvatica	2		

Associated species (3)

The following species, where occurring in "natural" situations, are confined in the county to woods on the more calcareous (often gypsiferous) strata, either in Triassic or Carboniferous rocks:—

	No. of Stands		No. of Stands
Acer campestre	4	Paris quadrifolia	1
Campanula trachelium	1	Polystichum aculeatum	7
Carex strigosa	2	Polystichum setiferum	7
Chrysosplenium alternifolium	4	Ranunculus auricomus	10
Euonymus europaeus	1	Sanicula europaea	8
Hordelymus europaeus	1	Sorbus torminalis	1
Lathraea squamaria	2	Swida sanguinea	1
Myosotis sylvatica	10	Vicia sylvatica	4
Orchis mascula	7	Viola reichenbachiana	9

Although not present in the stands surveyed, *Dipsacus pilosus* and *Lathyrus sylvestris* could be included in this group.

Many of these species exhibit a markedly disjunct, or local pattern of distribution in the county, a phenomenon for which, in some cases, it is difficult to find convincing explanations. *Ranunculus auricomus*, for instance, is present over a wide area in the south of the county, not only in woods but in scrub, hedgebanks and open roadsides; *Vicia sylvatica* seems to be associated particularly with adjacent saliferous beds (in the area of maximum development of this series, it persists in quantity on open banks); *Paris quadrifolia* is confined to very old, undisturbed fragments of wood; *Chrysosplenium alternifolium* and *Lathraea squamaria* are restricted to particular areas where they flourish, but are absent from large tracts of apparently suitable ground elsewhere, while *Hordelymus europaeus* is found in two places close to gypsiferous bands in company with *Polystichum aculeatum* and *Carex strigosa* in one instance, with *Polystichum setiferum* and *Carex strigosa* in the other, while in a third it grows in an old, bouldery, very wet wood with *Festuca altissima* and (formerly) with *Thelypteris phegopteris* on Carboniferous shale. On the other hand, *Myosotis sylvatica*, *Sanicula europaea* and *Viola reichenbachiana* seem to stretch throughout their potential range. It seems that we are now presented with several species which are at the limit of their range on the more base-rich soils, and that the existence of suitable stable habitats of this type determines their incidence.

27

2. Woods of the Lower Pennine Slopes on Carboniferous Shales or Boulder Clay

On the higher reaches of the Rivers Etherow, Goyt and Dane there are a limited number of examples of oakwood with species-rich ground layer where the floristic structure shows considerable affinity with the Keuper marl and woods of the plain, but also reveal a subtle transition to the type of upland woods on acid rocks. Seven of these examples were surveyed and the results are discussed below:—

Upper Canopy
Quercus petraea-robur intermediates are more frequent and *Quercus petraea s.s.* is present in two stands.

Lower Canopy
Sorbus aucuparia is present in all stands, and *Salix caprea* occurs in two. *Prunus padus* is present in three stands. *Corylus avellana* is less prominent, but *Betula spp.* are present throughout.

Tall Herb Layer
Anthriscus sylvestris is rare or absent, but *Dryopteris pseudo-mas*, *Myrrhis odorata* and *Luzula sylvatica* each occur in two stands.

Ground Layer
Allium ursinum, *Arum maculatum*, *Glechoma hederacea* and *Primula vulgaris* are rare or absent, but are replaced by *Equisetum sylvaticum* (6) *Hieracium vagum* (2) and *Crepis paludosa* (2). *Deschampsia flexuosa* and *Anthoxanthum odoratum* are also present. *Lysimachia nemorum* occurs in four stands.

Associated Species (3)
Only *Chrysosplenium alternifolium*, *Lathraea squamaria*, *Sanicula europaea* and (in one place) *Hordelymus europaeus* are present in this group of woods.

3. Wood on Outcrops of Triassic Sandstone or Carboniferous Grits

Woodlands of this type, with species-poor ground layer, have not been surveyed extensively, and are in any case, though widespread, much more fragmentary than the previous category. As a contrast, however, a list of species from a relict oakwood on gritstone rocks at about 1,250 ft. in the Crowden valley may be taken as typical:—

Upper Canopy	Quercus petraea.
Lower Canopy	Betula pubescens, Ilex aquifolium, Sorbus aucuparia.
Tall Herbs	Dryopteris dilatata, Dryopteris pseudo mas, Pteridium aquilinum, Thelypteris limbosperma, Hieracium vagum, Digitalis purpurea, Luzula sylvatica, Lonicera periclymenum.
Ground Layer	Deschampsia flexuosa, Vaccinium myrtillus, Calluna vulgaris, Empetrum nigrum, Molinia caerulea, Holcus mollis, Festuca ovina, Rubus sprengelii, Solidago virgaurea, Oxalis acetosella, Galium saxatile, Potentilla erecta.

28

CHESHIRE PLANT HABITATS. II.
SAND DUNES

Areas of dune slack which were formerly extensive between Wallasey and West Kirby and in small patches on the Dee shore have been greatly modified by development, particularly over the last fifty years. Housing and nurseries occupy large tracts, the slacks have been progressively drained and converted to pasture or used as rubbish tips and with the building of an embankment along almost the total length of the Irish Sea frontage fresh supplies of sand and shell fragments, important in the maintenance of a dune system, have been cut off. The Hoylake, Leasowe and Wallasey golf courses now incorporate almost all the "undeveloped" portions of the dune system; the latter two, due to the presence of the Leasowe embankment, consist largely of consolidated "grey dunes". Leaching is apparent from the presence of species such as *Jasione montana* and *Hieracium umbellatum* in quantity—both these are characteristic of sandy districts inland. The Hoylake dunes, still open to replenishment by fresh-blown sand, are markedly more calcareous and only here is it possible to see in Cheshire a full sequence of development from fore dunes to mature dunes. Even here the once extensive slacks which lay behind the dunes are now all dry, due to drainage operations on the golf course. The patches of blown sand down the Dee shore at Gayton form surface layers on top of boulder clay and cannot therefore be considered as dunes in the conventional sense: they are none the less the home of some dune plants and others not to be found elsewhere.

A table is appended showing the incidence of characteristic dune plants at each of four sites as observed 1964-1968.

1. Leasowe dunes and golf course (Grid ref: SJ 2792)

2. Hoylake golf course   (,,   ,,   ,,   2188)

3. Gayton and Heswall blown sand (,,   ,,   ,,   2680)

4. Wallasey golf course   (,,   ,,   ,,   2893)

It is instructive to compare the present situation with that found by E. Drabble (ref: Journal of Botany vol. 48) who compiled a list of plants observed in these localities over the period 1905-8. Compared with his findings the plants characteristic of moving dunes, e.g., *Cynoglossum officinale*, *Carlina vulgaris*, *Euphorbia paralias*, *Vulpia membranacea* and *Echium vulgare*, have apparently disappeared from the Wallasey area, and *Salsola kali* from Leasowe, while the calcicoles *Saxifraga tridactylites* and *Arabis hirsuta*, now only found in a few very small colonies, are very much reduced in numbers. By contrast, *Thalictrum minus* and *Rhynchosinapis monensis* seem to have neither increased nor decreased over the century since de Tabley wrote, and are still to be seen where he described them.

	1	2	3	4
Agropyron junceiforme..	o	o		o
A. pungens	o			
Agrostis tenuis	a	a	a	a
Aira caryophyllea				r
A. praecox		c	c	c
Allium vineale (var. compactum)		f		
Ammophila arenaria	a	a	c	a
Anthoxanthum odoratum		c	c	c
Anthriscus caucalis		r		
Anthyllis vulneraria	c	c	c	c
Aphanes arvensis s.l.		f		f
Arabidopsis thaliana		o		f
Arabis hirsuta				v r
Arenaria serpyllifolia subsp. serpyllifolia		c		c
Asparagus officinalis subsp. officinalis		o		
Beta vulgaris subsp. maritima	o	o		o
Blackstonia perfoliata			f	
Bromus mollis		c		c
Cakile maritima	o	f		
Campanula rotundifolia	c	c		a
Carex arenaria	a	a	c	a
C. flacca			f	
Centaurium erythraea	o			o
C. diffusum		c		c
Cerastium semidecandrum		c		c
Convolvulus arvensis		c		c
Coronopus didymus		c		
Crepis capillaris	c	c	c	c
Crocosmia x crocosmiflora		r		
Elymus arenarius	f	f	o	f
Equisetum variegatum		a		c
Erodium cicutarium subsp. cicutarium		f	c	f
E. glutinosum		o		
Erophila verna		c		c
Eryngium maritimum	r	r		
Euphorbia portlandica		o		

	1	2	3	4
Festuca ovina	c	c	f	c
F. rubra	a	a	a	a
Foeniculum vulgare		r		
Galium verum	c	c	f	c
Geranium molle		c		c
G. sanguineum			o	
Helictotrichon pubescens		f		
Hieracium umbellatum	c	f		a
Honkenya peploides	o	o		
Jasione montana	c		f	a
Leucanthemum vulgare			c	o
Leontodon taraxacoides	f	c		c
Lolium perenne	c	c	c	c
Lotus corniculatus	a	a	a	a
Lycium barbarum		o		
Myosotis ramosissima		r		
Ononis repens	a	a	c	a
Ornithogalum umbellatum		r		
Pastinaca sativa		f		c
Phleum arenarium		f		o
P. bertolonii	f	f		f
Pilosella officinarum	o			f
Pimpinella saxifraga	c			c
Plantago coronopus	f	f	o	f
Poa augustifolia		o		
P. pratensis agg.	c	c	c	c
Polygala vulgaris		c	f	c
Polypodium vulgare		o		
Primula veris				v r
Ranunculus bulbosus	c	c	c	c
Rhinanthus minor		f		f
Rhynchosinapis monensis	o			f
Rosa pimpinellifolia	c	c	f	a
Rubus caesius	c	a	c	a
Rumex acetosella			c	f
Sagina nodosa			r	

C

	1	2	3	4
Salix repens	c			a
Saxifraga tridactylites				v r
Sedum acre	c	c		c
S. album ..		f		
S. anglicum		o		
Silene vulgaris subsp. maritima		r		
Taraxacum Sect. Erythrospermae		c		
Thalictrum minus		r		
Thymus drucei		c	c	c
Trifolium arvense		a	a	a
T. campestre		f		f
T. striatum			r	
Trisetum flavescens		o		
Valerianella locusta subsp. dunensis		o		
Veronica arvensis		f		f
Vicia sativa agg.		o	o	c
V. hirsuta		f		
V. lathyroides		f		f
Viola canina		o		f

a : abundant
c : common
f : frequent
o : occasional
r : rare
vr : very rare

CHESHIRE PLANT HABITATS. III.

INDUSTRIAL WASTE LAND IN CENTRAL CHESHIRE

With the exception of a small outlier at Astbury, long since quarried away, there are no outcrops of limestone in Cheshire. The areas of waste ground, in places predominantly calcareous, which have resulted from the operations of the salt-based chemical industry in the centre of the county are therefore of interest in providing plant habitats unique in the area.

Sludge lagoons, into which chemical waste was pumped at different times, are the main features in the Northwich and Middlewich areas; at Winsford however the waste ground was formerly occupied by small salt works which stored brine in pits and evaporated it by combustion. This area is now a mosaic of damp hollows, ashes, remains of masonry and derelict railway tracks, as well as pits containing saline or calcareous mud, over which plant colonisation has been taking place for upwards of 40 years, and is therefore less homogeneous than the other sites. The complex of plant communities particularly of damp habitats is most interesting and variable, ranging from those reminiscent of bog pools on the fringes of nearby Delamere Forest through marshes with fen characteristics to residual saline zones where halophytic plants survive. The whole is superimposed upon heathy vegetation in which heather (*Calluna vulgaris*) is dominant.

At Plumley, (grid ref. SJ 7075) operations ceased about 1920 and the lime bed is being increasingly colonised by birch, hawthorn and willow scrub. The interest here is enhanced by close contiguity to a pool and associated marsh which is now developing into mature carr.

The large group of sludge lagoons in the Northwich district occupies the sites of subsidence flashes formed as a result of former brine pumping. One of these areas, Anderton (grid ref. SJ 6575) consists also of ashes and other non-calcareous waste, while a second, Marston (grid ref. SJ 6675) is the most recently used site and is as yet comparatively unfavourable to plant colonisation. The third, Witton (grid ref. SJ 6674), where pumping ceased about 1935, reproduces over a large area edaphic conditions remarkably similar to those of damp dune slacks, in which plants commonly found in such areas have become established presumably from the North Wales or Lancashire coasts. Willow scrub is well entrenched and becomes thicker annually. The sloping bank containing this waste is steep, dry and about 100 ft. high and approximates to fine limestone scree.

In the Middlewich district similar terrain though of lesser extent, is to be seen east of the Sandbach road at Cledford. Here a series of lagoons at different elevations are now mostly dry, but in one case due to the accident of topography the process of colonisation is excellently demonstrated by a series of concentric zones around a still saline pool. The inner fringe consists of a pure stand of *Agrostis stolonifera*, followed by one in which *Carex flacca*, *Festuca rubra*, *Dactylorhiza fuchsii*, *Dactylorhiza praetermissa* and hybrids are predominant; on the drier periphery, *Linum catharticum*, *Tussilago farfara* and *Sonchus arvensis* (both the latter species also found on the

33

brackish landward edge of salt marshes) are abundant. At a lower level an area of saline seepage occurs where *Puccinellia distans* and *Spergularia marina* form an intermittent cover.

Analysis of the species present in these areas shows that a relatively small proportion of the species present (approx. 10 per cent) are strictly calcicole: the predominant species are those characteristic of roadsides and disturbed ground throughout the county. Those favouring open dry or open damp situations (calcareous or not) are also well represented.

In fact the number of calcicoles present may be limited only by the distance separating the nearest colonies of suitable colonisers from central Cheshire. It is noteworthy that members of the Compositae and Orchidaceae, particularly reliant upon wind for seed dispersal, are present in large numbers. Species such as *Gentianella amarella*, *Botrychium lunaria* and *Selaginella selaginoides* might perhaps be expected to appear if source populations were available downwind (the prevailing quarter is N.W.—S.W.) It is to be hoped that observation of the process of colonisation in these most interesting areas will continue to be possible—fresh discoveries e.g. *Epipactis palustris* (1966), *Dactylorhiza incarnata* (1967) are still likely to be made.

A list of species found in these areas but absent or scarce in Cheshire as a whole is appended:—

	Witton "slack"	Witton "scree"	Plumley	Cledford	Winsford
Anacamptis pyramidalis		v r			
Blackstonia perfoliata ..	f	c	f		
Calamagrostis epigejos ..			c		
Dactylorhiza incarnata subsp. coccinea	vr				
Dactylorhiza praetermissa	a		c	c	c
Dactylorhiza praetermissa x fuchsii	c		f	f	f
Dactylorhiza praetermissa x purpurella			r		
Dactylorhiza purpurella			o		
Epipactis palustris ..	r				
Erigeron acer	o				
Euphrasia borealis ..	c				
Gymnadenia conopsea subsp. densiflora	a				
Hirschfeldia incana ..	c	f			
Hieracium grandidens ..		r			
Hieracium maculatum ..				o	
Hieracium severiceps ..			r		

34

	Witton "slack"	Witton "scree"	Plumley	Cledford	Winsford
Hieracium sublepistoides		o			
Inula conyza	f	f	f	f	
Ophioglossum vulgatum					r
Osmunda regalis ..					r
Pilosella praealta ..			o		
Pilosella officinarum x aurantiaca subsp. brunneocrocea ..			r		
Sagina nodosa	o				
Salix repens	c				

(Hieracium and Pilosella determined by J. N. Mills, P. D. Sell & C. West)

Semi-natural grassland in Cheshire represents a volatile vegetational state artificially maintained by grazing pressure. It is now confined to streambanks and steep slopes or field borders and hedgebanks, though occasionally it is possible to find isolated fields in the plain which are too hummocky or too wet to have been ploughed or drained thoroughly. In these instances many of the typical grassland species are still present.

In the Pennine zone there has been some "improvement" of grassland, but the area of old pasture and semi-natural hay meadow is larger.

Nine stands in the plain, in each case taken where Keuper marl substrata are sufficiently near to the surface to have an influence on the vegetation, and eight stands in the Pennines where Carboniferous shales form the ground rock are taken as representative of species-rich grassland.

Distinguishing features in the floristic composition of these communities are commented on below.

The following 15 species occur in 60 per cent of both sets of communities, and may be regarded as the main constituents of grassland in Cheshire as a whole:—

Agrostis tenuis	Luzula campestris
Anthoxanthum odoratum	Plantago lanceolata
Bellis perennis	Prunella vulgaris
Briza media	Ranunculus acris
Carex caryophyllea	Succisa pratensis
Centaurea nigra	Taraxacum spectabile agg.
Cynosurus cristatus	Trifolium pratense
Lotus corniculatus	

The following species occur in more than 60 per cent of the samples in each group:—

A	B
Ajuga reptans	Achillea millefolium
Betonica officinalis	Carex panicea
Carex flacca	Cerastium fontanum subsp. triviale
Rumex acetosa	Cirsium arvense
	C. palustre
	Conopodium majus
	Festuca rubra
	Leucanthemum vulgare

B—contd.

Holcus lanatus

Hypochoeris radicata

Lathyrus montanus

L. pratensis

Leontodon hispidus

Pilosella officinarum
subsp. officinarum

Sieglingia decumbens

Trifolium repens

Characteristically the samples of grassland which remain do not consist of wide areas of homogeneous vegetation but rather form a disjunct set of mosaics in which the elements of several communities are closely intermixed. In addition to species peculiar to grassland, it is possible to find within one field, woodland relics, marsh-loving species, and incipient scrub. On steep banks in some pastures a colony of gorse (*Ulex europaeus*) may develop on patches of superficial sand or leached clay, while on the richer clays hawthorn (*Crataegus monogyna*) with oak seedlings, bramble and rose species are characteristic. In hollows influenced by seepage or springs communities dominated by Carex or Juncus species occur depending on the nature and quantity of the ground water, and if the contour shape favours it, alder saplings will develop on a ground story of tall sedges and herbs e.g. *Scirpus sylvaticus, Filipendula ulmaria.*

The point to emphasise from the field experience is the dynamic nature of the intermixed communities within quite small areas, influenced by ground water, soil characteristics, nature of the underground strata, and by the pattern of land use practices. There are many examples where due to lack of grazing, the coarser grass species, particularly cocksfoot (*Dactylis glomerata*) become dominant at the expense of the less vigorous herbs, and where this community in turn is invaded by scrub-forming species.

The comparative predominance of many of the species in group B may be due to a variety of causes e.g. higher rainfall and therefore greater leaching of bases at surface, tending to greater acidity; greater number of species and therefore higher competition on the richer soils of group A.

The following species found in group A, are not found at all in group B: —*Agrimonia eupatoria, Helictotrichon pubescens, Ononis spinosa, Pimpinella major, Polygala vulgaris, Orchis morio, Senecio erucifolius, Silaum silaus;* most of these species are restricted to the Keuper marl series, or fen meadow.

Those found in group B but not in group A are:—*Alchemilla glabra, Botrychium lunaria, Campanula rotundifolia, Cirsium heterophyllum, Euphrasia anglica, Euphrasia borealis, Viola lutea.* All except *Campanula rotundifolia* are virtually confined to sub-montane grassland, while that species is found on well drained grassland on neutral-acid soils throughout the county.

Two other features are worthy of note:—The species which are particularly prominent in group B are also the main components of grassland on sandy soils and boulder clay in the plain—group B can therefore be said to be in many ways intermediate between the richer and poorer grasslands of the plain, with the additional admixture of the sub-montane elements.

In the hilly areas, transitions to grass heath in which the main species are *Nardus stricta*, *Deschampsia flexuosa*, *Galium saxatile*, and *Potentilla erecta*, are of frequent occurrence. These changes take place with an increase in altitude but also correlate with a change to siliceous sandstone/gritstone in the ground rock. An excellent sequence from species rich grassland to grass heath and incipient upland scrub can be seen on the east facing slope of White Nancy Hill, Bollington, SJ9477.

GROUP A—Keuper marl grassland

	44	76	57	87	64	65	54	78	77
	SW	NE	NW	NE	SE	NW	NE	SE	
Achillea millefolium	+						+	+	+
Agrimonia eupatoria	+	+					+	+	
Agrostis tenuis	+			+			+	+	+
Ajuga reptans	+	+	+	+	+	+	+	+	+
Alchemilla vestita		+				+	+		
A. xanthochlora		+			+			+	
Alopecurus pratensis					+		+		
Anthoxanthum odoratum	+	+	+	+	+		+	+	+
Bellis perennis	+	+	+	+	+		+	+	+
Betonica officinalis	+	+	+		+		+		+
Briza media		+	+		+		+	+	+
Carex caryophyllea	+	+	+	+	+	+	+	+	+
C. flacca		+	+	+	+	+	+	+	+
C. hirta				+	+		+	+	+
C. nigra									+
C. ovalis					+				+
C. panicea					+		+	+	+
Centaurea nigra			+	+	+		+	+	+
Centaurium erythraea					+				
Cerastium fontanum subsp. triviale					+		+	+	+
Cirsium arvense	+						+	+	+
C. palustre	+			+					
C. vulgare	+								
Conopodium majus			+				+	+	
Cynosurus cristatus	+	+	+	+	+	+	+	+	+
Dactylis glomerata		+					+	+	
Dactylorhiza fuchsii		+	+				+		+
Equisetum arvense			+	+				+	+

	44	76	57	87	64	65	54	78	77
	SW	NE	NW	NE	SE		NW	NE	SE
E. sylvaticum				+					+
Festuca rubra			+				+	+	+
Fragaria vesca							+		
Genista tinctoria		+	+				+		
Helictotrichon pubescens		+							
Holcus lanatus						+	+	+	+
Hypochoeris radicata	+				+		+	+	+
Juncus inflexus			+	+			+		
Lathyrus montanus		+			+		+		
L. pratensis		+			+			+	+
Leontodon hispidus		+	+				+	+	
Leucanthemum vulgare			+			+	+		
Linum catharticum					+		+		
Lolium perenne	+		+	+	+	+			
Lotus corniculatus	+	+	+	+	+	+	+	+	+
Luzula campestris	+		+	+	+	+	+	+	+
Myosotis discolor									+
Ononis spinosa					+		+		
Ophioglossum vulgatum			+	+			+		
Orchis morio			+						
Pedicularis sylvatica	+		+		+		+		+
Phleum pratense agg.		+				+			
Pilosella officinarum subsp. officinarum							+	+	+
Pimpinella major			+	+		+			+
P. saxifraga	+	+					+	+	
Plantago lanceolata	+	+	+	+	+		+	+	
Platanthera chlorantha									+
Poa pratensis		+					+	+	
Polygala serpyllifolia			+	+	+		+		
P. vulgaris		+							+
Potentilla anglica								+	
Potentilla erecta			+		+		+		+
Primula veris	+	+	+				+		+
P. vulgaris					+	+	+		
Prunella vulgaris	+		+	+	+	+	+	+	+
Ranunculus acris	+	+	+	+	+	+	+	+	+
R. bulbosus	+		+	+					+
Rumex acetosa		+	+	+			+	+	+
Sanguisorba officinalis		+							
Senecio erucifolius		+	+				+		
S. jacobea					+			+	
Sieglingia decumbens								+	+
Silaum silaus		+	+				+		
Succisa pratensis	+	+	+	+			+	+	+

GROUP A—Keuper marl grassland—*cont.*

	44 SW	76 NE	57 NW	87 NE	64 SE	65 NW	54 NE	78	77 SE
Taraxacum spectabile agg.	+	+	+	+			+		+
Trifolium medium			+		+		+		
T. pratense	+	+	+	+			+	+	+
T. repens					+	+	+		
Trisetum flavescens							+		
Veronica chamaedrys			+	+	+		+		
V. officinalis					+				+
V. serpyllifolia	+				+		+		
Viola riviniana						+	+	+	

GROUP A—Scrub species

	44 SW	76 NE	57 NW	87 NE	64 SE	65 NW	54 NE	78	77 SE
Betula pendula				+					
Crataegus monogyna				+		+			
Hypericum pulchrum						+			
Potentilla sterilis					+	+			
Prunus spinosa						+			
Quercus robur				+		+			
Ulex europaeus			+	+	+	+		+	
Vicia cracca						+			
V. sepium					+				

GROUP A—Woodland relicts

	44 SW	76 NE	57 NW	87 NE	64 SE	65 NW	54 NE	78	77 SE
Anemone nemorosa						+			
Arum maculatum					+				
Endymion non-scriptus					+				
Lysimachia nummularia						+			
Orchis mascula						+			
Ranunculus ficaria					+				
Rubus vestitus						+			

GROUP A—Marsh loving species

	44 SW	76 NE	57 NW	87 NE	64 SE	65 NW	54 NE	78	77 SE
Anagallis tenella	+								
Cardamine pratensis					+	+			+
Carex pulicaris				+		+			
Pulicaria dysenterica				+		+			

GROUP B—Upland grassland

	97 NW	97 NE	97 SE	96 NW	99 SE	98 SE	86 SE	85 NE
Achillea millefolium	+	+	+	+		+		+
A. ptarmica				+	+			
Agrostis canina subsp. montana				+	+	+		
A. tenuis	+	+		+		+	+	+

40

	97 NW	97 NE	97 SE	96 NW	99 SE	98 SE	86 SE	85 NE
Alchemilla glabra	+		+	+				
A. filicaulis subsp. vestita			+		+		+	
A. xanthochlora	+		+	+			+	
Anthoxanthum odoratum			+	+	+	+	+	
Bellis perennis			+		+	+	+	+
Betonica officinalis	+				+	+		
Blackstonia perfoliata								+
Botrychium lunaria			+	+				
Briza media	+	+			+		+	+
Campanula rotundifolia	+		+				+	+
Cardamine pratensis					+		+	
Carex caryophyllea	+		+	+			+	+
C. flacca	+	+	+	+				+
C. nigra			+					
C. ovalis			+	+	+		+	
C. panicea	+	+	+	+		+	+	
Centaurea nigra	+	+	+	+	+	+	+	+
Centaurium eythraea					+			
Cerastium fontanum subsp. triviale	+	+	+	+	+		+	
Cirsium arvense	+				+		+	+
C. heterophyllum			+					
C. palustre	+				+	+	+	+
C. vulgare	+							+
Conopodium majus	+	+	+	+	+		+	
Cynosurus cristatus	+	+	+	+	+	+	+	+
Dactylis glomerata	+		+	+				+
Dactylorhiza fuchsii			+		+	+		
Deschampsia caespitosa	+				+			
D. flexuosa	+		+					
Equisetum arvense						+	+	+
Euphrasia anglica					+			
E. borealis				+	+			
Festuca ovina					+			
F. rubra	+	+	+	+	+	+		+
Galium saxatile				+	+			
Genista tinctoria					+			
Gentianella amarella								+
Holcus lanatus	+	+	+	+	+	+		+
Hypericum pulchrum	+							+
Hypochoeris radicata	+	+	+	+	+	+	+	
Juncus articulatus					+		+	
Lathyrus montanus	+		+	+			+	+
L. pratensis	+	+	+	+			+	+
Leontodon autumnalis	+							+

41

GROUP B—Upland grassland—*cont.*

	97 NW	97 NE	97 SE	96 NW	99 SE	98 SE	86 SE	85 NE
Leontodon hispidus	+	+		+			+	+
Leucanthemum vulgare	+	+		+			+	+
Linum catharticum						+		+
Lolium perenne	+				+	+		+
Lotus corniculatus	+			+	+	+	+	+
L. uliginosus			+		+			
Luzula campestris	+	+	+	+			+	+
Nardus stricta	+				+		+	
Ophioglossum vulgatum	+				+		+	+
Pedicularis sylvatica							+	
Phleum pratense				+		+		
Pilosella officinarum subsp. officinarum	+				+	+	+	+
Pimpinella saxifraga					+	+		
Plantago lanceolata	+				+	+	+	+
Platanthera chlorantha				+	+			
Poa pratensis agg.	+	+			+	+		+
P. trivialis						+		
Polygala serpyllifolia					+	+	+	+
P. vulgaris						+		
Potentilla erecta	+	+			+		+	
Primula veris								+
Prunella vulgaris	+			+	+	+	+	+
Ranunculus acris	+	+	+	+	+	+	+	+
R. bulbosus	+							
R. repens				+	+	+	+	
Rumex acetosa	+				+	+	+	
Sagina procumbens	+				+			
Sanguisorba officinalis						+		
Senecio jacobea	+				+			
Sieglingia decumbens		+		+	+	+		+
Succisa pratensis	+	+	+	+	+	+	+	+
Taraxacum spectabile agg.			+	+	+		+	
Trifolium medium	+			+			+	+
T. pratense	+	+	+	+	+	+	+	+
T. repens	+			+	+	+	+	+
Trisetum flavescens								+
Ulex europaeus	+						+	
Veronica chamaedrys	+			+	+			+
V. officinalis	+			+	+			+
Vicia sepium	+	+			+			
Viola lutea					+			
V. riviniana					+		+	

GROUP B—Scrub species

	97 NW	97 NE	97 SE	96 NW	99 SE	98 SE	86 SE	85 NE
Ajuga reptans							+	
Crataegus monogyna							+	
Rosa arvensis				+				
R. canina				+				
Rubus vestitus				+				
Vicia cracca				+				

GROUP B—Woodland relicts

Athyrium filix-femina			+	
Equisetum sylvaticum			+	

The following habitat studies, representative of heath, moor, marsh, and open water, are given to illustrate the range of plant communities present in the county as observed during 1967-8.

1. **Heathland on Triassic sandstone, with peaty hollows and light scrub (½ mile from sea) Thurstaston Common, SJ 28NW, alt. 250 ft.**

Agrostis tenuis
Betula pubescens
Calluna vulgaris
Carex nigra
C. pilulifera
Cytisus scoparius
Deschampsia flexuosa
Drosera intermedia
D. rotundifolia
Dryopteris dilatata
Erica cinerea
E. tetralix
Eriophorum angustifolium
Galium saxatile
Gentiana pneumonanthe
Holcus mollis
Hypochoeris radicata
Juncus bulbosus
J. effusus
J. squarrosus
Lonicera periclymenum
Luzula multiflora
Molinia caerulea
Nardus stricta
Narthecium ossifragum
Ornithopus perpusillus
Pinus sylvestris
Potentilla erecta
Pteridium aquilinum
Quercus petraea
Rubus cardiophyllus
R. selmeri
Salix repens
Scirpus caespitosus
Scutellaria minor
Sorbus aucuparia
Ulex gallii

2. **Hill flush, stream and Alder carr, Kettleshulme Valley, SJ 97NE, alt. 800 ft.**

Alnus glutinosa
Anthoxanthum odoratum
Athyrium filix-femina
Caltha palustris
Cardamine flexuosa
Carex echinata
C. flacca
C. laevigata
C. panicea
Crepis paludosa
Deschampsia caespitosa
Dryopteris dilatata
Epilobium obscurum
Heracleum sphondylium
Holcus mollis
Ilex aquifolium
Lotus uliginosus
Lychnis flos-cuculi
Lysimachia nemorum
Populus tremula
Salix aurita
S. cinerea
Vicia sepium
Viola palustris

3. **High-level spring and flush, Charles Head, SJ 97NE, alt. 1,100 ft.**

Carex demissa
C. echinata
C. nigra
C. panicea
C. pulicaris

Hydrocotyle vulgaris
Juncus articulatus
J. effusus
Myosotis repens
Potamogeton polygonifolius

4. **Hill flush and marsh on Carboniferous shale, near Stirrup Wood, SJ 99SE, alt. 450 ft.**

Achillea ptarmica
Agrostis stolonifera
Alopecurus geniculatus
Angelica sylvestris
Cardamine pratensis
Carex demissa
C. echinata
C. flacca
C. laevigata
C. nigra
C. ovalis
C. pallescens
C. panicea
C. remota
C. sylvatica
Crepis paludosa
Dactylorhiza fuchsii

Deschampsia caespitosa
Juncus articulatus
J. subuliflorus
Lotus uliginosus
Lychnis flos-cuculi
Lysimachia nemorum
Mentha aquatica
Myosotis caespitosa
Poa trivialis
Pulicaria dysenterica
Ranunculus flammula
R. repens
Rumex acetosa
Sagina procumbens
Senecio aquaticus
Stellaria alsine
S. graminea

5. **Gritstone moorland, Cheshire Close, SJ 85, alt. 900 ft.**

Agrostis canina subsp. montana
A. tenuis
Anthoxanthum odoratum
Calluna vulgaris
Carex nigra
Cirsium palustre
Deschampsia caespitosa
D. flexuosa
Epilobium angustifolium
Eriophorum angustifolium
Festuca ovina
Galium saxatile
Holcus lanatus
Juncus bulbosus

Juncus effusus
J. squarrosus
Luzula multiflora
Molinia caerulea
Nardus stricta
Narthecium ossifragum
Potentilla erecta
Pteridium aquilinum
Rubus fruticosus agg.
Rumex acetosella
Ulex gallii
Vaccinium myrtillus
V. oxycoccus
V. vitis-idaea

6. **Wet meadow reclaimed from surrounds of peat moss, Brereton, SJ 86NW, alt. 250 ft.**

Agrostis stolonifera
Alopecurus geniculatus
Anthoxanthum odoratum
Bellis perennis
Briza media
Caltha palustris
Cardamine pratensis
Carex demissa
C. echinata
C. flacca
C. hirta
C. nigra
C. ovalis
C. panicea
C. paniculata
C. pulicaris
Centaurea nigra
Cerastium fontanum
  subsp. triviale
Cirsium palustre
Cynosurus cristatus
Dactylorhiza fuchsii
Eleocharis palustris
Equisetum fluviatile
E. palustre
Festuca rubra
Filipendula ulmaria

Galium palustre
Hydrocotyle vulgaris
Hypericum tetrapterum
Juncus articulatus
J. effusus
J. inflexus
Lathyrus montanus
L. pratensis
Lotus uliginosus
Lychnis flos-cuculi
Nardus stricta
Nasturtium officinale
Plantago lanceolata
Poa pratensis
Polygonum amphibium
Prunella vulgaris
Ranunculus acris
R. flammula
R. repens
Rumex acetosa
Stellaria alsine
Succisa pratensis
Taraxacum officinale
Trifolium pratense
Triglochin palustre
Vicia cracca

Peaty ditch nearby contained:—*Alnus glutinosa, Carex remota, Catabrosa aquatica, Ranunculus omiophyllus, Salix pentandra, Viburnum opulus, Viola palustris.*

7. **Series of 10 ponds at Hapsford (SJ 47NE) dug about 1940,* alt. 40 ft.**

Agrostis stolonifera	6	Callitriche stagnalis	1
Alisma plantago-aquatica	9	Cardamine pratensis	4
Alopecurus geniculatus	5	Carex curta	1
Apium inundatum	3	C. flacca	4
A. nodiflorum	2	C. hirta	2
Baldellia ranunculoides	4	C. otrubae	1
Berula erecta	2	C. ovalis	2
Bidens cernua	2	C. pseudocyperus	2

---

* Although the practice of marl digging has long been obsolete, the flora of this set of ponds approximates closely to the aspect of recently dug pits as given in De Tabley's Flora.

Carex rostrata	4	Lycopus europaeus	3
C. spicata	1	Mentha aquatica	1
Centaurium erythraea	2	Menyanthes trifoliata	2
Cerastium fontanum	2	Myosotis caespitosa	6
subsp. triviale		Nasturtium officinale	1
Cirsium palustre	1	Oenanthe fistulosa	7
Dryopteris dilatata	1	Poa trivialis	6
Eleocharis palustris	5	Polygonum amphibium	3
Epilobium palustre	4	Potamogeton natans	6
E. parviflorum	4	Potentilla palustris	6
Equisetum fluviatile	1	Prunella vulgaris	2
E. palustre	1	Pulicaria dysenterica	3
Galium palustre	4	Ranunculus flammula	1
Glyceria declinata	1	R. hederaceus	1
G. fluitans	6	R. repens	6
Holcus lanatus	4	R. sceleratus	5
Hottonia palustris	1	R. trichophyllus	1
Hydrocharis morsus-ranae	3	Rumex conglomeratus	2
Hydrocotyle vulgaris	3	R. hydrolapathum	2
Hypericum tetrapterum	1	Sagina procumbens	4
Iris pseudacorus	3	Salix cinerea	2
Juncus articulatus	8	Scirpus setaceus	4
J. bufonius	4	Scutellaria galericulata	1
J. bulbosus	2	Senecio aquaticus	1
J. effusus	7	Solanum dulcamara	2
J. inflexus	9	Sparganium emersum	4
J. subnodulosus	1	S. erectum	1
J. subuliflorus	3	Stellaria alsine	2
Leontodon taraxacoides	3	Taraxacum spectabile	1
Lotus uliginosus	1	Typha angustifolia	3
Lemna minor	3	T. latifolia	2
L. trisulca	3	Veronica catenata	2
Lychnis flos-cuculi	1	V. scutellata	1

8. **Ditch on Frodsham marsh, SJ 47NE, alt. 15 ft.**

Callitriche hamulata	Myosotis caespitosa
C. obtusangula	Myriophyllum spicatum
C. stagnalis	M. verticillatum
Catabrosa aquatica	Potamogeton berchtoldii
Ceratophyllum demersum	P. crispus
Elodea canadensis	P. natans
Glyceria fluitans	P. pectinatus
Hottonia palustris	P. pusillus
Lemna gibba	Ranunculus circinatus
L. minor	R. sceleratus
L. trisulca	Zanichellia palustris

D

9. Quoisley meres—Salix-Alder carr and Oak-Alder wood surrounding open water, and wet meadow on fen peat (SJ 54NW/NE), alt. 200 ft.

Ajuga reptans
Alisma plantago-aquatica
Alnus glutinosa
Alopecurus geniculatus
A. pratensis
Anemone nemorosa
Angelica sylvestris
Athyrium filix-femina
Bellis perennis
Berula erecta
Briza media
Calamagrostis canescens
Caltha palustris
Cardamine flexuosa
C. pratensis
Carex acutiformis
C. disticha
C. echinata
C. elata
C. hirta
C. nigra
C. ovalis
C. panicea
C. paniculata
C. riparia
Cerastium glomeratum
C. fontanum subsp. triviale
Cirsium palustre
Corydalis claviculata
Crataegus monogyna
Dactylis glomerata
Digitalis purpurea
Dryopteris dilatata
Epilobium hirsutum
E. obscurum
E. parviflorum
Equisetum fluviatile
E. palustre
Eupatorium cannabinum
Festuca rubra
Filipendula ulmaria
Frangula alnus
Galium aparine
G. palustre

Geranium robertianum
Glechoma hederacea
Glyceria fluitans
G. plicata
Hedera helix
Holcus lanatus
H. mollis
Hydrocotyle vulgaris
Hypericum tetrapterum
Iris pseudacorus
Juncus effusus
J. inflexus
J. subuliflorus
Lychnis flos-cuculi
Lycopus europaeus
Lysimachia vulgaris
Lythrum salicaria
Mentha aquatica
Myosotis caespitosa
M. discolor
Nasturtium officinale
Nymphaea alba
Phalaris arundinacea
Phragmites australis
Poa pratensis
P. trivialis
Plantago lanceolata
Potentilla palustris
Prunella vulgaris
Quercus robur
Ranunculus acris
R. flammula
R. repens
R. sceleratus
Rhinanthus minor
Rosa arvensis
R. canina
Rubus idaeus
Rumex acetosa
R. conglomeratus
Sagina procumbens
Salix cinerea
S. fragilis
Sambucus nigra

Scirpus lacustris
S. setaceus
Scutellaria galericulata
Silene dioica
Solanum dulcamara
Sparganium erectum
Stachys sylvatica
Stellaria alsine
S. graminea
Thelypteris palustris

Trifolium pratense
Triglochin palustris
Typha angustifolia
T. latifolia
Urtica dioica
Valeriana officinalis
Veronica beccabunga
V. catenata
V. serpyllifolia
Viburnum opulus

10. **Bollin Valley, Wilmslow, SJ 88SW, alt. 250 ft.**

Mosaic of damp grassland, wet springhead and marsh at foot, with scrub surround. Drift on Mottled sandstones.

Ajuga reptans
Alnus glutinosa
Alopecurus pratensis
Angelica sylvestris
Anthoxanthum odoratum
Bellis perennis
Briza media
Caltha palustris
Cardamine pratensis
Carex caryophyllea
C. flacca
C. hirta
C. pallescens
C. panicea
C. paniculata
Centaurea nigra
Cerastium fontanum
    subsp. triviale
Cirsium palustre
Conopodium majus
Crataegus monogyna
Cynosurus cristatus
Dactylorhiza purpuiella
Epilobium hirsutum
E. obscurum
E. parviflorum
Equisetum arvense
E. palustre
Festuca rubra
Filipendula ulmaria
Galium uliginosum
Holcus lanatus

Hypericum tetrapterum
Hypochoeris radicata
Juncus effusus
J. inflexus
Lathyrus pratensis
Lolium perenne
Lotus corniculatus
L. uliginosus
Luzula campestris
Lychnis flos-cuculi
Lysimachia nemorum
Myosotis discolor
Ophioglossum vulgatum
Plantago lanceolata
Poa trivialis
Polygala serpyllifolia
Potentilla erecta
Prunella vulgaris
Ranunculus acris
R. bulbosus
R. ficaria
R. flammula
R. repens
Rhinanthus minor
Rosa arvensis
Rumex acetosa
R. conglomeratus
Scirpus setaceus
S. sylvaticus
Stellaria alsine
Succisa pratensis
Taraxacum spectabile

49

10. **Bollin Valley, Wilmslow, SJ 88SW**—*cont.*

Trifolium dubium
T. pratense
Valeriana dioica
V. officinalis

Veronica beccabunga
V. chamaedrys
Vicia cracca
V. sepium

11. **Pickmere. Mere fringe and spring fed marsh, SJ 67NE alt. 80 ft.**

Achillea ptarmica
Agrostis stolonifera
Alnus glutinosa
Alopecurus geniculatus
Berula erecta
Butomus umbellatus
Calamagrostis canescens
Carex acutiformis
C. disticha
C. hirta
Cicuta virosa
Cirsium palustre
Epilobium hirsutum
E. parviflorum
Equisetum palustre
Filipendula ulmaria
Galium palustre
Glyceria x pedicellata
G. plicata
Hypericum tetrapterum
Iris pseudacorus
Juncus articulatus
J. bufonius
J. effusus
J. inflexus
J. subuliflorus
Lemna minor

Lotus uliginosus
Lychnis flos-cuculi
Lysimachia vulgaris
Mentha aquatica
Myosotis caespitosa
Myriophyllum spicatum
Nasturtium officinale
Nuphar lutea
Phalaris arundinacea
Phragmites australis
Poa trivialis
Polygonum amphibium
P. hydropiper
Potamogeton alpinus
P. crispus
P. pectinatus
P. perfoliatus
Ranunculus flammula
Rumex conglomeratus
Salix cinerea
S. fragilis
Scutellaria galericulata
Sparganium erectum
Stellaria alsine
S. graminea
Vicia cracca

12. **Streamhead and carr, below Bowstones, SJ 98SE, alt. 950 ft.**

Achillea ptarmica
Alnus glutinosa
Angelica sylvestris
Anthoxanthum odoratum
Athyrium filix-femina
Cardamine flexuosa
Carex nigra

Carex ovalis
C. panicea
C. paniculata
Centaurea nigra
Cirsium palustre
Corylus avellana
Crepis paludosa

Cynosurus cristatus
Dactylorhiza fuchsii
Deschampsia caespitosa
Dryopteris dilatata
Epilobium palustre
Equisetum palustre
E. sylvaticum
Filipendula ulmaria
Fraxinus excelsior
Galium palustre
Glyceria fluitans
Heracleum sphondylium
Holcus lanatus
H. mollis
Hypericum tetrapterum
Ilex aquifolium
Juncus articulatus
J. bulbosus
J. subuliflorus
Lathyrus pratensis
Lotus uliginosus
Lychnis flos-cuculi
Lysimachia nemorum
Menyanthes trifoliata

Molinia caerulea
Myosotis repens
Poa trivialis
Prunella vulgaris
Pulicaria dysenterica
Ranunculus acris
R. flammula
R. repens
Rubus accrescens
R. lindebergii
R. sprengelii
Salix aurita
S. cinerea
Sorbus aucuparia
Scirpus setaceus
Stellaria alsine
S. graminea
Succisa pratensis
Triglochin palustris
Valeriana dioica
V. officinalis
Viburnum opulus
Vicia cracca
V. sepium

13. **Wet meadow in Carboniferous shales, Handley Fold, SJ 98SE, alt. 800 ft.**

Alchemilla xanthochlora
Alopecurus geniculatus
Angelica sylvestris
Athyrium filix-femina
Briza media
Caltha palustris
Cardamine amara
C. flexuosa
C. pratensis
Carex acuta
C. panicea
Cirsium palustre
Crepis paludosa
Dactylorhiza maculata
Deschampsia caespitosa
Dryopteris dilatata
Epilobium obscurum
Equisetum fluviatile
E. palustre

Filipendula ulmaria
Galium palustre
Juncus acutiflorus
J. effusus
Lotus uliginosus
Lysimachia nemorum
Myosotis discolor
Petasites hybridus
Poa trivialis
Polygonum bistorta
Ranunculus acris
R. flammula
R. repens
Rumex acetosa
Stellaria alsine
Taraxacum spectabile agg.
Valeriana dioica
Veronica serpyllifolia

14. Spring flushes, marsh, wet grassland and stream gullies on Carboniferous shales, Bosley SJ 96NW, alt. 1,100 ft.

Achillea ptarmica
Agrostis stolonifera
A. tenuis
Alnus glutinosa
Angelica sylvestris
Anthoxanthum odoratum
Athyrium filix-femina
Betula pubescens
Briza media
Caltha palustris
Cardamine pratensis
Carex demissa
C. echinata
C. flacca
C. hostiana
C. nigra
C. ovalis
C. panicea
C. pulicaris
Cerastium fontanum
  subsp. triviale
Cirsium palustre
Crepis paludosa
Cynosurus cristatus
Dactylorhiza fuchsii
Deschampsia caespitosa
Dryopteris dilatata
Eleocharis palustris
Epilobium palustre
E. parviflorum
Equisetum palustre
Eriophorum angustifolium
Filipendula ulmaria
Galium palustre
G. uliginosum
Glyceria declinata
G. fluitans
Holcus lanatus
Hypericum tetrapterum

Juncus acutiflorus
J. articulatus
J. bulbosus
J. effusus
J. subuliflorus
Lotus uliginosus
Luzula campestris
Lychnis flos-cuculi
Lysimachia nemorum
Mentha aquatica
Myosotis caespitosa
M. repens
Pinguicula vulgaris
Poa subcaerulea
Prunella vulgaris
Ranunculus acris
R. flammula
R. hederaceus
R. repens
Rubus dasyphyllus
R. lindebergii
R. sprengelii
R. vestitus
Rumex acetosa
Sagina procumbens
Salix aurita
S. cinerea
S. pentandra
Stellaria alsine
Succisa pratensis
Thelypteris limbosperma
Trifolium repens
Triglochin palustris
Tussilago farfara
Valeriana dioica
V. officinalis
Veronica beccabunga
Viola palustris

Surrounding matrix of upland heath:—

Agrostis canina
  subsp. montana
Calluna vulgaris
Carex binervis
Deschampsia flexuosa

Festuca ovina
Juncus squarrosus
Melampyrum pratense
Molinia caerulea
Nardus stricta

15. **Damp grassland, springheads and marsh on drift covered Keuper marl slope, Kermincham, SJ 76NE, alt. 180 ft.**

Agrostis stolonifera
Alnus glutinosa
Anagallis tenella
Angelica sylvestris
Briza media
Cardamine pratensis
Carex acutiformis
C. demissa
C. flacca
C. hirta
C. pallescens
C. panicea
Cerastium fontanum
  subsp. triviale
Centaurium erythraea
Cirsium palustre
Dactylorhiza fuchsii
Epilobium hirsutum
E. palustre
E. parviflorum
Equisetum palustre
E. telmateia
Filipendula ulmaria
Galium palustre
G. uliginosum
Glyceria declinata
G. fluitans
Hypericum tetrapterum
Juncus acutiflorus
J. articulatus
J. bulbosus

Juncus effusus
J. inflexue
J. subuliflorus
Lathyrus pratensis
Leontodon taraxacoides
Lotus uliginosus
Lychnis flos-cuculi
Lysimachia nemorum
Mentha aquatica
M. arvensis
Odontites verna
Poa trivialis
Potentilla anserina
Prunella vulgaris
Pulicaria dysenterica
Ranunculus flammula
R. repens
Rumex acetosa
R. conglomeratus
Sagina procumbens
Scirpus setaceus
Solanum dulcamara
Stachys palustris
Stellaria alsine
S. graminea
Succisa pratensis
Taraxacum spectabile agg.
Trifolium pratense
Triglochin palustris
Vicia cracca

16. **Spring head and fen meadow on Keuper marl substrata with base rich inflow, Hatherton, SJ 64NE, alt. 180 ft.**

Achillea ptarmica
Alopecurus geniculatus
Anagallis tenella
Angelica sylvestris
Anthoxanthum odoratum
Berula erecta
Briza media
Caltha palustris
Cardamine pratensis
Carex flacca
C. nigra

C. otrubae
C. panicea
C. paniculata
Centaurea nigra
Cerastium fontanum
  subsp. triviale
Cirsium palustre
Cynosurus cristatus
Dactylorhiza fuchsii
D. praetermissa
Epilobium parviflorum

53

16. **Spring head and fen meadow, Hatherton**—*contd.*

Epipactis palustris
Equisetum palustre
E. telmateia
Eriophorum angustifolium
Eupatorium cannabinum
Festuca rubra
Filipendula ulmaria
Galium palustre
G. uliginosum
Gymnadenia conopsea
Hydrocotyle vulgaris
Hypericum tetrapterum
Iris pseudacorus
Juncus articulatus
J. bulbosus
J. effusus
J. inflexus
J. subnodulosus
Lathyrus pratensis
Lotus uliginosus
Lychnis flos-cuculi
Lysimachia vulgaris

Mentha aquatica
Oenanthe fistulosa
Parnassia palustris
Pedicularis palustris
Poa trivialis
Prunella vulgaris
Pulicaria dysenterica
Ranunculus flammula
Rumex acetosa
R. conglomeratus
Sagina procumbens
Scrophularia auriculata
Senecio aquaticus
Stellaria alsine
S. graminea
Trifolium pratense
Triglochin palustris
Valeriana dioica
V. officinalis
Veronica beccabunga
Vicia cracca
Viola palustris

17. **Fen peat, Alder carr, ditches, Norbury, SJ 54NE, alt. 270 ft.**

Agrostis canina
A. stolonifera
A. tenuis
Alnus glutinosa
Alopecurus geniculatus
A. pratensis
Anemone nemorosa
Briza media
Calamagrostis canescens
Callitriche stagnalis
Caltha palustris
Cardamine pratensis
Carex acutiformis
C. demissa
C. echinata
C. elata
C. hirta
C. nigra
C. ovalis
C. panicea
C. pulicaris
C. rostrata

Centaurea nigra
Cerastium glomeratum
C. fontanum
Cirsium dissectum
C. palustre
Cladium mariscus
Cynosurus cristatus
Dactylorhiza fuchsii
Deschampsia caespitosa
Epilobium obscurum
E. palustre
E. parviflorum
Equisetum palustre
Filipendula ulmaria
Galium palustre
G. uliginosum
Glyceria fluitans
Holcus lanatus
Hydrocotyle vulgaris
Juncus acutiflorus
J. articulatus
J. bufonius

J. effusus
J. subuliflorus
Lathyrus pratensis
Lotus uliginosus
Luzula campestris
Lychnis flos-cuculi
Lysimachia nummularia
L. vulgaris
Lythrum salicaria
Mentha aquatica
Menyanthes trifoliata
Molinia caerulea
Myosotis caespitosa
Nasturtium officinale
Oenanthe fistulosa
Pedicularis palustris
Phalaris arundinacea
Phragmites australis
Plantago lanceolata
Potentilla erecta
Prunella vulgaris
Ranunculus acris
R. flammula
R. lingua
R. repens
Rhinanthus minor
Ribes rubrum

Rosa canina
Rubus fruticosus agg.
Rumex acetosa
R. conglomeratus
Rorippa islandica
Sagina procumbens
Salix cinerea
S. fragilis
Sambucus nigra
Scirpus setaceus
Senecio aquaticus
Sieglingia decumbens
Solanum dulcamara
Stachys palustris
Stellaria graminea
Succisa pratensis
Thelypteris palustris
Trifolium pratense
T. repens
Triglochin palustris
Valeriana officinalis
Veronica beccabunga
V. catenata
V. scutellata
V. serpyllifolia
Vicia cracca
Viola palustris

18. **Strand line on mud and gravel, and shore fringe, Bosley Reservoir, SJ 96NW, alt. 600 ft.***

Agrostis stolonifera
Alopecurus aequalis
A. geniculatus
Apium inundatum
Bidens tripartita
Callitriche hamulata
Carex vesicaria
Deschampsia caespitosa
Gnaphalium uliginosum
Juncus articulatus
J. bufonius
J. effusus
Littorella uniflora
Lythrum portula
    subsp. portula
Mentha arvensis

Montia fontana subsp. fontana
Myosotis caespitosa
M. palustris
Myriophyllum alterniflorum
Plantago major
Polygonum amphibium
P. aviculare
P. hydropiper
Potentilla anglica
P. anserina
Ranunculus flammula
R. peltatus
Rorippa islandica
Senecio aquaticus
Trifolium repens

* *Limosella aquatica* and the moss *Physcomitrium sphaericum* occurred eight feet below the normal water level.

19. **Sandstone detritus below parapet, Beeston Castle, SJ 55NW, alt. 350 ft.**

Aphanes arvensis
Arabidopsis thaliana
Arenaria serpyllifolia
Cerastium semidecandrum
Erigeron acer
Erophila verna
Festuca rubra
Galium verum
Geranium molle
Lotus corniculatus
Myosotis ramosissima
Pilosella officinarum
 subsp. officinarum

Plantago coronopus
Sagina apetala
Saxifraga tridactylites
Trifolium arvense
T. campestre
T. dubium
Veronica arvensis
Vicia hirsuta
V. lathyroides
Vulpia bromoides

20. **Heathland with peaty pools and one area of active sphagnum, Lindow Common, SJ 88SW, alt. 240 ft.**

Betula pubescens
Calluna vulgaris
Carex nigra
Deschampsia flexuosa
Drosera rotundifolia
Empetrum nigrum
Erica tetralix
Eriophorum angustifolium
Juncus bulbosus
J. effusus
J. squarrosus
J. subuliflorus
Molinia caerulea
Nardus stricta
Narthecium ossifragum
Potamogeton polygonifolius

Potentilla erecta
Pteridium aquilinum
Quercus robur
Ranunculus flammula
Rubus idaeus
R. selmeri
R. Sect. Suberecti
R. scissus
Rumex acetosella
Salix cinerea
Scirpus caespitosus
Sorbus aucuparia
Ulex europaeus
U. gallii
Vaccinium myrtillus
V. oxycoccus

CHESHIRE PLANT HABITATS. VI.

SOME DATA ON CHESHIRE MARL PITS AND OTHER AQUATIC HABITATS

by K. G. Allenby

1. INTRODUCTION

Layers of marl, or marl derived boulder clay, cover large areas of the Cheshire Plain. It is basically a sand-clay mixture of variable appearance and composition containing up to approximately 4 per cent calcium carbonate. The marl was dug and spread on the fields chiefly during May to September, and acted as a manure due to both its lime content and its physical properties, giving body to sandy drift soils. Records show that the practice was in operation about the year 1300, reaching a peak in the 18th century, the last large scale marling occurring in the Delamere area in 1850 (Agriculture of Cheshire, W. B. Mercer). Many of the depressions left after excavation of marl became filled with water, and although in many cases natural silting has given marshy areas with little clear water and many ponds have been filled, open water marl pits are still very numerous in the fields in many areas of Cheshire; in some localities almost every field has at least one marl pit. Typically these pits are 10—30 metres in diameter and 1—2 metres deep; they occur singly or in groups of up to 12, usually with narrow connecting channels. Tree growth around the pits is usual where groups exist, but is less likely at single pits. With age the sides become inclined, giving a wide perimeter of marginal plant growth often showing marked zonation. Some ponds with apparently suitable conditions have no fringe of marginal plants (or true aquatics) and it is likely that continuous trampling of the shore by cattle, has prevented colonisation. Other ponds have become silted with little open water, often *Sphagnum* filled, and with *Salix* and later *Alnus* carr in the centre; here the characteristic flora includes *Manyanthes trifoliata,* and *Potentilla palustris* in the more open regions progressing with age to *Juncus* dominated marsh.

Although the numbers of ponds recorded and waters analysed is not as large as might have been wished, it is felt that the information given presents a general picture of the situation.

2. WATER ANALYSES

Analysis of many pond waters has shown that there is little variation. It is of interest to note that the calcium content of waters varies little between ponds where the soil in the immediate vicinity is calcareous as shown by plant species and analysis (2½ per cent calcium carbonate), and those surrounded by non-calcareous sandy soil (less than 0.1 per cent calcium carbonate). Waters were sampled during May to September, 1965/68.

(a) **pH Values** were determined 18—24 hours after sampling, and may have differed slightly from the original. Figures ranged from 6.3 to 9.0. 88 per cent lying between 6.7 and 7.4.

(b) **Total Dissolved Solids:** for pits with little tree cover were from 114 to 572 ppm, average 267 ppm. The effect of tree cover gave an increased figure, range 194 to 624 ppm. and average 388 pp.

(c) **Mineral Content** by ignition at 600°C. No trees—range 50–335 ppm, average 153 ppm. With trees—range 88–385 ppm, average 206 ppm. The increased dissolved solid and mineral content of waters from tree fringed pits is assumed to result from dissolved decomposing leaves, and the less dense surface vegetation of these pits. Considering the number of years over which the tree cover has been developing, the increase in soluble matter is not high.

(d) **Calcium Content**—No trees, 6–72 ppm, average 34 ppm. Tree cover, 9–84 ppm, average 49 ppm. The percentage of calcium in dissolved solids is similar—13 per cent in both cases.

(e) **Chloride Content**—No trees, 7–77 ppm, average 34 ppm, Tree cover, 7–125 ppm, average 49 ppm. These figures are identical on average to calcium values. Chloride figures for pits in coastal areas, squares SJ/28, 37, 45, 47 and 57 show no increase over inland waters. Some pits in built up areas have shown chloride increases of 500 per cent in winter, presumably due to the use of salt as an antifreeze.

(f) **Magnesium Content** for treeless ponds, 5–22 ppm, average 15 ppm.

(g) **Phosphate phosphorus** for treeless ponds, 0.01–0.20 ppm, average 0.07 ppm.

(h) **Nitrate nitrogen** for treeless ponds, 0.05 to 0.45 ppm. Values up to 25 ppm were found in a few samples due to the spreading of fertilisers on the surrounding areas.

(j) **Ammoniacal nitrogen** 0.10 to 2.0 ppm. Similar values with and without tree cover.

(k) **Total Kjeldahl nitrogen** for treeless ponds, 0.2–3.9 ppm, average 1.9 ppm., tree fringed ponds, 1.9–9.2 ppm. average 3.4 ppm. Values increase during the autumn due to rotting vegetation.

(l) **Bicarbonate:** 8—170 ppm, average 70 ppm. Tree cover appears to have no effect.

(m) **Manganese:** Nil to 2.0 ppm. It is of interest to note that aquatic plants contain a high concentration of manganese; marginals contain up to 700 ppm, rooted aquatics to 5,000 ppm, and free-floating plants up to 10,000 ppm, of this metal determined on dry material (Hydrobiologia 27.3/4. 29. 1/2). The manganese content of the water is about 1 in 2,000 of the total minerals present, whereas in plant ash the proportion has increased to about 1 in 10, the manganese thus having been concentrated 200 times. Values for the copper content of waters and plants show no concentration of this element.

THE EFFECT OF TREE COVER

Tree cover appears to give increased values for the amounts of dissolved solids, minerals and total nitrogen; the composition of the ash i.e. Calcium/ash and Chloride/ash ratios seem similar. Typically tree-fringed ponds are shallower than open ponds (silting by dead leaves) with clear brownish water having a blackish sheen. The number of species is much reduced and many small ponds with tree cover almost complete have only *Callitriche* spp. present. Ponds with appreciable tree cover have a species list about half that of open ponds but slight cover is often associated with an increased number of species due to a wide range of light intensities. Although light conditions are an important factor it is possible that some substance produced from decaying vegetation may act as a plant growth inhibitor.

Analysis of other waters

Larger pools and meres have a composition similar to marl pits. Canals vary very considerably and can be classified into two types:

(i) Low mineral content, often clear water with a good species variety, and in some areas luxuriant growth. These conditions obtain in the Llangollen and Macclesfield canals.

(ii) High mineral and suspended matter, with a very cloudy water; marginals are common as in previous type but submerged plants are much less common. The Shropshire Union and Trent and Mersey are in this category. The increasing volume of boat traffic along some of these canals will probably have quite substantial effects on future plant life.

Large areas of saline waters (Flashes) occur in the Sandbach/Middlewich/Winsford areas; plant species are typical but reduced in variety, and include *Aster tripolium* and *Samolus valerandi* as interesting marginals.

SUMMARY OF ANALYSES OF CHESHIRE WATERS

(Average values in parts per million)

Constituent	Small Ponds Trees	No Trees	Larger Pools	Canals	Saline Flashes
Total dissolved solids	267	388	380	200–1,000	To 10,000
Minerals (Ash)	153	206	223	110–800	To 4,000
Calcium	34	49	56	30–100	To 400
Chloride	34	49	28	30–90	To 4,000
Phosphate Phosphorous	0·07	—	—	—	—
Nitrate Nitrogen	0·25	0·25	—	∸	—
Ammoniacal Nitrogen	0·5	0·5	0·5–5·0	0·1–1·0	—
Kjeldahl Nitrogen	1·9	3·4	—	—	—
Bicarbonate	70	70	—	—	—
Chemical Oxygen Demand	48	48	—	—	—

3. THE OCCURRENCE AND DISTRIBUTION OF PLANT SPECIES IN CHESHIRE PONDS

The figures tabulated below are possibly understated since it was not practical to visit all ponds at sufficiently frequent intervals to cover all flowering periods. Ponds were recorded at random showing no preference for areas of greater interest. Nevertheless results should give a reasonably accurate impression of the plant distribution and abundance.

To show distribution on a broad scale records of species present are tabulated in four regional areas as follows:

North West

80 ponds recorded in 10 Km. squares No. SJ/28, 37, 38, 47, 57, 58, 67, 68.

North East

50 ponds recorded in 10 Km. squares No. SJ/77, 78, 87, 88, 97, 98, 99.

South West

145 ponds recorded in 10 Km. squares No. SJ/36, 44, 45, 46, 54, 55, 56, 64, 65, 66.

South East

66 ponds recorded in 10 Km. squares No. SJ/74, 75, 76, 85, 86, 96.

	North West		North East		South West		South East		Total	
	No.	%	No.	%	No.	%	No.	%	No.	%
Alisma plantago-aquatica	61	76	20	40	108	78	46	70	233	68
Lemna minor	55	70	29	58	89	61	41	62	214	63
Sparganium erectum	55	70	25	50	88	61	37	56	205	60
Potamogeton natans	42	53	19	38	88	61	32	49	181	53
Myosotis caespitosa	33	41	9	18	61	42	28	42	131	38
Lemna trisulca	24	33	11	22	38	26	19	29	92	27
Nasturtium officinale (agg.)	14	17	7	14	44	30	6	9	71	21
Veronica beccabunga	9	11	2	4	41	28	9	14	61	18
Typha latifolia	15	19	5	10	27	19	13	20	60	18
Bidens cernua*	16	20	3	6	25	17	12	18	56	17
Apium nodiflorum	19	24	2	4	27	19	6	10	54	16
Equisetum fluviatile	10	13	7	14	28	19	8	12	53	16
Elodea canadensis	25	31	6	12	10	7	7	11	48	14
Carex pseudocyperus	6	8	3	6	33	23	5	8	47	14
Oenanthe fistulosa	12	15	10	20	22	15	0	0	44	13
Potentilla palustris	3	4	12	24	13	9	10	15	38	12
Lycopus europaeus	2	2	2	4	24	17	6	9	34	10
Hydrocotyle vulgaris	6	8	5	10	14	10	8	12	33	10
Mentha aquatica	4	5	4	8	21	14	5	8	34	10
Iris pseudacorus	6	8	4	8	12	8	11	17	33	10
Berula erecta	2	2	0	0	21	14	1	1	24	7
Cicuta virosa	1	1	0	0	18	12	4	6	23	7
Ranunculus flammula	2	2	4	8	4	3	12	18	22	7
Eleocharis palustris	6	8	1	2	6	4	9	14	22	7
Hydrocharis morsus-ranae	8	10	1	2	12	8	0	0	21	6
Carex acutiformis*	2	2	0	0	8	6	8	12	18	5
Potamogeton crispus	2	2	2	4	10	7	4	6	18	5
Ranunculus aquatilis†	2	2	1	2	9	6	5	8	17	5
Carex otrubae	1	1	0	0	12	8	3	5	16	5
Myosotis palustris	5	6	1	2	6	4	1	1	13	4
Rorippa islandica	3	4	1	2	6	4	2	3	12	4
Apium inundatum	7	9	1	2	2	1	3	5	13	4

*Probably under-recorded.   † May include R. peltatus and trichophyllus.

	North West		North East		South West		South East		Total	
	No.	%	No.	%	No.	%	No.	%	No.	%
Oenanthe aquatica	1	1	0	0	6	4	5	8	12	4
Polygonum amphibium	2	3	1	2	2	1	6	9	11	3
Ranunculus trichophyllus	2	3	2	4	4	3	3	5	11	3
Menyanthes trifoliata	0	0	0	0	9	6	1	1	10	3
Nymphaea alba	4	5	2	4	2	1	1	1	9	3
Potamogeton obtusifolius	2	2	2	4	4	3	1	1	9	3
Equisetum palustre	0	0	0	0	8	6	1	1	9	3
Potamogeton berchtoldii	5	6	2	4	2	1	1	1	10	3
Typha angustifolia	3	4	1	2	3	2	2	3	9	3
Ranunculus peltatus	0	0	0	0	2	1	6	9	8	2
Lemna polyrhiza	1	1	0	0	7	2	0	0	8	2
Ceratophyllum demersum	4	5	1	2	0	0	1	1	6	2
Hottonia palustris	0	0	3	6	3	2	0	0	6	2
Myriophyllum spicatum	2	2	0	0	4	3	0	0	6	2
Carex paniculata	0	0	1	2	3	2	2	3	6	2
Carex remota	3	4	1	2	1	1	0	0	5	1
Bidens tripartita*	0	0	0	0	0	0	5	8	5	1
Ranunculus hederaceus	0	0	2	4	3	2	0	0	5	1
Azolla filiculoides	1	1	0	0	3	2	0	0	4	1
Carex riparia	0	0	0	0	2	1	2	3	4	1
Sparganium emersum*	1	1	0	0	1	1	2	3	4	1
Scutellaria galericulata*	0	0	2	4	2	1	0	0	4	1

* Probably under-recorded

The following species were found in less than four ponds: *Montia fontana, Lemna gibba, Veronica scutellata, V. catenata, Oenanthe crocata, Scirpus tabernaemontani* (3 records), *Scirpus lacustris, Catabrosa aquatica, Stratiotes aloides, Utricularia vulgaris* agg., *Ranunculus lingua, Scirpus fluitans, Carex rostrata, Lythrum portula, Baldellia ranunculoides* (2 records), *Potamogeton alpinus, Butomus umbellatus, Mimulus guttatus, Ceratophyllum submersum* (1 record).

The following species were not included in the survey, since they are more characteristic of marshy areas in general: *Epilobium spp., Juncus spp., Glyceria spp., Alopecurus geniculatus, Ranunculus sceleratus*.

PLATE 1. *Above:* Reed fringe, Hatchmere; *beneath:* Base-rich fen, valley near Hatherton.

PLATE 2. *Above:* Centre of Wybunbury Moss; *beneath:* Moors and hill grassland, the County march, upper R. Dane.

4. CHEMICAL COMPOSITION OF WATERS FOR SOME SPECIES

The range of values as parts per million is given of waters in which the species have been found growing.

Species	Mineral	Calcium	Chloride	Total Nitrogen
Lemna minor	90– 650	15– 70	30– 300	0·3–3·9
Lemna trisulca	75– 650	20– 70	10– 300	0·3–3·1
Lemna polyrhiza	70– 205	15– 60	15– 70	2·0–3·9
Typha latifolia	85– 425	20– 90	30–2000	1·2–3·5
Typha angustifolia	85–5000	30– 300	30–3000	—
Elodea canadensis	30– 800	10– 110	30– 300	0·3–2·5
Carex otrubae	80–7000	10– 250	20–3500	1·0–1·2
Oenanthe fistulosa	75– 180	20– 60	20– 50	0·2–2·5
Oenanthe aquatica	35– 380	10– 70	20– 125	1·2–9·2
Potamogeton crispus	80– 880	20– 90	20– 70	0·3–2·0
Potamogeton obtusifolius	40– 100	20– 60	15– 30	0·9–1·7
Potentilla palustris	90– 250	10– 60	20– 80	1·2–2·5
Berula erecta	80– 150	20– 55	20– 50	1·0–2·4
Eleocharis palustris	90– 900	10– 115	20– 300	0·3–3·9
Hydrocharis morsus-ranae	30– 145	20– 40	30– 70	2·0–2·5
Ranunculus aquatilis/peltatus	65– 170	10– 35	10– 45	0·2–2·5
Apium inundatum	90– 150	15– 30	30– 90	1·2–3·9
Iris pseudacorus	90– 800	20– 135	30– 125	2·2–9·2
Cicuta virosa	70– 145	10– 30	10– 15	—
Ranunculus trichophyllus	80– 425	15– 90	30– 70	—
Hottonia palustris	90– 260	10– 80	—	2·5
Ceratophyllum demersum	100– 800	40– 110	30– 70	—
Myriophyllum spicatum	60–5000	30– 300	30–3200	—
Potamogeton pectinatus	up to 5000	to 300	to 3500	—
Scirpus tabernaemontani	to 5000	to 300	to 3200	—

E*

5. MUD ANALYSES

For aquatic bottom rooted plants the mud composition may be of more importance than the water. Only a few analyses are available but the values tabulated below give some idea of variation.

Type	Loss on Ignition	Silica	Total Nitrogen	Calcium as Chalk	Acid soluble Minerals
Black mud	3	96	0·05	0·12	1·3
Black mud	22	73	1·0	1·5	5·5
Black mud	3	94	0·06	0·4	2·9
Grey/brown mud	13	79	0·3	0·2	7·2
Sandy	2	96	0·06	0·4	2·0
Reddish	16	68	1·56	0·25	15·8

Figures are as % of dried material after passing a 20 mesh screen.

6. AQUATIC PLANT ANALYSES

Analyses of plant material vary greatly within species, and in general show little correlation between time of year, environment, etc., Some values are given in the Table below and were determined on well washed and dried material. Ash contents were done at 600° C. The Calcium values are for the total present; washing for half a minute with a 1 in 100 solution of hydrochloric acid gives much reduced figures indicating that 20–60 per cent of the Calcium occurs as an external deposit on the plant surfaces. No relationship between this Calcium value and the Calcium or Bicarbonate content of the water is evident. The ash content of marginals appears to be less than that of true aquatics (see table on p.65).

AQUATIC PLANT ANALYSES % DRY BASIS

SPECIES	PART	ASH Range	ASH Av.	CALCIUM Range	CALCIUM Av.	CHLORION Range	CHLORION Av.	NITROGEN × 6.25 Range	NITROGEN × 6.25 Av.
Lemna minor ...	W	7·1–13·6	10·4	1·27–1·78	1·55	0·66–1·31	1·10	14·9–33·2	25·1
Lemna trisulca ...	W	9·4–19·5	14·9	0·94–2·02	1·47	1·18–2·10	1·57	10·0–30·0	23·0
Lemna polyrhiza ...	W	10·5–13·5	11·5	1·40–1·46	1·43	1·16–1·82	1·48	24·6–33·5	29·0
Lemna gibba ...	W	10·2–12·5	11·2	0·97–1·50	1·16			16·9–29·7	20·3
Hydrocharis morsus-ranae ...	L	12·0–14·6	13·2	0·71–0·93	0·82	1·33–2·22	1·81		
Elodea canadensis ...	L & S	10·4–17·4	13·3	1·05–3·40	1·55	0·31–1·35	0·96	11·3–27·6	20·0
Ceratophyllum demersum ...	L & S	10·8–16·1	13·5	0·50–1·11	0·80	1·60–2·11	1·86	12·4–23·0	17·5
Potamogeton crispus ...	L	12·1–14·0	12·9	1·10–1·68	1·42	1·04–1·83	1·42		
Potamogeton natans ...	L	5·4–8·0	7·1	0·43–1·38	0·89				
Sparganium erectum ...	L	6·3–10·0	7·8	0·65–1·64	1·07				
Sagittaria sagittifolia ...	L	4·7–15·1	9·8	0·55–1·55	0·90				
Carex acutiformis ...	L	4·2–6·1	5·0	0·15–0·56	0·31				
Alisma plantago-aquatica ...	L	7·3–12·8	10·8	0·72–2·3	1·19				

L—Leaves   S—Stems   W—Whole plant

FLORA

EXPLANATORY NOTES

1. Nomenclature and order are after the *List of British Vascular Plants* (J. E. Dandy, 1958) with subsequent amendments reported in BSBI proceedings and Watsonia. Numbers of Hieracia are taken from the BSBI Atlas of Critical Species. English names are largely taken from the draft BSBI "List of recommended names of wild plants".

2. Where species described by Flora of Cheshire as flourishing c. 1875 have not been found during the period of survey (1964-1969, to which period all records refer unless otherwise stated), mention is made after each family; last records have been inserted, where later than the Flora reference, with authority and source, where traced.

3. Species of alien or garden origin which have been observed as casual occurrences in ephemeral habitats are commented on in a tailpiece to each family.

4. All references are to 5 × 5 km. squares within the National Grid 100 km. grid square SJ, unless otherwise stated.

5. The frequency scale used in assessing the incidence of each species is as follows (total recording units 110 5 × 5 km. squares):

very common 81—110
common 53—80
frequent 27—52
occasional 14—26
local 7—13
rare 2—6
very rare 1

6. The symbol ! indicates that the plant has been seen by the author *in situ* or that it has been verified by him.

PTERIDOPHYTA

Lycopodiaceae

1/4 Lycopodium clavatum L. *Stagshorn Moss*
Very rare. 1. Floor of abandoned sand pit with high water table where recolonisation by various plant communities is well advanced. 86SW! 1966 et seq.

Species apparently extinct

1/1 Huperzia selago (L.) Bern. ex Sobranti & Mart. (Goyt Valley, SJ98, 1900, *H. G. Willis* per *F. H. Perring.*)

1/2 Lepidotis inundata (L.) C. Börner (W. Hodge, Lancs. Nat. 5, 1912-13, p. 44, Delamere).

Selaginellaceae

Species apparently extinct

2/1 Selaginella selaginoides (L.) Link.

Equisetaceae

4/1 Equisetum hyemale L. *Rough Horsetail*
Very rare. 1. Marshy edge of sandhills along a line of seepage, Hoylake, 28NW!, 1968, in a habitat exactly like that "near Gayton" mentioned by De Tabley, p. 381.

4/4 Equisetum variegatum Schleich. ex Weber & Mohr *Variegated Horsetail*
Rare. 4. Locally abundant on sand dunes from Wallasey to Gayton. Inland on sand heap, 88SE, *A. Gibson.*

4/5 Equisetum fluviatile L. *Water Horsetail*
Very common. 94. Shallow water of ponds, meres and ditches throughout.

4/6 Equisetum palustre L. *Marsh Horsetail*
Very common. 93. Marshes, waterlogged pastures, mere and pond fringes.

4/7 Equisetum sylvaticum L. *Wood Horsetail*
Frequent. 45. Woods, wood borders and banks, particularly in east Cheshire in sessile oakwoods on Carboniferous shales and mixed woods on glacial sand. In the plain less common on scrubby banks on leached clay and sandy soils.

Polypodiaceae

4/9 Equisetum arvense L. *Common Horsetail*
Very common. 108. Grassland, arable, disturbed and waste ground, roadsides throughout.

4/10 Equisetum telmateia Ehrh. *Great Horsetail*
Common. 65. Marshy woods, damp wood borders and hedgebanks; swampy alluvial flats under alder carr; less commonly in unshaded spring fed marshes and damp canal banks.

OSMUNDACEAE

5/1 Osmunda regalis L. *Royal Fern*
Local. 7. Fen margin of sphagnum bog 57SE! Alder carr 87SW! Peaty hollows on remnant of heath 66NE!, 87NW! damp sandstone rock faces 46SE, *A. Gibson*; 38, *N. Povey*. Canal side, 78NW *P. Newton*! Recently extinct—sandstone quarry face 88SW, 1964; ditchside, Carrington Moss, 79SW, 1965. Almost totally absent from its former range of habitats, it now favours damp sandstone cuttings.

POLYPODIACEAE

8/1 Pteridium aquilinum (L.) Kuhn *Bracken*
Very common. 107. Well drained often detrital soils, woods and wood margins, heath surrounds, slopes where woodland has been felled, undisturbed roadside banks on sandy soils, gritstone slopes.

11/1 Adiantum capillus-veneris L. *Maidenhair Fern*
Well established on brickwork of Thurstaston station 28NW!

13/1 Blechnum spicant (L.) Roth *Hard Fern*
Frequent. 33. Common in Pennine woods, damp rock faces, streamsides and moorland gullies. In plain, rare in peaty ditches and damp banks on heathland and in woodland on glacial sands or Triassic sandstone.

14/1 Phyllitis scolopendrium (L.) Newm. *Hart's-tongue Fern*
Frequent. 45. (1) Deeply shaded sides of cloughs on Keuper series (often among dominant *Allium ursinum*) Bollin, Weaver and Dane valleys. (2) Damp shaded banks and walls, particularly in Wirral.

15/1 Asplenium adiantum-nigrum L. *Black Spleenwort*
Occasional. 14. Damp shaded sandstone outcrops on Delamere Ridge; interstices of stonework elsewhere; canal banks and bridges.

15/4 Asplenium marinum L. *Sea Spleenwort*
Very rare. 1. Crevices in Triassic sandstone cliffs, Hilbre Island, a long known site.

15/5 Asplenium trichomanes L. *Maidenhair Spleenwort*
Local. 13. Sandstone and gritstone walls, and in mortared interstices.

15/7 Asplenium ruta-muraria L. *Wall Rue*
Frequent. 49. Rare on sandstone outcrops; more frequently on walls.

16/1 Ceterach officinarum DC. *Rusty-back Fern*
Rare. 3. Naturalised on wall near Lyme Park gates, 98SW *Mrs. G. Mackie*; railway bridge, Audlem, 64 SE, *G. Meredith*; wall at Capenhurst, 37NE, *Mrs. N. F. McMillan.*

18/1 Athyrium filix-femina (L.) Roth *Lady Fern*
Very common. 102. Wet patches in woods, shaded stream and river banks, ditchsides, hedge bottoms. Fringes of meres in alder carr. Abundant on Pennine stream and gully banks.

19/1 Cystopteris fragilis (L.) Bernh. *Brittle Bladder-fern*
Rare. 3. Wall of Rostherne churchyard, 78SW, *P. Oswald!* the exact place whence it was thought to have disappeared by De Tabley: canal stonework, 96NW! (North Rode), 98NE, *Mrs. G. Mackie.*

21/1 Dryopteris filix-mas (L.) Schott *Male Fern*
Very common. 106. Woods, shaded stream and hedgebanks throughout the county.

21/2 Dryopteris pseudo-mas (Woll.) Holub & Pouzar (*D. borreri* Newm.) *Scaly Male Fern*
Occasional. 18. Pennine streams and gully banks both in shade and in the open; particularly on wet friable shale slopes. Small colonies also in Weaver and Bollin valleys, and heathy woods in S. Wirral.

21/6 Dryopteris carthusiana (Villar) H. P. Fuchs (*D. lanceolatocristata* (Hoffm.) Alston) *Narrow Buckler-fern.*
Occasional. 23. Peat mosslands, in active sphagnum and in more consolidated but saturated peat, sometimes in shade. Rarely in swampy alluvial flats under alder carr.

21/7 Dryopteris dilatata (Hoffm.) A. Gray *Broad Buckler-fern*
Very common. 106. Abundant in all wooded situations on clay, peat, sandstone, gritstone; Pennine streams and gullies. Major constituent of ground flora in Birch woods on peat mosses, and sessile oak woods in hills.

22/1 Polystichum setiferum (Forsk.) Woynar *Soft Shield-fern*
Local. 13. Steep wooded banks; most luxuriant and often more abundant locally than *P. aculeatum*: more catholic in soil preferences e.g. Carboniferous shale 99SW, Keuper waterstones 46SW, 38, and Boulder clay in 28NW. Elsewhere on Keuper marl in similar sites to *P. aculeatum.* The two species however rarely grow together.

Azollaceae

22/2 Polystichum aculeatum (L.) Roth *Hard Shield-fern*
Local. 10. Steep wooded cloughs on Keuper marl exposures usually in heavy shade.

24/1 Thelypteris limbosperma (All.) H. P. Fuchs (*T. oreopteris* (Ehrh.) Slosson) *Mountain Fern*
Occasional. 24. Gullies, streamsides and damp banks, often in shaded or lightly wooded situations. Common in Pennine zone, rare elsewhere.

24/2 Thelypteris palustris Schott *Marsh Fern*
Rare. 3. Alder carr fringe of two meres in SW of county 54NW! 54NE! and fenny margin of Wybunbury Moss 65SE!

25/1 Polypodium vulgare L. *Polypody*
Frequent. 41. Sandstone outcrops, sand dunes and walls in Wirral and West Cheshire. On stone walls in Pennines.

Species apparently extinct

9/1 Cryptogramma crispa (L.) R.Br. ex Hook.

21/5 Dryopteris cristata (L.) A. Gray.

24/3 Thelypteris phegopteris (L.) Slosson (Hb. Manchester Mus., Stirrup Wood, 1876).

24/4 Gymnocarpium dryopteris (L.) Newman.

MARSILEACEAE

Species apparently extinct

26/1 Pilularia globulifera L.
Formerly in abundance at Fishpool, Delamere, now drained and overgrown; cf. also Lancs. Nat. 5 p.44.

AZOLLACEAE

27/1 Azolla filiculoides Lam. *Water Fern*
Established in several ponds in the Chester district and Wirral; 37SE, 47SW, *T. Edmondson*. 45NW, Aldersey, *K. G. Allenby;* 38, 28NW, *Miss V. Gordon;* 46SW, *K. S. Cansdale.* For earlier history cf. N.W.Nat., vols. 15-22, passim.

28/1 Botrychium lunaria (L.) Sw. *Moonwort*
Rare. 3. Pennine grassland on Carboniferous shale with *Platanthera chlorantha, Ophioglossum vulgatum, Viola lutea* (96NW! 97SE! 98SE *A. Gibson*). While apparently extinct in the plain, it formerly grew with *P. chlorantha* on Keuper marl (cf. De Tabley p. 300).

29/1 Ophioglossum vulgatum L. *Adder's Tongue*
Frequent. 31. Hill grassland on Carboniferous shales in large colonies; alluvial meadows near coast; in small colonies in flushed sloping Keuper marl grassland; damp railway embankments on same soils.

SPERMATOPHYTA

GYMNOSPERMAE

PINACEAE

32/1 Larix decidua Mill. *European Larch*
Occasional. 20. Planted in woods and coverts.

33/1 Pinus sylvestris L. *Scots Pine*
Common. 59. Widely planted and also self sown, particularly on lighter loams and sandy drift soils. The pines in the Oakmere district have every appearance of ancient origin.

Plantations of conifers are infrequent in Cheshire except in Delamere Forest and the gathering grounds of reservoirs in some Pennine valleys. Here the species include **31/1 Picea abies** (L.) Karst. (*Norway Spruce*) **Pinus nigra** Arnold subsp. **nigra** (*Austrian pine*) and subsp. **laricio** (Poir.) Palibin (*Corsican Pine*), **Picea sitchensis** Carr. (*Sitka spruce*), **Pseudotsuga menziesii** (Nisb.) Franco (*Douglas Fir*), in addition to the two previous species.

TAXACEAE

35/1 Taxus baccata L. *Yew.*
Occasional. 21. Planted in most localities.

ANGIOSPERMAE

DICOTYLEDONES

RANUNCULACEAE

36/1 Caltha palustris L. *Marsh Marigold*
Very common. 99. Marshy woods, ditches, swampy stream and river sides, alder carr; tolerates considerable shade.

Ranunculaceae

43/1 Anemone nemorosa L. *Wood Anemone*
Very common. 87. Woods, wood borders, scrubland, hedgebanks.
Throughout the county except at highest levels, particularly on clay soils.

45/1 Clematis vitalba L. *Traveller's Joy*
Local. 10. Scrub and hedgebanks in Wirral; garden escape 46SW, 64SE,
67NE, 74. While its origins in Cheshire have been doubted (cf. De Tabley
p.1) it is thoroughly established in North Wirral and may in fact be
indigenous, on the analogy of the North Wales coast population.

46/1 Ranunculus acris L. *Meadow Buttercup*
Very common. 108. Pasture and meadow on all except peaty soils.

46/2 Ranunculus repens L. *Creeping Buttercup*
Very common. 110. Damp pastures, marshes, ponds, roadsides, woods,
disturbed ground throughout the county.

46/3 Ranunculus bulbosus L. *Bulbous Buttercup*
Very common, 85. Sand dunes, pastures and meadows on light soils; well
drained grassy slopes on marl and Carboniferous shale.

46/10 Ranunculus auricomus L. *Goldilocks*
Occasional. 20. Semi-natural woodland and hedgebanks on Keuper
marl in open or light shade. Most frequent in area of the former Forest of
Mondrum. Plants with abortive petals are frequent in this area; elsewhere
fully formed petals are usual.

46/11 Ranunculus lingua L. *Great Spearwort*
Local. 13. Small mere surrounds in reed swamp fringe in *Phragmites* zone;
large ponds with developing fen vegetation; relict fens; water of high base
status.

46/12 Ranunculus flammula L. *Lesser Spearwort*
Very common. 85. Mere, pond fringes, mosslands; peaty hollows and
ditches on heath and moorland, Pennine flushes; particularly characteristic of wet humified peat.

46/15 Ranunculus sceleratus L. *Celery-leaved Crowfoot*
Very common. 97. Muddy surrounds of meres, ponds, ditches. Rare in
Pennine zone. Tolerates highly nitrogenous conditions, often one of the
last flowering plants to survive in stagnant or contaminated ponds. Also
persists at drained pond sites.

46/16 Ranunculus hederaceus L. *Ivy-leaved Water Crowfoot*
Frequent. 46. Muddy margins of ponds and ditches, springheads.

46/17 Ranunculus omiophyllus Ten. (*R. lenormandii* F. W. Schultz) *Round leaved Water Crowfoot*
Occasional. 23. Pennine flushes, runnels, springheads. Rarely springs and small streams in plain.

46/19 Ranunculus fluitans Lam. *River Water Crowfoot*
Occasional. 16. Unpolluted regularly flowing streams and rivers, Gowy, Dane, Weaver tributaries, Shropshire Union Canal.

46/20 Ranunculus circinatus Sibth. *Fan leaved Water Crowfoot*
Rare. 5. Frodsham marsh ditches and large meres in north centre, e.g. Tatton, Tabley: tolerant of brackish water. Locally abundant.

46/21 Ranunculus trichophyllus Chaix *Thread leaved Water Crowfoot*
Occasional. 23. Ponds with circulating water.

46/22 Ranunculus aquatilis L. *Common Water Crowfoot*
Frequent. 39. Ponds with circulating water; slow flowing streams and ditches.

46/22b Ranunculus peltatus Schrank
Rare. 6. Reservoirs and large ponds. Locally abundant.

46/23 Ranunculus baudotii Godr. *Brackish Water Crowfoot*
Rare. 4. Salt marsh pools and brackish ditches, 27! conf. C. D. K. Cook. 57NE, *T. Edmondson*; 29! 37SW!

46/24 Ranunculus ficaria L. *Lesser Celandine*
Very common. 103. Woodlands and wood borders, scrubland, shady hedgerows, particularly on damp humus rich soils. Subsp. **bulbifera** (M.-Jones) Lawalrée:—96NW, 98SW; no doubt under recorded.

49/1 Aquilegia vulgaris L. *Columbine*
Established on roadsides near habitation 78NW, 88NW, 87NW, 76NW/SW, 75NE, 65SW, 64NE, 37NE, 45NE/SE.

50/1 Thalictrum flavum L. *Meadow Rue*
Rare. 5. Alluvial riverside meadows on lower Dee; ditchsides on alluvial flats of lower Gowy, Weaver and Helsby Brook. 36NE, 47NE, 57NW!, *T. Edmondson* 47SE!, 45NW *P. Newton and A. Gibson*.

50/3 Thalictrum minus L. subsp. **arenarium** (Butcher) Clapham *Lesser Meadow Rue*
Rare. 2. Hoylake sand dunes, 28NW! Sandy bank, Irby 28NE!

Papaveraceae

Species apparently extinct

37/1 Trollius europaeus L.

46/5 Ranunculus arvensis L. (N.W. Nat. 3, 1928, p.197, Heswall).

46/7 R. sardous Crantz.

46/9 R. parviflorus L.

48/1 Myosurus minimus L.

BERBERIDACEAE

53/1 Berberis vulgaris L. *Barberry*
Rare. 4. Hedgerows, 57SW *T. Edmondson*; 46SW! 54NE! 65SE, *Mrs. A. Blacklay.*

54/1 Mahonia aquifolium (Pursh) Nutt. *Oregon Grape*
Local. 13. Established in ornamental woods and coverts; hedgebanks near habitation, probably bird sown.

NYMPHAEACEAE

55/1 Nymphaea alba L. *White Water-lily.*
Frequent. 38. Meres and larger pools; occasionally ponds, sphagnum filled hollows and peaty pools.

56/1 Nuphar lutea (L.) Sm. *Yellow Water-lily*
Frequent. 40. Meres and larger pools, ornamental lakes.

CERATOPHYLLACEAE

57/1 Ceratophyllum demersum L. *Spined Horn-wort*
Occasional. 21. Ponds, ditches and canals in the northern half of the county, often forming a dense impenetrable mass.

57/2 Ceratophyllum submersum L. *Spineless Horn-wort*
Very rare. 1. Pond near Gt. Budworth 67NE 1968 *K. G. Allenby*! conf. C. A. Stace. Not previously recorded in the county. Other non-fruiting populations appear to be intermediate between this and *C. demersum fide* C.A.S.

PAPAVERACEAE

58/1 Papaver rhoeas L. *Field Poppy*
Frequent. 27. Regularly on sandy arable and waste ground in Wirral; sporadic arable weed elsewhere.

58/2 Papaver dubium L. *Long-headed Poppy*
Common. 62. Arable and disturbed ground, open roadsides, especially on light soils.

58/6 Papaver somniferum L. subsp. **hortense** Hussenot *Opium Poppy*.
Occasional on rubbish tips and waste ground; persistent in some localities.

62/1 Chelidonium majus L. *Greater Celandine*
Common. 71. Hedgebanks and roadsides near habitation, never in quantity at any one site.

63/1 Eschscholzia californica Cham. occurs as a garden outcast on rubbish tips.

Species apparently extinct

58/5 Papaver argemone L.

61/1 Glaucium flavum Crantz (L.N.F.C. 1953, p.15, Denhall.)

FUMARIACEAE

65/2 Corydalis bulbosa (L. emend Mill.) DC. has been recorded once as a garden escape (77NE).

65/3 Corydalis claviculata (L.) DC. *White Climbing Fumitory*
Frequent. 36. Heathy birchwood on glacial sand and Triassic sandstone outcrops; Alder carr surrounds of meres; wooded outer margins of moss-lands. Appears to require peaty soil.

65/4 Corydalis lutea (L.) DC. *Yellow Fumitory*
Established on a few roadsides, 38, 45NE, 67SW, 64SE, 78SE.

66/4-10 Fumaria officinalis L. agg. *Common Fumitory*
Common. 65. Arable, waste and disturbed ground.

66/4 Fumaria bastardii Bor. has been recorded only on waste ground, Thurstaston, 28NW! and along a field border Ollerton 77NE! in 1968.

66/6b Fumaria muralis Sonder ex Koch subsp. **boraei** (Jord.) Pugsl. 22. The prevalent taxon in arable ground.

66/8 Fumaria officinalis L. s.s. is more characteristic of waste and disturbed ground but also occurs occasionally in similar situations to *F. muralis* subsp. *boraei*.

66/2 Fumaria capreolata L. & **66/3 F. purpurea** Pugsl. are recorded for SJ28 in the BSBI Atlas, det. *Pugsley* (undated) but have not been found during the survey.

CRUCIFERAE

67/2 Brassica napus L. *Rape, Cole*
Common. 57. *B. napus/rapa*: Any attempt to construct an accurate account of the separate distribution of these species would be presumptuous on the records available. Collectively they are common on arable and disturbed ground, and consist entirely of cultivation relicts.

67/4 Brassica nigra (L.) Koch *Black Mustard*
Local. 9. Ditches, riverbanks and streamsides; rarely on waste ground.

69/1 Rhynchosinapis monensis (L.) Dandy *Isle of Man Cabbage*
Very rare. 1. Locally common on sand dunes, Wallasey and Leasowe 29! in the same area noted in De Tabley's Flora, p.21.

70/1 Sinapis arvensis L. *Charlock*
Common. 68. Arable and disturbed ground, particularly on light soils.

71/1 Hirschfeldia incana (L.) Lagr.-Foss. *Hoary Mustard*
Rare. 2. Large colony on lime waste beds, Northwich. 67NE/SE! conf. *C. A. Stace*. First present in this area c. 1920, cf. L. & C. Nat. 15, p.44 (as *Brassica adpressa*).

72/1 Diplotaxis muralis (L.) DC. *Annual Wall Rocket.*
Local. 7. Open sandy ground on the coast; nurseries on light soils in the Altrincham district.

72/2 Diplotaxis tenuifolia (L.) DC. *Perennial Wall Rocket.*
Rare. 2. Waste ground, Frodsham; City walls, Chester.

74/1 Raphanus raphanistrum L. *Wild Radish*
Common. 62. Arable and disturbed ground. White, yellow and veined colour forms are all found.

77/1 Cakile maritima Scop. *Sea Rocket.*
Rare. 3. Sand dunes and foreshore, Gayton to Wallasey.

78/1 Conringia orientalis (L.) Dumort. *Hare's-ear Cabbage.*
Sporadic in a few places on industrial waste ground in 38, 47NE, 57NW, 77NW.

79/2 Lepidium campestre (L.) R.Br. *Pepperwort*
Local. 12. Persistent on industrial waste; casual in farmyards and nurseries.

79/3 Lepidium heterophyllum Benth. *Smith's Cress.*
Rare. 5. Railway ballast.

79/6 Lepidium latifolium L. *Dittander*
Old established patch at Meols, 29, *Miss V. Gordon*; railway precinct, Chester Northgate, 1970, *T. Edmondson*.

80/1 Coronopus squamatus (Forsk.) Aschers. *Swine-Cress*
Local. 12. Damp open waste ground, e.g. canal sides, muddy farm tracks and gateways.

80/2 Coronopus didymus (L.) Sm. *Lesser Swine-Cress*
Rare. 4. Locally abundant on sand dunes, Hoylake and Wallasey golf courses; casual elsewhere on sandy ground.

81/1 Cardaria draba (L.) Desv. *Hoary Cress*
Local. 11. Well established along the banks of the Dee from Thurstaston to Parkgate; isolated long-lived patches on the banks of the Bridgewater and Trent and Mersey canals; casual on rubbish dumps and waste ground elsewhere.

84/1 Thlaspi arvense L. *Field Penny-cress*
Local. 9. Nurseries and disturbed ground, roadsides and tips.

85/1 Teesdalia nudicaulis (L.) R.Br. *Shepherd's Cress*
Rare. 5. Open sandy ground; sandstone detritus, Storeton, 38 *Miss V. Gordon*; sandpit edges, 56 NE, *P. Newton*! Wybunbury 74!; sandy surrounds of Sound Common, 64NW *Mrs. G. Mackie*! Sandy bank, 67SW! Decreasing.

86/1 Capsella bursa-pastoris (L.) Medic. *Shepherd's Purse*
Very common. 104. Arable and disturbed ground, open roadsides, rubbish tips, throughout the county.

88/5 Cochlearia danica L. *Danish Scurvy-grass*
Local. 7. Low sandstone cliffs and grassy banks close to the sea; behind Leasowe embankments; inland on railway ballast, 37NW/NE, 57SE.

88/6 Cochlearia anglica L. *English Scurvy-grass*
Local. 9. Salt marshes and creeks.

95/1 Erophila verna (L.) Chevall. *Whitlow Grass*
Local. 9. Open dry situations; sand dunes near coast; railway ballast, sandpits, wall tops inland.

96/1 Armoracia rusticana Gaertn., Mey. & Scherb. *Horse Radish*
Common. 72. Roadsides; railway banks; waste ground; rubbish tips.

97/1 Cardamine pratensis L. *Lady's Smock*
Very common. 105. Damp grassland and marshes throughout the county. Pond fringes, ditch and stream sides. The double flowered form is rare and is only recorded from 68SE and 98NW.

97/2 Cardamine amara L. *Large Bitter-cress*
Common. 72. Shaded stream and river banks and alluvial flats, particularly on Keuper marl and Carboniferous shale; apparently absent in a large part of the west of the county.

Cruciferae

97/4 Cardamine flexuosa With. *Wavy Bitter-cress*
Very common. 98. In similar areas to *C. amara*, but also in unshaded marshy ground along streams, ditches; damp shaded hedgebanks. Not so selective in soil requirements; any damp open, but shaded situation.

97/5 Cardamine hirsuta L. *Hairy Bitter-cress*
Common. 56. Nursery and garden weed; tracks and pathsides; walls; sandy grassland on Triassic sandstone outcrops.

98/1 Barbarea vulgaris R. Br. *Winter Cress*
Common. 67. Ditch, stream, and river banks; less commonly on waste ground and roadsides.

100/4 Arabis hirsuta (L.) Scop. *Hairy Rock-cress*
Very rare. 1. Small colony on sand dunes of Wallasey golf course 29!

102/1 Nasturtium officinale R. Br. **sensu lato** (*Rorippa nasturtium-aquaticum* (L.) Hayek s.l.) *Watercress.*
Very common. 89. Streams, ditches, and slow flowing rivers; ponds with some circulating water. Many observers have not distinguished the segregates, but **N. microphyllum** (Boenn.) Reichb. has been recorded from SJ/38, 37SE, 47NE/SW/SE, and from 28 and 88 *fide* Critical Atlas; the hybrid, **N. officinale x microphyllum** from SJ/47NE, 57NE/SE & *fide* Critical Atlas from 56, 88 & 98.

102/3 Rorippa sylvestris (L.) Bess. *Creeping Yellow-cress*
Occasional. 17. Allotment and garden weed on sandy soils; river banks on alluvial silt.

102/4 Rorippa islandica (Oeder) Borbás *Marsh Yellow-cress*
Common. 65. Muddy pond margins, ditches, canal banks between the stonework, strand lines of larger waters.

102/5 Rorippa amphibia (L.) Bess. *Great Yellow-cress*
Occasional. 20. River banks and canal sides. Occurs along Dee, Bollin, Dane and Macclesfield Canal.

104/1 Hesperis matronalis L. *Dame's Violet*
Local. 11. Established on railway banks, hedgebanks; rubbish tips.

105/1 Erysimum cheiranthoides L. *Treacle Mustard*
Casual on waste ground, 78NE, 88SW, 88NE, 65SE. Persistent for a few years, 46NW.

106/1 Cheiranthus cheiri L. *Wallflower*
Long naturalised on the walls of Beeston Castle, 55NW! Sandstone walls at Burton, 27, *Miss V. Gordon;* Chester 46NW!

PLATE 3. *Above: Botrychium lunaria* (Moonwort), upland meadow near Wincle (page 71); *beneath: Ranunculus auricomus* (Goldilocks), wood border, Darnhall (page 72).

PLATE 4. *Above: Drosera rotundifolia* (Sundew), Lindow Common, Wilmslow (page 110); *beneath: Primula veris x vulgaris* (False Oxlip), meadow, Darnhall (page 125).

107/1 Alliaria petiolata (Bieb.) Cavara & Grande *Garlic Mustard*
Very common. 96. Streamsides, roadsides, waste ground.

108/1 Sisymbrium officinale (L.) Scop. *Hedge Mustard*
Very common. 82. Disturbed ground, roadsides, industrial waste, decreasing eastwards.

108/4 Sisymbrium orientale L. *Eastern Rocket*
Local. 10. Railway ballast, waste ground: well established and spreading in Wirral.

108/5 Sisymbrium altissimum L. *Tall Rocket*
Occasional. 23. Disturbed and waste ground; often abundant on tips.

109/1 Arabidopsis thaliana (L.) Heynh. *Thale Cress*
Frequent. 41. Open sandy situations; sand dunes; Triassic sandstone outcrops and walls; sandy grassland; nurseries on light soils; railway ballast.

67/1 Brassica oleracea L. **70/2 Sinapis alba** L. **98/3 Barbarea intermedia** Bor. & **98/4 B. verna** (Mill.) Aschers. have been found rarely as cultivation relics; **74/3 Raphanus sativus** L., **79/1 Lepidium sativum** L., **92/1 Lobularia maritima** (L.) Desv. **Iberis umbellata** L., **76/3 Rapistrum orientale** (L.) Crantz, **110/1 Camelina sativa** (L.) Crantz, as garden outcasts or casuals on waste ground and rubbish tips; **Lunaria annua** L. is found as a garden escape near habitations.

Species apparently extinct

79/4 Lepidium ruderale L., Morley 1927, coll. *A. Pollitt*

111/1 Descurainia sophia (L.) Webb ex Prantl (Carrington, casual, 1924, L.&C. Nat. 16 p.285).

RESEDACEAE

112/1 Reseda luteola L. *Dyer's Rocket*
Frequent. 38. Open and disturbed ground, ashes, railway embankments, industrial waste, river banks, sandy roadsides; sandy exposures on Dee shore.

112/2 Reseda lutea L. *Wild Mignonette*
Occasional. 23. Open and disturbed ground, cinder banks; railway ballast and lime waste.

VIOLACEAE

113/1 Viola odorata L. *Sweet Violet*
Local. 12. Open woods, shaded hedgebanks; all sites except 64SW/SE near habitation and usually with white flowers, suggesting garden origin; with blue flowers and apparently indigenous in this small area where associated with uppermost Keuper marl.

113/4 Viola riviniana Reichb. *Common Violet*
Very common. 99. Hill grassland, Keuper marl grassland; woods, wood borders, hedgebanks and scrubland on shale and clay.

113/5 Viola reichenbachiana Jord. ex Bor. *Pale Wood Violet*
Occasional. 17. Open woodland and hedgebanks where Keuper marl exposed at surface. Plants with intermediate characteristics, suggesting introgression, occur where this and the preceding species are contiguous.

113/6 Viola canina L. *Heath Violet*
Rare. 3. Sand dunes, 28NW/SE! 29! Hoylake and Wallasey golf courses.

113/9 Viola palustris L. subsp. **palustris** *Marsh Violet*
Frequent. 41. Pennine hill flushes, peaty surrounds of mosslands; peaty pools and ditches on heathland; markedly commoner in east of county.

113/11 Viola lutea Huds. *Mountain Pansy*
Rare. 4. Old pastures on Carboniferous shale above 1,250 ft. (97NE! SW, SE! 96NE!).

113/12a Viola tricolor L. *Wild Pansy*
Frequent. 27. Arable and disturbed ground, sandpit edges, tips.

113/13 Viola arvensis Murr. *Field Pansy*
Common. 66. Arable and disturbed ground, particularly on sandy soils; railway ballast.

Viola arvensis x tricolor
Rare on sandy arable and waste ground, 27! 54NE! 56NW!

Viola x wittrockiana Hort. occurs occasionally on rubbish tips.

Species apparently extinct

113/12b Viola tricolor L. subsp. **curtisii** (E. Forst.) Syme ("very rare" on Wirral Dunes 1924 L.&C. Nat. 16, p.133).

POLYGALACEAE

114/1 Polygala vulgaris L. *Common Milkwort*
Occasional. 20. Sand dunes, flushed grassland, particularly old pastures on Keuper marl.

114/2 Polygala serpyllifolia Hose *Heath Milkwort*
Frequent. 30. Rough grassland in Pennines; leached banks on clay grassland in plain. Grass heath on Triassic sandstone.

GUTTIFERAE

115/1 Hypericum androsaemum L. *Tutsan*
Established on hedgebanks, 38, 98NE, where probably bird sown.

115/5 Hypericum perforatum L. *Common St. John's Wort*
Common. 77. Well drained banks and scrub on clay and sandy soils; canal and railway embankments, roadsides, sandpit edges, lime waste beds.

115/6 Hypericum maculatum Crantz subsp. **obtusiusculum** (Tourlet) Hayek *Imperforate St. John's Wort*
Occasional. 23. Wood borders, scrub and hedgebanks, chiefly on Keuper marl, but also recorded from boulder clay.

115/8 Hypericum tetrapterum Fr. *Square-stemmed St. John's Wort*
Very common. 81. Marshes, mere and pond fringes, springs and flushes.

115/9 Hypericum humifusum L. *Trailing St. John's Wort*
Occasional. 18. Open situations on sandstone; sand pits; sandy grassland; nurseries on light soils. Two places in Pennines on open banks.

115/11 Hypericum pulchrum L. *Slender St. John's Wort*
Frequent. 31. Open situations on heathy wood borders, scrubland and hedgebanks on clay, sand and Carboniferous series. A small number of plants at each site even when "pioneers", e.g. at disused clay and sand pits.

115/12 Hypericum hirsutum L. *Hairy St. John's Wort*
Rare. 4. Wood borders and hedgebanks on Keuper marl and calcareous drift, Dee Valley 44! 45NW, *A. Gibson & P. Newton*; 46SW, *Mrs. G. Mackie*; 57NE, *T. Edmondson*, where doubted by De Tabley (p.59)—cf. for reinstatement of J. Harrison's record, Lancs. Nat., 3, p. 408.

115/13 Hypericum montanum L. *Mountain St. John's Wort*
Very rare. 1. A few plants were found twenty yards inside the county boundary at Lower Kinnerton (36SW) by *T. Edmondson*! in 1969. Colonies occur along the railway banks at intervals from Mold (a limestone district) towards Chester, of which this is apparently the last outpost.

115/4 Hypericum calycinum L. is reported as established near gardens.

Species apparently extinct

115/14 Hypericum elodes L. ("not found in Delamere forest", 1923, L.&C. Nat. 16, p.135); A specimen (coll. *A. Pollitt*) labelled "Dunham on the Hill, 5 vii 1925" is now in the Grosvenor Museum, Chester.

Caryophyllaceae

Species apparently extinct

122/1 Elatine hexandra (Lapierre) DC. (The Dibbin, Bromborough (38)
1953; N.W. Nat. n.s., 1, p.100, *Mrs N. F. McMillan.*)

CARYOPHYLLACEAE

123/1 Silene vulgaris (Moench) Garcke subsp. **vulgaris** *Bladder Campio*
Frequent. 28. Dry waste and disturbed ground, roadsides, railway ballast
tips, particularly near the coast.

123/2 Silene vulgaris subsp. **maritima** (With.) A.&D. Löve *Sea Campion*
Rare. 2. Sandstone outcrops at Hoylake and Hilbre.

123/6 Silene gallica L. *Small flowered Campion*
Very rare. 1. A small, white-flowered colony in a sandy farm lane, 28NW
Mrs. E. Hall!, 1968.

123/13 Silene dioica (L.) Clairv. *Red Campion*
Very common. 106. Woods, wood borders, shaded hedgebanks, ditche
and streamsides throughout.

123/14 Silene alba (Mill.) E. H. L. Krause *White Campion*
Common. 69. Arable and disturbed ground, especially on light soils.

Silene alba x dioica
Rare. 6. Observed on roadsides and field borders in 28NW/NE/SE
45SW/SE, 74(all!)

124/3 Lychnis flos-cuculi L. *Ragged Robin*
Very common. 90. Marshes, wet meadows, pond fringes.

127/8 Dianthus deltoides L. *Maiden Pink*
Very rare. 1. Fragment of sand dune, Hoylake 28NW! 1965.

129/1 Saponaria officinalis L. *Soapwort*
Occasional. 14. Well established on fringes of sand dunes on coastal strip.
Naturalised on roadsides or casual on rubbish tips elsewhere.

131/2 Cerastium arvense L. *Field Mouse-ear Chickweed*
Very rare. 1. Several large patches in ungrazed grassland on Hilbre Island,
Mr. & Mrs. D. Parish, 1968! apparently the only surviving locality (cf.
De Tabley p.47).

131/3 Cerastium tomentosum L. *Dusty Miller*
Garden escape on roadsides and waste ground, 29, 98NE, 64NE, 45SE.

31/7 Cerastium fontanum Baumg. subsp. **triviale** (Link) Jalás (*C. holosteoides* Fr.) *Common Mouse-ear Chickweed*
Very common. 110. Abundant in a wide variety of habitats throughout the county, including sand dunes, grassland, arable, disturbed and waste ground, marshes, pond fringes.

31/8 Cerastium glomeratum Thuill. *Sticky Mouse-ear Chickweed*
Frequent. 43. Trampled mud in gateways; farm tracks; sandy grassland.

31/10 Cerastium diffusum Pers. (*C. atrovirens* Bab.) *Dark-green Mouse-ear Chickweed*
Local. 10. Sand dunes, and cinders of railway ballast inland.

31/12 Cerastium semidecandrum L. *Little Mouse-ear Chickweed*
Rare. 6. Locally common on sand dunes and open sandy grassland. Beeston Castle 55NW! Field near Oakmere 56NE! sandy bank 66NW!

32/1 Myosoton aquaticum (L.) Moench *Water Chickweed*
Local. 10. In some quantity, low lying ditches near R. Dee (47SW! 36SE!); 45NW, *F. Tyrer*; Riversides near Darnhall 66SW! 65NW! and Audlem 64SW! 64SE, *G. Meredith*! Rostherne Mere outflow, 78SW, *P. H. Oswald*! Brereton Pool 76NE, *F. Tyrer*, Bollin Bank 88SW, *G. M. Kay*.

33/1 Stellaria nemorum L. *Wood Stitchwort*
Local. 8. Damp stream banks in old woodland on Keuper marl, mottled sandstone or Carboniferous shale; along Bollin, Goyt and Upper Dane valleys.

33/2 Stellaria media (L.) Vill. *Chickweed*
Very common. 110. Arable, disturbed and waste ground, hedgebanks, roadsides throughout the county.

33/3 Stellaria pallida (Dumort.) Piré *Lesser Chickweed*.
Rare. 2. Sand dunes at Hoylake and Gayton. (28NW/SE)!

133/4 Stellaria neglecta Weihe *Greater Chickweed*
Frequent. 42. Wooded streamsides and damp wooded alluvial flats particularly on Keuper marl derived soils.

133/5 Stellaria holostea L. *Greater Stitchwort*
Very common. 101. Woods, wood borders, scrub, hedgebanks on well drained soils throughout the county.

133/7 Stellaria graminea L. *Lesser Stitchwort*
Very common. 103. Marshes, ditches, mere and pond fringes, streamsides, damp hedgebanks throughout the county.

Caryophyllaceae

133/8 Stellaria alsine Grimm *Bog Stitchwort*
Very common. 103. Marshes, streams, springs, flushes, pond fringes and
wet muddy situations throughout the county.

136/1 Sagina apetala Ard. *Common Pearlwort*
Occasional. 22. Sandstone outcrops and detritus in west of county;
gritstone walls in Pennine zone.

136/3 Sagina maritima Don *Sea Pearlwort*
Rare. 3. Inland edge of salt marsh 27! conf. F. N. Hepper; 47NW *A.*
Gibson! Inland bank of seawall 29!

136/4 Sagina procumbens L. *Procumbent Pearlwort*
Very common. 97. Roadsides, pathsides, marshes, garden weed; open
damp areas throughout.

136/10 Sagina nodosa (L.) Fenzl *Knotted Pearlwort*
Rare. 4. Relict sand dunes 28SE! Lime beds, 67SE! Upland flush on
Carboniferous shale 96NW, *P. Newton!*

139/1 Honkenya peploides (L.) Ehrh. *Sea Sandwort*
Rare. 4. Loose sand above spring tide level.

140/1 Moehringia trinervia (L.) Clairv. *Three-nerved Sandwort*
Common. 74. Woods and wood borders, dry sloping wooded stream
banks; light and clay soils.

141/1 Arenaria serpyllifolia L. *Thyme-leaved Sandwort*
Occasional. 21. Sand dunes; sandy grassland; sandstone outcrops, lime-
waste beds. The prevalent form is subsp. **serpyllifolia**; subsp. **leptoclados**
(Reichb.) Guss., was recorded in 28NW! 37NE! and 46NW det F. N.
Hepper. Intermediates also occur.

141/6 Arenaria balearica L. *Balearic Pearlwort*
Reported as naturalised in several localities in Wirral, e.g. West Kirby,
Ness, Burton. First records L.&C. Nat., 9, p.25 and 10, p.128, at Brom-
borough (1917).

142/1 Spergula arvensis L. *Corn Spurrey*
Very common. 89. Arable and disturbed ground, particularly on light soils.

143/1 Spergularia rubra (L.) J.&C. Presl *Sand Spurrey*
Occasional. 18. Open sandy and gravelly ground on sandstone and
glacial drift, sandpit edges, clinkers of railway tracks.

143/3 Spergularia rupicola Lebel ex Le Jolis *Cliff Sand Spurrey*
Rare. 2. Plentiful on sandstone cliffs at Hoylake and Hilbre!

143/4 Spergularia media (L.) C. Presl *Greater Sand Spurrey*
Rare. 4. Higher levels of salt marshes.

Chenopodiaceae

143/5 Spergularia marina (L.) Griseb. *Lesser Sand Spurrey*
Local. 10. Higher levels of salt marsh, and brackish marsh; also saline ground inland (66NE, 76NW).

123/8 Silene armeria L. Wirral, 1967, *E. Hardy*, **123/12 S.noctiflora** L., waste ground Broadheath (78NE), 1968, *P. Newton!* and **127/1 Dianthus armeria** L., gravel drive, Alderley (87NW), *G. M. Kay!* have occurred as casuals. **127/2 D. barbatus** L. occurs as a garden outcast on rubbish dumps.

Species apparently extinct

125/1 Agrostemma githago L. (except as bird seed casual.)

135/1 Moenchia erecta (L.) Gaertn., Mey., & Scherb.

136/9 Sagina subulata (Sw.) C. Presl.

ILLECEBRACEAE

148/1 Scleranthus annuus L. *Annual Knawel*
Local. 7. Open sandy and gravelly soils, particularly on sandpit edges: railway track, 37NW.

146/3 Herniaria hirsuta L. occurred on railway ballast, SJ 9286 in 1967, *A. Gibson* conf. A. Melderis.

PORTULACACEAE

149/1 Montia fontana L. *Blinks*
Frequent. 29. Hill flushes in Pennines; shore line of meres and pools; streamsides at water level. All the material examined from the hill region (SJ/97, 99, SE/00) is subsp. **fontana**; subsp. **variabilis** Walters occurs in 57SW (conf. S. M. Walters), 74. subsp. **amporitana** Sennen occurs in 45SE & 54NE.

149/2 Claytonia perfoliata Donn ex Willd. *Spring Beauty*
Occasional. 19. Gardens, nurseries and hedge bottoms; open sandy disturbed and waste ground.

149/3 Claytonia sibirica L. *Pink Purslane*
Occasional. 24. Naturalised particularly in damp woods and streamsides in east and north east Cheshire; also in Delamere Forest and Wirral.

CHENOPODIACEAE

154/4 Chenopodium album L. *White Goosefoot*
Very common. 86. Arable and disturbed ground, tips; exhibits a wide variety of growth forms; abundant in manured fields of root crops.

85

Chenopodiaceae

154/14 Chenopodium rubrum L. *Red Goosefoot*
Occasional. 19. Arable and waste ground, tips; farmyard rubbish dumps.

155/1 Beta vulgaris L. subsp. **maritima** (L.) Thell. *Sea Beet*
Rare. 5. Spring tide lines and sea walls; open parts of sand dunes.

156/1 Atriplex littoralis L. *Shore Orache*
Rare. 6. Spring tide level around Wirral; sea wall and marsh, Leasowe.

156/2 Atriplex patula L. *Common Orache*
Common. 76. Arable and disturbed ground, rubbish tips.

156/3 Atriplex hastata L. *Hastate Orache*
Occasional. 23. Sand and shingle at spring high tide level; low lying pastures subject to flood, lower Weaver valley; inland, occasional in arable fields and farmyards.

156/4 Atriplex glabriuscula Edmondst. *Babington's Orache*
Rare. 3. Shore line at Gayton, 28SE!, 28NW!, Frodsham salt marshes, 47NW, *A. Gibson.*

157/1 Halimione portulacoides (L.) Aellen *Sea Purslane*
Rare. 5. Salt marshes and creeks.

158/1 Suaeda maritima (L.) Dumort. *Annual Seablite*
Local. 7. Sides of creeks and channels in salt marshes.

160/2 Salicornia dolichostachya Moss *Glasswort*
Very rare. 1. Salt marsh, Burton 27! det. *Miss V. Gordon.* For first record cf L.&C. Nat., 13, p.75.

160/3 Salicornia europaea L. *Glasswort*
Rare. 4. Inner fringes of salt marshes.

154/1 Chenopodium bonus-henricus L. has been recorded by some observers but has not been substantiated by specimens; **154/10 C. pratericola** Rydb. is recorded as a casual in B.E.C. Rep., 1943-4. p.749, and **159/2 Salsola pestifer** A. Nels. as a dock alien, L.N.F.C., 1957, p.20.

Species apparently extinct

154/11 Chenopodium murale L.

156/5 Atriplex laciniata L.

159/1 Salsola kali L. (Leasowe, 1908, Drabble, J. Bot 48, p.155 (1910)).

TILIACEAE

162/2 Tilia cordata Mill. *Small leaved Lime*
Rare. 2. Apparently indigenous in old woodland in the Lower Weaver valley (57NE)! where other calcicolous species are found. Planted in 98SE.

Tilia cordata x platyphyllos (*T. vulgaris* Hayne) *Common Lime*
Frequent. 36. Ornamental or planted woodland.

MALVACEAE

163/1 Malva moschata L. *Musk Mallow*
Local. 10. Shaded river banks 44! 57NE!; canal bank 65SW; roadsides or casual elsewhere.

163/2 Malva sylvestris L. *Common Mallow*
Frequent. 51. Roadsides, hedgebanks, disturbed ground; absent except as casual in east of the county.

163/4 Malva neglecta Wallr. *Dwarf Mallow*
Rare. 6. Open sandy ground and field borders, 28SE, 36NE, 46NW, 57NE, 75SW, 64SE. Rarely persists.

Althaea rosea (L.) Cav. & **Sidalcea** spp. occur in the Chester area as garden outcasts on rubbish tips and waste ground. **Hibiscus trionum** L. (det. Kew) has been observed in some quantity in Frodsham station yard in 1969 (*T. Edmondson*).

LINACEAE

166/4 Linum catharticum L. *Purging Flax*
Frequent. 47. Damp flushed grassland on Keuper marl and calcareous clay; rarely on Carboniferous shales; calcareous waste in Northwich, Middlewich and Winsford areas; open spots on canal towpaths.

166/2 Linum usitatissimum L. is occasionally found on rubbish tips and waste ground.
Species apparently extinct

166/1 Linum bienne Mill. (sp. in Hb. Manch., 1874, Burton; cf. De Tabley p.64), last record Lancs. Nat., 6, p.341 (Bidston, 1913).

167/1 Radiola linoides Roth plentiful on heaths a century ago (sp. Hb. Liverpool Museum, Flaxmere, 1912, cf. Lancs. Nat., 5, p.178).

GERANIACEAE

168/1 Geranium pratense L. *Meadow Cranesbill*
Common. 55. Stream and river banks, wet alluvial meadows, Dee, Bollin, Weaver and Dane valleys; rare in upland meadows and hedgebanks.

168/3 Geranium endressii Gay *French Cranesbill*
Naturalised for many years by roadsides, 78SE! 87SE!

168/6 Geranium phaeum L. *Dusky Cranesbill*
Established by two roadsides, 87NE!

168/7 Geranium sanguineum L. *Bloody Cranesbill*
Rare. 2. Dee coast from Thurstaston to Gayton, on small vestiges of blown sand 28NW! 28SE! amongst gorse and bracken scrub.

168/9 Geranium pyrenaicum Burm.f. *Mountain Cranesbill*
Local. 11. Well established and abundant on roadsides and hedgebanks in S.W.Wirral; elsewhere a few persistent patches on canal banks; casual in 56NE and 67SW.

168/11 Geranium dissectum L. *Cut-leaved Cranesbill*
Common. 58. Arable and disturbed ground, roadsides, usually on light soils, decreasing north-eastwards.

168/12 Geranium rotundifolium L. *Round-leaved Cranesbill*
Very rare. 1. Triassic sandstone detritus, 27 *Miss V. Gordon*! First record from this site (1915) L.&C. Nat., 9, p.270.

168/13 Geranium molle L. *Dove's-foot Cranesbill*
Frequent. 50. Open situations usually on sandy soils; dunes, sandpits, roadsides, arable fields.

168/14 Geranium pusillum L. *Small-flowered Cranesbill*
Local. 7. Open sandy and arable ground, sandpits: 38, *Mrs. N. McMillan*; 45SE! with *Aphanes arvensis, Viola arvensis*; 56NE, *Mrs. G. Mackie*; 88 SW, *A. Gibson*; 57NW, 74! 36NE, *T. Edmondson*.

168/15 Geranium lucidum L. *Shining Cranesbill*
Local. 7. Established on a few road and path sides; no doubt a garden escape 37NE, 55NW, 46SW, 86SE, 45NE, 46SE, 64SE.

168/16 Geranium robertianum L. *Herb Robert*
Very common. 103. Woods, wood borders, shaded stream and river banks; ditch sides and hedgebanks throughout; rarely on railway ballast.

169/3 Erodium cicutarium (L.) L'Hérit. *Storksbill*
Occasional. 15. Open dry situations; sand dunes and sandy waste ground near the coast; sandpit edges, sandy waste ground; rubbish tips inland; subsp. **cicutarium** occurs in all observed situations. **E. glutinosum** Dumort. apparently occurs only on sand dunes, and is recorded in the Critical Atlas for 29.

Species apparently extinct

168/10 Geranium columbinum L. (Spec. in Hb. Liverpool Museum, ex Burton Point, 1915/6).

OXALIDACEAE

170/1 Oxalis acetosella L. *Wood Sorrel*
Very common. 100. Woodland on sand, clay, and shale; wood borders and hedgerows. Ascends into high Pennines as a woodland relic.

170/2 Oxalis corniculata L. & **170/3 O. stricta** L. have each been recorded once as garden escapes.

BALSAMINACEAE

171/2 Impatiens capensis Meerb. *Orange Balsam*
Large colony established in old meander of R. Mersey, Statham, 68NE! (Recorded in N.W. Nat., 13, 1938, p.247).

171/3 Impatiens parviflora DC. *Small Balsam*
Rare. 5. Established in a few waste, usually shady places, 28NE, 88NW/NE, 98NE/SW.

171/4 Impatiens glandulifera Royle *Himalayan Balsam*
Frequent. 46. Abundant on river and stream banks in north and east of the county and along the Dee. Waste ground, roadsides near houses and rubbish dumps elsewhere.

ACERACEAE

173/1 Acer pseudoplatanus L. *Sycamore*
Very common. 106. Woods and hedges on clay soil throughout the county; regenerating freely.

173/3 Acer campestre L. *Field Maple*
Frequent. 35. Woods and hedgerows. Apparently indigenous on Keuper marl and drift in lower Dee and Weaver valley south of Winsford; planted elsewhere.

173/2 Acer platanoides L. is occasionally planted in parklands and ornamental woods.

Leguminosae

175/1 Aesculus hippocastanum L. *Horse Chestnut*
Very common. 81. Ornamental and planted woodland.

176/1 Ilex aquifolium L. *Holly*
Very common. 103. Woods, scrub, hedges throughout.

177/1 Euonymus europaeus L. *Spindle-tree*
Rare. 4. Old woods on Keuper marl, 66SE! 44! 78SE, 88SE, *P. Newton.*

178/1 Buxus sempervirens L. Obviously originally planted, occurs rarely in woods.

180/1 Frangula alnus Mill. *Alder Buckthorn*
Frequent. 37. Mere fringes in alder carr; wooded surrounds of mosslands; sides of peaty ditches. Common in east central Cheshire and in the south; absent elsewhere.

Species apparently extinct

179/1 Rhamnus catharticus L.

183/2 Lupinus arboreus Sims *Tree Lupin*
Locally naturalised on sandy ground, 28SE! 38 *Mrs. N. F. McMillan;* 57NW, *T. Edmondson.*

185/1 Genista tinctoria L. *Dyer's Greenweed*
Frequent. 30. Grassland and scrubland on Keuper marl, Carboniferous shale and calcareous drift. Characteristic of damp undisturbed usually flushed pastures and meadows, often on steep banks. Much reduced over the last century.

187/1 Ulex europaeus L. *Gorse*
Very common. 105. Open banks, scrubland on well drained sandy soils and sandstone outcrops, boulder clay; leached grassland on Keuper series; hill grassland reverting to scrub, gritstone faces, quarry spoil.

187/2 Ulex gallii Planch. *Western Gorse*
Frequent. 40. Heath on sandstone outcrops and sandy surrounds of mosslands; uncommon in Pennine zone. Intermediates between this and *U. europaeus* have occasionally been found.

188/1 Cytisus scoparius (L.) Link *Broom*
Very common. 89. Roadside banks, incipient scrubland, woodland and wood borders on sandy glacial drift soils and sandstone detritus; also coloniser of sandpits and railway cuttings.

189/1 Ononis repens L. *Restharrow*
Local. 11. Abundant on sand dunes, rare inland on pastures on sandy drift soils. Plants intermediate between this and *O. spinosa* grow on the old bank of the Dee, Shotwick 37SW!

189/2 Ononis spinosa L. *Spiny Restharrow*
Frequent. 27. Grassland on Keuper marl and calcareous drift in Wirral.

190/2 Medicago sativa L. *Lucerne*
Occasional. 14. Established on railway sidings and sandy soils (including sand dunes) in Wirral and west of Delamere ridge; casual on waste ground elsewhere.

Medicago x varia Martyn: A few plants occurred in a sandpit at Sandiway (67SW) in 1965!

190/3 Medicago lupulina L. *Black Medick*
Very common. 81. Sandy grassland; open and disturbed ground, particularly sandy or gravelly tracks and roadsides.

191/2 Melilotus officinalis (L.) Pall. *Common Melilot*
Occasional. 24. Open dry waste ground. Tolerant of high salinity e.g. in Winsford district. Some recorders may have included **191/1 M. altissima** Thuill. under this taxon.

191/3 Melilotus alba Medic. *White Melilot*
Local. 12. Persistent and abundant on sandy waste ground in Wirral, and on railway ballast. Rubbish tip casual elsewhere.

192/2 Trifolium pratense L. *Red Clover*
Very common. 108. Grassland throughout the county, both undeveloped and "improved"; roadsides, waste ground, etc.

192/4 Trifolium medium L. *Zigzag Clover*
Very common. 89. Scrubland, hedgebanks, and grassland, particularly on clay or shale.

192/9 Trifolium arvense L. *Hare's-foot*
Occasional. 17. In quantity on sand dunes and open sandy ground, near the coast; inland on sandy or cindery ground, e.g. sandpit edges, railway ballast, industrial waste.

Leguminosae

192/10 Trifolium striatum L. *Soft Trefoil*
Very rare. 1. Sandy ground at Gayton (28SE), *Miss V. Gordon*!

192/17 Trifolium hybridum L. *Alsike Clover*
Common. 62, Reseeded pastures and meadows, roadsides, field borders, waste ground.

192/18 Trifolium repens L. *White Clover*
Very common. 110. Grassland throughout the county, roadsides, waste ground, etc.

192/19 Trifolium fragiferum L. *Strawberry Clover*
Rare. 5. Brackish marshes.

192/21 Trifolium campestre Schreb. *Hop Trefoil*
Frequent. 45. Sandy grassland; sand dunes, occasionally dry open banks on clay soils and on roadsides.

192/23 Trifolium dubium Sibth. *Lesser Yellow Trefoil*
Very common. 93. Grassland and open habitats on sand or clay, e.g. paths, roadsides, industrial waste, cinder tracks.

193/1 Anthyllis vulneraria L. subsp. **vulneraria** *Kidney Vetch*
Rare. 5. Sand dunes; sandy waste ground near the coast. Rare casual inland on calcareous waste.

195/1 Lotus corniculatus L. *Birdsfoot-Trefoil*
Very common. 109. Dry grassland, open sandy ground.

195/3 Lotus uliginosus Schkuhr *Large Birdsfoot Trefoil*
Very common. 106. All damp habitats; pond, marsh, alder carr, mere fringe, canal and ditch sides, etc.; occasionally on drier clay banks.

197/1 Galega officinalis L. *Goat's Rue*
Established by a few roadsides and canal banks; 88NW/NE/SW, 87NE, 46NW/47SE, 57SE.

202/1 Ornithopus perpusillus L. *Birdsfoot*
Frequent. 30. Open sandy ground, sand pit edges, sandstone outcrops, reclaimed sandy heaths, leached dunes; rare in sandy arable fields. Often with *Jasione montana, Aira praecox*.

206/1 Vicia hirsuta (L.) Gray *Hairy Tare*
Common. 58. Arable and disturbed ground, sandpit edges, open habitats on light soils but decreasing in north and east of the county.

206/2 Vicia tetrasperma (L.) Schreb. *Smooth Tare*
Rare. 5. Disturbed ground and roadsides.

206/4 Vicia cracca L. *Tufted Vetch*
Very common. 107. Mere and pond fringes, ditches and canal banks, roadsides, scrubland, hedgerows throughout the county to 1,250 ft.

206/10 Vicia sylvatica L. *Wood Vetch*
Rare. 6. Woods and wood borders in close conjunction with saliferous beds of Keuper marl, in one area persisting in open as woodland relict. 44! 66NW! where recorded in De Tabley's Flora a century ago, 66NE! 66SE! 86NW! 88SW, *A. Gibson*!

206/11. Vicia sepium L. *Bush Vetch*
Very common. 101. Woods, wood borders, scrubland, hedgebanks, road-sides, canal banks throughout the county, particularly on clay soils.

206/14 Vicia sativa L. agg. *Common Vetch*
Common. 76. Arable, disturbed and waste ground, roadsides: sandy grassland. Scarce in Pennine zone and foothills. The following treatment is suggested by C. A. Stace and Miss E. Pickering in the light of their current research, as yet unpublished:—

subsp. **sativa.** Usually large and robust with a large pod markedly compressed between the seeds. Flowers usually bicolorous. Relic of cultivation, on roadsides, field borders and waste ground.

subsp. **nigra** (L.) Ehrh. Very variable in stature, the largest sorts as robust as many subsp. *sativa.* Pod variable in size, not or only slightly compressed between the seeds. Flowers bi- or concolorous. In "native" and disturbed habitats.

Var. 1. "**V. bobartii**" sorts; small and slender and usually markedly heterophyllus. Pod black and not constricted between seeds. Flowers usually concolorous. Locally common on sand dunes in Wirral and grassland over Triassic sandstone and sandy moraine, e.g. in the Delamere area.

Var. 2. "**V. segetalis**" sorts; variable in stature, intermediate in many ways between **V. bobartii** sorts and subsp. **sativa.** Pod variously coloured, usually not constricted between the seeds. Flowers usually bicolorous. Field borders, roadsides, and disturbed ground but also on dunes and sandy ground near the coast.

206/16 Vicia lathyroides L. *Spring Vetch*
Rare. 4. Sand dunes (28NW! 29!) Sandy grassland (55NW, *Miss V. Gordon*! 56NE!).

207/4 Lathyrus pratensis L. *Meadow Vetchling*
Very common. 106. Grassland on clay; roadsides, hedgebanks, mere and pond fringes, canal and ditch sides.

93

Rosaceae

207/6 Lathyrus sylvestris L. *Narrow-leaved Everlasting Pea*
Very rare. 1. Wooded slope on lower Weaver (57NW!) where it has evidently persisted since at least 1891 (cf. C. R. Billups, J. Bot., 44, p.427 and W. Hodge, Lancs. Nat. 3, p.408). This appears to confirm *J. Harrison's* 1850 record which was suspected by De Tabley, who was not well acquainted with the Weaver valley. Occurring with other typical marl wood border vegetation, it seems undoubtedly native.

207/8 Lathyrus latifolius L. *Broad-leaved Everlasting Pea*
Naturalised on railway banks near habitation, 37SE, 57NW, 58SE.

207/11 Lathyrus montanus Bernh. *Bitter Vetch*
Frequent. 51. Common on hill grassland on Carboniferous shales and on grassland slopes in plain where characteristic of leached marl soils reverting to scrub. Decreasing westwards.

184/1 Laburnum anagyroides Medic. **190/6 Medicago arabica** (L.) Huds., **191/1 Melilotus altissima** Thuill., **191/4 Melilotus indica** (L.) All., **192/20 Trifolium resupinatum** L., occur rarely on rubbish tips as casuals; **206/6 Vicia villosa** Roth is well established in a wet meadow, Lindow 88SW.; **207/1 Lathyrus aphaca** L. is sometimes generated from bird seed.

Species apparently extinct

185/2 Genista anglica L. known at heathy pits near Ness until 1943, *H. E. Green*!

192/1 Trifolium ornithopodioides L. (sp. Hb. Liv. Mus. 1935, Grange Hill); Thurstaston 1942, L.N.F.C.

192/13 T. subterraneum L.

192/24 T. micranthum Viv.

206/12 Vicia lutea L.

207/2 Lathyrus nissolia L.

ROSACEAE

209/1 Spiraea salicifolia L. *Willow Spiraea*
Occasional. 14. Naturalised in hedgerows.

210/2 Filipendula ulmaria (L.) Maxim. *Meadow Sweet*
Very common. 106. Marshes and wet places throughout the county in a wide variety of habitats, e.g. woods, ditches, mere and pond fringes, canal sides.

211/1 Rubus chamaemorus L. *Cloudberry*
Confined to two areas on the high blanket bog moors, on the edge of peat bogs at 1500 ft. plus, with *Empetrum nigrum*, *Calluna vulgaris* and *Vaccinium myrtillus*. Webb's site (cf. De Tabley, p. 116) still flourishes.

211/6 Rubus idaeus L. *Raspberry*
Very common. 89. Woods and wood borders, hedgebanks, roadsides, particularly on sandy soils.

211/9 Rubus caesius L. *Dewberry*
Sand dunes, river banks. 7. Abundant on "grey" dunes at Hoylake (28NW) and Wallasey (29NW) and on sand over boulder clay at Gayton (28SE). Banks of the river Dee below Chester and calcareous clay elsewhere in Wirral. To the rear of the former sand dune area in North-west Wirral hybrids between *R. caesius* and other members (named and unnamed) of Sect. *Triviales* and *R. ulmifolius* are common, characterised by inability to form mature fruit.

211/11 Rubus fruticosus L. **sensu lato** *Blackberry**

Sect. *Suberecti* P. J. Muell.

211/11/2 Rubus scissus W.C.R. Wats.
16. The commonest suberect bramble in the county, this occurs often in abundance on the margins of peat mosses and peaty heaths particularly in the Eastern-central areas, e.g. around Lindow Moss, Carrington Moss, Stretton Moss, Brookhouse Moss, etc. There is also a good deal of the plant in woods on sandy soils and in rough grass heath in the Pennine area. When growing in shade the plants are often weaker and the foliage more lax and limp and the armature less pronounced.

211/11/4 Rubus opacus Braun ex Focke
7. Detected on several remnants of heath in the Delamere and Wilmslow areas, at Bradley common (54NW) and Knutsford Heath (77NW) where it was evidently called *R. plicatus* by De Tabley. Note, however, that another plant called *R. plicatus* by De Tabley still exists on the northwest part of Lindow Common; this, while close to the true *R. plicatus* has glandular panicles and is an undescribed species. Sandy heaths among *Erica cinerea, Calluna vulgaris, Deschampsia flexuosa*. Features: suberect in habit, strong prickles, white flowers.

211/11/13a Rubus accrescens A. Newton
21. A common bramble of the Pennines and the foothills; peat mosses, heaths, e.g. Dane's Moss, Soss Moss; upland woods on gritstone slopes; particularly in birch woods on drained mosslands. It has affinities with *R. opacus* and *R. carpinifolius*. Features: early white flowers, green stems and foliage, eglandular, much less heavily armed than *R. carpinifolius* and lacking the characteristic prickly pedicels of that species.

---

* The following account is based entirely on observations made by the author and/or E. S. Edees.

Rosaceae

Sect. *Triviales* P. J. Muell.
211/11/16 Rubus eboracensis W. C. R. Wats.
11. Hedges, old sandpits. The prevalent plant of the "*Corylifolius*" group in west and central Cheshire. Features: pink flowers, rhomboid terminal leaflet, leaves felted on back.

211/11/21 Rubus balfourianus Bloxam ex Bab.
8. Hedgerows, stream banks. Apparently restricted to the east central plain where Keuper marl is near the surface, preferring damp rich soils. Commonest in Mobberley district where over 50 bushes have been counted growing with *Rubus dumetorum* and *Rosa dumetorum*. In 77NW, the bush mentioned by De Tabley in Lennards wood is still *in situ*, and a flourishing colony is established on the lime waste beds nearby at Plumley. Features: large mauve flowers with short stamens and hairy anthers, long flowering period (mid-May to October), rhomboidal terminal leaflet.

211/11/22 Rubus warrenii Sudre
6. A well-marked and constant member of the *Triviales*, this species is common along a band of the sub-Pennine country from Hyde to Congleton, roughly between 700 and 1,000 ft. It is the highest growing member of the group (above the level at which *R. dumetorum* fades out). This species was first named by De Tabley as *R. concinnus* Warren, and was well understood by his contributors, Webb and Baker, who both remarked its abundance between Hazel Grove and Whaley Bridge and in the Tame valley, where it thrives today. Features: small roundish leaflets, pinkish flowers, glandular stem.

211/11/29 Rubus rubriflorus Purchas
3. This very local but readily distinguishable species of the Section was first found in hedgebanks along the Macclesfield canal at Astbury (86SE) by E. S. Edees. It has since been located along the same canal at Sutton (96NW) and in small colonies in hedges in the Swettenham area, e.g. south of Swettenham church (86NW). Features: sessile lower leaflets, stems with glands and short prickles in addition to longer prickles, and, as the name suggests, flowers of deep reddish pink.

211/11/30 Rubus scabrosus P. J. Muell
One of the more readily identifiable species of Sect. *Triviales*, with a very prickly stem and pink flowers. A small colony was discovered on Bickerton hill (55NW) by E. S. Edees, and another occurs near Black Hall farm, Bexton (77NW).

211/11 Rubus dumetorum agg.
82. The commonest bramble in Cheshire, occurring throughout the county below 500 ft. in woods and hedgerows, particularly on clay soils and in damp places generally, and usually the first Rubus species to colonise waste ground and railway banks is a clearly recognisable but unnamed member of the *Triviales* section, with early white flowers, sessile

lower leaflets often absorbed into ternate leaves, fruits of often few drupelets and a glandular stem densely crowded with prickles of various sizes. It is a most aggressive plant and quickly forms large low impenetrable scrub if allowed. Referred to by De Tabley's contributors under a variety of names (*R. dumetorum* var. *diversifolius* Lindl. perhaps the most popular version) it was equated by Watson with *R. myriacanthus* Focke, from which, however, it differs in its smaller flower size and less floriferous panicles. It is also very common in the surrounding counties of Lancashire and the west Midlands. In the south and south west of the county particularly, the quality of the armature appears less hystrican and it may be that we have here another closely related species. In the present state of ignorance about the limits of species definition within Sect. *Triviales* we can do no better than record these plants as an aggregate.

Sect. *Sylvatici* P. J. Muell

211/11/34 Rubus gratus Focke
14. A frequent bramble around the old mosslands in the north of the county, e.g. Carrington Moss, Stretton Moss, with *R. scissus* and *R. dasyphyllus*; also on the sandy banks and woods in the same district, extending into the Oakmere area through Delamere forest. Features: Large leaves, large pink flowers with erect sepals and hairy anthers, and stamens much longer than styles.

211/11/42 Rubus calvatus Lees ex Bloxam
9. Rough grassland reverting to scrub, on sandy soil derived from drift, sandstone or gritstone. Most frequent on the Pennine hill slopes, e.g. between Langley and Macclesfield forest where found with other upland species, e.g. *R. eifeliensis* and *R. lindebergii*; isolated colonies elsewhere. Features: convex leaves hard beneath, some teeth on terminal leaflet recurved, stamens suffused pink.

211/11/47 Rubus carpinifolius Weihe & Nees
8. Relict heaths, heathy scrub and wood borders on low ground, e.g. Sound Common (64NW). Features: stem strongly armed with yellow, red-based prickles, pedicels densely clothed with pricklets, flowers pinkish.

211/11/52 Rubus selmeri Lindeb.
57. Surrounds of old mosslands, relict heaths, hedges on sandy drift soils. A useful indicator of former mosslands and heathland, the sites correlating remarkably well with the extent of "commons and wastes" on Burdett's map of 1777. Features: robust in habit, leaves thick, dark green, panicle rachis heavily armed with falcate prickles, petals pink, notched, stamens equalling styles. Flowers into October. Characteristic plants can be observed on Lindow Common where it is the prevalent bramble of the heath margin.

Rosaceae

211/11/53 Rubus questieri Muell. & Lefev.
1. A large colony of a plant approaching this species (*fide* E. S. Edees) was discovered in 1968 on the margins of old Keuper marl woodland in the Weaver valley below Hall o' th' Hey farm (57NE). The same plant occurs extensively on both sides of the Weaver over a limited area. Features: pink flowers and styles, narrow leaflets with large simple serration and felted undersides.

211/11/54 Rubus laciniatus Willd.
A few bushes, presumably bird sown, were found in 1969 near Knutsford golf course.

211/11/59 Rubus lindleianus Lees
66. A tall-growing, late-flowering bramble, the predominant member of Sect. *Sylvatici* in Cheshire. Common in hedgebanks and woods on sandy or the better-drained clay soils, but absent above 600 ft. Features: terminal leaflet with wavy edges and wedge-shaped base; flowers white, panicles long, wide and much-branched.

211/11/64 Rubus robii (W. C. R. Wats.) A. Newton
31. This bramble, probably the "obscure *R. villicaulis* of Cheshire" of De Tabley, is to be found in woods, wood borders and hedgerows throughout a large part of central and southern Cheshire, particularly on clay and Keuper marl soils. It is closely allied to *R. polyanthemus*, but differs in the eglandular panicle rachis, the shape of the panicle and the pentagonal, flat terminal leaflet, often relatively long-stalked. The pink flowers and the thick, felted leaflets are points of similarity. Of the two, this species occurs in far greater numbers throughout the county as a whole.

211/11/66 Rubus macrophyllus Weihe & Nees
5. A much-misused name in the past, probably on account of the propensity of many Rubi to become large leaved in semi-shade. The true plant (det. E. S. Edees) is only known in woods and hedgebanks in five areas. Features: leaflets large, the terminal convex, often with parallel sides, prickles relatively sparse and weak, flowers pink, very few prickles in the panicle.

211/11/77 Rubus amplificatus Lees
4. Hedgerows and banks. Appears to be confined to the margins of Thurstaston common (below Thurstaston hill), Bickerton hills (Larkton Lane near Broxton Hall) and the vicinity of Ness (track between village and shore), in each case on sandy soil. A specimen from Eastham Wood (38), coll. *J. A. Wheldon*, 1896, in Hb. Manch. was determined by Rogers as *R. lentiginosus* Lees. Features: dull apple green foliage, short but stout recurved prickles and white flowers with pink sutured anthers.

11/11/103 Rubus incurvatus Bab.
5. Rough grassland slopes above Langley (97SW/SE), heathy banks in Peckforton hills (55NW) and Sound common (64NW), in hedgebanks in the Rostherne area and elsewhere. A specimen from Langley in the Manchester Museum (coll. *Bailey*) was determined by W. M. Rogers as *R. pyramidalis* Kalt. but is, in fact, this species (conf. E. S. Edees). The glossy green concave leaves with white felted backs, and large pink cup-shaped flowers, are distinctive, and are identical with Welsh bushes. The 55NW record was first made by Wolley-Dod (Pennsylvania) and a bush was subsequently re-discovered and confirmed by E. S. Edees. A large colony was subsequently discovered nearby. A Rostherne bush was known to C. Bailey, and was determined as *R. incurvatus* by Focke. A small colony of a similar plant, but with white flowers, grows near the landmark on Overton hill and compares well with similar populations in Staffordshire. It is not clear whether this is, in fact, *R. incurvatus* with white flowers, or another closely related species. Bushes of *R. incurvatus x vestitus* occur at Langley.

11/11/104 Rubus castrensis W-Dod.
4. Confined to the area west and south west of the Triassic sandstone of Peckforton hills, whence it was described in J. Bot. 44, p.63 (1906). Features: light green foliage, leaves often in threes, white flowers.

11/11/113 Rubus polyanthemus Lindeb.
23. Well distributed throughout the county in hedges and heath fringes, on sandy soils and grass heath, scrub in the Pennine zone; a useful indicator of old heath margins. Features: sometimes difficult to distinguish from *R. robii* (p. 98) but with convex leaflets, the terminal oval rather than pentagonal, and usually with sparse glands in the panicle. Not normally found with *R. robii*, which prefers clay soils.

11/11/123 Rubus cardiophyllus Muell. & Lefev.
29. Hedges, banks on clay or sand. Frequent, particularly in south and west Cheshire and Wirral. Features: long stalked terminal leaflet, leaflets white felted beneath, flowers white, cup-shaped.

11/11/125 Rubus lindebergii P. J. Muell.
9. Grass heath and upland pasture in the Pennines with an outlier on Peckforton hills. The first record for Cheshire, made by C. Bailey from the Langley district (Hb. Manchester Museum) was determined by W. M. Rogers. E. S. Edees has seen and confirmed several of the populations. Features: strong prickles, small leaves with leaflets white-backed, white flowers.

11/11/126 Rubus errabundus W. C. R. Wats.
A small colony of this species was determined by E. S. Edees from Eastham wood, Bromborough (38) in 1968.

Rosaceae

Sect. *Discolores* P. J. Muell.

211/11/129 Rubus ulmifolius Schott
49. This species is ecologically the obverse of *R. sprengelii* and is confined apart from one outlier, to the south and west of the county, where it i often the only Rubus species to be found on alluvial, clay or marl soils. Th distribution is very similar to those of *Tamus communis, Torilis japonica Agrimonia eupatoria* and *Senecio erucifolius*; it often grows in this compan in hedgerows and scrub. Hybrids with *R. vestitus* and species of Sect *Triviales* are not uncommon.

211/11/132 Rubus winteri P. J. Muell. ex Focke
1. A solitary bush of this species was discovered and named by E. S Edees at Overton heath (44). Superficially similar to *R. ulmifolius* in it chalky-white-backed leaflets, it has white filaments exceeding red styles carpels and receptacle pilose, and hairy anthers.

211/11/139 Rubus procerus P. J. Muell. *"Himalayan Giant"*
2. Well-established as a garden escape in the Bowdon, Hale and Knutsford areas, where it quickly forms dense, high-growing thickets. Features white-backed leaves, large pink flowers similar to *R. gratus*; extremely robust.

Sect. *Sprengeliani* (Focke) W. C. R. Watson

211/11/146 Rubus sprengelii Weihe
47. This bramble, one of the most elegant and common species in the county, is found in heathy hedgebanks, woods on sand or peat, rough grassland, and scrub in the Pennine zone, and in *Quercus petraea* woods on Carboniferous rocks. It ascends to about 1,250 ft. near Crowden (the highest growing Rubus species except for *R. chamaemorus*). Features low growing, rose pink flowers in diffuse panicles, stamens shorter than styles. The distribution reflects accurately the extent of primeval wood on sandy and peaty soils in the uplands.

Sect. *Appendiculati* (Genev.) Sudre.

211/11/165 Rubus vestitus Weihe & Nees
44. This species is one of the well-marked, widely distributed species in Cheshire, although the map shows an interesting distribution pattern due to a peculiar combination of ecological characteristics. Often the only bramble in old mixed oak woodland on Keuper marl soils, it is also a prominent member of the grass-heath/moorland boundary community in the north east and south east of the county, and also occurs, along with other species, in heath fringes and occasionally on clay soils, thus over-lapping both with *R. ulmifolius* on the one hand and the characteristic species of heath and moorland on the other, while forming the dominant ground layer in a major woodland community. Both pink and white flowered varieties occur.

211/11/178 Rubus criniger (E. F. Linton) Rogers
4. Hedges and scrub on sandy drift soils. Several colonies of this species are present in the Newchurch common and Whitegate areas (66NW/NE). It also occurs around the edge of old peat mosses in north Cheshire and south Lancashire. Features: dull green foliage, hairy stem, white flowers with hairy anthers, panicles often nodding.

211/11/179 Rubus eifeliensis Wirtg.
7. A common species in the south east corner of the county, particularly in the Pennine foothills, e.g. north of Rainow, on the west slope of Bosley Cloud, but with outliers on the sandy moraine in the Gawsworth and Alderley districts. Extends into Staffordshire. Features: stem very hairy but not glandular, flowers white, large.

211/11/182a Rubus wirralensis A. Newton
One of the most widespread brambles in central and southern Wirral, the Dee valley, and also occasionally found farther east, is a pink-flowered, slightly glandular species with obovate, mucronate terminal leaflets. In the past this has been determined as "*R. mucronulatus*", but while it has some affinity with that species it lacks several conclusive features, e.g. hairy anthers, large flowers (*fide* E. S. Edees, B. A. Miles) and cannot be so described. It is also known from S. & W. Lancs., N. Wales, and Connemara.

211/11/201 Rubus taeniarum Lindeb.
5. A colony of this interesting species was first discovered in the county by E. S. Edees in a heathy hedgebank near Doddington in 1968. Further finds were afterwards made in the Swettenham district—first an isolated colony in scrub on the Dane Valley terrace (76NE), then a considerable number of bushes on the fringes of the ancient Swettenham heath (86NW). Other small colonies grow near Stretton Moss and Knutsford heath. Features: pink, cup-shaped petals, spreading sepals, hooked prickles in the panicle which is more glandular than the stem, dark green compact leaves with felted backs.

211/11/204 Rubus radula Weihe ex Boenn.
1. While there are a few populations in Cheshire which approach *R. radula* closely (a fairly widespread example of this grows in the Wilmslow-Mobberley area), the true plant has been found in one place only (hedge between Winsford and Darnhall, 66SW, 1966, *E. S. Edees*). I have seen specimens of the true plant (coll. *Wolley-Dod* c.1900) from Aldford and Edge in herb. B.M.

211/11/212 Rubus echinatus Lindley
5. Hedgerows on sandy or clay soils. Probably rather more widespread, at least in the west of the county than present records indicate. Features: leaflets with incised toothing, stem hairy, purplish, flowers pink, cup-shaped, flowering from August onwards.

Rosaceae

211/11/213 Rubus echinatoides (Rogers) Sudre
4. Isolated bushes only in 77NW, 86NW, 86SE in relict heath situations; 99SE in open woodland. The plant at 77NW (Bexton) was noted by De Tabley as "*R. reuteri*". Features: superficially similar to *R. dasyphyllus* but with white notched petals, felted leaflets, stem without hair and with prickles confined to the main angles.

211/11/221 Rubus wolley-dodii Sudre
1. A small colony of bushes has been refound in Edge Park whence this species was described. It has never been found anywhere else and is likely to be of spontaneous local origin, hardly deserving specific rank.

211/11/224 Rubus rubristylus W. C. R. Wats.
10. Occurs in large quantity over a wide area of south west Cheshire, around the fringes of the Peckforton hills, on sandy soils, and in the Malpas district on sandy and clay soils. Originally described from an Edge Park specimen as *R. oigocladus* var. *newbouldii* (Set No. 66), it is also found in thickets and hedgerows elsewhere in south Cheshire and extends through Shropshire into south west Staffordshire. Features: dark green foliage and pinkish-white flowers with red styles which are particularly noticeable when the flowers are first opening. Grows at Oldcastle heath with *Rubus leightoni* and *Rosa tomentosa*.

211/11/225 Rubus adenanthoides A. Newton
2. Confined to the vicinity of the Peckforton hills (45SE, 55NW) where it is present in large quantity on heathy road and pathsides. Features: similar to *R. dasyphyllus* in flowers and armature, but with greyer foliage, slanting prickles and rhomboid terminal leaflets. A bush thought to be this species was also found near Utkinton (56NE). The same plant has been recognised in Oxfordshire, Yorkshire, Northumberland, the Lake District and the Isle of Man.

211/11/226 Rubus subtercanens W. C. R. Wats.
3. Colonies of this species were found in four places during 1968—one at Dinsdale Hollow, Frodsham (57NW), one near Kingsley (57NE) and two others in 56NE—one near Fishpool in company with *R. gratus* and *R. euryanthemus*, the other near Utkinton with a number of other species. All these sites are on the borders of heathy woods on sandy soils. Features: pinkish-white flowers with red-based styles, ovate dark green leaves sometimes with pedate lower leaflets, hairy panicle rachis with strong armature, the whole with a purplish cast. I have seen specimens of the same taxon from S. Lancashire (Walton, Aughton, Cunscough, Hesketh Bank) coll. *J. H. Lewis* in Hb. Manchester Museum, and also from Shropshire, Herefordshire, Middlesex and Co. Meath.

211/11/229 Rubus bloxamii Lees
1. On a heathy bank at the edge of Rudheath (grid ref. 7471) in company with many other Rubus species, *Hieracium vagum, Agrostis tenuis, Quercus robur* and *Betula pubescens*. An outlier of the main populations of this species which is mainly found in the midlands (south Staffordshire/ Leicestershire) and the south. Features: hystrican stem, dome-shaped panicle, white flowers and terminal leaflet very jagged on the upper edge.

211/11/246a Rubus newbouldii Babington, J. Bot. 25, p.20 (1887).
6. Recently recognised at five sites: (1) Lane to Moors brook (57NW); (2) Hedge bank between Prestbury and Wilmslow (87NE); (3) between Marple and Strines, along the canal (98NE); (4) Hedgerow, Antrobus (68SW); (5) Banks close to the Goyt (99SW); (1, 2, & 3) confirmed by E. S. Edees. Features: the general appearance of the plants is dark green with a purple tinge; terminal leaflets oval, stem hystrican, petals white. The species has close affinity with several others, e.g. *R. rubristylus* and *R. granulatus*, with which it has been confused. This species has a wide distribution in South Yorkshire, Lancashire, Derbyshire and Lincolnshire.

211/11/248a Rubus distractiformis A. Newton (*R. warrenii* Bloxam, MS.)
23. Prevalent in north east Cheshire where in many places it is the dominant Rubus species. Woods, hedges on clay, peat or sand. Outliers in the Etherow valley, around Oakmere, and in the Pennine foothills. Features: stem hairy and slightly glandular, with straight prickles, climbing and scrambling over hedges, leaves mostly ternate held erect from the barren stems, white flowers with narrow petals, heavily armed in panicle; light green in appearance. The name "*R. distractus* P. J. Muell" was given to a plant of this species from Rudyard, Staffordshire by Dr. W. O. Focke (Hb. Manchester Museum, 27 viii 1889, coll. *W. H. Painter*): it has received a variety of other names at different times.

211/11/252 Rubus euryanthemus W. C. R. Wats.
7. A frequent bramble near the outer periphery of the old peat mosses and peaty heaths, e.g. Oakhanger Moss; Fishpool, Delamere; eastern fringes of Dane's Moss (along Macclesfield canal banks, Sutton); Rudheath. This species may well have been the *R. radula* of De Tabley. It was named by W. M. Rogers *R. pallidus* var. *leptopetalus*. Features: petals narrow, white, stem thickly covered with glands "like a field of corn".

211/11/284 Rubus rufescens Muell. & Lefev.
2. Several large colonies of this species have been discovered at the edge of old woodland along the river Weaver above and below Sutton bridge, on Keuper marl (57NW, 58SW). It has not been found elsewhere in Cheshire but occurs in some quantity on the opposite side of the Mersey in south Lancashire. Features: stem glandular, flowers pink with erect sepals at early fruiting stage, buds discoid, fruit only partly fertile. The species was named by W. M. Rogers *R. rosaceus* var. *infecundus*, and has a wide distribution in England and Scotland.

Rosaceae

211/11/310 Rubus leightoni Lees ex Leighton
4. (1) Hedge near Swanley (65SW), along Shropshire Union canal, on the site of Ravensmoor common; (2) wood border near Heronbridge along river Dee (46SW); (3) common in the lower Wych district (44); (4) hedges near Handley (45SE); (1, 3 & 4) confirmed by E. S. Edees. On low-lying sandy clay or marl slopes and wood borders. This beautiful bramble, the *R. radula* var. *anglicanus* of W. M. Rogers, was first described from the neighbouring county of Shropshire by Leighton (Flora of Shropshire, 1841). Its main situations in Cheshire are close to the border with Flintshire. Features: stem with prickles, glands and hairs, flowers large, showy, pink, stamens much longer than styles, leaflets narrow, white-backed, the terminal relatively long-stalked.

Sect. *Glandulosi* P. J. Muell.

211/11/330 Rubus murrayi Sudre
2. This bramble, the *R. atrorubens* Wirtg. of Webb in De Tabley's Flora (p.110) is still to be found in some quantity in the same locality "around College Fields Farm" (64SE). It was rediscovered and confirmed by E. S. Edees. An isolated bush has also been found in a wood border at Handley (45SE). Features: flowers white, styles red, stem hystrican; heavily armed in the panicle where the main prickles are very deflexed; the leaves are small, dark green with the lower leaflets pedate and the terminal leaflet ovate.

211/11/348 Rubus hylocharis W. C. R. Wats.
15. A widespread species almost always in woods and wood borders, preferring old river terraces, but also on clay and shale. Under a variety of names, e.g. *R. hystrix*, *R. rosaceus* var. *sylvestris*, this was well-known as a Wirral plant, many well-marked specimens in local herbaria coming from the Eastham and Bromborough areas. Features: Petals narrow, deep pink, sepals erect, stem hystrican. The thin leaves often expand to very large size in shade.

211/11/354 Rubus infestus Weihe ex Boenn.
1. The Flitto Gate bramble, which De Tabley referred to as "a distinctive form of *R. koehleri*" and which still occupies a few yards of hedge on Flitto Gate lane, answers well to Watson's description of this species and may perhaps be it. It compares well with Bloxam's Coventry specimen in Hb. Manchester Museum, which was accepted as this species by W. C. R. Watson, who however determined a specimen of this plant (in Hb. CGE) "*R. schleicheri*".

211/11/356 Rubus dasyphyllus (Rogers) Druce
64. The commonest Cheshire bramble with glandular and hairy stem. Surrounds of old peat mosses, heathy and sandy woods, hedgerows and

banks on well-drained soil throughout the county. Ascends to c. 1,250 ft. on hills, often with *R. sprengelii* and *Rosa canina*. Features: petals narrow, salmon pink, leaves often in threes or fours, jaggedly toothed, stem hystrican. Shade grown plants often less characteristically armed, and leaves less coriaceous.

212/2 Potentilla palustris (L.) Scop. *Marsh Cinquefoil*
Common. 68. Meres and ponds; persists among developing willow or alder carr in shaded waters.

212/3 Potentilla sterilis (L.) Garcke *Barren Strawberry*
Common. 80. Woodland banks, wood borders and hedgebanks, particularly on clay and Keuper marl.

212/5 Potentilla anserina L. *Silverweed*
Very common. 102. Open habitats on sandy soils, pond and mere, etc. surrounds, muddy tracks and farmyards. Sand dunes, upper levels of salt marshes; absent only at highest levels.

212/7 Potentilla recta L. *Sulphur Cinquefoil*
Rare. 2. Established on three ditch sides in lower Weaver and Frodsham marshes, far from habitation.

212/8 Potentilla norvegica L. *Norwegian Cinquefoil*
Casual on waste ground, 38. Persistent on ashes of railway ballast, 47NW *T. Edmondson*!

212/13 Potentilla erecta (L.) Räusch. *Common Tormentil*
Very common. 99. Characteristic of leached and acid soils throughout the county. Sandstone and gritstone outcrops, grassland or grass reverting to heath or moorland, dry peat and birch woods on reclaimed mossland.

212/14 Potentilla anglica Laichard. *Trailing Tormentil*
Very common. 82. Banks on clay or light soils, cinder tracks and railway ballast. The hybrids **P. anglica x erecta** and **P. anglica x reptans** are present in the county and may have been recorded as *P. anglica* by some observers.

212/15 Potentilla reptans L. *Creeping Cinquefoil*
Very common. 99. Roadsides, hedgebanks and disturbed ground, particularly on clay soils.

215/1 Fragaria vesca L. *Wild Strawberry*
Common. 55. Wood borders, scrub and hedgebanks, particularly on Keuper marl and Carboniferous shale. Lime waste beds.

215/3 Fragaria ananassa Duchesne *Garden Strawberry*
Established on railway banks, 37NE/SE, 47SE, 88SE.

216/1 Geum urbanum L. *Wood Avens*
Very common. 91. Woods, wood borders, shaded hedgebanks throughout, but avoiding sandy and peaty soils.

105

216/3 Geum rivale L. *Water Avens*
Local. 11. Damp stream and canal banks, in small quantity at each site. The hybrid **G. rivale x urbanum = G. x intermedium** Ehrh. has been found only on a wooded stream bank, Wybunbury (74) by *K. G. Allenby*, 1968, with both parents.

218/1 Agrimonia eupatoria L. *Agrimony*
Frequent. 51. Scrubland, grassland, particularly on Keuper marl or calcareous drift. Almost confined to south and south-west of the county.

220/3 (2) Alchemilla filicaulis Buser subsp. **vestita** (Buser) M. E. Bradshaw. *Ladies Mantle*
Frequent. 32. Grassland; old pasture and banks on Keuper marl; hay meadows and flushed grassland on Pennine hill slopes.

220/3 (8) Alchemilla xanthochlora Rothm. *Ladies Mantle*
Frequent. 37. Hay meadows; grassy stream and river banks in eastern half of the county. Rare elsewhere.

220/3 (10) Alchemilla glabra Neygenf. *Ladies Mantle*
Local. 12. Pennine and sub-pennine grassland on Carboniferous shale; Bollin Valley on Keuper marl.

221/1 Aphanes arvensis L. sensu lato *Parsley Piert*
Occasional. 18. Sand dunes; sandy grassland; Triassic sandstone detritus; arable ground on light soils. **A. microcarpa** (Boiss. & Reut.) Rothm. was determined by *S. M. Walters* from 57NW(Helsby Hill); other records are given in the Critical Atlas for SJ28, 46, 47, 55.

221/1 Sanguisorba officinalis L. *Great Burnet*
Frequent. 30. Old meadows and flushed grassland slopes in Pennines; stream and canal banks, chiefly on Keuper marl and Carboniferous shale derived soils.

223/2 Sanguisorba minor Scop. subsp. **muricata** Briq. (*Poterium polygamum* Waldst. & Kit.) *Fodder Burnet*
Persistent on sandy roadside bank, 75NW, *K. G. Allenby*!

225/1 Rosa arvensis Huds. *Field Rose*
Very common. 105. Woods and wood borders, hedgerows, scrubland, particularly on clay soils.

225/4 Rosa pimpinellifolia L. *Burnet Rose*
Rare. 3. Locally abundant: sand dunes.

225/8 Rosa canina L. agg. *Dog Rose*
Very common. 104. Wood borders and hedgerows, scrubland.

Approximately 70 specimens were submitted to Mrs. H. Vaughan, who has kindly made the following determinations, based on A. H. Wolley-Dod's supplement to J. Bot. 1930 (cf. also J. Bot. 58, p.137, 1920):—

225/8 p.p. Rosa canina L.

*Group 1. *Lutetianae*

var. **lutetiana** (Lem.) Baker. 55NW, 57NE, 67NE/SW, 76NW, 77SW, 78SE, 97NE, 98SW. The commonest form of the Cheshire plain, particularly on light and sandy soils and boulder clay.

var. **sphaerica** (Gren.) Dum. 37NW, 56NE, 85.

var. **flexibilis** (Desegl.) Rouy 28NE.

var. **senticosa** (Asch.) Baker f. **mucronulata** (Desegl.) W.-Dod. 55SE, 57 NE.

*Group 2. *Transitoriae*

var. **spuria** (Pugsl.) W.-Dod. 45NE, 54NE, 55NW, 77NE.

var. **globularis** (Franch.) Dum. 96NW.

var. **rhynchocarpa** (Rip.) Rouy 55SE.

var. **ramosissima** Ran. 28NE, 64NW, 76NW.

var. **dumalis** (Bechst.) Dum. 97NE, 98SE, 87SE (f. *cladioleia* Rip.)

*Group 3. *Dumales*

var. **stenocarpa** (Desegl.) Rouy 54NE, 85, 87SW.

var. **fraxinoides** H. Br. f. **recognita** Rouy 54SE, 56NE.

*Group 4. *Andegavenses*

var. **verticillantha** (Mer.) Baker. 67SW.

225/8 p.p. Rosa dumetorum Thuill.

var. **typica** W.-Dod f. **semiglabra** (Rip.) W.-Dod. 28NE, 55NW, 64NW, 67NW, 76NW, 77SW, 78SE, 97NW/NE. The widespread form on Keuper marl and Carboniferous shales.

var. **ramealis** (Pugsl.) W.-Dod. 97NE.

var. **gabrielis** (F. Ger.) R. Kell. 97SE.

var. **calophylla** Rouy 54NE, 75NE.

var. **sphaerocarpa** (Pugsl.) W.-Dod. 67SW.

225/9 p.p. Rosa coriifolia Fr.

var. **typica** Chr. f. **implexa** (Gren.) W.-Dod. 96NW, east and north east of Bosley reservoir in some quantity. A submontane species of the Pennine foothills.

225/9 p. p. Rosa afzeliana Fr.

var. **glaucophylla** (Winch.) W.-Dod. 97SE, Macclesfield forest, on the bank of Clough brook. A submontane species of the Pennine foothills.

Rosaceae

225/11 Rosa tomentosa Sm. *Downy Rose*
44. Oldcastle heath, with *Rubus rubristylus* and *Rubus leightoni* ; 57NE, Weaver bank (var. *scabriuscula* Sm. f. *foetida*).

225/12 Rosa sherardii Davies
var. **woodsiana** 57NE, 85, on calcareous soil, 97NE.
var. **typica** W.-Dod. f. **pseudomollis** 85, SK 06NE, Gradbach.

226/1 Prunus spinosa L. *Blackthorn*
Very common. 96. Woods, hedges and scrub throughout the county.

226/2 Prunus domestica L. subsp. **domestica** *Plum.*
Naturalised in hedgerows, always near habitation past or present; subsp. **insititia** (L.) C. K. Schneid. is occasionally found in hedgerows in west and central Cheshire.

226/4 Prunus avium (L.) L. *Wild Cherry*
Common. 60. Constituent of semi-natural mixed oakwoods particularly on Keuper marl and Carboniferous shale series, Weaver, Dane, Bollin valleys. Many fine specimens reach height of 80 feet.

226/6 Prunus padus L. *Bird Cherry*
Local. 13. Pennine and sub-Pennine oakwoods, thickets and streamsides.

229/2 Crataegus monogyna Jacq. *Hawthorn*
Very common. 110. Woods and hedges throughout.

232/1 Sorbus aucuparia L. *Rowan*
Very common. 91. All types of woodland and hedgerows; particularly characteristic of sandy soils, gritstone faces, and peaty surrounds of old mosslands.

232/4/1 Sorbus intermedia (Ehrh.) Pers.
An isolated tree was found in a thicket at Landican, 28NE!, 1968.

232/5/1 Sorbus aria (L.) Crantz *White Beam*
Local. 18. Isolated trees in old mixed woodland, perhaps bird sown.

232/7 Sorbus torminalis (L.) Crantz *Wild Service Tree*
Several trees in wood on Keuper marl, Darnhall, 66SW! 1967 et seq.

233/1 Pyrus communis L. *Pear*
Old established trees have been seen at Willaston, 37NW, (*E. Hardy*, 1969 per F. Perring) and in the Weaver valley, 57NE (Liv. Bot. Soc. 1969)

234/1 Malus sylvestris Mill. *Crab Apple*
Very common. 83. Subsp. **sylvestris** is the prevalent form in mixed oak wood both in the plain on Keuper marl and in the Pennine foothills. Subsp. **mitis** (Wallr.) Mansf. is more characteristic of hedgerows and less remote woods, but intermediates occur throughout the range.

224/1 Acaena anserinifolia (J. R. & G. Forst.) Druce was established at Spital, 1948-56, *J. P. Savidge*, L.N.F.C., 1957, p.20.

226/7 Prunus laurocerasus L. is planted ornamentally and occurs in game coverts.

235/5 Sedum anglicum Huds. *English Stonecrop*
Very rare. 1. Locally abundant on Hoylake sand dunes.

235/6 Sedum album L. *White Stonecrop*
Local. 7. Naturalised on sandstone outcrops and dunes in west of county.

235/8 Sedum acre L. *Wall-pepper*
Frequent. 27. Open dry situations on sand, sandstone outcrops, gravel, railway ballast, industrial waste (lime and cinders in Northwich/Middlewich areas). Gritstone walls in Pennine area.

236/1 Sempervivum tectorum L. *Houseleek*
Roof of Kermincham Hall, 76NE!; Kettleshulme 97NE!

238/1 Umbilicus rupestris (Salisb.) Dandy *Wall Pennywort*
Rare. 6. Triassic sandstone outcrops and old walls in south west of county.

235/2 Sedum telephium L. & **235/11 Sedum reflexum** L. are found rarely as garden escapes.

239/8 Saxifraga tridactylites L. *Rue-leaved Saxifrage*
Rare. 2. Sand dunes, Wallasey golf course, 29! slope below Beeston Castle, 55NW!

239/9 Saxifraga granulata L. *Meadow Saxifrage*
Rare. 5. Lightly shaded riverside banks on Keuper marl, Bollin and Peover Brook and bank at Burton.

240/1 Tellima grandiflora (Pursh) Torr. & Gray
Established for at least thirty years by roadside, Disley 98SE; by a shaded stream 78NE!

241/1 Tolmiea menziesii (Pursh) Dougl. ex Lindl.
Established in damp woodland 88SW, *Mrs. G. Mackie!*

242/1 Chrysosplenium oppositifolium L. *Opposite-leaved Golden Saxifrage*
Very common. 81. Swampy alluvial flats, streamsides, marshes and flushes in old woodland; shaded damp rocks and gullies in Pennines. Scarce west of Delamere ridge.

Droseraceae

242/2 Chrysosplenium alternifolium L. *Alternate-leaved Golden Saxifrage*
Local. 9. Swampy alluvial flats in old woodland; shaded stream banks on Keuper marl; one site (98SE) on Carboniferous shale. Confined to a restricted area of east central Cheshire. (cf. *Saxifraga granulata, Stellaria nemorum*)

239/3 Saxifraga hirculus L. was still at Knutsford Moor in 1842, cf. J. B. Wood, Phytologist, i, 700. **Saxifraga spathularis x umbrosa,** *"London Pride,"* & **239/15 S. hypnoides** L. have been found as garden outcasts and on rubbish dumps.

PARNASSIACEAE

243/1 Parnassia palustris L. *Grass of Parnassus*
Very rare. 1. Base rich flush on Keuper marl, 64NE. *Mrs. A. Blacklay!* The characteristic tall, late flowering fen plant.

GROSSULARIACEAE

246/1 Ribes rubrum L. (*R. sylvestre* (Lam.) Mert. & Koch) *Red Currant*
Frequent. 41. Similar situations to *R. nigrum* but also on damp wooded banks in addition to alluvial flats.

246/3 Ribes nigrum L. *Black Currant*
Frequent. 31. Often in quantity on wooded alluvial flats, particularly where derived from Keuper marl substratum.

246/6 Ribes uva-crispa L. *Gooseberry*
Frequent. 42. Woods and wood borders, hedgerows, streamsides.

DROSERACEAE

247/1 Drosera rotundifolia L. *Sundew*
Local. 11. Sphagnum bogs, Black Lake 57SW! Flaxmere 57SE! Abbott's Moss 56NE! Newchurch Common 66NW! Wybunbury Moss 65SE! Brookhouse Moss 86SW, *B. Green.* Lindow Moss 88SW! Brereton Moss 64SE, *G. Meredith.* Wet sphagnum on heaths, Thurstaston 28NW! Bickerton 55SW! Sound 64NW! Lindow 88SW! Greatly decreased in comparison with De Tabley's account.

247/3 Drosera intermedia Hayne *Long-leaved Sundew*
Very rare. 1. One patch on damp heath with *Erica tetralix, Molinia caerulea, D. rotundifolia,* Thurstaston Common, 28NW, *Miss V. Gordon!*

Species apparently extinct

247/2 Drosera anglica Huds. (Abbott's Moss, 1918, L. & C. Nat. 16, p.179).

249/1 Lythrum salicaria L. *Purple Loosestrife*
Common. 63. Meres, ponds, and reservoir fringes; stream, ditch and canal sides.

250/1 Lythrum portula (L.) D. A. Webb subsp. **portula** (*Peplis portula* L.) *Water Purslane.*
Local. 7. Locally common below high water level at Disley reservoir 98SE!, Langley reservoir 97SW & SE! Bosley reservoir 96NW *K. Allenby!* pond margin 86NW *K. Allenby!* Damp tracks, 28NW, 55NW, *Miss V. Gordon.*

Lythrum junceum Banks & Solander was observed as a casual on waste ground in Altrincham, 1969.

251/2 Daphne laureola L. *Spurge Laurel*
One site in Styal woods, 88SW, *P. Newton*; apparently indigenous.

254/1 Epilobium hirsutum L. *Great Hairy Willow-herb*
Very common. 107. Marshes, ditch, canal and stream sides, mere and pond fringes throughout.

254/2 Epilobium parviflorum Schreb. *Small-flowered Hairy Willow-herb*
Common. 73. Marshes, mere and pond fringes, walls.

254/3 Epilobium montanum L. *Broad-leaved Willow-herb*
Very common. 90. Woods in Pennines; waste and disturbed ground, roadsides, walls, canal towpaths, ditch sides elsewhere.

254/5 Epilobium roseum Schreb. *Pale Willow-herb*
Casual on waste ground, 88NW, *A. Gibson* 1965; recorded at intervals from Altrincham, Sale, Chester and Bromborough areas since 1912. e.g. L.N.F.C., 1957, p.21.

254/6 Epilobium adenocaulon Hausskn. *American Willow-herb*
Local. 11. Open sandy and waste ground e.g. sandpit edges, clinkers, railway sidings; persistent but not aggressive at Winsford and around Ellesmere Port, casual elsewhere. A large colony which appeared above the strand line around Oakmere in 1965 when the water level was low has not reappeared. Confirmed by T. D. Pennington in 37SE, 47SE, 56NE.

H   111

Onagraceae

254/7 Epilobium tetragonum L. subsp. **tetragonum.** *Square-stemmed Willow-herb*
Very rare. 1. One plant from a collection of Epilobia on sandy shore of Oakmere 56NE was thus identified by T. D. Pennington.

254/9 Epilobium obscurum Schreb. *Short-fruited Willow-herb*
Common. 73. Marshes, stream and ditch sides, pond margins throughout.

254/10 Epilobium palustre L. *Marsh Willow-herb*
Very common. 96. Hill flushes in Pennine zone. Marshes, mere and pond fringes in the plain.

254/13 Epilobium nerterioides A. Cunn. *New Zealand Willow-herb*
Waste ground (railway ballast), Ellesmere Port 47NW *Mrs. E. Hall*! 1968. Other recent records are given in L.N.F.C., 1957, p.21

254/14 Epilobium pedunculare A. Cunn. (*E. linnaeoides* Hook. f.)
Established on walls, 47NE, since 1938, *Miss V. Gordon*; Alderley Edge, 87SE, *Mrs. S. Gregory*.

255/1 Epilobium angustifolium L. (*Chamaenerion angustifolium* (L.) Scop.)
Rosebay Willow-herb
Very common. 110. Abundant in a variety of open situations; disturbed and waste ground, rubbish tips, dry heathy woods following felling, drained peat mosses following burning; quarry faces and gritstone exposures in the Pennines.

256/1 Oenothera biennis L. *Evening Primrose*
Occasional. 16. Light dry soils; established on sand dunes, railway embankments, industrial waste.

256/2 Oenothera erythrosepala Borbás *Large-flowered Evening Primrose*
Local. 8. Sand dunes, waste ground, railway embankments. First record West Kirby, L. & C. Nat., 7, p.163.

Oenothera biennis x erythrosepala was determined by Kew from Mouldsworth, 57SW, *T. Edmondson*. Some coastal plants also appear to be this hybrid.

258/1 Circaea lutetiana L. *Common Enchanter's Nightshade*
Common. 78. Wooded banks on loamy soils; tolerant of deep shade, where it carpets the ground in late summer.

258/2 Circaea intermedia Ehrh. *Intermediate Enchanter's Nightshade*
Very rare. 1. Streamside in Cotterill Clough 88SW! May also be still present in the Marple district.

259/1 Myriophyllum verticillatum L. *Whorled Water-milfoil*
Very rare 1. Ditches on Frodsham Marshes, 57NE!

259/2 Myriophyllum spicatum L. *Spiked Water-milfoil.*
Frequent. 30. Meres, large ponds, canals, ditches. Flowering more profusely in the western part of the county.

259/4 Myriophyllum alterniflorum DC. *Alternate-flowered Water-milfoil.*
Rare. 3. Locally abundant in Bosley Reservoir 96NW! Disley reservoir 98SE! Pond on Hilbre Island where it has been known since 1872! Another recent record in L.N.F.C., 1956, p.19 28SE, has not been confirmed.

260/1 Gunnera tinctoria (Molina) Mirb.
Established along two stream banks, 87SW/SE.

261/1 Hippuris vulgaris L. *Mare's-tail*
Rare. 4. Capesthorne Mere, 87SW! where recorded in De Tabley a century ago. Brereton Pool, 76NE, *Mrs. G. Mackie*; Pool at Frankby, 28NW, *Mrs. E. Hall*; Pool at Plumley 77NW, *P. Newton*!

262/1 Callitriche stagnalis Scop. *Water Starwort*
Very common. 99. Ponds, ditches, streams, canals; Seasonally waterlogged and muddy hollows.

262/2 Callitriche platycarpa Kütz. *Water Starwort*
Rare. 6. Probably under recorded. Ditches.

262/3 Callitriche obtusangula Le Gall. *Water Starwort*
Local. 7. Low lying ditches along the Dee and Gowy basins.

262/4 Callitriche hamulata Kütz. ex Koch (*C. intermedia* Hoffm.) *Water Starwort*
Occasional. 26. Upland streams and pools; less commonly in ditches and streams elsewhere.

262/5 Callitriche hermaphroditica L. *Autumnal Starwort*
Local. 9. In larger meres in the north of the county, (Mere Mere, Tatton Mere, Tabley Mere); Redesmere, and in Macclesfield Canal.

Umbelliferae

265/1 Swida sanguinea (L.) Opiz (*Thelycrania sanguinea* (L.) Fourr.) *Dogwood*
Occasional. 21: except in extreme south where there are bushes in hedges
and semi-natural woods, planted in ornamental woods and small coverts.
Most records for the north of the county are probably for *Swida sericea*
(L.) Holub.

ARALIACEAE

268/1 Hedera helix L. *Ivy*
Very common. 107. Woods, wood borders, scrub and hedgebanks throughout.

UMBELLIFERAE

269/1 Hydrocotyle vulgaris L. *Marsh Pennywort*
Common. 60. Pennine hill flushes and small streams; mere and pond
fringes; peaty pools and ditches on heaths and edges of mossland.

270/1 Sanicula europaea L. *Sanicle*
Frequent. 42. Old established mixed woodland chiefly on steep well
shaded slopes where Keuper marl or Carboniferous shale exposed at
surface, but rare in the central plain.

272/1 Eryngium maritimum L. *Sea Holly*
Rare. 3. Outer margin of sand dunes, 28NW! 28SE! 29!

273/1 Chaerophyllum temulentum L. *Rough Chervil*
Common. 63. Wood borders, scrubland, hedgebanks on clay and sandy
soils, becoming scarcer eastwards.

274/1 Anthriscus caucalis Bieb. *Bur Chervil*
Rare. 2. Sand dunes, Hoylake, 28NW! sandy roadside, 75NW *K. G.
Allenby*!

274/2 Anthriscus sylvestris (L.) Hoffm. *Cow Parsley*
Very common. 107. Woods, hedgebanks, roadsides throughout the
county, to approx. 800 ft.

276/1 Myrrhis odorata (L.) Scop. *Sweet Cicely*
Frequent. 38. River and stream sides, hedgebanks in east of county;
rare on roadsides, railway embankments westwards.

277/1 Torilis japonica (Houtt.) DC. *Upright Hedge-parsley*
Common. 69. Wood borders, scrub and hedgebanks on clay soils particularly Keuper marl; decreasing eastwards and northwards.

280/1 Smyrnium olusatrum L. *Alexanders*
Rare. 4. Locally common. Hedgebanks and roadsides in 28/29 near the coast.

282/1 Conium maculatum L. *Hemlock*
Occasional. 25. Open disturbed and waste ground, river banks, roadsides, tips; frequent west of Delamere ridge; rare elsewhere.

285/1 Apium graveolens L. *Wild Celery*
Local. 10. Brackish pools and ditches; river banks, lower reaches of River Weaver.

285/2 Apium nodiflorum (L.) Lag. *Fool's Watercress*
Very common. 89. Meres, ponds, ditches, streams, canals.

285/4 Apium inundatum (L.) Reichb. f. *Lesser Marshwort*
Occasional. 19. Ponds where water level fluctuates seasonally, and where bed shelves gradually. More frequent west of Delamere ridge. In quantity at Bosley and Langley Reservoirs on silt where level also fluctuates.

287/1 Sison amomum L. *Stone Parsley*
Rare. 5. Undisturbed hedgebanks west of Delamere ridge on calcareous drift. Decreasing. The Frankby colony (LNFC 1956, p.19) appears to be lost through road works; the Capenhurst colony (cf. N.W.Nat., 5. p.267) still thrives. 36NE, *P. Newton*, 37SE/47SE, *T. Edmondson*! 36SE! 56SW!

288/1 Cicuta virosa L. *Cowbane*
Frequent. 30. Meres and ponds in centre and south of the county, usually on outer fringe of "reed" swamp. No less common than it was a century ago.

293/1 Conopodium majus (Gouan) Loret *Pignut*
Very common. 99. Woodland, wood borders, scrub on clay and sandy soils. Woodland relict in grassland.

294/1 Pimpinella saxifraga L. *Burnet Saxifrage*
Frequent. 41. (1) In the Pennine zone characteristic of well-drained grassland on Carboniferous shales. (2) In central Cheshire on well drained old pasture on Keuper marl banks. (3) Common west of Delamere ridge on sand dunes and calcareous boulder clay grassland.

294/2 Pimpinella major (L.) Huds. *Greater Burnet Saxifrage*
Occasional. 21. Wood borders, hedgebanks and scrub on Keuper marl series but confined (apart from one colony) to north and central Cheshire. This distribution pattern is unique and cannot be correlated with any observable combination of factors: Keuper marl is however at or close to the surface throughout this area.

115

Umbifelliferae

295/1 Aegopodium podagraria L. *Goutweed*
Very common. 102. Hedgebanks, roadsides, particularly damp shaded areas near habitation.

297/1 Berula erecta (Huds.) Coville *Lesser Water-parsnip*
Frequent. 49. Mere and pond fringes; ditch, stream, and canal sides. Thinning out eastwards.

300/1 Oenanthe fistulosa L. *Tubular Water Dropwort*
Frequent. 33. Ponds and marl pits in Central and West Cheshire; ditches on Frodsham marshes; absent in north and east.

300/4 Oenanthe lachenalii C. C. Gmel. *Parsley Water Dropwort*
Local. 7. Landward fringes of salt marshes.

300/5 Oenanthe crocata L. *Hemlock Water Dropwort*
Frequent. 33. Common in west of county (Wirral, Dee and Lower Weaver Valleys) rare elsewhere; streams and ditch sides, swampy woods.

300/6 Oenanthe aquatica (L.) Poir. *Fine-leaved Water Dropwort*
Frequent. 29. Ditches, ponds, slow flowing streams: shade tolerant, decreasing NE-wards.

301/1 Aethusa cynapium L. *Fool's Parsley*
Common. 62. Arable and disturbed ground; garden and nursery weed.

302/1 Foeniculum vulgare Mill. *Fennel*
Rare. 4. Sandy waste ground near the coast; railway bank, 46NW! rubbish tip, 88SW.

303/1 Silaum silaus (L.) Schinz & Thell. *Pepper Saxifrage*
Occasional. 15. Old grassland on Keuper marl or calcareous drift; damp fen meadows.

307/1 Angelica sylvestris L. *Angelica*
Very common. 108. Marshes; ditches, stream and river sides; mere and pond fringes; alluvial flats; damp places in woods.

307/2 Angelica archangelica L. *Garden Angelica*
Rare. 4. Ditches near the Manchester Ship Canal at intervals from Warburton to Ellesmere Port. (cf. N.W. Nat., 13 p.166, 1938, Lymm & Thelwall).

310/1 Pastinaca sativa L. *Wild Parsnip*
Occasional. 15. Established on lime waste beds, industrial waste, dunes; casual on rubbish tips.

311/1 Heracleum sphondylium L. *Hogweed, Cow Parsnip*
Very common. 108. Woods, hedgebanks, roadsides, disturbed ground throughout.

311/2 Heracleum mantegazzianum Somm. & Levier *Giant Hogweed*
Local. 13. Well established along the River Bollin from Hale westwards; isolated clumps by roadsides elewhere.

314/1 Daucus carota L. *Wild Carrot*
Frequent. 40. Grassland and scrub in south Wirral and along Dee shore. Well-drained hedgebanks on clay in the south of the county; sandpit edges in centre and east.

Bupleurum lancifolium Hornem. occurs as a bird seed casual in gardens and waste ground; **291/2 Carum carvi** L. occurred in an untended arable field, 1965, 86SW!; **286/1 Petroselinum crispum** (Mill.) Nyman has been found on rubbish tips where it may become established for a few years; **277/2 Torilis arvensis** (Huds.) Link and **289/1 Ammi majus** L. occurred on waste ground at Altrincham in 1969.

Species apparently extinct

275/1 Scandix pecten-veneris L. (Morley, 1924, coll. *A. Pollitt*).

277/3 Torilis nodosa (L.) Gaertn. (Burton Point, 1910, Hb. Liverpool Museum).

283/4 Bupleurum tenuissimum L., Bromborough, 1927, L.B.S.

309/3 Peucedanum ostruthium (L.) Koch, Poynton, 1918 (Adamson, J. Bot. 57, p.92, 1919).

CUCURBITACEAE

315/1 Bryonia cretica L. (*B. dioica* Jacq.) *White Bryony*
Frequent. 28. Wood borders and hedgerows, mainly confined to the Dee valley, lower Weaver Valley, lower Bollin valley. Very much in the same areas as mentioned by De Tabley, it is difficult to determine the factors governing the distribution.

EUPHORBIACEAE

318/1 Mercurialis perennis L. *Dog's Mercury*
Very common. 97. Often dominant ground flora in old woodland; hedgebanks, particularly on Keuper marl and Carboniferous shales.

318/2 Mercurialis annua L. *Annual Mercury*
Persistent for two years on sandy waste ground, 1966/67, 64SE, *G. Meredith*!

319/9 Euphorbia helioscopia L. *Sun Spurge*
Common. 69. Arable and waste ground.

319/10 Euphorbia peplus L. *Petty Spurge*
Common. 53. Arable and disturbed ground, nursery and garden weed.

319/12 Euphorbia portlandica L. *Portland Spurge*
Very rare. 1. Hoylake sand dunes! First localised record, W. Whitewell
J. Bot. 38, p.277, 1900.

319/16 Euphorbia cyparissias L. *Cypress Spurge*
Rare. 2. Well established and spreading, sandy ground Wallasey golf
course 29! roadside near habitation 57NW, *T. Edmondson.*

Species apparently extinct

319/11 Euphorbia exigua L. (Hb. Manchester Museum, Woodchurch, 1885).

319/13 E. paralias L. (West Kirby, 1913, *C. Waterfall*).

POLYGONACEAE

320/1 Polygonum aviculare L. **sensu lato** *Knotgrass*
Very common. 105. Arable disturbed and waste ground throughout the
county. While not mapped separately, *P. aviculare s.s.* and *P. arenastrum*
Bor. both occur. The former appears to be the more prevalent form. **320/1
(4) P. arenastrum** Bor. is recorded from 77NW (det. Kew), 45NE/SE,
65SW, 87SE, 98NE.

320/2 Polygonum oxyspermum Meyer & Bunge ex Ledeb. subsp. **raii** (Bab.)
Webb & Chater (*P. raii* Bab.) *Ray's Knotgrass*
Rare. 3. Above the strand line at Gayton, West Kirby and Leasowe.

320/6 Polygonum bistorta L. *Bistort*
Common. 70. Wood borders and hedgebanks, stream and river banks,
often in large patches. In the Pennine districts appears as a component of
hill meadows; becomes more associated with habitation westwards; almost
absent west of Delamere ridge.

320/8 Polygonum amphibium L. *Amphibious Bistort*
Very common. 91. Meres, pits, reservoirs, ponds, marshes, alluvial
flats subject to winter immersion. Both terrestrial and aquatic forms occur.

320/9 Polygonum persicaria L. *Persicaria*
Very common. 103. Arable and disturbed ground, rubbish tips.

320/10 Polygonum lapathifolium L. *Pale Persicaria*
Common. 69. Arable and disturbed ground, rubbish tips.

320/12 Polygonum hydropiper L. *Water-pepper*
Very common. 82. Ponds, meres, reservoir fringes; stream and ditch sides.
Characteristic of seasonally wet open habitats; occurring in places also in
damp arable ground.

PLATE 5. *Above:* Triassic sandstone scarp, Harthill, Bickerton Hills; *beneath: Quercus petraea* oakwood near Wincle (page 24).

H*

PLATE 6. *Above:* Marbury Mere from Wirswall; *beneath:* Shropshire Union Canal near Wrenbury.

PLATE 7. *Above: Ranunculus peltatus* (Crowfoot) and *Polygonum amphibium* (Amphibious Bistort), Bosley Reservoir (pages 73 and 118); *beneath: Viola reichenbachiana* (Pale Wood Violet), Aston (page 80).

PLATE 8. *Above: Vicia sylvatica* (Wood Vetch), Vale Royal (page 93); *beneath: Rubus caesius* (Dewberry), dunes, West Kirby (page 95).

PLATE 9. *Above: Andromeda polifolia* (Bog Rosemary), Saltersley Moss, Wilmslow (page 124); *beneath: Hottonia palustris* (Water Violet), Brookheys covert near Altrincham (page 125).

PLATE 10. *Above:* Damp heath, Thurstaston (page 44); *beneath: Gentiana pneumonanthe* (Marsh Gentian), Thurstaston Common (page 127).

PLATE 11. *Above: Utricularia minor* (Lesser Bladderwort), boggy pool with Sphagnum, near Oakmere (page 134); *beneath: Cotula coronopifolia* (Buttonweed), brackish ditches, Leasowe (page 145).

PLATE 12. *Above: Dactylorhiza purpurella* (Northern Marsh Orchid) and hybrids, Lime beds, Plumley (page 159); *beneath: Platanthera chlorantha* (Greater Butterfly Orchid) and *Leucanthemum vulgare* (Ox-eye Daisy), upland meadow near Wincle (pages 158 and 145).

320/14 Polygonum minus Huds. *Lesser Water-pepper*
Rare. 2. Several colonies with *P. hydropiper, Juncus bufonius* in peaty hollows in rides on the edge of Tatton Park (77NE), an outlier of the former Knutsford Heath lying close to the area where this species was prevalent a century ago, 1969! A large number of luxuriant plants on dumped soil from Bramhall area with other *Polygonum* spp. Poynton 98 SW, 1969, *C. A. Stace.*

320/15 Polygonum convolvulus L. *Black Bindweed*
Common. 77. Arable fields and disturbed ground, tips particularly on light soils.

320/19 Polygonum cuspidatum Sieb. & Zucc. *Japanese Knotweed*
Common. 73. Roadsides, railway banks and waste ground, decreasing southwards and away from the centres of population.

320/20 Polygonum sachalinense F. Schmidt. *Giant Knotweed*
Local. 7. Occasionally established in old shrubbery, river banks 78NE, 88SW, 77NE, 28NE, 37NW, 46NW, 58SE.

320/22 Polygonum campanulatum Hook. f. *Lesser Knotweed*
Rarely naturalised, 57SW, *T. Edmondson*! det. Kew.

325/1 Rumex acetosella L. *Sheep's Sorrel*
Very common. 106. Grassland, heath and mossland on sandstone, gritstone and sandy morraine soils; sandpit edges, arable and disturbed ground on sandy soils, walls.

325/2 Rumex acetosa L. *Sorrel*
Very common. 109. Grassland and woodland, particularly on clay soils. Hedgebanks, roadsides throughout.

325/4 Rumex hydrolapathum Huds. *Great Water Dock*
Common. 56. Canal fringes, meres, and occasionally ponds.

325/5 Rumex alpinus L. *Monk's Rhubarb*
Rare. 4. Six colonies by moorland roadsides, 98NE, *A. Gibson*; 97NE! 97SE *Mrs. S. Gregory* ! 86NE!

325/8 Rumex longifolius DC. *Butter Dock*
Very rare. 1. A large colony on mature gritstone quarry spoil heaps at about 1200ft, Billinge Hill, 97NE! conf. J. E. Lousley. Not previously recorded for Cheshire.

325/11 Rumex crispus L. *Curled Dock*
Very common. 102. Waste and disturbed ground, roadsides etc.

Ulmaceae

325/12 Rumex obtusifolius L. *Broad-leaved Dock*
Very common. 108. Arable, disturbed and waste ground, roadsides, farmyards.

325/14 Rumex sanguineus L. *Wood Dock*
Common. 77. Woods and wood borders, hedgebanks on light and clay soils.

325/15 Rumex conglomeratus Murr. *Clustered Dock*
Very common. 88. Pond and mere margins, canal and stream sides, waterlogged areas.

325/18 Rumex maritimus L. *Golden Dock*
Rare. 3. Muddy surrounds of Baddiley mere, 55NE! (conf. J. E. Lousley), 54SE, *P. Newton*! Damp peat, Fishpool, Delamere 56NE!

URTICACEAE

326/1 Parietaria judaica L. (*P. diffusa* Mert. & Koch) *Pellitory of the Wall*
Occasional. 21. Sandstone outcrops and old walls particularly west of Delamere ridge.

328/1 Urtica urens L. *Small Nettle*
Frequent. 51. Arable and disturbed ground, tips, particularly on sandy soils.

328/2 Urtica dioica L. *Stinging Nettle*
Very common. 109. Woods, wood borders, ditches, roadsides, farmyards; damp humus rich situations throughout.

327/1 Soleirolia soleirolii (Req.) Dandy has been recorded as a greenhouse escape in 38, 78NE, 88SW, 55NE

CANNABIACEAE

329/1 Humulus lupulus L. *Hop*
Common. 55. Wood borders and hedgerows; a few patches in the open on sand dunes.

ULMACEAE

330/1 Ulmus glabra Huds. *Wych Elm*
Very common. 96. Woods, hedgerows throughout the county to 800 ft.

330/2 Ulmus procera Salisb. *English Elm*
Common. 64. Woods, hedgerows, often planted, decreasing towards the east of the county.

330/3 Ulmus angustifolia (Weston) Weston is widely planted on the Stamford estates.

MORACEAE

331/1 Ficus carica L. occurs rarely on rubbish tips.

MYRICACEAE

333/1 Myrica gale L. *Bog Myrtle*
Rare. 5. Locally abundant on drained mosslands, with *Molinia* and *Vaccinum oxycoccus*; Stretton 68SW! Hatchmere 57SE! Danes Moss 97 SW! peaty hollow by upland stream 96NE! Decreasing as old peatlands are reclaimed for agriculture.

BETULACEAE

335/1 Betula pendula Roth *Silver Birch*
Common. 75. Less common than *B. pubescens* on heath and moorland ; also in marl and clay woods. Planted in ornamental coverts.

335/2 Betula pubescens Ehrh. *Downy Birch*
Common. 72. The dominant tree on sandy and peaty soils in the plain; heath on sandstone and morraine, springing up in quantity on drained mossland. Pennine woods and cloughs. Intermediates between *B. pubescens* and *B. pendula* are also common.

336/1 Alnus glutinosa (L.) Gaertn. *Alder*
Very common. 107. Marshes; river and stream sides; mere and pond fringes. A major constituent of climax woodland in all wet and marshy places.

CORYLACEAE

337/1 Carpinus betulus L. *Hornbeam*
Occasional. 24. Planted ornamentally and in coverts.

338/1 Corylus avellana L. *Hazel*
Very common. 103. Woods and hedges throughout, becoming scarcer in Pennine district.

FAGACEAE

339/1 Fagus sylvatica L. *Beech*
Very common. 97. Woods throughout the country, occasionally hedge-rows.

Salicaceae

340/1 Castanea sativa Mill. *Sweet Chestnut*
Common. 58. Planted ornamentally.

341/1 Quercus cerris L. *Turkey Oak*
Local. 10. Planted woodlands, parklands.

341/2 Quercus ilex L. *Holm Oak*
Rarely in ornamental woods and coverts.

341/3 Quercus robur L. *Common Oak*
Very common. 105. Major constituent of semi-natural woodland on clay soils. Many specimens intermediate between this and *Q. petraea* occur particularly on gritstone and sandstone rocks.

341/4 Quercus petraea (Mattuschka) Liebl. *Durmast Oak*
Frequent. 28. Well defined examples in Pennine clough woods and on sandstone and gritstone exposures.

SALICACEAE

342/1 Populus alba L. *White Poplar*
Occasional. 32. Planted ornamentally.

342/2 Populus canescens (Ait.) Sm. *Grey Poplar*
Local. 13. Hedgerows; copses; planted and suckering freely.

342/3 Populus tremula L. *Aspen*
Frequent. 42. Pennine cloughs and peat moss surrounds; usually on saturated soils.

342/4 Populus nigra L. subsp. **betulifolia** (Pursh) Wettst. *Black Poplar*
Rare. 3. Stream banks 78SE, 64SE, 67NW.

342/5 Populus x canadensis Moench *Black Italian Poplar*
Frequent. 39. River banks, coverts, plantations.

342/6 Populus gileadensis Rouleau *Balm of Gilead*
Occasionally planted and suckering; 38, 68NE, 77NE, 88SW, 99SW.

343/1 Salix pentandra L. *Bay Willow*
Occasional. 21. Mere and mossland surrounds in south and centre of county; streamsides and damp woods on Carboniferous shales in Pennines.

343/2 Salix alba L. *White Willow*
Frequent. 46. Stream and river banks, ditch sides. Obviously planted in most localities.

343/4 Salix fragilis L. *Crack Willow*
Very common. 96. Stream, ditch and river sides, obviously planted in some localities.

343/5 Salix triandra L. *Almond Willow*
Rare. 2. Planted? in mixed woodland, 86NW, 86SW.

343/9 Salix viminalis L. *Osier*
Common. 56. Pond sides, ditch and stream banks; often planted.

343/11 Salix caprea L. *Goat Willow*
Common. 74. Similar terrain to the next species but more frequently in damp woods.

343/12b Salix cinerea L. subsp. **oleifolia** Macreight (*S. atrocinerea* Brot.)
Grey Willow
Very common. 101. An early coloniser of marshy ground—ponds, meres, alluvial flats, ditch, stream and river sides, peaty pools.

343/13 Salix aurita L. *Eared Willow*
Occasional. 19. Moorland flushes and streamsides; rare in plain, in marshes and peaty pools on heaths.

343/16 Salix repens L. *Creeping Willow*
Occasional. 17. Subsp. **argentea** (Sm.) G. & A. Camus: sand dunes; lime beds, Northwich. Subsp. **repens:** damp heathland and mossland; damp sand or peat soils.

Salix Hybrids

S. x smithiana Willd. (*S. cinerea x viminalis*) is occasionally found in swampy thickets where it may have been planted.

S. x reichardtii A. Kerner (*S. caprea x cinerea*) is widespread in marshy situations, particularly in the centre and east of the county.

S. x rubra Huds. (*S. purpurea x viminalis*) is occasionally planted, e.g. near Rostherne Mere and Heatley.

S. x subsericea Doell (*S. cinerea x repens*) is found on the lime waste beds of central Cheshire and on the Wallasey sand dunes.

S. x capreola J. Kerner ex Anderss. (*S. aurita x caprea*) and **S. x multinervis** Doell (*S. aurita x cinerea*) occur occasionally in wet woods on the Pennine foothills.

ERICACEAE

344/2 Ledum groenlandicum Oeder *Labrador Tea*
Very rare. 1. Several plants on wooded parts of Danes Moss, *J. Godwin* 97SW! On Saltersley Moss, 88SW, until exterminated by peat cutting (1966).

Monotropaceae

345/1 Rhododendron ponticum L. *Rhododendron*
Common. 70. Undercover in plantation and coverts.

350/1 Andromeda polifolia L. *Bog Rosemary*
Rare. 5. Active sphagnum mosses: Flaxmere 57SE! Abbott's Moss 56NE! Wybunbury Moss 65SE! Brookhouse Moss 86SW; a fragment of Saltersley Moss saved by Cheshire Conservation Trust 88SW! Decreasing. Specimens exist in Hb. Manchester Museum from Dane's Moss (1906).

351/1 Gaultheria shallon Pursh *Shallon*
Rare. 4. Well established in a few plantations, 38, 57NW, 88SW, 97SW.

356/1 Calluna vulgaris (L.) Hull *Ling, Heather*
Common. 68. Dominant constituent of heath on Triassic sandstone exposures and sands of post glacial morraine; gritstone outcrops and margins of blanket bog in Pennines.

357/1 Erica tetralix L. *Cross-leaved Heath*
Frequent. 35. Sphagnum mosses and damp peaty hollows on heaths and moors.

357/4 Erica cinerea L. *Bell-Heather*
Occasional. 22. Heaths on Triassic sandstone outcrops and glacial sand; rare on dry gritstone outcrops in Longdendale.

358/1 Vaccinium vitis-idaea L. *Cowberry*
Local. 10. Dry gritstone edges and moorland over 1,000 ft. though formerly also on Peckforton hills. One small patch at 450 ft. near Frodsham (57NW), *T. Edmondson*, in area where other sub-montane species survive.

358/2 Vaccinium myrtillus L. *Bilberry*
Frequent. 40. Heathland on the sandstone of the Delamere ridge; mossland surrounds in eastern plain; abundant in Pennine moorlands.

358/4 Vaccinium oxycoccus L. *Cranberry*
Occasional. 19. Active Sphagnum mosses in plain amongst *Molinia caerulea* and on damp peat and sphagnum patches in relict mosslands or Pennine blanket bog. Often the last survivor of active sphagnum community on drained mosslands.

MONOTROPACEAE

362/1 Monotropa hypopitys L. sensu lato *Yellow Birdsnest*
Very rare. 1. This species is not listed in De Tabley's Flora, although it appears in the Cheshire list in Topographical Botany (Watson, 1883) to which he contributed. A small colony has been seen in an oakwood at Hooton (SJ 37) by *N. Povey* in 1964 and since (cf. E. Hardy, Liverpool Daily Post 22/6/64 & 31/8/64, and Critical Atlas).

364/1 Empetrum nigrum L. *Crowberry*
Occasional. 18. Peat mosses in plain, 57SW, 57SE, 56NE, 65SE, 88SW, 86SW; in Pennines, drier edges of peat "haggs" on blanket bog; better drained hill slopes on thin peat above 1,500 ft.

365/5/1 Limonium binervosum (G. E. Sm.) C. E. Salmon *Rock Sea-Lavender*
Very rare. 1. Two small colonies on west facing rocks of Hilbre Island, 1968, *Mr. & Mrs. D. Parish*! confirming long known locality.

366/1 Armeria maritima (Mill.) Willd. *Thrift*
Rare. 6. Occasional plants on higher levels of salt marshes.

Species apparently extinct

365/1 Limonium vulgare Mill. (L. & C. Nat. 17. p.88, 1924, Bromborough).

367/3 Primula veris L. *Cowslip*
Frequent. 43. Keuper marl grassland, unploughed pasture, railway cuttings, scrub; common in south of county, rare north of gridline 65.

Primula veris x vulgaris *False Oxlip*
Rare. 6. Wood borders and scrub on Keuper marl, where colonies of both parents are contiguous, 66SW! 77SE! 44! 64 NE/SE *G. Meredith*, 57NE, *T. Edmondson*.

367/5 Primula vulgaris Huds. *Primrose*
Common. 73. Hedgebanks, woodland, wood borders and scrub; most prevalent on Keuper marl exposures; also damp railway cuttings and embankments.

368/1 Hottonia palustris L. *Water Violet*
Occasional. 17. Ponds and ditches in three disjunct areas, Frodsham marshes and lower Gowy, south and west of Nantwich, and in the north east. Flowering regularly at most sites.

370/1 Lysimachia nemorum L. *Yellow Pimpernel*
Common. 75. Damp woodland banks, particularly on Keuper marl and Carboniferous shales; flushed grassland and marshy banks on same series.

370/2 Lysimachia nummularia L. *Money-wort*
Occasional. 26. Woods, wood borders, hedgebanks, Weaver valley; a few patches on Shropshire Union Canal banks and other damp shaded spots. Casual on rubbish tips.

Oleaceae

370/3 Lysimachia vulgaris L. *Yellow Loosestrife*
Frequent. 48. Mere and larger pond fringes; less commonly on river, stream and ditch sides.

370/5 Lysimachia punctata L. *Dotted Loosestrife*
Local. 10. Established by several roadsides; garden outcast on rubbish tips.

372/1 Anagallis tenella (L.) L. *Bog Pimpernel*
Local 13. Springs and flushes on Keuper series, 44, 57NW/SW; 67NW; 76NE; 66SE; 64NE/SW. Damp heath 54NW/NE. Dune slack remnants 28NW, 29.

372/2 Anagallis arvensis L. subsp. **arvensis.** *Scarlet Pimpernel*
Common. 80. Arable and disturbed ground; nursery and garden weed, rubbish tips. Decreasing eastwards; absent in Pennine zone. Forma *azurea* from 56NE, 28SE & 78NE.

373/1 Glaux maritima L. *Sea Milkwort*
Local. 12. Higher levels of salt marshes. Tidal embankments.

374/1 Samolus valerandi L. *Brookweed*
Rare. 5. Brackish marshes; Hilbre Island, 37SW, 47NE; brine springs in Weaver Valley, 66NE/SE!

Species apparently extinct

372/4 Anagallis minima (L.) E. H. L. Krause.

OLEACEAE

376/1* Fraxinus excelsior L. *Ash*
Very common. 104. Woods, scrub and hedges throughout the county.

378/1 Ligustrum vulgare L. *Common Privet*
Occasional. 21. In old woodland, particularly in central Weaver valley; hedgerows in Dane valley. Probably planted in some coverts and near habitation.

378/2 Ligustrum ovalifolium Hassk.
Hedgerows near towns, rubbish tips.

---

*375/1 Buddleia davidii Franch. (*Buddleiaceae*) has been found as a garden outcast on rubbish tips.

379/1 Vinca minor L. *Lesser Periwinkle*
Local. 13. Woods and hedgebanks, mostly near habitation.

GENTIANACEAE

382/1 Centaurium pulchellum (Sw.) Druce *Lesser Centaury*
Rare. 2. Remnants of dune slacks at Leasowe (29)! and Hoylake (28NW)!

382/4 Centaurium erythraea Rafn. *Common Centaury*
Common. 72. Open situations on glacial sand and clay including sand dunes, sand pit edges, clay pits; grassland on Keuper marl and Carboniferous shale.

383/1 Blackstonia perfoliata (L.) Huds. *Yellow-wort*
Frequent 27. Open grassland on Keuper marl and calcareous boulder clay; surrounds of marl pits; lime waste beds.

384/1 Gentiana pneumonanthe L. *Marsh Gentian*
Very rare. 2. One patch on damp peat Thurstaston Common, 28NW! with *Molinia caerulea, Erica tetralix, Juncus squarrosus.* Greatly reduced over the last century due to destruction of habitat and lowering of water table through drainage, etc. Survived at Rudheath till c.1910 (per *C. Irwin*) on site now covered by birch wood. Three plants on fragment of Oxton Heath (28NE), where once abundant, 1969; Merseyside Nats. Assoc. per F. Perring.

385/3 Gentianella amarella (L.) Börner subsp. **amarella** *Felwort*
Very rare. 1. One small colony on grass covered limestone spoil, 85! with *Primula veris, Blackstonia perfoliata, Linum catharticum.*

Species apparently extinct

382/6 Centaurium littorale (Turner) Gilmour

385/1 Gentianella campestris (L.) Börner

MENYANTHACEAE

386/1 Menyanthes trifoliata L. *Bogbean*
Frequent. 39. Ponds with good water circulation in process of development to fen. Rare in moorland flushes and mere fringes.

387/1 Nymphoides peltata (S. G. Gmel.) Kuntze *Fringed Waterlily*
Very rare. 1. Established in Oulton Mere, (56SE) for at least a century.

388/1 Polemonium caeruleum L. (*Polemoniaceae*) has been recorded as a garden escape in 78NE, 88NE, 97NE! Persistent in the last station, 1966-9.

Boraginaceae

BORAGINACEAE

392/2 Symphytum officinale L. agg. *Comfrey*
Very common. 83. Confined to roadsides, field borders, hedgebanks and disturbed ground. Specimens determined by F. H. Perring include (1) the hybrid *S. officinale x asperum* = *S. x uplandicum* Nyman. (2) intermediates between *S. x uplandicum* & *S. officinale*. (3) *S. officinale* var. *patens* and var. *ochroleucon*. The cream flowered plants however occur close to pale purple forms and cannot be regarded as the "native" plant of E. England. The majority of Cheshire populations probably fall into category (2).

395/1 Pentaglottis sempervirens (L.) Tausch *Alkanet*
Occasional. 20. Roadsides, hedgebanks, near habitation.

397/1 Lycopsis arvensis L. *Bugloss*
Local. 13. Persistent in old sandpits in south of county, and allotments on sandy soil in Wirral; sporadically in arable fields elsewhere.

400/1 Myosotis palustris (L.) Nath. subsp. **palustris** (*M. scorpioides* L.) *Water Forget-me-not*
Very common. 81. Mere and pond fringes, canal, ditch and stream sides.

400/2 Myosotis repens G. Don (*M. secunda* A. Murr.) *Creeping Forget-me-not*
Local. 9. Pennine rills and flushes and one spring gully on Bunter Sandstone (57SW) where the associated species approximate closely to those of the Pennine habitats.

400/4 Myosotis caespitosa K. F. Schultz *Tufted Forget-me-not*
Very common. 91. Pond and mere margins, ditch, canal, and stream sides.

400/7 Myosotis sylvatica Hoffm. *Wood Forget-me-not*
Frequent. 30. Old woodland on Keuper marl and Carboniferous shale; often in large quantity on damp banks and alluvial flats, Bollin and Weaver valleys. Occasionally garden escape on roadsides near houses.

400/8 Myosotis arvensis (L.) Hill *Field Forget-me-not*
Common. 62. Arable land particularly on sandy soils; disturbed roadsides.

400/9 Myosotis discolor Pers. *Changing Forget-me-not*
Frequent. 29. Occurs in two habitats:—(1) Old pastures on sandy soils, sand dunes. (2) Flushed grassland and marshes on Keuper marl and Carboniferous shale.

400/10 Myosotis ramosissima Rochel *Early Forget-me-not*
Rare. 2. Sand dunes, West Kirby (28NW)! Sandy detritus, Beeston Castle Rock (55NW)!

393/1 Borago officinalis L. has occurred as a casual on waste ground or rubbish tips in 47NE, 75NW, 78NE. **403/1 Echium vulgare** L. occurred on dunes at Leasowe in 1962, *P. Newton.*

Species apparently extinct

389/1 Cynoglossum officinale L., (Dee Banks L. & C. Nat., 7, p.60; "disappearing" at Wallasey (1919) L. & C. Nat., 12, p.138. Gravel pit, Delamere, 1923, L. & C. Nat., 16, p. 199).

401/3 Lithospermum arvense L., Agden, 1928, coll. *A. Pollitt*

CONVOLVULACEAE

405/1 Convolvus arvensis L. *Field Bindweed*
Frequent. 52. Sand dunes, arable and waste ground particularly on light soils, railway banks.

406/1 Calystegia sepium (L.) R.Br. *Hedge Bindweed*
Very common. 91. Hedgerows, waste ground, fences and railings. Rare in Pennine districts. Subsp. **roseata** Brummitt: edge of Hoylake golf course, formerly part of dune system, 28NW! Sep. 1968. Stanlow, *T. Edmondson*, 47NW, 1967.

406/2 Calystegia pulchra Brummitt & Heywood (*C. dahurica* (Herb.) G. Don).
Spreading on waste ground and near gardens: Waste ground, Altrincham 78NE! Railings at Offerton 98SW! Hedge near garden, Oakhanger 75NE! 36SE. 57NE *T. Edmondson*. Records of R. K. Brummitt in the Critical Atlas:—SJ28, 38, 56, 88.

406/3 Calystegia silvatica (Kit.) Griseb. *Great Bindweed*
Common. 56. Hedgerows, roadsides, waste ground, fences and railings. The dominant Calystegia near towns. *Polygonum cuspidatum* has a similar distribution.

Calystegia silvatica x C. sepium (*C. x lucana*), Compstall, 99SE 1968, *C. A. Stace*

Species apparently extinct

406/4 Calystegia soldanella (L.) R. Br. ("not known in Wirral in 1924" L. & C. Nat., 16, p.133).

407 Cuscuta spp. Sporadic past occurrences are given in De Tabley, p.207. *C. europaea* L. appeared briefly on potatoes in the Weaver valley—G. Owen, MS. Flora and J. Bot. 59, p.355, 1921.

Scrophulariaceae

409/1 Lycium barbarum L. (*L. halimifolium* Mill.) *Duke of Argyll's Tea Tree*
Local. 13. Increasing on sand dunes and sandy waste ground in Wirral and at Weaver mouth; industrial waste and sandpits in south.

410/1 Atropa bella-donna L. *Deadly Nightshade*
Rare. 4. Established for at least forty years on waste ground at Helsby, 47SE and Runcorn Docks, 58SW; casual at Chester, 46NW. Malpas churchyard, 44, 1969, *Mrs. M. W. Cullen.*

411/1 Hyoscyamus niger L. *Henbane*
Very rare. 1. Sporadic in occurrence on sandy waste ground; sand quarry, Mouldsworth, 57SW, *T. Edmondson*, 1967.

413/1 Solanum dulcamara L. *Bittersweet*
Very common. 103. Damp woods, wood borders, ditches, canal and streamsides, mere and pond sides, most commonly as undershrub in Alnus/Salix scrub, or inner fringe of reed swamp.

413/3 Solanum nigrum L. *Black Nightshade*
Occasional. 17. Arable and disturbed ground, tips.

413/4 Solanum sarrachoides Sendtn.
Occurred at Hoylake police station in 1966, *Miss V. Gordon.*

415/1 Datura stramonium L. *Thorn Apple*, appears in gardens and on waste ground particularly in hot summers; it has been recorded since 1956 in the following areas :— 28NE, 46NW, 47NW, 56NW, 57NW, 75NW, 78NE, 87NE/SW.

416/1 Verbascum thapsus L. *Aaron's Rod*
Occasional. 26. Open sandy ground at the base of Triassic sandstone outcrops e.g. Burton Point, Beeston Castle; well drained slopes, e.g. railway embankments, and industrial waste tips. One site in open woodland (44); bank on lime beds, 77NW; casual on rubbish tips.

416/4 Verbascum lychnitis L. *White Mullein*
Rare. 2. A large colony of this species was observed 1966-70 on ballast and embankments of abandoned railway line at Malpas, 44! Another colony was found on a recent embankment, 47NE, 1969, *F. W. Clarke*

420/3 Linaria repens (L.) Mill. *Pale Toadflax*
Local. 8. Railway ballast and embankments, 88NE, 78SE, 37SE, 47NE/SE, 57NW, 65SW, 74. Increasing.

Linaria repens x vulgaris (L. x sepium Allman)
Extensive colonies with both parents, railway sidings, 37SE, 47SE
T. Edmondson!

420/4 Linaria vulgaris Mill. *Toadflax*
Common. 65. Sandy banks, hedgerows in Wirral and Dee Valley; industrial
waste and railway banks inland. Decreasing north and eastwards.

421/1 Chaenorhinum minus (L.) Lange *Small Toadflax*
Occasional. 14. Abundant where present on ballast of abandoned railway
tracks.

423/1 Cymbalaria muralis Gaertn., Mey. & Scherb. *Ivy-leaved Toadflax*
Frequent. 42. Walls, particularly west of Delamere ridge.

424/1 Scrophularia nodosa L. *Figwort*
Very common. 99. Woodland, wood borders and hedgebanks; ditch and
stream sides. Occasionally in open disturbed ground e.g. quarries. Widespread throughout the county.

424/2 Scrophularia auriculata L. (*S. aquatica* L.) *Water Figwort*
Common. 62. By slow flowing water, marshes, ditches, river and stream
sides, often in shaded portions. Rare in east of county (east of grid line 80).

425/1 Mimulus guttatus DC. *Monkey-flower*
Occasional. 26. Canal and ditch sides; well established and most frequent
along Shropshire Union Canal.

425/3 Mimulus moschatus Dougl. ex Lindl. *Musk.*
Rare. 6. Established by a few streams and mere sides: 78NW, Dunham,
P. Newton. 78SE, *P. Newton!* 87NW, *Miss K. Simpson*; 98SE, *A. Gibson*;
67SW, *R. E. Thomas*; garden escape, 38, *Mrs. N. F. MacMillan.*

426/1 Limosella aquatica L. *Mudwort*
Very rare. 1. Several hundred plants, many flowering, were found on
almost bare but waterlogged mud about eight feet below normal water
level in 1969 at Bosley reservoir (96NW)! An interesting link between
colonies at Rudyard lake, Staffordshire (Hb. Manchester Museum)
and Combs reservoir (Flora of Derbyshire, pp.63, 260). All these are
canal feeders, built in the first half of the 19th century. Associated species
were *Myriophyllum alterniflorum* and seedlings of *Rorippa islandica*,
Gnaphalium uliginosum, Apium inundatum and *Juncus bufonius.*

429/1 Digitalis purpurea L. *Foxglove*
Very common. 104. Woods, wood borders, scrub and hedgebanks on
leached clay, sandy and gritstone soils; rock faces and quarries.

Scrophulariaceae

430/1 Veronica beccabunga L. *Brooklime*
Very common. 101. Mere and pond fringes, ditch, stream and canal sides; marshes.

430/3 Veronica catenata Pennell *Pink Water Speedwell*
Occasional. 23. Pond fringes, ditch and stream sides. Frequent west of Delamere ridge; isolated sites in south of county, absent elsewhere.

430/4 Veronica scutellata L. *Marsh Speedwell*
Occasional. 18. Never in any quantity; mere and pond fringes, streamsides, flushes and marshes.

430/5 Veronica officinalis L. *Heath Speedwell*
Frequent. 48. Common in hill grassland in east of the county, thinning out westwards as an element in old pastures and hedgebanks on clay and sandy soils.

430/6 Veronica montana L. *Wood Speedwell*
Common. 75. Woods and shaded banks, particularly on Keuper marl and Carboniferous shale but also on boulder clay.

430/7 Veronica chamaedrys L. *Germander Speedwell*
Very common. 102. Open woods, wood borders, scrub and hedgebanks on clay and sandy soils; grassland throughout the county.

430/13 Veronica serpyllifolia L. *Thyme-leaved Speedwell*
Common. 68. Damp grassland, muddy tracks.

430/15 Veronica arvensis L. *Wall Speedwell*
Frequent. 38. Sandy grassland; sand dunes; sand pit edges, railway ballast, arable fields on light soils, old walls.

430/20 Veronica hederifolia L. agg. *Ivy Speedwell*
Frequent. 43. Woods and wood borders on Keuper marl and sandstones in dry situations; garden and allotment weed on light soils.

430/21 Veronica persica Poir. *Buxbaum's Speedwell*
Frequent. 37. Arable and waste ground, tips.

430/23 Veronica agrestis L. *Green Field Speedwell*
Occasional. 17. Arable and garden weed.

430/24 Veronica filiformis Sm. *Slender Speedwell*
Local. 11. Established on damp banks in 38; grassy stream bank far from habitation 65SW; naturalised from garden outcasts, 98NW/SW, 87NE, 86NW/SW, 28NE, 37NW/SE, 47SW.

432/1 Pedicularis palustris L. *Red-rattle*
Rare. 2. Fen meadow on mineral peat, 65NE, *P. Newton & E. Teague*!
Base rich flush on Keuper marl, 64NE, *Mrs. A. Blacklay*!

432/2 Pedicularis sylvatica L. *Lousewort*
Frequent. 39. Flushed grassland in Pennines on Carboniferous shales and in plain on clay grassland slopes. Characteristic of patches on damp slopes reverting to heathland with *Ulex europaeus, Lathyrus montanus, Polygala serpyllifolia.* Decreasing westwards.

433/2 Rhinanthus minor L. *Yellow Rattle*
Common. 54. Sand dunes, old pastures on Keuper marl and Carboniferous shales, usually in flushed areas; marshy banks, damp roadsides. The vast majority of plants observed flower in May-June.

434/3 Melampyrum pratense L. *Common Cow-Wheat*
Local. 11. Dry heaths, slopes on Triassic sandstone or gritstone edges usually with *Calluna* and *Erica cinerea*, in relict *Quercus petraea—Betula* woods. Helsby Hill, Peckforton, Lyme Park, Wincle. On *Sphagnum* at Wybunbury Moss. Rare with *Erica tetralix* in *Molinietum*, Crowden, on blanket bog.

435/1 Euphrasia officinalis L. **sensu lato** *Eyebright*
Frequent. 27. Pennine grassland; rare in Keuper marl grassland; fringes of heaths; lime waste beds. The following determinations of the microspecies of this aggregate have been made by P. F. Yeo.

435/1/13 Euphrasia nemorosa (Pers.) Wallr.
37NE/SE, 64NW, 77SE, 78SE, 96NW; roadsides, canal towpaths, heath fringes, pastures on clay.

435/1/15 Euphrasia confusa Pugsl.
66NW, 78SE, 96NW/NE, 97SW; heathy upland pastures, lowland heath fringes.

Euphrasia confusa x tetraquetra
Large patches on edge of sand dunes, Hoylake, 28NW.

435/1/18 Euphrasia borealis (Towns.) Wetts. "*E. brevipila*"
67SE, 77NW, 97NE, 98SE, 99SE; lime waste beds, abundant; upland pastures and meadows on Carboniferous shales. Both glandular and eglandular forms occur.

435/1/22 Euphrasia anglica Pugsl.
96NW/NE, 97SE; upland pastures on Carboniferous shales, often with *Pilosella officinarum, Viola lutea, Veronica officinalis, Lathyrus montanus,* etc.

436/1 Odontites verna (Bellardi) Dumort. *Red Bartsia*
Frequent. 30. Damp grassland on boulder clay or Keuper marl; usually in quantity where it occurs. Subsp. **serotina** (Wettst.) E. F. Warb. appears to be the prevalent form but both this and subsp. **verna** are recorded in the Critical Atlas.

133

Verbenaceae

416/7 Verbascum nigrum L., **420/2 Linaria purpurea** (L.) Mill. occur rarely on waste ground and rubbish tips; **418/1 Antirrhinum majus** L. is naturalised on sandstone walls in Wirral and occurs as a garden outcast on waste ground in the Chester area; **437/1 Parentucellia viscosa** (L.) Caruel occurred as a casual in reseeded ground, 1968, 99SW, *C. A. Stace*; and **424/5 Scrophularia vernalis** L. in shrubbery in 78SE in 1965. **430/9 Veronica longifolia** L. has been observed as a garden escape in 78SE.

Species apparently extinct

416/10 Verbascum virgatum Stokes (Burton, 1913, *C. Waterfall* and N. W. Nat. 4, p.205, 1929).

OROBANCHACEAE

439/1 Lathraea squamaria L. *Toothwort*
Local. 10. Old woodlands; steep cloughs on Carboniferous shales and Keuper marls. Goyt, Bollin, lower Weaver and Dane valleys. Usually parasitic on sycamore, hazel or elm.

Species apparently extinct

440/3 Orobanche rapum-genistae Thuill.

LENTIBULARIACEAE

441/3 Pinguicula vulgaris L. *Common Butterwort*
Very rare. 1. One moorland flush with *Carex hostiana*, *C. pulicaris* and other *Carex* and *Juncus* spp. on Carboniferous shale, 96NW, *P. Newton & K. Allenby*!

442/1 Utricularia vulgaris L. **sensu lato** *Greater Bladderwort*
Rare. 6. Ponds and ditches on Keuper marl or calcareous drift, 37NW, 44, 47SW/SE, 88SW, seldom flowering; ditch on Wybunbury moss, 65SE. Specimens examined (in the vegetative state) all appear referable to **U. neglecta** Lehm. but in the Critical Atlas the following determinations are given, based on flowering material: **U. vulgaris**, SJ/47; **U. neglecta**, SJ38/68/65.

442/4 Utricularia minor L. *Lesser Bladderwort*
Very rare. 1. Two bog pools near Abbott's moss (56NE). Flowering regularly.

VERBENACEAE

Species apparently extinct

444/1 Verbena officinalis L. (Shotwick, N.W. Nat. 4, p.151, 1929).

LABIATAE

445/3 Mentha arvensis L. *Corn Mint*
Frequent. 34. Arable land on light soils; silt or gravel surrounds of ponds, reservoirs; canal stonework.

445/4 Mentha aquatica L. *Water Mint*
Very common. 100. Marshes, pond and mere fringes; canal, ditch and stream sides.

Mentha aquatica x arvensis = M. x verticillata L.
Local. 12. Ditch and canal sides, frequently in absence of either parent.

Mentha aquatica x spicata = M. x piperita L. *Peppermint*
Rare. 5. Streamside, 96NW! Macclesfield canal banks, 98NE, 96NW, 86SE, 85, 99SW (det. R. M. Harley).

445/5 Mentha spicata L. *Spearmint*
Local. 10. Established by a few roadsides and on waste ground. Var. **citrata** Druce was determined by R. M. Harley from 38.

Mentha spicata x longifolia (L.) Huds.
Rare. 6. 36NE, 46NW, 47NW, *T. Edmondson*. 86NE, *Mrs. S. Gregory*, det. R. M. Harley. 44! 67SW, *R. E. Thomas*!

Mentha x villosa Huds. var. **alopecuroides** (Hull) Briq.
Roadside 74! waste ground 47NW *T. Edmondson*, det. R. M. Harley; 88SW!

446/1 Lycopus europaeus L. *Gipsy-wort*
Very common. 95. Pond and mere fringes; stream, ditch and canal sides.

448/3 Thymus drucei Ronn. *Thyme*
Rare. 3. Locally common on dune remnants, Wallasey, Hoylake, Gayton.

451/2 Calamintha ascendens Jord. *Common Calamint*
Very rare. 1. Top of sandstone cliff at Saighton, where noted in De Tabley's flora, 46SW, *K. S. Cansdale*!

453/1 Clinopodium vulgare L. *Wild Basil*
Rare. 5. Wood borders and scrub on Keuper marl and calcareous drift. 57NW! with *Inula conyza* and *Lathyrus sylvestris*. 38, *Miss M. Henderson*; 37NW, *Mrs. G. Mackie*; 36 NE; 37SE! with *Pimpinella saxifraga, Silaum silaus, Genista tinctoria, Senecio erucifolius*. Decreasing.

455/4 Salvia horminoides Pourr. *Wild Clary*
Very rare. 1. Sandy grassland, Denhall, 27, *K. Cansdale, N. F. McMillan, & H. E. Green*

Labiatae

457/1 Prunella vulgaris L. *Self-heal*
Very common. 103. Scrub, pasture and meadowland throughout the county particularly on clay soils. Occasionally persistent in reseeded grassland.

458/1 Betonica officinalis L. *Betony*
Common. 71. Grassland and scrubland on Keuper marl soils, persistent despite rank growth and leaching; rare in Pennine grassland on Carboniferous shale.

459/3 Stachys arvensis (L.) L. *Field Woundwort*
Frequent. 36. Arable ground, particularly on sandy soils.

459/6 Stachys palustris L. *Marsh Woundwort*
Common. 74. River, ditch, stream and canal sides; less frequently on mere and pond fringes.

Stachys palustris x sylvatica = S. x ambigua Sm.
Local. 9. Marshes, river and canal banks, usually with both parents.

459/7 Stachys sylvatica L. *Hedge Woundwort*
Very common. 108. Woods, wood borders, scrub, hedgebanks, roadsides throughout the county.

460/1 Ballota nigra L. *Black Horehound*
Frequent. 47. Roadsides and hedgebanks in west and south of the county.

461/1 Lamiastrum galeobdolon (L.) Ehrend. & Polatschek. (*Galeobdolon luteum* Huds.) *Yellow Archangel*
Common. 61. A conspicuous element in the ground flora of woods, particularly on Keuper marl, and Carboniferous shales.

462/1 Lamium amplexicaule L. *Henbit*
Local. 7. Sandy arable ground; casual except in Wirral.

462/3 Lamium hybridum Vill. *Cut-leaved Dead-nettle*
Occasional. 21. Arable ground, particularly on light soils.

462/4 Lamium purpureum L. *Red Dead-nettle*
Common. 79. Nursery and garden weed; roadsides, arable ground, particularly on sandy and peaty soils.

462/5 Lamium album L. *White Dead-nettle*
Common. 71. Hedgebanks, stream and ditch sides, rarely far from habitation, most frequent in centre and south of county. Rare or absent in Pennine zone.

462/6 Lamium maculatum L. *Spotted Dead-nettle*
Occasional. 16. Hedgebanks near houses; casual on rubbish tips.

463/1 Leonurus cardiaca L. *Motherwort*
Very rare. 1. A patch by a pathside at Storeton (38) has been known since 1915 (L. & C. Nat. 16, p.143).

465/4 Galeopsis tetrahit L. **sensu lato** *Common Hemp-nettle*
Common. 79. arable and disturbed ground, roadsides, occasionally in wood borders and hedgebanks. Both *G. tetrahit* and *G. bifida* Boenn. occur, the latter less commonly, but have not been distinguished by most recorders.

465/5 Galeopsis speciosa Mill. *Large-flowered Hemp-nettle*
Frequent. 45. Arable and disturbed ground. Locally abundant in north central Cheshire particularly in root crops on peaty soils.

467/1 Glechoma hederacea L. *Ground Ivy*
Very common. 95. Woods, wood borders, scrub, hedgebanks throughout.

469/1 Scutellaria galericulata L. *Skull-cap*
Common. 72. Mere and pond fringes, ditch and canal sides.

469/2 Scutellaria minor Huds. *Lesser Skull-cap*
Rare. 4. Four remaining sites in the county associated with sphagnum in acid flushes on sandstone 57SW! gritstone SE/00SE!; damp peat on Thurstaston Common, (28NW), *Miss V. Gordon!*, Brereton Heath 76SE!

470/4 Teucrium scorodonia L. *Wood Sage*
Very common. 92. Woods, woodborders, hedgebanks, scrubland on well drained, particularly sandy soils. Rough slopes and rock exposures on sandstone and Carboniferous gritstone.

471/2 Ajuga reptans L. *Common Bugle*
Very common. 83. Open woods, wood borders, scrubland, damp hedge-banks, especially on Keuper Marl and Carboniferous shale.

466/1 Nepeta cataria L. has been recorded as a probable garden escape in 36NE, 66NW.

Species apparently extinct

445/2 Mentha pulegium L.
452/1 Acinos arvensis (Lam.) Dandy.
465/1 Galeopsis angustifolia Ehrh. ex Hoffm.
468/1 Marrubium vulgare L. (Neston, 1915, L. & C. Nat. 8, p.172).

PLANTAGINACEAE

472/1 Plantago major L. *Great Plantain*
Very common. 109. Agricultural grassland, road and path sides, disturbed ground.

Campanulaceae

472/2 Plantago media L. Hoary Plantain
Very rare. 1. One colony only on Carboniferous shale, 96NW, *P. Newton &*
K. Allenby, 1967!

472/3 Plantago lanceolata L. Ribwort Plantain
Very common. 108. All types of grassland, roadsides, disturbed and waste
ground.

472/4 Plantago maritima L. Sea Plantain
Local. 12. Higher levels of salt marshes, in brackish alluvial plain of lower
Weaver, and on Frodsham marsh.

472/5 Plantago coronopus L. Buck's-horn Plantain
Local. 11. Abundant on rocks close to the coast, higher levels of salt
marshes and sand dunes; inland on sandstone detritus, Beeston Castle
rock, 55NW!

473/1 Littorella uniflora (L.) Aschers. Shore-weed
Rare. 6. Locally abundant in shallow lakes and reservoirs on sandy
substrata, 56NE Oakmere, 78SW Mere Mere; 97SW/SE, 96NW, 98SE,
reservoirs.

CAMPANULACEAE

474/1 Wahlenbergia hederacea (L.) Reichb. Ivy Campanula
Very rare. 1. Two sites in hill flushes, SE00SE, *Mrs. G. Mackie!* One of
these colonies, close to Woodhead, recalls the reference in How, Phyt.
Brit. p.19 (1650) "on a watery bank . . . in a lane near Woodhead, in
Cheshire."

475/1 Campanula latifolia L. Giant Bellflower
Occasional. 24. Steep wooded stream and river banks particularly on
Keuper marl exposures. A plant of mature undisturbed woodland.

475/2 Campanula trachelium L. Nettle-leaved Bellflower
Rare. 2. Woodland banks on Keuper marl and calcareous drift in extreme
SW of the county—44! 45SW! in the same place as recorded by Wolley-
Dod in De Tabley's Flora.

475/3 Campanula rapunculoides L. Creeping Campanula
Rare. 3. Well established on three roadsides (27, 37SW, 87NE)

475/7 Campanula rotundifolia L. Harebell
Very common. 83. Sand dunes; sandy grassland and well drained banks
in the plain. Pennine pastures and meadows in dry, open situations.

479/1 Jasione montana L. Sheep's-bit
Frequent. 30. Sand dunes, sandy grassland, heathy banks, sandpit edges.

475/6 Campanula glomerata L. & **475/11 C. medium** L. have been recorded as garden outcasts on waste ground in the Chester area.

481/1 Sherardia arvensis L. *Field Madder*
Local. 7. Sandy grassland (57NW, 56NE, 67SW, 87NE, 64SE). Casual garden introduction (75NW). Railway embankment (47NE).

484/1 Cruciata ciliata Opiz (*C. chersonensis* (Willd.) Ehrend.) *Crosswort*
Frequent. 38. Wood borders, scrub, and hedgebanks, shaded streamsides on clay soils. Absent in the north and east of the country. Similar distribution to *Agrimonia eupatoria, Rubus ulmifolius, Torilis japonica* and *Primula veris.*

485/1 Galium odoratum (L.) Scop. *Woodruff*
Frequent. 39. Open banks and damp flushes in woodland on Keuper marl and Carboniferous shales, more rarely on Boulder clay. Goyt, Dane, Weaver and Bollin valleys.

485/3 Galium album Mill. (*G. mollugo* Huds.) *Hedge Bedstraw*
Rare. 6. Sandy bank of disused railway, Thurstaston, 28NW! railway banks, 98SW, 88NE, *A. Gibson*; canal bank, 99SW, *Mrs. G. Mackie*; grassy river bank, 36NE, *T. Edmondson*; tip 88SW!

485/4 Galium verum L. *Lady's Bedstraw*
Frequent. 34. Dry grassland on sand and Carboniferous shale, sand dunes, Triassic sandstone detritus; well drained railway and canal banks.

485/5 Galium saxatile L. *Heath Bedstraw*
Common. 71. Distribution almost the obverse of *Cruciata ciliata.* Well drained banks and grassland on sandstone, gritstone and glacial sand; part of typical community of grass heath dominated by *Deschampsia flexuosa.*

485/8 Galium palustre L. *Marsh Bedstraw*
Very common. 106. Marshes and wet places throughout the county. Both subsp. **palustre** and subsp. **elongatum** (C. Presl) Lange are present.

485/10 Galium uliginosum L. *Fen Bedstraw*
Occasional. 15. Flushes and spring fed marshes on river and stream banks; wet meadows.

485/12 Galium aparine L. *Goosegrass*
Very common. 105. Woods, wood borders, scrub, hedgebanks, arable and disturbed ground, roadsides throughout the county except at the highest levels.

Valerianaceae

CAPRIFOLIACEAE

487/1 Sambucus ebulus L. *Danewort*
Rare. 2. River Mersey bank, Sale, 79SE, *P. Newton*; allotment border, Kingston, near Hyde, 99NW!

487/2 Sambucus nigra L. *Elderberry*
Very common. 107. Understorey in woods, wood borders, hedgerows, stream banks throughout the county.

487/3 Sambucus racemosa L. *Red berried Elder*
Naturalised in shrubberies, 98NE, *A. Gibson*; 96NE, *C. A. Stace*

488/3 Viburnum opulus L. *Guelder Rose*
Very common. 89. Understorey in damp woods throughout the county; hedgerows; mere and pond fringes, alder carr, stream sides.

489/1 Symphoricarpos rivularis Suksd. *Snowberry*
Frequent. 50. Hedgerows near gardens; naturalised in woodland, stream and river banks, often far from habitation, presumably bird sown.

491/3 Lonicera periclymenum L. *Honeysuckle*
Very common. 102. Woods, hedgerows, heathland; woodland surrounds of drained mosslands.

ADOXACEAE

493/1 Adoxa moschatellina L. *Moschatel*
Common. 78. Woods and wood borders on shaded banks, e.g. around the bases of tree trunks. Most abundant in mature woodland on Keuper marl.

VALERIANACEAE

494/1 Valerianella locusta (L.) Betcke *Lamb's Lettuce*
Rare. 6. Sand dunes; cinders on railway ballast inland.

495/1 Valeriana officinalis L. *Valerian*
Common. 79. Swampy alluvial valleys; alder carr; stream and ditch sides.

495/2 Valeriana pyrenaica L.
One colony established on a stream bank at Disley, 98SE, *A. Gibson*

495/3 Valeriana dioica L. *Marsh Valerian*
Occasional. 22. Spring fed marshes on Keuper marl and calcareous drift; hill flushes on Carboniferous shale.

496/1 Centranthus ruber (L.) DC. *Red Valerian*
Rare. 5. Established on sandstone faces west of the Delamere ridge.

497/1 Dipsacus fullonum L. *Teasel*
Frequent. 31. Grassland—banks on Keuper marl: 44, 66SE. River banks, disturbed and waste ground, rubbish tips elsewhere.

497/2 Dipsacus pilosus L. *Small Teasel*
Rare. 5. Shaded banks of River Weaver on Keuper marl, 57NE, *T. Edmondson & Miss V. Gordon*; shaded stream banks 66SE! 64SW! 64SE *G. Meredith!* Wooded bank of River Dee in place recorded by Wolley-Dod nearly a century ago, 45SW!

498/1 Knautia arvensis (L.) Coult. *Field Scabious*
Frequent. 30. Hill grassland on Carboniferous shale. Grassy banks on sandy or clay soils in plain.

500/1 Succisa pratensis Moench *Devil's-bit Scabious*
Very common. 83. Characteristic of damp grassland either flushed or leached on clay or shale soils; also on waterlogged and peaty soils.

502/1 Bidens cernua L. *Nodding Bur-Marigold*
Very common. 82. Mere and pond surrounds; ditch and canal sides. Prefers open muddy situations, but persists in spite of silting and overgrowth. Var. *radiata* DC. 87SW, pond near Jodrell Bank; 98NW, Hazel Grove golf course road; 54NW, Bradley; 66SE, 44, 67NE, 55NE.

502/2 Bidens tripartita L. *Trifid Bur-Marigold*
Frequent. 50. Similar situations to *B. cernua* but less common; more characteristic of larger ponds and meres. Muddy shore of Bosley reservoir (96NW) where subject to fluctuating water level.

503/1 Galinsoga parviflora Cav. *Gallant Soldier*
Local. 7. Nursery and garden weed in light soils. Waste ground, barely persistent. For an early record, cf. L. & C. Nat., 12, p.137 (Ness Gardens).

503/2 Galinsoga ciliata (Raf.) Blake *Shaggy Soldier*
Local. 8. Nurseries and allotments, waste ground; often persistent but not aggressive; 38, *Mrs. N. F. McMillan* det. W. S. Lacey. 37NE, *Miss M. Sanders!* 77SW! 78NE, *P. Newton!*

506/1 Senecio jacobaea L. *Ragwort*
Very common. 108. A persistent weed of all types of pasture, occasionally in wood edges and scrubland; disturbed ground and roadsides throughout the county.

506/2 Senecio aquaticus Hill *Marsh Ragwort*
Very common. 88. Wet muddy situations e.g. surrounds of ponds; marshes, streamsides, waterlogged pastures.

Senecio aquaticus x jacobaea = S. x ostenfeldii Druce has been recorded from 56SW and 98SW, but may in fact be more frequent.

506/3 Senecio erucifolius L. *Hoary Ragwort*
Frequent. 41. Old pastures and scrubland particularly on Keuper marl substratum, and calcareous drift in S. Wirral.

506/4 Senecio squalidus L. *Oxford Ragwort*
Frequent. 47. Increasing on dry waste ground; cinders, railway ballast and yards, gravel pits. "Thoroughly established" at Northwich c. 1910, Lancs. Nat., 3, p.224, *W. Hodge*.

506/6 Senecio sylvaticus L. *Heath Groundsel*
Frequent. 41. Rough dry heathy slopes on sandstone, gritstone and glacial sand.

506/7 Senecio viscosus L. *Sticky Groundsel*
Frequent. 45. Dry disturbed and waste ground, e.g. cinders and railway ballast, rubbish tips.

506/8 Senecio vulgaris L. *Groundsel*
Very common. 107. Open arable and disturbed ground. Radiate forms (some perhaps deriving from *S. squalidus x vulgaris*) are spreading on waste ground in and near towns and have been recorded in 31 squares. For early records cf. Lancs. Nat. 3, p.224 (1910) & B.S.B.I. proc., 1935, p.32.

506/13 Senecio fluviatilis Wallr. *Broad-leaved Ragwort*
Rare. 3. Several large patches on the sandy banks of the Dee south of Chester, (45NW/SW) Garden escape on damp slope, Marple (98NE).

508/1 Tussilago farfara L. *Coltsfoot*
Very common. 110. Early coloniser of open waste ground, roadsides etc., throughout the county; tolerant of high salinity; in hill pastures and meadows, apparently a member of the indigenous community.

509/1 Petasites hybridus (L.) Gaertn., Mey. & Scherb. *Butterbur*
Common. 74. Streams and river banks; swampy alluvial flats, particularly in shade. Female plants occur throughout the range.

509/2 Petasites albus (L.) Gaertn. *White Butterbur*
Established on damp streambank, 78NW, *P. Newton*!

509/3 Petasites japonicus (Sieb. & Zucc.) F. Schmidt *Giant Butterbur*
Persistent colony on open river bank near nursery, 78SE, *Mrs. C. Ashburn!*
Another colony has appeared half mile downstream, 1969, *P. Newton.*
For another recent record cf. J. Bot. 78, p.103, 1940.

509/4 Petasites fragrans (Vill.) C. Presl. *Winter Heliotrope*
Local. 11. In large patches by roadsides, usually near habitation.

512/1 Inula helenium L. *Elecampane*
Rare. 3. Established in three places on stream and river banks, 38, 76SE,
78NE!

512/4 Inula conyza DC. *Ploughman's Spikenard*
Rare. 6. Calcareous band in Keuper marl bank of lower Weaver where
doubted by De Tabley 57NW! Lime waste beds in Northwich and Middlewich districts 67NE/SE, 77NW, 76NW/SW. For earlier confirmation of
J. Harrison's 1850 record, cf, J. Bot. 44, p.427, 1906.

513/1 Pulicaria dysenterica (L.) Bernh. *Fleabane*
Common. 72. Ditches, stream and canal sides, damp banks on neutral
soils (particularly clay). Marshes with percolating water.

515/1 Gnaphalium sylvaticum L. *Wood Cudweed*
Rare. 2. A small colony at edge of sandpit, Sandiway, 67SW, *R. E. Thomas!*
A large population in colonised area of a sandpit in Upper Mottled
Sandstones, 57SW, *T. Edmondson!* with *Cladonia* spp., *Centaurium
erythraea, Jasione montana, Festuca ovina,* etc.

515/4 Gnaphalium uliginosum L. *Marsh Cudweed*
Common. 72. Arable and disturbed ground, roadsides, damp muddy farm
tracks; open situations on sand or clay.

516/1 Anaphalis margaritacea (L.) Benth. *Pearly Everlasting*
Well established among indigenous vegetation, bank on south side of road
below Bowstones, 98SE!

518/1 Solidago virgaurea L. *Golden Rod*
Frequent. 46. Wood borders and scrub on sandy banks, and either glacial
morraine or sandstone in plain: gritstone rock faces and damp ledges in
woodland or relict woodland in Pennines.

518/2 Solidago altissima L. (*S. canadensis* L.) *Garden Golden Rod*
Local. 13. Naturalised on railway banks, roadsides and stable tips near
towns.

519/1 Aster tripolium L. *Sea Aster*
Local. 12. Creeks and landward fringe of salt marshes—inland at Winsford
and Sandbach. Var. *discoideus* Rchb. f. occurs but is less common than
the rayed form.

K   143

Compositae

519/6 Aster novi-belgii L. agg. *Michaelmas Daisy*
Local. 12. Large patches established on railway embankments and waste ground near towns.

521/1 Erigeron acer L. *Blue Fleabane*
Rare. 6. Dry, open situations; sandstone detritus Beeston Castle, 55NW! Burton Point, 37SW, *P. Newton*. Lime waste beds Northwich area, 67NE/67SE!/77NW! Cinder tip, Betley Road, 74, *K. Allenby*

522/1 Conyza canadensis (L.) Cronq. *Canadian Fleabane*
Rare. 3. Sandy waste ground, 29, *Miss M. Thornton*; in quantity near Hoylake Gasworks, (28NW!) where first noted by J. D. Massey in 1942. Waste ground, Chester 46NW!

524/1 Bellis perennis L. *Daisy*
Very common. 109. Grassland throughout the county, roadsides, etc.

525/1 Eupatorium cannabinum L. *Hemp Agrimony*
Common. 59. Stream and ditch sides, usually in partly shaded situations; damp hedgebanks.

528/1 Achillea millefolium L. *Yarrow*
Very common. 109. Dry grassland particularly on sandy and clay soils; roadsides and disturbed ground.

528/3 Achillea ptarmica L. *Sneezewort*
Very common. 85. Marshes, waterlogged pastures on clay and shales; canal and ditch sides.

531/1 Tripleurospermum maritimum (L.) Koch subsp. **inodorum** (L.) Hylander
ex Vaarama *Scentless Mayweed*
Very common. 92. Arable and disturbed ground. Rare in Pennine zone. Subsp. **maritimum** occurs on the upper limits of salt marshes and strand line on Mersey and Dee shores and the lower Weaver.

532/1 Matricaria recutita L. *Wild Chamomile*
Very common. 84. Arable and disturbed ground.

532/2 Matricaria matricarioides (Less.) Porter *Pineapple Weed*
Very common. 109. Open disturbed and waste ground, pathsides, farm-yards throughout the county. First records: G. C. Druce (J. Bot. 44, p.426, 1906) between Wybunbury and Crewe, 1904, E. & H. Drabble (J. Bot. 48, p.154, 1910), thoroughly established near Birkenhead and Wallasey, 1905-8.

533/1 Chrysanthemum segetum L. *Corn Marigold*
Occasional. 18. Arable and waste ground; persistent at some sites, appearing in quantity every few years when ground under root crops.

144

533/2 Leucanthemum vulgare Lam. (*Chrysanthemum leucanthemum* L.) *Ox-eye Daisy*
Very common. 96. Grassland on clay and sandy soils; upland meadows, roadsides, railway banks, open waste ground, e.g. sandpits, lime waste beds, cinders.

533/4 Tanacetum parthenium (L.) Schultz-Bip. (*Chrysanthemum parthenium* (L.) Bernh.) *Feverfew*
Frequent. 47. Hedgebanks, roadsides and walls near habitation; rubbish tips.

533/5 Tanacetum vulgare L. (*Chrysanthemum vulgare* (L.) Bernh.) *Tansy*
Common. 59. Stream and river banks, also disturbed ground, tips and railway banks.

534/1 Cotula coronopifolia L. *Buttonweed*
Very rare. 1. Naturalised since about 1880 on saline marsh and along ditches behind embankment, Leasowe (29). (cf. C. Bailey, Manch. L.P.S. 25, p.219, 1886; J. Bot. 32, p.24, 1894; Manchester City News, 5 & 12 September, 1885; B.E.C. Rep., 1885/6.).

535/1 Artemisia vulgaris L. *Mugwort*
Very common. 102. A wide variety of open habitats:—arable and disturbed ground, industrial waste, refuse tips, railway banks, river banks.

535/6 Artemisia absinthium L. *Wormwood*
Local. 9. Waste ground, (78NE, 88NW/SW, 47SW, 36NE, 37NE); River banks, (79SW, 78NW); roadside (27).

535/7 Artemisia maritima L. *Sea Wormwood*
Very rare. 1. Small colony on margin of salt marsh, Bromborough, where recorded in De Tabley, 38, *Mrs. N. F. McMillan*!

537/1 Carlina vulgaris L. *Carline Thistle*
Very rare. 1. One colony on sandy embankment, Newchurch Common, (56NE), *H. Marsden*! Formerly more widespread in this district (*fide* G. Owen, MS Flora of the Northwich district).

538/1 Arctium lappa L. *Great Burdock*
Very rare. 1. Several colonies on bank of Aldford Brook, 45NW! 1970, the same area in which the species was found a century ago (cf. De Tabley, p.172).

538/4 Arctium minus Bernh. sensu lato *Burdock*
Very common. 105. Woods or wood borders, scrubland; hedgebanks, roadsides, waste ground. The vast majority of the Cheshire plants belong to subsp. **minus**; subsp. **nemorosum** (Lejeune) Syme is recorded from wood borders on Keuper marl and calcareous clay:—36SE, 44, 64SW! 47SW, *T. Edmondson*. 45NW, 56NW, 58SE, *Dr. F. Tyrer*. 67NW, *Mrs N. Kelcey*.

Compositae

539/1 Carduus tenuiflorus Curt. *Slender Thistle*
Rare. 2. Sandstone outcrop, Burton Point (37SW)! River Weaver bank, (57NE), *T. Edmondson, Miss V. Gordon.*

539/3 Carduus nutans L. *Musk Thistle*
Rare. 4. Casual on arable and waste ground; persistent in the extreme south of the county in arable fields, 64SE, *G. Meredith* and on waste ground in the Chester area, 36NE, *T. Edmondson.*

539/4 Carduus crispus L. *Welted Thistle*
Occasional. 19. Wood borders, hedgebanks, scrubland on Keuper marl and calcareous clay; Weaver & Dee valleys mainly.

540/2 Cirsium vulgare (Savi) Ten. *Spear Thistle*
Very common. 109. Grassland, arable, disturbed and waste ground, roadsides throughout the county.

540/3 Cirsium palustre (L.) Scop. *Marsh Thistle*
Very common. 106. Marshes and damp grassland throughout the county; canal, ditch, and streamsides, mere and pond surrounds; damp woods, scrubland; Pennine hill flushes.

540/4 Cirsium arvense (L.) Scop. *Creeping Thistle*
Very common. 110. Grassland, arable, disturbed and waste ground, roadsides throughout the county.

540/7 Cirsium heterophyllum (L.) Hill *Melancholy Thistle*
Rare. 2. Steeply sloping hill pasture on Carboniferous shale, 97SE!, near *Botrychium lunaria* and *Ophioglossum vulgatum* etc. Neglected allotment at Compstall, 99SE, *Mrs. G. Mackie*

540/8 Cirsium dissectum (L.) Hill *Meadow Thistle*
Very rare. 1. Two colonies in fen meadow surrounding small mere, 54NE, *P. Newton!* Not recorded in Cheshire previously.

542/1 Onopordum acanthium L. *Scotch Thistle*
Very rare. 1. A few plants were seen on waste ground near Hoylake railway station in 1968 (28NW!) in exactly the same area noted by De Tabley (p.169) in 1867.

544/1 Centaurea scabiosa L. *Greater Knapweed*
Rare. 3. Persistent on waste ground: 47NW, 57NW/SE.

544/6 Centaurea nigra L. *Lesser Knapweed*
Very common. 110. Well drained grassland, hedgebanks, railway embankments, roadsides throughout the county.

545/1 Serratula tinctoria L. *Saw-wort*
Very rare. 1. One colony on Keuper marl bank on grassland among light scrub, 66SW!, with *Primula veris, Pimpinella saxifraga, Carex caryophyllea, Betonica officinalis*, etc.

546/1 Cichorium intybus L. *Chicory*
Occasional. 19. Arable and disturbed ground; not persistent at any one site but occurring most years somewhere in the county.

547/1 Lapsana communis L. *Nipplewort*
Very common. 100. Woods and wood borders, shaded stream banks; arable and disturbed ground, roadsides, old walls.

549/1 Hypochoeris radicata L. *Cat's Ear*
Very common. 108. Grassland, especially on well drained soils throughout. Rough grassy and heathy banks on clay and sandy soils; coloniser of sandpits and waste ground; roadsides.

550/1 Leontodon autumnalis L. *Autumnal Hawkbit*
Very common. 98. Well drained pastures on sand, clay, Carboniferous shale, and gritstone soils.

550/2 Leontodon hispidus L. *Rough Hawkbit*
Frequent. 43. Hill grassland on Carboniferous shales and on Keuper marl grassland in plain. Decreasing westwards.

550/3 Leontodon taraxacoides (Vill.) Mérat *Lesser Hawkbit*
Occasional. 15. Found in three distinct habitats. (1) Dry sandy pastures and consolidated dunes, 56NE and Wirral coast. (2) Lime waste beds in Northwich district. (3) Damp soils, e.g. pond surrounds, 37NW, 47SE. Flushes on marl soils, 76NE and Carboniferous shales, 98SW, 99SW.

551/1 Picris echioides L. *Bristly Ox-Tongue*
Rare. 4. Open river bank on Keuper marl outcrop in lower Weaver valley, 57NW! Boulder clay cliffs, Thurstaston, 1965, *Miss V. Gordon*. Casual on waste ground Altrincham and Broadheath 78NE, 1968-9! Chester 36NE, 1969, *T. Edmondson*.

552/1 Tragopogon pratensis L. subsp. **minor** (Mill.) Wahlenb. *Goat's Beard*
Common. 77. Usually isolated plants on roadsides, canal path sides, streamsides and disturbed ground in process of recolonisation.

555/1 Mycelis muralis (L.) Dumort. *Wall Lettuce*
Frequent. 38. Woodland banks on Keuper marl; walls and rock faces in Pennine zone and west Cheshire.

556/2 Sonchus arvensis L. *Corn Sow-Thistle*
Common. 78. Brackish ditches and inner fringes of salt marshes. Arable ground, open industrial waste.

556/3 Sonchus oleraceus L. *Sow-Thistle*
Very common. 92. Arable, disturbed and waste ground, roadsides.

556/4 Sonchus asper (L.) Hill *Prickly Sow-Thistle*
Common. 78. Arable, disturbed and waste ground.

557/3 Cicerbita macrophylla (Willd.) Wallr. *Blue Sow Thistle*
Established on three roadsides near habitation (46NW, 87NW, 88NW) and on bank of R. Bollin (88SW!)

558/1 [107] Hieracium exotericum Jord. ex Bor., agg.
In some quantity on canal bank and abandoned railway at North Rode (96NW)! conf. P. D. Sell & C. West.

558/1 [109] Hieracium grandidens Dahlst.
Lime waste beds, Northwich, 67SE! det. P. D. Sell & C. West.

558/1 [110] Hieracium severiceps Wiinst.
Lime waste beds, Plumley, 77NW!, det. P. D. Sell & C. West. Abandoned railway line from Hartford to Winsford, 56NE/66NW!, det. J. N. Mills.

558/1 [111] Hieracium sublepistoides (Zahn) Druce
Lime waste beds, Northwich, 67SE! det. P. D. Sell & C. West.

558/1 [172] Hieracium maculatum Sm. *Spotted Hawkweed*
Lime waste beds, Middlewich, 76SW! det. J. N. Mills.

558/1 [174] Hieracium diaphanum Fr.
Local. 8. Open waste ground; quarry faces and spoil; walls, railway embankments and ballast. Determined by J. N. Mills from the following localities: 37SE, 67SE, 77NW, 87NE, 96NW, 97NW. 99SW, SK09NW.

558/1 [177] Hieracium strumosum (W. R. Linton) A. Ley
Local. 8. Quarry faces and walls; roadsides in Pennines. Determined by J. N. Mills in the following areas: 66NE, 97NE/SE, 98SE, 99SW/SE.

558/1 [184] Hieracium vulgatum Fr. *Common Hawkweed*
Frequent. 32. Locally abundant on open waste ground, e.g. cinder banks, lime waste beds, railway embankments, quarry spoil and rock faces, walls. Determined by J. N. Mills in ten localities.

558/1 [240] Hieracium umbellatum L.
Frequent. 28. Abundant on sand dunes; open waste ground, e.g. cinder banks and lime waste beds; sandy banks in areas enclosed from heathlands, with *Agrostis tenuis, Jasione montana, Crepis capillaris, Solidago virgaurea, Campanula rotundifolia.* Determined by J. N. Mills in the following localities: 67SE, 77NW, 86NW, 88SW.

558/1 [241] Hieracium vagum Jord. *Leafy Hawkweed*
Common. 72. Open woods and well drained banks, particularly on leached clay and sandy soils; canal and railway embankments, lime waste beds and cinders. A form with long white hairs but without the glandular phyllary hairs distinctive of *H. perpropinquum* has been included with this taxon. Determined by J. N. Mills in ten localites.

558/1 [245] Hieracium perpropinquum (Zahn) Druce
Rare. 5. Waste ground, railway embankments, hedgebanks. Determined by J. N. Mills: 47NE, 57NE, 68SW, 77SW; by F. H. Perring, 75SW.

558/2 [2] Pilosella officinarum C. H. & F. W. Schultz subsp. **officinarum**
(*Hieracium pilosella* L.) *Mouse-ear Hawkweed*
Very common. 81. Open dry situations; grassland on glacial sand, clay, Keuper marl, Carboniferous shale, sand dunes, lime waste beds. The lime waste bed plants are different from the plants of the rest of the county, but have not yet been named as a segregate.

558/2 [6b] Pilosella aurantiaca C. H. & F. W. Schultz subsp. **brunneocrocea**
(Pugsl.) Sell & West (*Hieracium brunneocroceum* Pugsl.) *Orange Hawkweed*
Occasional. 17. Established in a few places on roadsides and hedgebanks; abundant at Mobberley clay pit (78SE) and Plumley lime beds (77NW/SW), both open calcareous habitats. Determined by J. N. Mills in four localities.

Pilosella aurantiaca subsp. **brunneocrocea x P. officinarum**
In some quantity at Plumley lime beds, *Mrs G. Mackie*, det. J. N. Mills, P. D. Sell & C. West.

558/2 [7] Pilosella praealta (Vill. ex Gochnat) C. H. & F. W. Schultz
(*Hieracium praealtum* Vill. ex Gochnat)
Lime waste beds, Plumley, 77NW!, det. J. N. Mills.

559/2 Crepis vesicaria L. subsp. **taraxacifolia** (Thuill.) Thell. *Beaked Hawksbeard*
Established on a limited area at Neston, where first discovered by H. E. Green (cf. B.S.B.I. Proc. 1941-2, p.494).

559/5 Crepis biennis L. *Rough Hawksbeard*
Rare colonist on railway embankments, 88NE, 98NW, *A. Gibson*!

559/6 Crepis capillaris (L.) Wallr. *Smooth Hawksbeard*
Very common. 86. Sandy grassland and dunes; well-drained banks on clay; sandpit edges and open waste ground.

559/8 Crepis paludosa (L.) Moench *Marsh Hawksbeard*
Occasional. 14. Pennine streamsides, cloughs and flushes, usually in shade of Alder and Willow, or sessile oak.

149

Compositae

560/1 Taraxacum officinale Weber **sensu lato** (Sect. *Vulgaria* Dt.)* *Dandelion*
Very common. 109. Arable, disturbed and waste ground, roadsides throughout the county.

560/3 Taraxacum spectabile Dahlst. **sensu lato** (Sect. *Spectabilia* Dt.)* *Broad-leaved Marsh Dandelion*
Occasional. 22. Damp grassland and old pastures, chiefly on Keuper marl and Carboniferous shale.

560/4 Taraxacum laevigatum (Willd.) DC **sensu lato** (incl. Sect. *Erythrospermae* Dt.)* *Lesser Dandelion*
Rare. 3. Locally common on sand dunes, 27!, 28NW!, 29!

544/3 Centaurea cyanus L. has been recorded as a casual on waste ground and farmyards (79SW, 87NW/NE, 88NW); **Helianthus annuus** L., **H. rigidus** (Cass.) Desf., **511/1 Calendula officinalis** L., **526/1 Anthemis tinctoria** L. (46NW, 1966), **527/1 Chamaemelum nobile** (L.) All. (88SW), **533/3 Leucanthemum maximum** (Ram.) DC. (*Chrysanthemum maximum* Ram.) (37NE, 47NW, 87NE, 88SW) and **Bupthalmum salicifolium** L. (36NE) are found as garden outcasts on rubbish dumps; **501/1 Rudbeckia laciniata** L. (38), **507 Doronicum** spp. (74, 77SW, 86SW, 97NW, 98NE), **536/1 Echinops sphaerocephalus** L. (78NW) are found on roadsides outside gardens; **504/1 Ambrosia artemisiifolia** L., A. **trifida** L., and A. **psilostachya** have been recorded as poultry feed casuals by Miss V. Gordon at Ness; **Centaurea diluta** Ait. and **Guizotia abyssinica** (L.f.) Cass. were seen by C. E. Shaw on a tip at Cheadle Heath in 1968; the former also appeared on waste ground at Altrincham (78NE)! in 1969.

Species apparently extinct

514/1 Filago vulgaris Lam. (*F. germanica* (L.) L.) (by Flaxmere, 1924, L. & C. Nat., 17, p.43).

---

*The following taxa have been determined by Dr. A. J. Richards for about 60 specimens gathered from various parts of the county:

Sect. *Vulgaria*: T. hamatum R. (78SE, 29); T. recurvilobum Lindb. f. (78SE); T. marklundii Lindb. f. (88SW); T. melanthoides Dt. (97SE); T. subcyanolepis M.P. Chr. (78SE); T. duplidentiformis Dt. (28NW); T. perhamatum Dt. (98SW) T. longisquameum Lindb. f. (57SW); T. hamatiforme Dt. (57SW),

Sect. *Spectabilia*: T. cimbricum Wiinst. (damp grassland on Keuper marl and Carboniferous shale, 78SE, 88SW, 44, 47SE, 54NW, 57 NW/NE, 98SW, 97SE); T. spectabile Dt. (98SE); T. norstedtii Dt. (57SW, 97SE); T. euryphyllum (Dt.) M.P. Chr. (98SE, 77SE); T. maculigerum Lindb. f. (98SW/SE, 97SE, 77SE); T. praestans Lindb. f. (29); T. faroense Dt. (97SE, 77SE).

Sect. *Erythrospermae*: T. brachyglossum Dt. (28NW); T. lacistophyllum Dt. (29).

Records for "*T. palustre*" both in De Tabley and the Critical Atlas are attributable to Sect. *Spectabilia*

514/5 Filago minima (Sm.) Pers. (by Delamere station, 1922, L. & C. Nat. 16, p.197). Specimens of *F. vulgaris* (Delamere, vii 1927, *A. Pollitt*) and *F. minima* (Newchurch Common, viii 1927, *A. Pollitt*), are in Grosvenor museum, Chester.

549/2 Hypochoeris glabra L.

552/2 Tragopogon porrifolius L. (Upton, 1919, L. & C. Nat., 16, p.141, L.B.S., 1927).

MONOCOTYLEDONES

ALISMATACEAE

561/1 Baldellia ranunculoides (L.) Parl. *Lesser Water-plantain*
Rare. 3. Spring-fed ponds, Dunham-on-the-Hill (47SE)!; Thurstaston (28NW!); brackish ditch at Burton (27!). Decreasing. Recent records (cf. L.N.F.C., 1954, p.14, 1956, p.20), at Willaston, Childer Thornton (37) and Storeton (28SE) have not been confirmed.

562/1 Luronium natans (L.) Raf. *Floating Water-plantain*
Local. 11. Macclesfield canal and Peak Forest canal from Hyde to Congleton. First record in these canals, cf. R. S. Adamson, J. Bot. 57, p.94 1919.

563/1 Alisma plantago-aquatica L. *Water-plantain*
Very common. 102. Meres, ponds, canals, streams, ditches. All aquatic habitats up to c. 750 ft.

565/1 Sagittaria sagittifolia L. *Arrow-head*
Local. 21. Canals and ditches. The length of Peak forest and Macclesfield canals; Shropshire Union canal; Frodsham marshes.

BUTOMACEAE

566/1 Butomus umbellatus L. *Flowering Rush*
Occasional. 24. Rare in meres; more frequently in canals in the west and south of the county, often in non-flowering state; ditches on Frodsham marshes and lower Gowy.

HYDROCHARITACEAE

567/1 Hydrocharis morsus-ranae L. *Frog-bit*
Frequent. 28. Almost confined to the south and west of the county; probably introduced elsewhere; commonest in ponds and ditches immediately to the west of the Peckforton ridge, where the more calcareous Irish Sea drift is present.

Potamogetonaceae

568/1 Stratiotes aloides L. *Water Soldier*
Rare. 4. Apparently introduced in three ponds in Wirral, one near Chester and one near Alderley Edge.

570/1 Elodea canadensis Michx. *Canadian Pondweed*
Common. 68. Canals, meres, ponds, ditches; often the only aquatic vegetation in ponds; not so aggressive elsewhere.

571/1 Lagarosiphon major (Ridl.) Moss
Persistent in Peak forest canal at Hyde, 99NW, *Mrs. G. Mackie.*

SCHEUCHZERIACEAE

Species apparently extinct

573/1 Scheuchzeria palustris L. (not recorded since 1896—cf. J. Bot. 34, p.136, when it was seen at Wybunbury Moss by E. S. Marshall).

JUNCAGINACEAE

574/1 Triglochin palustris L. *Marsh Arrow Grass*
Common. 61. Marshes, flushes, occasionally canal sides and pond fringes.

574/2 Triglochin maritima L. *Sea Arrow Grass*
Local. 9. Salt marshes, from Burton to Runcorn.

POTAMOGETONACEAE

577/1 Potamogeton natans L. *Broad-leaved Pondweed*
Very common. 94. Ponds, meres, canals, ditches; most luxuriant and often dominant in still or slow flowing water 3 feet or less deep.

577/2 Potamogeton polygonifolius Pourr. *Bog Pondweed*
Local. 9. Peaty pools on relict heaths, Lindow, Sound, Brereton; moorland runnels with sphagnum and bryophytes (conf. J. E. Dandy from 99NE)

577/5 Potamogeton lucens L. *Shining Pondweed*
Rare. 3. Short stretch of Macclesfield canal (conf. J. E. Dandy from 98NE/SE).

577/6 Potamegeton gramineus L. *Various-leaved Pondweed*
Known at Hatchmere between c. 1850 and 1920. Two recent records are given by J. P. Savidge in L.N.F.C. Proc., 1956, p.21. (Ledsham and Neston).

577/7 Potamogeton alpinus Balb. *Reddish Pondweed*
Local. 11. Peak Forest and Macclesfield Canals throughout (conf. J. E. Dandy 98SE); Redesmere 87SE! Pickmere 67NE! pool near Alderley Edge 88SW!

577/8 Potamogeton praelongus Wulf. *Long-stalked Pondweed*
Very rare. 1. A solitary plant was found at Quoisley (Shropshire Union canal) in 1967! where the species was recorded by Sir George Taylor in 1947 (per J. E. Dandy).

577/9 Potamogeton perfoliatus L. *Perfoliate Pondweed*
Occasional. 22. Canals, larger meres; slow flowing water up to six feet deep. (conf. J. E. Dandy from 78SW).

577/13 Potamogeton pusillus L. *Lesser Pondweed*
Very rare. 1. Ditches on Frodsham marshes, 47NE, det. J. E. Dandy.

577/14 Potamogeton obtusifolius Mert. & Koch *Blunt-leaved Pondweed*
Occasional. 17. Several places along Peak Forest and Macclesfield Canals; ponds usually where other aquatic plants scarce, on sandy substratum. (conf. J. E. Dandy from 47SW, 99SW).

577/15 Potamogeton berchtoldii Fieb. *Small Pondweed*
Occasional. 25. Ponds and smaller meres. Frodsham marsh ditches. (conf. J. E. Dandy from 47NE).

577/16 Potamogeton trichoides Cham. & Schlecht. *Hair-like Pondweed*
Very rare. 1. Peak Forest Canal, Apethorne, 99SW! conf. J. E. Dandy Rarely flowering.

577/17 Potamogeton compressus L. *Grass-wrack Pondweed*
Rare. 5. Confined to northern stretch of Macclesfield and Peak Forest Canal. (det. J. E. Dandy, 98NE, 99SW).

577/19 Potamogeton crispus L. *Curled Pondweed*
Common. 58. Ponds, canals, ditches, unpolluted slow-flowing streams.

577/21 Potamogeton pectinatus L. *Fennel-leaved Pondweed*
Common. 53. Ponds, meres, canals, ditches; tolerant of some salinity e.g. in R. Weaver, Frodsham marshes, Leasowe, Burton Point.

Species apparently extinct

577/3 Potamogeton coloratus Hornem. Willey Moor, now drained. 54NW, 1902, *A. H. Wolley-Dod* per J. E. Dandy; see also J.Bot. 57, p.129, 1919.

578/1 Groenlandia densa (L.) Fourr. (Delamere, 1884, per J. E. Dandy).

Liliaceae

579/2 Ruppia maritima L. *Beaked Tasselweed*
Very rare. 1. Salt pans on Burton Marsh, 27!

580/1 Zannichellia palustris L. *Horned Pondweed*
Local. 7. Brackish ditches, Frodsham Marshes; spring fed ponds (36NE, 36SE, 54NW)! Sandy borders of meres (78SE, 87SW)!

584/1 Narthecium ossifragum (L.) Huds. *Bog Asphodel*
Local. 12. Remnants of active sphagnum or wet peaty pools on Pennine moorland; on wetter portions of heaths, e.g. Lindow, Thurstaston, Sound. Waterlogged peat, Hatchmere; active sphagnum, Wybunbury.

588/1 Convallaria majalis L. *Lily-of-the-Valley*
Local. 8. Not consistently part of any identifiable community; apparently naturalised in a few woods.

589/3 Polygonatum multiflorum (L.) All. *Solomon's Seal*
Local. 8. Naturalised but long persistent at Vale Royal, Bolesworth, Aston, Eaton, Marple. Smaller growth form with endemic woodland vegetation on east bank of Weaver, 66NW!

591/1 Asparagus officinalis L. *Asparagus*
Rare. 3. Established on sand dunes and sandy waste ground, 28NW! 37SW! 46NW, *T. Edmondson*.

592/1 Ruscus aculeatus L. *Butcher's Broom*
Rarely naturalised in old shrubberies, 37SW, 88SW, 98NW, *A. Gibson*.

595/1 Tulipa sylvestris L. *Wild Tulip*
A patch still present in the Aldersey district, 45NE, 1969, *Miss M. Gillison*. (cf. N. W. Nat. 11 p.161).

597/1 Gagea lutea (L.) Ker-Gawl. *Yellow Star-of-Bethlehem*
Very rare. 1. Several hundred plants on a flushed, shaded slope with *Viola reichenbachiana*, *Veronica montana*, *Ranunculus ficaria* etc., *Mrs. Rylands*, 44! The plants have been known to flower annually for at least 70 years.

598/1 Ornithogalum umbellatum L. *Star-of-Bethlehem*
Rare. 5. Sand dunes of Hoylake golf course. Garden relic elsewhere.

600/1 Endymion non-scriptus (L.) Garcke *Bluebell*
Very common. 101. Woodland, wood borders throughout; occasional relict in grassland; typically with *Pteridium* and *Holcus mollis* under medium shade on leached well drained soils on sand and clay.

603/1 Paris quadrifolia L. *Herb Paris*
Rare. 2. Old oakwoods on Keuper marl, 44! 54SE! apparently extinct in
Arley district where it was known in the 1930's to A. W. Boyd.

593/1 Lilium martagon L. was recorded as a garden outcast at Hoylake in
1965. **600/2 Endymion hispanicus** (Mill.) Chouard has been recorded a few
times outside gardens.

JUNCACEAE

605/1 Juncus squarrosus L. *Heath Rush*
Frequent. 41. Characteristic plant of eroded *Callunetum*; heaths, drained
mosslands on peat. Moorlands on thin peaty soils; rough grassland
pathsides, with *Nardus stricta*.

605/2 Juncus tenuis Willd. *Slender Rush*
Occasional. 22. Increasing in open situations periodically subject to
waterlogging, particularly canal towpaths. For an early record cf. Marriott,
N.W. Nat. 2, p.29, 1927.

605/5 Juncus gerardii Lois. *Mud Rush*
Local. 12. Brackish marshes. Locally abundant on higher levels of salt
marshes.

605/7 Juncus bufonius L. *Toad Rush*
Very common. 100. Open damp situations in a variety of habitats; arable
and waste ground; muddy tracks and roadsides, damp sand, marshes,
pond fringes, brackish marshes.

605/8 Juncus inflexus L. *Hard Rush*
Very common. 100. Wet places, particularly on clay soils throughout.
The hybrid *J. x diffusus* (*J. effusus x J. inflexus*) has been looked for but
not observed. It was recorded by R. S. Adamson from Rainow (J. Bot. 57
p.94, 1919)

605/9 Juncus effusus L. *Soft Rush*
Very common. 110. Abundant in wet places throughout.

605/10 Juncus subuliflorus Drej. (*J. conglomeratus* L.) *Compact Rush*
Very common. 85. Marshes and wet places throughout, especially waterlogged pastures and rough moorland.

605/14 Juncus maritimus Lam. *Sea Rush*
Rare. 2. Upper portions of two salt marshes, 28NW! 29!

605/17 Juncus subnodulosus Schrank *Blunt-flowered Rush*
Local. 8. Base rich flushes on Keuper marl; fen meadows.

605/18 Juncus acutiflorus Ehrh. ex Hoffm. *Sharp-flowered Rush*
Common. 62. Hill flushes, marshes, waterlogged pastures. Often the dominant species in rough marshy pastures in Pennines.

605/19 Juncus articulatus L. *Jointed Rush*
Very common. 104. Marshes throughout the county.

605/22 Juncus bulbosus L. *Bulbous Rush*
Frequent. 47. Hill flushes; damp peat and pools on heaths, sphagnum mosses. Proliferous form often submerged in flooded sand pits and peaty pools.

606/1 Luzula pilosa (L.) Willd. *Hairy Woodrush*
Frequent. 49. Old woodland particularly on Keuper marl or Carboniferous shales; characteristic of dry open humus-free banks.

606/3 Luzula sylvatica (Huds.) Gaudin *Greater Woodrush*
Occasional. 22. Damp shaded woodland and river banks; rare away from Pennine valleys. Humidity rather than soil appears to be limiting factor.

606/8 Luzula campestris (L.) DC. *Field Woodrush*
Very common. 100. Dry grassland; old pastures on sandy and neutral soils.

606/9 Luzula multiflora (Retz.) Lejeune *Heath Woodrush*
Common. 64. Heathland and moorland on well drained soils; dry mossland on peat.

AMARYLLIDACEAE

607/5 Allium vineale L. *Crow Garlic*
Local. 8. Locally abundant on Hoylake sand dunes (28NW!); casual on sandy waste ground elsewhere. Var. *compactum* is the prevalent form.

607/6 Allium oleraceum L. *Field Garlic*
Very rare. 1. A few plants were found by A. J. Farmer at Denhall (27) in 1946 (N. W. Nat., 21, p.105); about a dozen were also seen in Sept. 1966 by Mrs. H. E. Gribble in the same place (per Miss V. Gordon). Verge trimming is thought to account for the sporadic appearances.

607/12 Allium ursinum L. *Ramsons*
Common. 70. Woods; damp humus-rich areas. Often the dominant ground layer in damp heavily shaded woods on Keuper series, and Carboniferous shales. Shaded river and streamsides.

612/1 Galanthus nivalis L. *Snowdrop*
Rarely naturalised near habitation, 37SE, 86NE, etc.

614/1 Narcissus pseudonarcissus L. *Wild Daffodil*
Local. 9. Locally abundant in old woodland, central Weaver and Dane valleys and Alderley area on sandy drift soils and river terraces; garden forms are found as relics elsewhere.

IRIDACEAE

615/1 Sisyrinchium bermudiana L. *Blue Eyed grass*
Very rare. 1. A solitary plant was found on the bank of Bridgewater Canal (78NW) by *P. Newton* in 1966. It was still thriving in 1969!

616/4 Iris pseudacorus L. *Yellow Flag*
Very common. 97. Mere and pond fringes, canal and ditch sides.

618/1 Crocus nudiflorus Sm. *Autumnal Crocus*
Rare. 5. Roadsides, 78NW, 98NE. River Mersey bank, 88NW. Banks of river Bollin, 78SE, 88SW; both these sites are amongst indigenous vegetation well above flood level.

620/1 Crocosmia x crocosmiflora (Lemoine) N.E.Br. *Montbretia*
Naturalised on sand dunes, Hoylake, 28NW! roadside near habitation, 47SE, *T. Edmondson*

DIOSCOREACEAE

622/1 Tamus communis L. *Black Bryony*
Common. 53. Woods, wood borders, scrub and hedgebanks west of grid line 70 on clay soils; rarer eastwards.

ORCHIDACEAE

625/1 Epipactis palustris (L.) Crantz *Marsh Helleborine*
Rare. 2. Two colonies totalling approx. 100 plants, Northwich lime beds, 67SE, *P. Newton*! Growth form similar to plants of dune slacks. One colony in base rich marsh on Keuper marl, 64NE! The characteristic tall fen plant.

625/2 Epipactis helleborine (L.) Crantz *Broad Helleborine*
Occasional. 26. Woods and wood borders. A large number of colonies, each consisting of only a few plants have been observed in or at the edge of old woodland. No soil preferences are apparent.

Orchidaceae

628/1 Listera ovata (L.) R. Br. *Twayblade*
Occasional. 19. Wood borders and damp open scrub on Keuper marl, calcareous drift and Carboniferous shale. It has a particular affinity for damp railway embankments where spring lines emerge from these strata and where there is minimal interference. Characteristic associates include *Primula vulgaris, Carex flacca, Blackstonia perfoliata, Dactylorhiza fuchsii, Linum catharticum, Genista tinctoria, Ononis spinosa.*

636/1 Gymnadenia conopsea (L.) R. Br. subsp. **densiflora** (Wahlenb.) G.
    Camus, Bergon & A. Camus *Fragrant Orchid*
Rare. 2. Locally abundant on lime waste beds, Northwich, 67SE! with a distinct scent of cloves. Small colony in base rich marsh on Keuper marl, 64NE!

638/1 Platanthera chlorantha (Custer) Reichb. *Greater Butterfly Orchid*
Rare. 3. Pennine meadows; flushed grassland on Carboniferous shales (96NW! 97NE!). Old pasture along Peover Brook, on drier parts of a flushed bank on Keuper marl (77SE!) Formerly along Peover Brook in quantity (cf. De Tabley).

640/1 Ophrys apifera Huds. *Bee Orchid*
Very rare. 1. Approx. 20 plants were found by *T. Edmondson* on calcareous soil during 1968, growing with *Blackstonia perfoliata* and *Linum catharticum* (37NE)! About a dozen plants and some seedlings were visible in 1969.

642/5 Orchis morio L. *Green-winged Orchid*
Rare. 2. Alluvial meadow at Leasowe, 29! 1967: small number of plants in old damp pasture on Keuper marl, 57NE! 1968, in a district where it has long been known. Other recent record c. 1950, Shotwick 37SW (cf. E. Hardy, Liverpool Daily Post 31/5/1954.)

642/7 Orchis mascula (L.) L. *Early Purple Orchid*
Local. 12. Confined to old woodland or less commonly grassland banks flushed by calcareous water on Keuper marl strata, Bollin, Weaver valleys, or drift in the west of the county. Recently extinct due to scrub growth, 64SE. Much reduced over the past century.

643/1 Dactylorhiza fuchsii (Druce) Soó subsp. **fuchsii** *Common Spotted*
    Orchid
Common. 74. Flushed grassland and marshes on Keuper marl and Carboniferous shales. Lime waste beds in Central Cheshire.

Dactylorhiza fuchsii x praetermissa
Local. 8. With both parents, alluvial meadows, lime waste and clay pits.

158

PLATE 13. *Above: Rubus chamaemorus* (Cloudberry), Cat and Fiddle Moors (page 94); *beneath: Lathraea squamaria* (Toothwort), Cotterill Clough (page 134).

L

PLATE 14. *Above: Dipsacus pilosus* (Small Teasel), bank of R. Weaver near Winsford (page 141); *beneath: Dactylorhiza maculata* subsp. *ericetorum* (Heath Spotted Orchid), Brindley Lea (page 159).

Orchidaceae

643/2 Dactylorhiza maculata (L.) Soó subsp. **ericetorum** (E. F. Lint.) P. F. Hunt & Summerheyes *Heath Spotted Orchid*
Occasional. 14. Peat soils; Crowden, Hatchmere, Faddiley, Wybunbury surrounds. Marshes on mineral soils: Bradley, Audlem, Bosley, Dane Valley.

643/3 Dactylorhiza incarnata (L.) Soó subsp. **coccinea** (Pugsl.) H. Harr. f. *Early Marsh Orchid*
Very rare. 1. A small colony of this dune plant was found on the Northwich lime beds (67SE) near *Epipactis palustris, Salix repens* and *Dactylorhiza praetermissa* in 1968 by R. E. Thomas!

643/4 Dactylorhiza praetermissa (Druce) Soó *Southern Marsh Orchid*
Occasional. 20. Alluvial water meadows, 57NW/NE; residual dune slack, 28NW; in large quantity on lime beds, 67NE/SE, 77NW/SW, 76NW; clay pit, 78SE; marshes flushed by base rich ground water on Keuper marl or calcareous clay elsewhere.

643/5 Dactylorhiza purpurella (T. & T. A. Steph.) Soó. *Northern Marsh Orchid*
Rare. 2. Plumley (lime beds), det. R. H. Roberts & P. F. Hunt; Bollin Bank, Wilmslow (flushed grassland) *Mrs G. Mackie*, det. P. F. Hunt.

Dactylorhiza purpurella x praetermissa
Plumley, 77NW!, det. P. F. Hunt.

Dactylorhiza purpurella x fuchsii
Plumley, 77NW!, conf. P. F. Hunt.

645/1 Anacamptis pyramidalis (L.) Rich. *Pyramidal Orchid*
Very rare. 1. Two plants on a bank of lime bed, Northwich, 67SE, *P. Newton!*, 1964 et seq.

Species apparently extinct

625/6 Epipactis phyllanthes G. E. Sm. (N. W. Nat., 22, p.280 and Watsonia 2).

627/1 Spiranthes spiralis (L.) Chev. (Caldy, 1917, L. & C. Nat., 16, p.144).

628/2 Listera cordata (L.) R. Br.

631/1 Hammarbya paludosa (L.) Kuntze (Sink Moss, 1837—cf. J. Bot., 38, p.74, 1900.)

635/1 Coeloglossum viride (L.) Harton.

637/1 Pseudorchis albida (L.) A. & D. Löve.

L*   159

Sparganiaceae

638/2 Platanthera bifolia (L.) Rich. (due to former confusion of *Platanthera* spp., the incidence of this species in Cheshire is regarded as unconfirmed.)

ARACEAE

646/1 Acorus calamus L. *Sweet Flag*
Frequent. 27. Large ponds and ornamental lakes; canals.

649/1 Arum maculatum L. *Cuckoo Pint*
Common. 77. Woods, wood borders, shady hedgebanks, often in damp humus rich situations; particularly on Keuper marl and clay soils. Tolerant of deep shade.

647/1 Calla palustris L.
Presumably planted, occurs on the margin of a pool in 87NE.

LEMNACEAE

650/1 Lemna polyrhiza L. *Great Duckweed*
Local. 13. Ponds or small meres. Virtually confined to west of county.

650/2 Lemna trisulca L. *Ivy Duckweed*
Very common. 84. Ponds, ditches, canals, meres.

650/3 Lemna minor L. *Duckweed*
Very common. 105. Ponds, ditches and canals in slow flowing or stagnant waters.

650/4 Lemna gibba L. *Gibbous Duckweed*
Frequent. 32. Canals, ditches, ponds; virtually confined to canals in south and east Cheshire stations.

SPARGANIACEAE

652/1 Sparganium erectum L. *Bur-reed*
Very common. 98. Mere, pond fringes; ditch, stream and canal sides. subsp. **neglectum** (Beeby) Schinz & Thell. appears to be the prevalent form; subsp. **microcarpum** (Neumer) Domin has also been distinguished.

652/2 Sparganium emersum Rehm. *Unbranched Bur-reed*
Frequent. 29. Large ponds, ditches and canal sides, (Peak Forest and Macclesfield Canals). Most widespread in alluvial flats of Gowy and Frodsham marshes.

652/4 Sparganium minimum Wallr. *Small Bur-reed*
Very rare. 1. One spring fed pond on calcareous drift, 28SE!

653/1 Typha latifolia L. *Great Reedmace*
Very common. 97. Meres and ponds, stagnant ditches, tolerating deep shade, persisting in ponds until last stages of silting, the raft of roots effectively suppressing competition from other species.

653/2 Typha angustifolia L. *Lesser Reedmace*
Frequent. 46. Meres and large ponds. Typically appears in deeper water than the previous species, but where the two grow together, plants intermediate in leaf width and inflorescence characters occur.

654/1 Eriophorum angustifolium Honck. *Common Cotton-grass*
Frequent. 44. Sphagnum mosses, sphagnum filled pools; wet peaty hollows and pools on old mossland. Moorlands and blanket bog.

654/4 Eriophorum vaginatum L. *Harestail Cotton-grass*
Frequent. 31. Abundant on wet peat on Pennine moorland and blanket bog. Wet sphagnum on heaths and mossland in the plain where less widespread than *E. angustifolium.*

655/2 Scirpus caespitosus L. *Deer-grass*
Local. 9. Wet peaty areas on highest moors, also in similar ground but in small quantity on Thurstaston Heath (28NW), Lindow Common (88SW) and Brookhouse Moss (86SW).

655/3 Scirpus maritimus L. *Sea Club-rush*
Occasional. 18. Inner fringe of salt and brackish marshes and ditches, spreading up Weaver valley to Vale Royal; also inland at Marbury Mere (54NE).

655/4 Scirpus sylvaticus L. *Wood Club-rush*
Occasional. 19. Commonest in constantly spring fed marshes on banks of Bollin and tributaries, also in similar places in S.E. of county. Alder carr at Redesmere (87SW/SE) 45NW and 86NE.

655/8 Scirpus lacustris L. *Bulrush*
Occasional. 16. Outer fringes of meres and lagoons, rarely in large ponds.

655/9 Scirpus tabernaemontani C. C. Gmel. *Glaucous Bulrush*
Local. 13. Landward fringe of salt marsh and brackish ditches, Frodsham marsh, and lower Weaver valley, rarely in saline spring fed ponds in lower Weaver district.

Cyperaceae

655/10 Scirpus setaceus L. *Bristle Club-rush*
Frequent. 48. Open wet places, spring fed marshes, hill flushes.

655/12 Scirpus fluitans L. *Floating Club-rush*
Rare. 3. Spring fed pond at Thurstaston, 28NW! peaty pools on relict heaths, 64NE, 75SW!, *K. G. Allenby*.

656/2 Eleocharis acicularis (L.) Roem. & Schult. *Needle Spike-rush*
Very rare. 1. Forming lawns above the *Littorella* zone at two old established reservoirs in the Macclesfield district (97SW!), normally submerged but flowering fitfully when exposed in dry summers. Associated with *Gnaphalium uliginosum, Juncus bufonius, Lythrum portula, Bidens tripartita*, but often forming a pure sward.

656/3 Eleocharis quinqueflora (F. X. Hartmann) Schwarz *Few-flowered Spike-rush*
Very rare. 1. Several small patches in remnant of dune slack, Leasowe, 29!, with *Anagallis tenella, Carex serotina*.

656/4 Eleocharis multicaulis (Sm.) Sm. *Many-stemmed Spike-rush*
Very rare. 1. Two bog pools near Oakmere, 56NE! with *Nymphaea alba, Ultricularia minor, Sphagnum* spp.

656/5 Eleocharis palustris (L.) Roem. & Schult. *Common Spike-rush*
Very common. 83. Margins of ponds, meres, reservoirs.

656/6 Eleocharis uniglumis (Link) Schult. *Slender Spike-rush*
Rare. 3. Brackish marshes, lower Weaver 57NW! 57NE! Salt marsh, Leasowe 29!

657/2 Blysmus rufus (Huds.) Link *Saltmarsh Flat Sedge*
Very rare. 1. A small area on brackish marsh, Hoylake, 28NW, *A. Gibson!* 1966 et seq.

661/1 Cladium mariscus (L.) Pohl. *Great Fen Sedge*
Rare. 3. Fen margin of a small mere 54NE! Base rich inflow water Wybunbury Moss 65SE! Hatchmere (57SE) 1970, *J. Cullen*.

663/1 Carex laevigata Sm. *Smooth Sedge*
Local. 10. Marshy hill streamsides and runnels, often under shade of alder. Two sites in Bollin and one in lower Weaver in spring fed marsh on valley slopes.

663/2 Carex distans L. *Distant Sedge*
Rare. 4. Landward edge of salt marshes 28NW/SE! 27! 37NE, *Miss M. Sanders!*

663/4 Carex hostiana DC. *Tawny Sedge*
Very rare. 1. In quantity in one hill flush, 96NW. *P. Newton & K. G. Allenby!*, 1967 et seq.

663/5 Carex binervis Sm. *Ribbed Sedge*
Rare. 5. Rough upland pasture on well drained gritstone slopes. Grass heath on Triassic sandstone, Moor's Brook (57SW), *T. Edmondson*!

663/8 Carex demissa Hornem. *Common Yellow Sedge*
Frequent. 34. Flushes and springheads, particularly in hills, also on marshy slopes and open peaty hollows in plain.

663/10 Carex serotina Mérat *Small Yellow Sedge*
Very rare. 1. Remnant of damp slack, Leasowe (29)! with *Anagallis tenella, Eleocharis quinqueflora.*

663/11 Carex extensa Gooden. *Long-bracted Sedge*
Rare. 3. Higher levels of salt marshes, West Kirby to Parkgate.

663/12 Carex sylvatica Huds. *Wood Sedge*
Frequent. 33. Scrubland; open banks in old woodland on Keuper marl, boulder clay and Carboniferous shale.

663/15 Carex pseudocyperus L. *Cyperus Sedge*
Common. 60. Mere fringes and particularly in marl pits throughout the county, persisting in spite of silting and shade development.

663/16 Carex rostrata Stokes *Bottle Sedge*
Frequent. 39. Sphagnum bogs and peaty pools; large ponds usually with extensive swamp fringes; ponds partly colonised by *Sphagnum* spp.

663/17 Carex vesicaria L. *Bladder Sedge*
Rare. 6. In quantity on shores of Bosley reservoir (96NW)!, pools 66SW! 64NW! 64SE! 99SE! Silted lagoons Eaton Park 45NW!

663/20 Carex riparia Curt. *Great Pond Sedge*
Occasional. 14. Rostherne Mere (78SW), Quoisley Mere (54NW), Pool at Arley (67NE); abundant in low lying ditches and ponds west of Delamere ridge—lower Weaver, middle Dee, Frodsham marshes. Similar distribution to *C. disticha.*

663/21 Carex acutiformis Ehrh. *Lesser Pond Sedge*
Common. 76. Stream, ditch and canal sides; meres, ponds; marshy alluvial flats and alder carr. Often the dominant vegetation in marshes with constant but shallow percolating water.

663/22 Carex pendula Huds. *Pendulous Sedge*
Frequent. 29. Wet seepage areas on shaded banks—old woodland on Keuper marl, boulder clay, and Carboniferous shale.

663/23 Carex strigosa Huds. *Thin Spiked Wood Sedge*
Rare. 5. Alluvium in steep heavily shaded cloughs on Keuper marl; Bollin valley and Cotterill Clough (88SW)! along R. Weaver downstream from Church Minshull (65NE! 66SW! 57NW!).

Cyperaceae

663/24 Carex pallescens L. *Pale Sedge*
Local. 9. In small quantity at all discovered sites; wet meadow 47SE; damp grassland or scrubland on unploughed banks elsewhere.

663/26 Carex panicea L. *Carnation Sedge*
Common. 74. Flushed grassland; edges of marshes on valley slopes; hill flushes.

663/28 Carex limosa L. *Bog Sedge*
Very rare. 1. One small patch in spongiest part of Wybunbury Moss (65SE), *P. Oswald*!

663/31 Carex flacca Schreb. *Glaucous Sedge*
Very common. 85. Coloniser of clay pits and lime waste beds; sand dunes and slacks; damp grassland; margins of flushes and spring fed marshes.

663/32 Carex hirta L. *Hairy Sedge*
Very common. 95. Waterlogged ground, marshes, pond surrounds; damp road and path sides.

663/34 Carex pilulifera L. *Pill Sedge*
Occasional. 20. Dry sandy banks on remnants of heathland; rough upland pastures.

663/36 Carex caryophyllea Latourr. *Spring Sedge*
Frequent. 50. Flushed grassland on Carboniferous shale, Keuper marl, and calcareous drift. Characteristic of old pasture, e.g. on steep valley slopes, stream banks.

663/46 Carex elata All. *Tufted Sedge*
Rare. 4. Fen margins of four meres; Rostherne, 78SW! Hatchmere, 57SE, *Mrs. G. Mackie*!, Quoisley Meres 54NW! 54NE!

663/47 Carex acuta L. *Slender Tufted Sedge*
Local. 8. Pond at Halton Moss (58SE), upland flush 98SE! conf. J. Faulkner; ditches on alluvial flats of R. Gowy and Frodsham marshes 46NE! 47SW, 47SE, *T. Edmondson* conf. A. C. Jermy, canal sides, 37SE, 36NE, *T. Edmondson* conf. A. C. Jermy.

Carex acuta x nigra
47SW, *T. Edmondson* det. A. C. Jermy.

663/50 Carex nigra (L.) Reichard *Common Sedge*
Very common. 87. Wet peaty situations, mosslands and pools throughout the county; mere, pond and ditch fringes; marshes; occasionally in damp grassland. Exhibits a variety of growth forms according to water regime and soil.

663/54 Carex paniculata L. *Greater Tussock Sedge*
Common. 64. Meres and ponds; canal sides; wet alluvial flats in alder
carr. Up to 1000 ft. in alder swamp below Bowstones Farm (98SE).

C. paniculata x remota = C. x boenninghausiana Weihe
Alder swamp, 56SE!

663/56 Carex diandra Schrank *Lesser Tussock Sedge*
Very rare. 1. One small colony was found in a pool being colonised by
Sphagnum spp. and *Menyanthes trifoliata*, 65NW!, 1968.

663/57 Carex otrubae Podp. *False Fox-sedge*
Common. 61. Pond, ditch, and canal margins; brackish ditches, e.g. on
Frodsham marshes. Abundant on west side of Delamere ridge and in
smaller quantity in centre of county. Isolated plants only east of grid line
70.

Carex otrubae x remota = C. x pseudoaxillaris K. Richt.
Ditchsides near both parents, 47SE, *T. Edmondson*! 65NE, *R. E. Thomas
& P. Newton*!

663/60 Carex disticha Huds. *Brown Sedge*
Occasional. 14. Marshy surrounds of Pickmere, Quoisley Mere; brackish
marshes and ditches, lower Weaver and Gowy valleys; alluvial meadows
near coast and along middle Dee. Similar distribution to *C. riparia*.

663/61 Carex arenaria L. *Sand Sedge*
Rare. 4. Locally abundant in sand dunes, Wallasey to Gayton. Railway
ballast 57NW, *T. Edmondson*. Also recorded inland from the banks of
Oakmere, 56NE, in 1956 but not confirmed in this survey.

663/67 Carex spicata Huds. *Spiked Sedge*
Occasional. 21. Scrubland, hedgebanks, chiefly on Keuper marl and drift
in West Cheshire.

663/69 Carex elongata L. *Elongated Sedge*
Rare. 2. Border of pond, Wrenbury (64NW), *Mrs. A. Blacklay*! Side of
Shropshire Union canal, with *Geum rivale*, 54NE!

663/70 Carex echinata Murr. *Star Sedge*
Occasional. 26. Flushes and peaty pools in hills; sphagnum bogs, springs,
and flushes in plain and damp open spots in peaty mere surrounds.

663/71 Carex remota L. *Remote Sedge*
Very common. 84. Canal banks; sides of wooded pools, streams and pits,
often in deep shade in alder carr.

Gramineae

663/72 Carex curta Gooden. *White Sedge*
Occasional. 23. Edges of mosslands and old pits colonised by *Sphagnum* spp. Wet peaty places; rarely by peaty runnels on Pennine blanket bog.

663/74 Carex ovalis Gooden. *Oval Sedge*
Very common. 82. Damp grassland on leached soils, reclaimed marshes and peat mosses; waterlogged pastures.

663/80 Carex pulicaris L. *Flea Sedge*
Local. 11. Springs and flushes in hills; open spots in fen meadows (86SW/54NE); flushed grassland on Keuper marl (57SW/57NE/66SW); damp heath (54NW).

Species apparently extinct

659/1 Schoenus nigricans L.

660/1 Rhynchospora alba (L.) Vahl. (Very rare at Hatchmere, 1912, Lancs. Nat., 5, p.179).

663/7a Carex lepidocarpa Tausch

663/33 Carex lasiocarpa Ehrh.

663/65 Carex divulsa Stokes

663/81 Carex dioica L. (specimen in Liverpool Museum herbarium, Hale Moss, 1884).

GRAMINEAE

665/1 Phragmites australis (Cav.) Stend. (*P. communis* Trin.) *Reed*
Common. 63. Mere and large pool fringes; occasionally stream, river and ditch sides; rarely around springs. Rare in east Cheshire.

667/1 Molinia caerulea (L.) Moench *Purple Moor-grass*
Common. 53. Dominant on drained mossland and large areas of damp peaty moorland in the Pennines; also on peaty portions of heathland. At Stretton Moss and the north end of Hatchmere it occurs with *Myrica gale* in areas where formerly base rich fen species were recorded.

668/1 Sieglingia decumbens (L.) Bernh. *Heath Grass*
Frequent. 47. Damp grassland near springs and flushes where sandstone or gritstone meets clay, marl or shale; grassland on leached clay soils. Commonest in Pennine grassland.

669/1 Glyceria fluitans (L.) R.Br. *Floating Sweet-grass*
Very common. 102. Wet areas, except on peat.

669/2 Glyceria plicata Fr. *Plicate Sweet-grass*
Common. 58. Ponds, ditches and streamsides.

Glyceria fluitans x plicata = G. x pedicillata Townsend
Noted at Pickmere, 67NE!, 46NE, and 98NW, *A. Gibson*, but is probably more frequent than these records indicate.

669/3 Glyceria declinata Bréb. *Small Sweet-grass*
Common. 64. Ponds, ditches, marshes, waterlogged pastures.

669/4 Glyceria maxima (Hartm.) Holmberg *Reed-grass*
Common. 55. Canals and ditches; appears to require a slow current.

670/1 Festuca pratensis Huds. *Meadow Fescue*
Common. 69. Pastures and meadows, rarely in undisturbed grassland; roadsides, waste ground.

670/2 Festuca arundinacea Schreb. *Tall Fescue*
Frequent. 39. Open disturbed and waste ground, roadsides, particularly in the west of the county.

670/3 Festuca gigantea (L.) Vill. *Giant Fescue*
Very common. 89. Woods and wood borders, particularly on clay and shale soils.

670/4 Festuca altissima All. *Wood Fescue*
Very rare. 1. A large colony was rediscovered by C. A. Stace (1967) in a steep rocky wood in the Etherow valley, 99SE! The plant is dominant over an area which is constantly saturated by springs emanating from the Carboniferous shale ground rock. Further smaller colonies have since been found in a similar wood nearby. The large colony was originally found (when in Derbyshire) by J. Whitehead in 1875 (cf. Linton, Flora of Derbyshire p.318).

670/5 Festuca heterophylla Lam. *Various-leaved Fescue*
Very rare. 1. A colony of this species was observed under a field hedge and along a farm track, Ollerton, 77NE! 1968, conf. C. A. Stace.

670/6 Festuca rubra L. *Red Fescue*
Very common. 98. A major constituent of undisturbed grassland throughout the county, but avoiding peat and waterlogged soils. Forms of this species occur abundantly on sand dunes and higher parts of salt marshes.

670/8 Festuca ovina L. *Sheep's Fescue*
Frequent. 48. Grassland on well drained soils; upland pastures on gritstones and shales; heathland on sandstones and glacial sand; sand dunes, lime waste beds.

670/9 Festuca tenuifolia Sibth. *Fine-leaved Sheep's Fescue*
This species is recorded in the Critical Atlas for SJ/77, where it grows on Knutsford Heath. Some populations also occur in the upland rough pastures in SJ/99SE. Probably under recorded through unfamiliarity.

x Festulolium loliaceum (Huds.) P. Fourn.
Has been seen at Marbury, 54NE!, and near Hartford, *J. G. Kelcey* (67SW), both in damp meadows. It is apparently rare, but may have been overlooked.

671/1 Lolium perenne L. *Rye-grass*
Very common. 107. Agricultural grassland and roadsides; old pastures on clay and shale soils.

671/2 Lolium multiflorum Lam. *Italian Rye-grass*
Frequent. 50. Reseeded pastures, field borders, roadsides; rubbish tips.

672/2 Vulpia bromoides (L.) Gray *Squirrel-tail Fescue*
Occasional. 15. Open sandy or gravelly situations; Triassic sandstone detritus and old sandstone walls; sandpits and railway ballast.

672/3 Vulpia myuros (L.) C. C. Gmel. *Ratstail Fescue*
Very rare. 1. A small colony was found in a disused railway siding, 45NE in 1968 by *A. Gibson & R. E. Thomas*!

673/1 Puccinellia maritima (Huds.) Parl. *Salt Marsh Grass*
Local. 11. The dominant grass on middle levels of salt marshes, Runcorn to Bromborough, and Dee shore.

673/2 Puccinellia distans (L.) Parl. *Reflexed Salt Marsh Grass*
Local. 7. Brackish marshes, Leasowe, Frodsham, Burton; inland close to saline workings, Winsford, Middlewich, Sandbach.

676/1 Poa annua L. *Annual Meadow Grass*
Very common. 110. Arable and disturbed ground, roadsides, pathsides and temporarily open areas on all soils.

676/6 Poa nemoralis L. *Wood Meadow Grass*
Frequent. 28. Old woods under high canopy on damp banks; no apparent soil preference.

676/9 Poa compressa L. *Flattened Meadow Grass*
Very rare. 1. Old wall of Dodleston churchyard, 36SE!

676/10 Poa pratensis L. *Meadow Grass*
Very common. 100. Pasture and meadow on sand, clay, shale or marl.

676/11 Poa angustifolia L. *Narrow leaved Meadow Grass*
Rare. 2. This early flowering *Poa* has only been found on Hoylake and Wallasey sand dunes, 28NW & 29! conf. C. A. Stace.

676/12 Poa subcaerulea Sm. *Spreading Meadow Grass*
Local. 11. This grass appears to be widespread in upland pastures and meadows, and on sand dunes in Wirral. It is also recorded from lime waste at Northwich 67SE! and sandy grassland, 66NW, conf. C. A. Stace.

676/13 Poa trivialis L. *Rough Meadow Grass*
Very common. 95. Damp woods, ditches, stream, and canal sides, marshes, roadsides, disturbed ground.

676/15 Poa chaixii Vill. *Broad leaved Meadow Grass*
Abundant in a plantation, Willaston, 37NW, *Miss V. Gordon.*

677/1 Catabrosa aquatica (L.) Beauv. *Water Whorl-grass*
Occasional. 15. Erosion pools on canal sides; ditches, particularly on drained mosslands in south of the county and Frodsham marshes. The lectotype of subsp. **minor** (Bab.) Perring & Sell was found at Hoylake in 1804, but this sub-species has not been detected in the survey.

678/1 Dactylis glomerata L. *Cock's-foot*
Very common. 110. Grassland throughout the county; roadsides, arable and disturbed ground.

679/1 Cynosurus cristatus L. *Crested Dog's-tail*
Very common. 105. A major constituent of grassland throughout the county, particularly on clay soils.

680/1 Briza media L. *Quaking Grass*
Common. 69. Damp pastures and meadows, particularly on Keuper marl and Carboniferous shale; edges of flushes and springs on grassland slopes; drier hummocks on marshy surrounds of meres.

681/1 Melica uniflora Retz. *Wood Melick*
Frequent. 47. Old woodland on Keuper marl or Carboniferous shales; dry banks on mineral soils. Can tolerate heavy shade.

683/2 Bromus ramosus Huds. *Hairy Brome*
Common. 63. Undisturbed woods and wood borders; shaded hedgebanks on clay, marl or Carboniferous shale.

683/5 Bromus sterilis L. *Barren Brome*
Common. 71. Disturbed ground on light soils; roadsides; sandstone detritus and walls. Becoming scarce east and northwards.

Gramineae

683/10 Bromus hordaceus L. subsp. **hordaceus** (*B. mollis* L.) *Soft Brome*
Common. 78. Arable and disturbed ground, roadsides, agricultural field borders. Subsp. **thominii** (Hardouin) Hylander (**683/12**) occurs on open sandy ground, 66NW, *R. E. Thomas*, conf. C. A. Stace, and on Frodsham marshes, 47NE, *T. Edmondson*, det. Kew.

683/13 Bromus lepidus Holmberg *Slender Brome*
Rare. 3. Waste ground, roadsides. Probably under-recorded. Plumley, 77NW, *C. A. Stace*; 88NE, 98SE, *A. Gibson*.

683/19 Bromus carinatus Hook. & Arn. *California Brome*
Waste ground, 88NW, *A. Gibson*; 47SE, *C. E. Shaw*; 36NE, *T. Edmondson*; established on Dee bank, Chester, 46NW, *Miss V. Gordon*.

684/1 Brachypodium sylvaticum (Huds.) Beauv. *Slender False Brome*
Very common. 81. Woods, wood borders, hedgebanks, particularly on well-drained slopes in moderate shade on Keuper marl and clay. Often the dominant ground cover grass in these situations. Rare in the Pennine district.

685/1 Agropyron caninum (L.) Beauv. *Bearded Couch-grass*
Frequent. 41. Wood borders, wooded stream and river banks, particularly on Keuper marl and Carboniferous shales.

685/3 Agropyron repens (L.) Beauv. *Couch-grass*
Very common. 104. Arable and disturbed ground, field borders, roadsides, tips.

685/4 Agropyron pungens (Pers.) Roem. & Schult. *Sea Couch-grass*
Local. 8. Higher portions of salt marshes.

685/5 Agropyron junceiforme (A. & D. Löve) A. & D. Löve *Sand Couch-grass*
Rare 3. Open portions of sand dunes, Wallasey to Gayton.

686/1 Elymus arenarius L. *Lyme Grass*
Rare. 5. Seaward side of sand dunes; ballast casual, 57NW.

687/1 Hordeum secalinum Schreb. *Meadow Barley*
Local. 9. Damp low-lying meadows and sides of drainage ditches, lower Gowy, Weaver and Dee valleys, where land is subject to occasional flooding by brackish water. Canal bank, Burland 65SW! 1969. *Myosoton aquaticum* and *Thalictrum flavum*, inter alia, have a similarly restricted distribution.

687/2 Hordeum murinum L. *Wall Barley*
Frequent. 37. Disturbed and waste ground, roadsides, particularly on light soils. Common in Wirral and hinterland of Dee and Mersey; waste land and tips elsewhere.

688/1 Hordelymus europaeus (L.) Harz *Wood Barley*
Rare. 3. Restricted to steep sides of two undisturbed cloughs where calcareous bands crop out in Keuper marl, 58SW! 88SW! and one rocky wood on Carboniferous shale where constant spring line maintains wet, open conditions, 99SE! Its presence here was known to J. Whitehead in 1875 (cf. Linton, Flora of Derbyshire p.323.)

691/1 Trisetum flavescens (L.) Beauv. *Yellow Oat Grass*
Frequent. 45. Upland meadows on Carboniferous shale; elsewhere in old pastures and banks in dry open situations, particularly on clay.

693/2 Helictotrichon pubescens (Huds.) Pilg. *Hairy Oat Grass*
Rare. 3. Grassland on Keuper marl, 66SE, *A. Gibson*! 76SW! sand dunes, Hoylake, 28NW!

694/1 Arrhenatherum elatius (L.) Beauv. ex J. & C. Presl *False Oat Grass*
Very common. 106. Arable, disturbed and waste ground, field borders, roadsides, canal and railway banks throughout the county.

695/1 Holcus lanatus L. *Yorkshire Fog*
Very common. 105. Grassland, waste ground, roadsides throughout.

695/2 Holcus mollis L. *Creeping Soft-grass*
Very common. 105. Woods, scrub, hedgebanks throughout: major element of vegetation in shaded situations on leached clay and sandy soils. Persists after felling of tree cover on bracken covered banks and slopes.

696/1 Deschampsia caespitosa (L.) Beauv. *Tufted Hair-grass*
Very common. 107. Woods and marshes throughout the county; waterlogged grassland and *Juncetum*; hill flushes.

696/3 Deschampsia flexuosa (L.) Trin. *Wavy Hair-grass*
Very common. 87. Heaths, woodlands, hedgebanks on sandy soils; dominant grass on higher Pennine slopes with thin soils; rock faces, quarries. Indicative of transition to heath, moor or heathy woodland on acid soils.

697/1 Aira praecox L. *Early Hair-grass*
Frequent. 33. Open sandy ground, dunes. Early coloniser of disused sandpits. Thin soils around Triassic sandstone outcrops.

697/2 Aira caryophyllea L. *Silvery Hair-grass*
Occasional. 18. Open sandy and (particularly) gravelly ground; sand dunes; beds of disused railway tracks; disused sandpits.

699/1 Ammophila arenaria (L.) Link *Marram Grass*
Rare. 2. Abundant on seaward side of sand dunes.

Gramineae

700/1 Calamagrostis epigejos (L.) Roth *Bushgrass*
Local. 9. Clay banks on coast—Hilbre, *R. E. Thomas*; Eastham, 38, *Mrs. N. F. McMillan*. Damp hedgebanks on Keuper marl, Darnhall, 66SE! Warmingham 76SW! Large but shallow pond, Dunham Park, *P. Newton*, 78SW! In quantity, swampy surrounds of Plumley limebeds under Salix, 77NW/SW! Under plantation of conifers, Dawpool, 28NW!

700/2 Calamagrostis canescens (Weber) Roth *Purple Smallreed*
Rare. 6. Swampy fringes of meres among alder carr or tall herb community Rostherne, 78SW! Pickmere, 67SE! Capesthorne, 87SW! Marbury, 54SE! Quoisley, 54NW! Canal bank 65SW!

700/3 Calamagrostis stricta (Timm) Koel. *Narrow Smallreed*
Very rare. 1. Fringe of Oakmere, 56NE! The water level at Oakmere fluctuates unpredictably; *C. stricta* is present at the highest horizon on sand around the north and east sides; also on peat surrounding a subsidiary pool at the north west end.

701/2 Agrostis canina L. *Brown Bent-grass*
Occasional. 24. Wet meadows, mere fringes, damp places on heaths; swampy alluvial flats (subsp. *canina*); rough grassland on Pennine slopes (subsp. *montana* (Hartm.) Hartm).

701/3 Agrostis tenuis Sibth. *Common Bent-grass*
Very common. 107. A major constituent of "unimproved" grassland throughout the county. Dry leached soils on Keuper marl; well-drained banks and slopes on boulder clay, sandstone, and gritstone in the Pennines.

701/4 Agrostis gigantea Roth *Black Bent-grass*
Frequent. 28. Arable and disturbed ground, e.g. sand-pit edges, roadsides. Probably under-recorded.

701/5 Agrostis stolonifera L. *Creeping Bent-grass*
Very common. 103. Damp bare places; pond and mere fringes; ditches and streamsides; canal-sides; roadsides; muddy farm tracks; arable and disturbed ground; waste ground.

707/1 Phleum bertolonii DC. *Cat's-tail*
Occasional. 14. Sand dunes (28NW, 29); rarely in old pastures on Keuper marl.

707/2 Phleum pratense L. *Timothy*
Very common. 99. Agricultural grassland, field borders and roadsides. Pastures and meadows on clay soils.

707/5 Phleum arenarium L. *Sand Cat's-tail*
Rare. 2. A member of the early flowering annual community on open but stable dunes, including *Cerastium semidecandrum, Erophila verna, Myosotis ramosissima, Vicia lathyroides*, etc.

708/2 Alopecurus pratensis L. *Meadow Foxtail*
Very common. 104. Agricultural grassland, meadows, roadsides, arable and disturbed ground.

708/3 Alopecurus geniculatus L. *Marsh Foxtail*
Very common. 100. Marshes; ponds, ditches, waterlogged pastures, higher levels of salt marshes and seasonally wet areas.

708/4 Alopecurus aequalis Sobol. *Orange Foxtail*
Rare. 2. Shore of Langley reservoir (97SE)!, 1965; Bosley reservoir (96NW)!, when the water level was unusually low.

709/1 Milium effusum L. *Wood Millet*
Frequent. 52. Old woodland on Keuper marl or Carboniferous shales; dry slopes in medium shade.

712/2 Anthoxanthum odoratum L. *Sweet Vernal Grass*
Very common. 110. Grassland throughout the county, especially on sandstone, gritstone, peat, and leached clay soils; occasionally in woods.

713/1 Phalaris arundinacea L. *Reed-grass*
Very common. 103. Ditches, streamsides, canal sides, mere fringes, Alder carr.

713/2 Phalaris canariensis L. *Canary Grass*
Occasional. 16. Common and recurrent on rubbish tips and waste ground.

714/1 Parapholis strigosa (Dum.) C. E. Hubbard *Sea Hard-grass*
Rare. 2. Bare patches, inner margins of salt marshes, Denhall, 27!, Leasowe 29!

715/1 Nardus stricta L. *Mat-grass*
Frequent. 43. Dominant over areas of upper hill slopes where distinctive of derelict pastures on gritstone rocks; also on similar areas in Delamere and Peckforton districts on Triassic sandstone; occasional on dry sandy heathland elsewhere and locally abundant in derelict pastures on boulder clay.

716/2 Spartina anglica C. E. Hubbard (*Spartina townsendii* auct. non Groves) *Cord Grass*
Rare. 4. Locally abundant; dominant on higher salt marsh from West Kirby to Burton Point, and at Stanlow. For notes on its history and biology in the Dee estuary, cf. M. C. Taylor & E. M. Burrows, J. Ecol. 56: 795-809, 1968, and references given there.

718/1 Echinochloa crus-galli (L.) Beauv. *Cockspur*
Rubbish tips, 88NE/SW; 55NW, *Mrs. A. Blacklay*; 75 NW, *C. E. Shaw*; 64SE, arable field, *G. Meredith*.

173

Gramineae

671/3 **Lolium temulentum** L. (Adswood and Wilmslow), **Hordeum jubatum L.,** 720/1 **Setaria viridis** (L.) Beauv., **S. italica** (L.) Beauv., **720/3 S. lutescens** (Weigel) Hubbard, **Panicum miliaceum** L., and **Zea mays** L. have been found on waste ground and rubbish tips; species of Bamboo (especially *Pseudosasa japonica* (Steud.) Mikano) are found occasionally in ornamental woods and coverts. **701/6 Agrostis avenacea** J. F. Gmel. was found on a roadside at Pott Shrigley in 1970 by C. A. Stace.

Species apparently extinct

672/1 **Vulpia membranacea** (L.) Dum. (Wallasey, 1908, cf. Drabble, J. Bot. 48, 1910).

673/5 **Puccinellia rupestris** (With.) Fern. & Weath.

674/1 **Catapodium rigidum** (L.) C. E. Hubbard (Wallasey, 1908, cf. Drabble, J. Bot. 48, 1910).

674/2 **Catapodium marinum** (L.) C. E. Hubbard.

676/14 **Poa palustris** L. (SJ 79, det. Kew, per F. H. Perring; cf. L. & C. Nat. 7, p.296).

708/5 **Alopecurus bulbosus** Gouan

ADDENDA

211/11/223a **Rubus porphyrocaulis** A. Newton.
4. A low-growing, 3-leaved bramble with hairy purplish glandular stem and white flowers, this species is locally common in oakwoods of the Etherow and Goyt valleys.

The following additional records should be included both in the species list and maps: **13/1 Blechnum spicant** (pp.68, 194), add 56NW; **109/1 Arabidopsis thaliana** (pp. 79, 207), add 56NW; **131/8 Cerastium glomeratum** (pp.83, 209), add 78SE; **149/2 Claytonia perfoliata** (pp. 83, 210), add 78SE; **187/2 Ulex gallii** (pp. 91, 203), add 56NW; **211/11/129 Rubus ulmifolius** (pp.100, 190), add 78NW; **211/11/248a Rubus distractiformis** (pp.103, 219), add 57SW; **238/1 Umbilicus rupestris** (pp.109, 207), add 56NW; **326/1 Parietaria judaica** (pp.120, 216), add 56NW; **423/1 Cymbalaria muralis** (pp.131, 210), add 56NW; **462/1 Lamium amplexicaule** (pp.136, 206), add 56NW, 78SE; **577/2 Potamogeton polygonifolius** (p.152), add 77SW.

PLATE 15. *Above: Gagea lutea* (Yellow Star of Bethlehem), wood near Malpas (page 154); *beneath: Epipactis palustris* (Marsh, Helleborine), flush near Hatherton (page 157).

PLATE 16. *Above: Paris quadrifolia* (Herb Paris), shaded bank near Malpas (page 155); *beneath: Carex elongata* (a Sedge), canal bank near Wrenbury (page 165).

NOTES ON DISTRIBUTION MAPS

Distribution maps are reproduced for most species occurring in more than 3 and less than 53 areas. Species occurring outside these limits are considered to be either too fragmentary or too widespread to enable any significant conclusions to be drawn from perusal of the maps, at least on a county scale. A few maps of common species have, however, been included where it is felt the distributional facts are unusually instructive.

Of the species included, a large number exhibit patterns of a random type, i.e. their incidence cannot be correlated with clear cut observable factors or combinations of factors. Most arable weeds mapped, for instance, can occur wherever conditions are locally suitable. These species are, it is suggested, those for which the ecological requirements are widely satisfied in the county, and those for which the constraints of climate, altitude, soil and water regime are not so restrictive either separately or in combination to enable a precise pattern to emerge. Even here, broad tendencies—i.e., greater frequency in east or west—are observable, but the species themselves do not behave exclusively enough, or required habitats are too evenly spread, to enable a distinctive pattern to emerge.

Several species occurring in $\frac{1}{4}$ to $\frac{1}{2}$ the areas fall into this category; indeed, the distribution of some actively colonising species may be a matter of pure chance. Of similar complexity, but more rewarding are those species with complex but distinguishable patterns due to their compound but clear cut habitat preferences, e.g. *Juncus squarrosus* for acid, peaty or sandy soils, *Genista tinctoria* for old pasture.

There are obvious limits to the information which can be gleaned from a perusal of dot maps alone. An attempt has been made to point to the most characteristic distributions, which are grouped according to "affinities", and maps showing specific features of obvious importance to many species are included as a basis for correlation.

Attention should be drawn to the maps of species which might have been thought to conform to a recognisable "affinity" but which, in fact, do not. Examples of this feature are:

> Blackstonia perfoliata
> Hypericum pulchrum
> Valeriana dioica
> Veronica scutellata

It is true that all of these species may be exhibiting a random pattern due to the semi-relict nature of their habitats in the county; it is curious, however, that the evidence of De Tabley in these instances supports a similar status a century ago.

Finally, it is instructive to note instances of well-marked patterns exhibited by particular species which do not conform to any group. Examples of this are:

Pimpinella major
Galeopsis speciosa
Bryonia cretica

It is likely that in these cases the factors governing their unique distributions are ascertainable but undefined; research on the ecology of these species might well have interesting results. One should remember also that few patterns, even within "affinities" are exactly identical, and that explanation of micro-variation is illusory.

The maps are arranged in the following order:

(i) Distribution maps arranged and numbered according to the lists of "affinities" given below.

(ii) Maps of species with "random" distributions, arranged in alphabetical order.

(iii) Base map, map showing number of species recorded per square during the survey, and maps showing topographical features of importance to plant distribution (these maps are to be found on the pull-out pages, pp. 227, 229).

AFFINITY 1. SPECIES WITH PREDOMINANTLY COASTAL DISTRIBUTION.

a. *Species confined to coastal and estuarine areas*.*

1. Agropyron pungens
2. Apium graveolens
3. Armeria maritima
4. Atriplex littoralis
5. Baldellia ranunculoides
6. Carex distans
7. C. extensa
8. Cochlearia anglica
9. Glaux maritima
10. Halimione portulacoides
11. Honkenya peploides
12. Juncus gerardii
13. Oenanthe lachenalii
14. Plantago maritima
15. Polygonum oxyspermum subsp. raii
16. Ranunculus baudotii
17. Smyrnium olusatrum
18. Spergularia media
19. Suaeda maritima
20. Thymus drucei
21. Trifolium fragiferum
22. Triglochin maritima
23. Viola canina

b. *Species of coastal and inland saline areas*

1. Aster tripolium
2. Puccinellia distans
3. Samolus valerandi
4. Scirpus maritimus
5. S. tabernaemontani
6. Spergularia marina

---

* cf. also *Plantago coronopus*, map not included.

c. *Species predominantly coastal but with some inland sites*

1. Anthyllis vulneraria (lime waste inland).
2. Atriplex hastata (occasional arable weed).
3. Carex arenaria (railway ballast inland)
4. Cerastium diffusum (railway ballast inland).
5. Cerastium semidecandrum (sandy ground inland).
6. Cochlearia danica (railway ballast inland).
7. Diplotaxis muralis (occasional weed of nurseries and waste ground).
8. Leontodon taraxacoides (marshes and sandy areas inland).
9. Ononis repens (sandy areas inland).
10. Vicia lathyroides (sandy detritus inland).

These lists illustrate the ability of some sub-littoral species to tolerate inland habitats. The case of *Leontodon taraxacoides* (1c8) seems to point to the existence of separate races with differing habitat requirements.

AFFINITY 2. SPECIES WITH A PRONOUNCED WESTERLY DISTRIBUTION.

a. *Species with a predominantly westerly or south-westerly distribution, very rare or absent east of grid line 7.*

1. Agrimonia eupatoria
2. Aira caryophyllea
3. Allium vineale
4. Apium inundatum
5. Arenaria serpyllifolia
6. Azolla filiculoides
7. Carex spicata
8. Clinopodium vulgare (relict)
9. Coronopus squamatus
10. Cruciata ciliata
11. Erophila verna
12. Galium verum
13. Hydrocharis morsus-ranae
14. Lemna polyrhiza
15. Ononis spinosa
16. Primula veris
17. Rubus caesius
18. R. ulmifolius
19. Silaum silaus
20. Sison amomum (relict)
21. Tamus communis
22. Trifolium arvense
23. Veronica catenata
24. Viola odorata
25. Vulpia bromoides

This is a long list which may well conceal several micro-affinities, e.g. the more calcareous clays derived from "Irish Sea" drift, more low-lying marshes and ponds, higher summer sunshine, may be crucial factors.

b. *Species with a main focus in lower estuarine alluvium of Gowy, Weaver and Dee tributaries, elsewhere in low-lying marshes.*

1. Callitriche obtusangula
2. Carex acuta
3. C. disticha
4. C. riparia
5. Hordeum secalinum
6. Juncus subnodulosus
7. Thalictrum flavum

Myosoton aquaticum is most luxuriant in this area.

177

c. *Species very common west of Delamere ridge, decreasing eastwards in varying degrees with a marked aversion to the more acid soils and altitude greater than 200 feet.*

1. Carex otrubae
2. C. pseudo-cyperus
3. Oenanthe crocata
4. Oenanthe fistulosa
5. Scrophularia auriculata

AFFINITY 3. SPECIES WITH A PRONOUNCED EASTERLY DISTRIBUTION.

a. *Species in all or most moorland areas, scattered in the plain (often strongly represented near the Delamere ridge), rare or absent west of grid line 5.*

1. Carex demissa
2. C. echinata
3. Equisetum sylvaticum
4. Eriophorum angustifolium
5. Knautia arvensis
6. Lathyrus montanus
7. Leontodon hispidus
8. Polygala serpyllifolia
9. Sieglingia decumbens
10. Veronica officinalis
11. Viola palustris

b. *Species with a strong concentration across the centre of the county.*

1. Erica tetralix
2. Juncus squarrosus
3. Molinia caerulea

c. *Distributions correlating with sandstone and gritstone outcrops*

1. Blechnum spicant
2. Luzula sylvatica
3. Melampyrum pratense
4. Nardus stricta
5. Vaccinium myrtillus

d. *Species in most or all moorland areas, rare in plain, where confined to Sphagnum pattern.*

1. Empetrum nigrum
2. Narthecium ossifragum
3. Potamogeton polygonifolius
4. Scirpus caespitosus

e. *Species confined to lowland Sphagnum*

1. Andromeda polifolia
2. Drosera rotundifolia
3. Myrica gale

f. *Species intermediate between d and e, apparently tolerating degraded peat in addition to active Sphagnum.*

1. Carex curta
2. Eriophorum vaginatum
3. Vaccinium oxycoccus

g. *Species confined to ground over 1,000 feet.*

1. Carex binervis
2. Myosotis repens
3. Vaccinium vitis-idaea*

---

* Formerly found in the Peckforton hills at 750 feet, and recently discovered near Frodsham (one small patch) at 450 feet.

178

h. *Species in almost all areas east of grid line 7, very scarce westwards.*

1. Alchemilla xanthochlora   2. Myrrhis odorata

Polygonum bistorta exhibits similar features, but extends further westwards; the further west, the closer to habitation.

i. *Species very concentrated in moorland areas, thinly scattered elsewhere and decreasing westwards (perhaps relict in the plain, cf. incised valley affinity, 4b).*

1. Carex laevigata
2. Crepis paludosa
3. Dryopteris pseudo-mas
4. Prunus padus
5. Quercus petraea
6. Salix aurita
7. Thelypteris limbosperma

j. *Species with a dense concentration in east-central and north-central Cheshire, but absent from moorland.*

1. Chrysosplenium alternifolium
2. Dryopteris carthusiana
3. Frangula alnus

Compare the distributions of *Rubus accrescens*, *R. distractiformis* and *R. scissus* in the alphabetical section.

k. *Species present in most moorland areas and most prevalent in the north-east*

1. Montia fontana   2. Ranunculus omiophyllus

l. *Species most concentrated in the north-east but also present on eastern and southern fringe*

1. Geum rivale
2. Salix pentandra
3. Scirpus sylvaticus
4. Stellaria nemorum

m. *Species with a distinct south-eastern tendency.*

1. Alchemilla glabra
2. Botrychium lunaria*
3. Viola lutea

Compare the distributions of *Rubus eifeliensis* and *R. lindebergii*. *Corydalis claviculata* (3m 4) appears to combine characteristics of 3c (sandstone), 3e and 3j.

AFFINITY 4. CORRELATIONS BASED CHIEFLY ON PHYSICAL FACTORS.

a. *Species with a marked similarity of 'clusters' in the north-west, south and north-east of the county, correlating well with relict fen or marshes with more eutrophic water.*

1. Calamagrostis canescens
2. Carex elata
3. Catabrosa aquatica
4. Hottonia palustris
5. Ranunculus lingua
6. Thelypteris palustris
7. Utricularia vulgaris
8. Zannichellia palustris

---

* Formerly present in the plain also, on the more calcareous soils.

b. *Incised valleys; several species display this pattern in part, but the following are particularly well fitted.*

1. Agropyron caninum
2. Alchemilla filicaulis subsp. vestita
3. Campanula latifolia
4. Carduus crispus
5. Carex pallescens
6. C. pendula
7. C. strigosa
8. C. sylvatica
9. Dipsacus fullonum
10. D. pilosus (relict)
11. Galium odoratum
12. Geranium pratense
13. Hordelymus europaeus
14. Lamiastrum galeobdolon
15. Lathraea squamaria
16. Lysimachia nummularia
17. Melica uniflora
18. Milium effusum
19. Myosotis sylvatica
20. Phyllitis scolopendrium*
21. Polystichum aculeatum
22. P. setiferum
23. Ribes rubrum
24. Stellaria neglecta
25. Vicia sylvatica (relict)

c. *Canals. The following species show a distinct correlation with this habitat; it is, however, noteworthy that some are not confined to canals and others are only present in one particular canal or portion of one.*

1. Acorus calamus
2. Butomus umbellatus
3. Ceratophyllum demersum
4. Glyceria maxima
5. Lemna gibba
6. Luronium natans
7. Mentha x piperita
8. Mimulus guttatus
9. Potamogeton alpinus
10. P. compressus
11. P. lucens
12. P. pectinatus
13. P. perfoliatus
14. Rumex hydrolapathum
15. Sagittaria sagittifolia
16. Sparganium emersum

d. *Heath, grass heath and moor species of wide altitudinal range. The following are characteristic of well-drained soils derived from glacial drift, sandstone and gritstone up to c. 800 feet.*

1. Aira praecox
2. Carex pilulifera
3. Erica cinerea
4. Festuca ovina
5. Solidago virgaurea
6. Ulex gallii

e. *Heath and grass heath species more restricted in altitudinal range and soil preferences, much commoner on post-glacial sand than on sandstone derived soils.*

1. Aphanes arvensis
2. Hieracium umbellatum
3. Jasione montana
4. Ornithopus perpusillus
5. Senecio sylvaticus
6. Galium saxatile†

---

* More westerly habitats are usually on walls.

† The map of G. *saxatile* links both types of heath affinity and is considered to indicate well the extent of acid soils.

f. *Species on the more calcareous soils, coupled with centre of distribution in the south.*

1. Acer campestre
2. Hypericum hirsutum
3. Ranunculus auricomus
4. Viola reichenbachiana

g. *Old pasture on medium soils. The following are spread throughout the county but are considered to correlate well with unimproved pasture, meadow and light scrub on clay, shale and calcareous sand-derived soils of medium reaction.*

1. Carex caryophyllea
2. Genista tinctoria
3. Ophioglossum vulgatum
4. Pimpinella saxifraga
5. Sanguisorba officinalis
6. Sanicula europaea
7. Senecio erucifolius
8. Trisetum flavescens

h. *Built-up areas and waste ground. The following species show a close similarity with the distribution of these features (northerly and north-westerly chiefly). Note the high proportion of relatively recent arrivals.*

1. Angelica archangelica
2. Artemisia absinthium
3. Ballota nigra
4. Calystegia sylvatica
5. Cardaria draba
6. Chaenorrhinum minus
7. Conium maculatum
8. Daucus carota
9. Festuca arundinacea
10. Galinsoga ciliata
11. Hordeum murinum
12. Lamium amplexicaule
13. Malva sylvestris
14. Pastinaca sativa
15. Polygonum cuspidatum
16. Silene vulgaris
17. Sisymbrium orientale

AFFINITY 5. SOME INTERESTING INDIVIDUAL DISTRIBUTIONS

1. Ranunculus fluitans—correlates with unpolluted rivers and streams.
2. Asplenium adiantum-nigrum—excellent fit with the sandstone outcrops plus isolated records from stonework in the Pennine foothills.
3. Polypodium vulgare
4. Umbilicus rupestris—sandstone faces and walls in the extreme west of the county; reduced in Wirral, probably due to the demolition of old sandstone walls. Cf. *Rubus castrensis, R. rubristylus.*

OTHER SPECIES MAPPED

Anagallis tenella
Agrostis canina
A. gigantea
Arabidopsis thaliana
Asplenium ruta-muraria
A. trichomanes

Berula erecta
Bidens tripartita
Blackstonia perfoliata
Brassica nigra
Briza media
Bryonia cretica

181

Calamagrostis epigejos
Callitriche hamulata
C. hermaphroditica
Cardamine amara
Carex pulicaris
C. rostrata
C. vesicaria
Cerastium glomeratum
Chenopodium rubrum
Chrysanthemum segetum
Chrysosplenium oppositifolium
Cicuta virosa
Claytonia perfoliata
C. sibirica
Clematis vitalba
Convolvulus arvensis
Crocus nudiflorus
Cymbalaria muralis
Dactylorhiza maculata
D. praetermissa
D. praetermissa x fuchsii
Elodea canadensis
Epilobium adenocaulon
Epipactis helleborine
Erigeron acer
Erodium cicutarium
Euphrasia officinalis agg.
Fumaria muralis subsp. boraei
Galeopsis speciosa
Galium uliginosum
Geranium dissectum
G. lucidum
G. molle
G. pyrenaicum
Helictotrichon pubescens
Hieracium diaphanum
H. vagum
H. vulgatum
Hippuris vulgaris
Hypericum humifusum
H. maculatum
H. pulchrum
Impatiens glandulifera
Inula conyza
Juncus bulbosus
J. tenuis
Lamium hybridum

Lepidium heterophyllum
Linum catharticum
Listera ovata
Littorella uniflora
Luzula pilosa
Lycium barbarum
Lycopsis arvensis
Lysimachia punctata
L. vulgaris
Lythrum portula
Malva moschata
M. neglecta
Melilotus alba
Mentha arvensis
M. x verticillata
Menyanthes trifoliata
Mycelis muralis
Myosotis discolor
Myosoton aquaticum
Myriophyllum spicatum
Narcissus pseudo-narcissus
Nuphar lutea
Nymphaea alba
Oenanthe aquatica
Oenothera biennis
O. erythrosepala
Odontites verna
Orchis mascula
Osmunda regalis
Papaver rhoeas
Parietaria judaica
Pedicularis sylvatica
Petasites fragrans
Phleum bertolonii
Pilosella aurantiaca
Pimpinella major
Platanthera chlorantha
Poa nemoralis
P. subcaerulea
Polygala vulgaris
Populus tremula
Potamogeton berchtoldii
P. obtusifolius
Primula veris x vulgaris
Prunus avium
Ranunculus aquatilis
R. circinatus

R. hederaceus
R. peltatus
R. trichophyllus
Reseda lutea
Rhinanthus minor
Ribes nigrum
R. uva-crispa
Rorippa amphibia
R. sylvestris
Rubus accrescens
R. balfourianus
R. calvatus
R. cardiophyllus
R. carpinifolius
R. castrensis
R. criniger
R. dasyphyllus
R. distractiformis
R. dumetorum agg.
R. eboracensis
R. echinatoides
R. echinatus
R. eifeliensis
R. euryanthemus
R. gratus
R. hylocharis
R. incurvatus
R. leightonii
R. lindebergii
R. lindleianus
R. macrophyllus
R. newbouldii
R. opacus
R. polyanthemus
R. robii
R. rubriflorus
R. rubristylus
R. scissus
R. selmeri
R. sprengelii
R. subtercanens

R. taeniarum
R. vestitus
R. warrenii
R. wirralensis
Sagina apetala
S. nodosa
Salix repens
Saxifraga granulata
Scirpus fluitans
S. lacustris
S. setaceus
Scleranthus annuus
Scutellaria minor
Sedum acre
Senecio squalidus
S. viscosus
S. vulgaris (radiate forms)
Sherardia arvensis
Sisymbrium altissimum
Solanum nigrum
Spergularia rubra
Spiraea salicifolia
Stachys arvensis
Swida sanguinea
Symphoricarpos rivularis
Taraxacum spectabile agg.
Teesdalia nudicaulis
Tragopogon pratensis
Typha angustifolia
Urtica urens
Valeriana dioica
Verbascum thapsus
Veronica agrestis
V. arvensis
V. filiformis
V. hederifolia
V. persica
V. scutellata
Vicia tetrasperma
Vinca minor
Viola tricolor

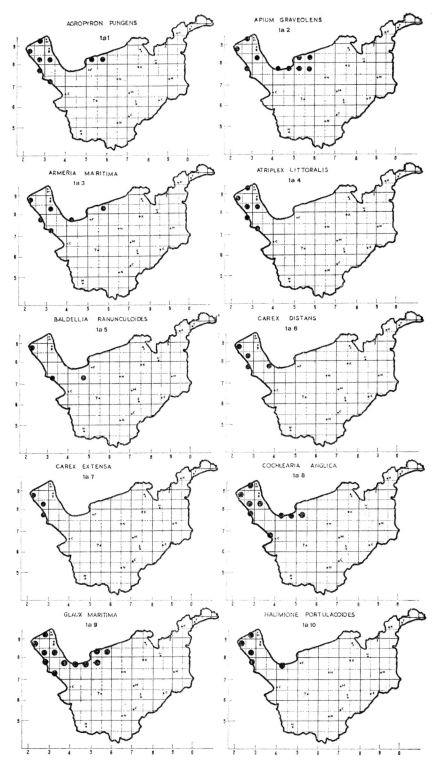

185

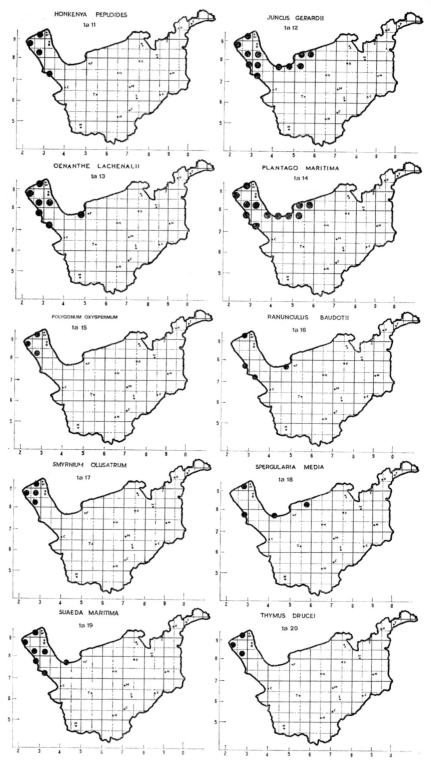

186

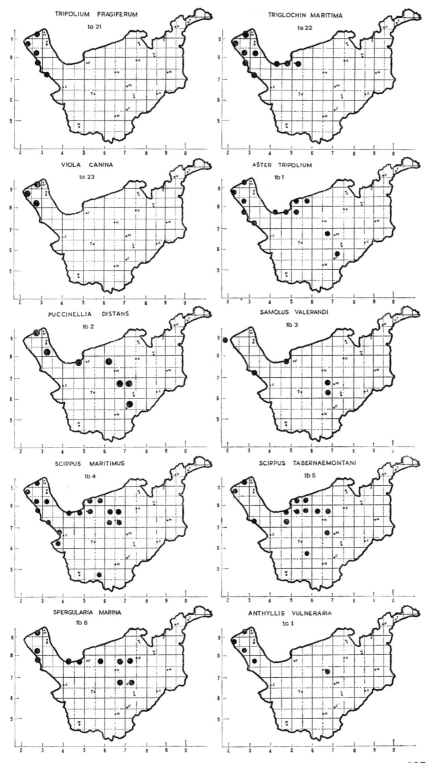

TRIFOLIUM FRAGIFERUM
1a 21

TRIGLOCHIN MARITIMA
1a 22

VIOLA CANINA
1a 23

ASTER TRIPOLIUM
1b 1

PUCCINELLIA DISTANS
1b 2

SAMOLUS VALERANDI
1b 3

SCIRPUS MARITIMUS
1b 4

SCIRPUS TABERNAEMONTANI
1b 5

SPERGULARIA MARINA
1b 6

ANTHYLLIS VULNERARIA
1c 1

187

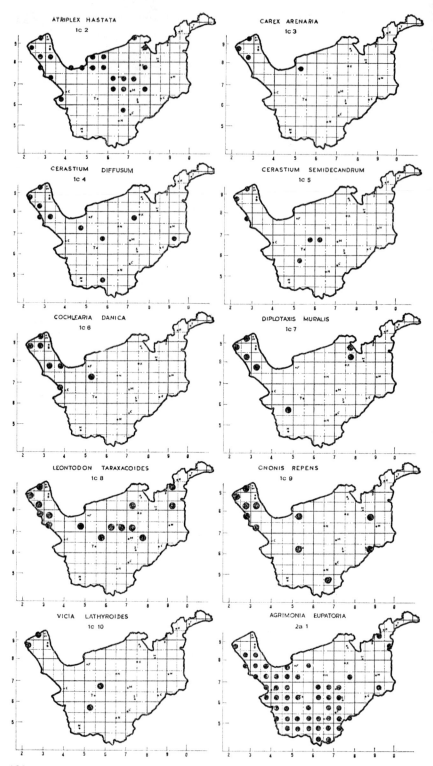

188

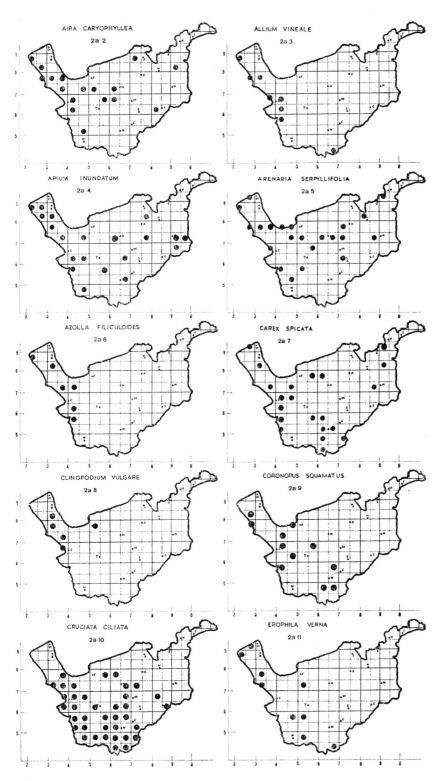

AIRA CARYOPHYLLEA
2a 2

ALLIUM VINEALE
2a 3

APIUM INUNDATUM
2a 4

ARENARIA SERPYLLIFOLIA
2a 5

AZOLLA FILICULOIDES
2a 6

CAREX SPICATA
2a 7

CLINOPODIUM VULGARE
2a 8

CORONOPUS SQUAMATUS
2a 9

CRUCIATA CILIATA
2a 10

EROPHILA VERNA
2a 11

189

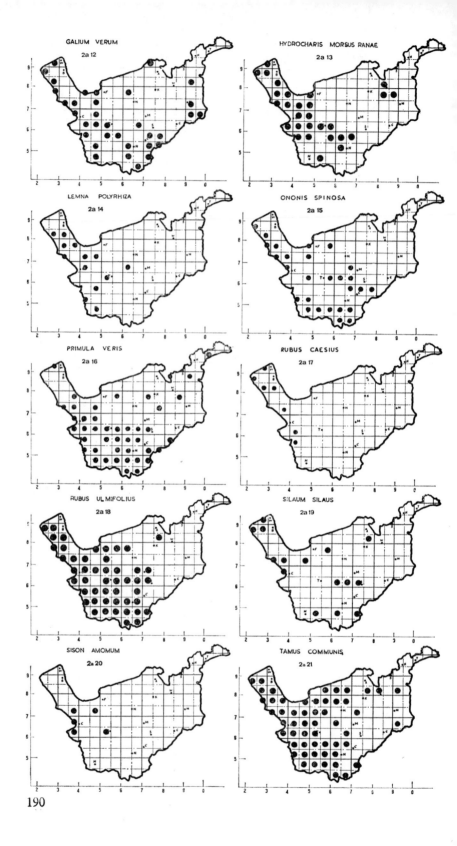

GALIUM VERUM
2a 12

HYDROCHARIS MORSUS RANAE
2a 13

LEMNA POLYRHIZA
2a 14

ONONIS SPINOSA
2a 15

PRIMULA VERIS
2a 16

RUBUS CAESIUS
2a 17

RUBUS ULMIFOLIUS
2a 18

SILAUM SILAUS
2a 19

SISON AMOMUM
2a 20

TAMUS COMMUNIS
2a 21

190

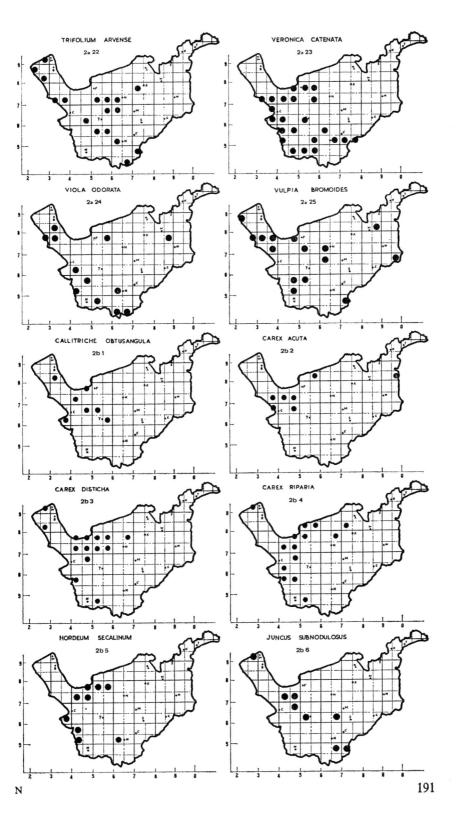

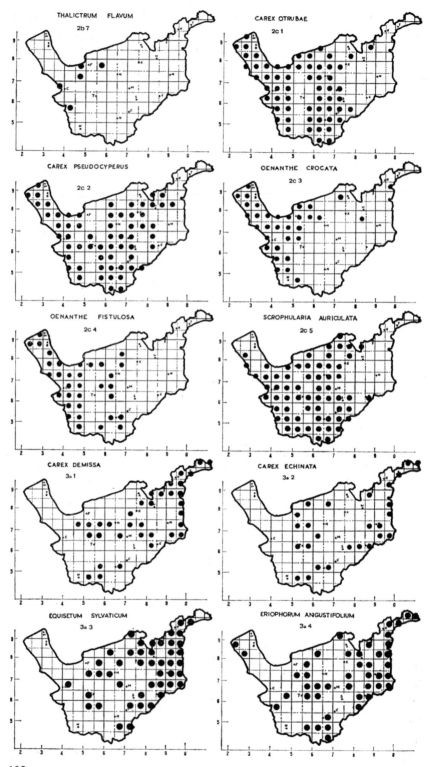

THALICTRUM FLAVUM
2b 7

CAREX OTRUBAE
2c 1

CAREX PSEUDOCYPERUS
2c 2

OENANTHE CROCATA
2c 3

OENANTHE FISTULOSA
2c 4

SCROPHULARIA AURICULATA
2c 5

CAREX DEMISSA
3a 1

CAREX ECHINATA
3a 2

EQUISETUM SYLVATICUM
3a 3

ERIOPHORUM ANGUSTIFOLIUM
3a 4

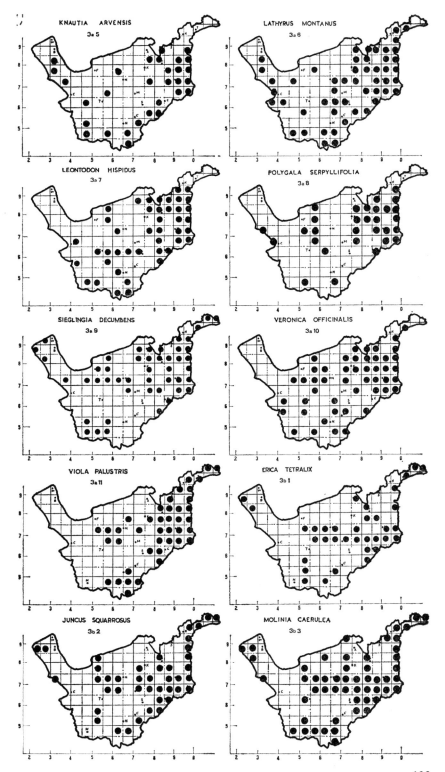

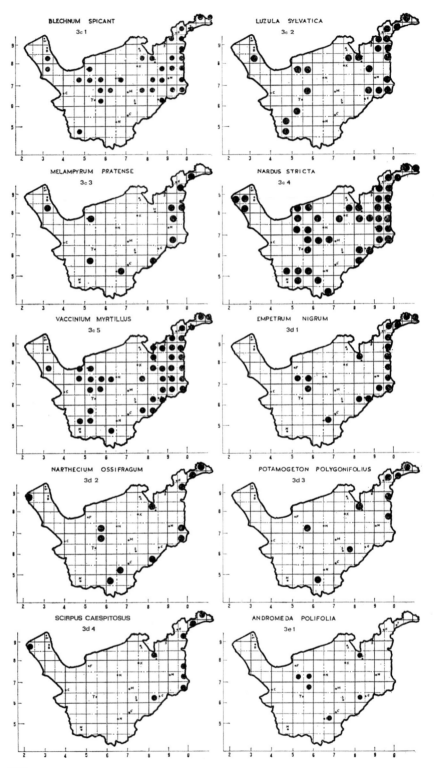

194

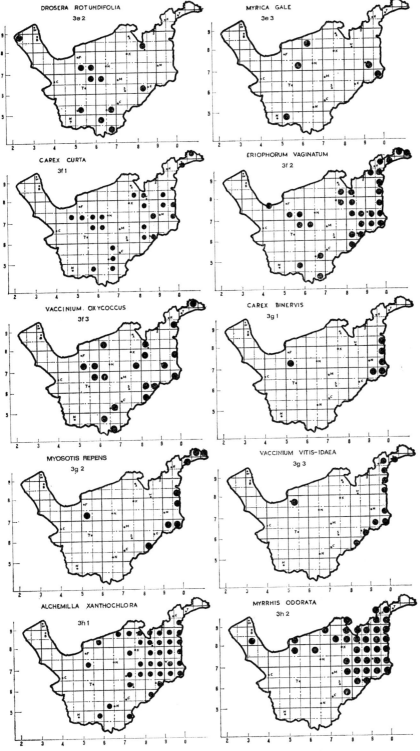

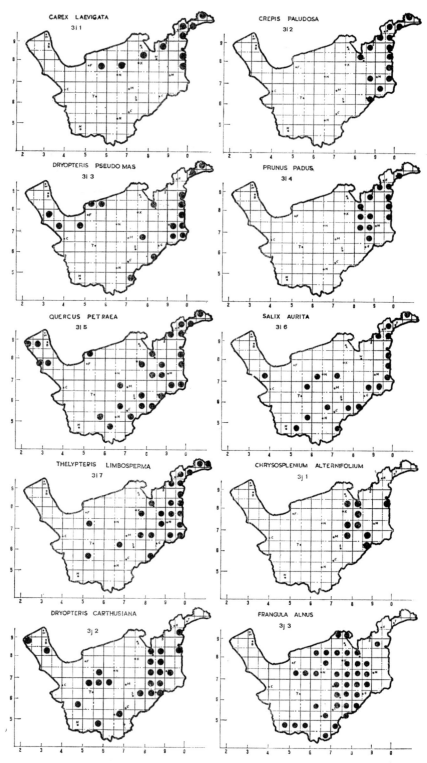

196

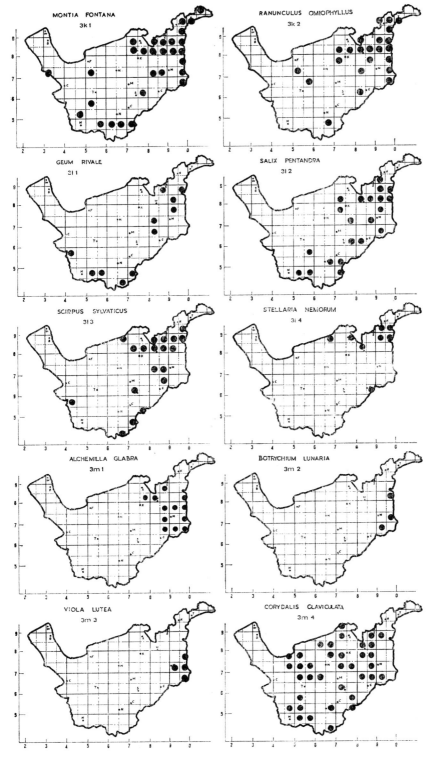

MONTIA FONTANA
3k 1

RANUNCULUS OMIOPHYLLUS
3k 2

GEUM RIVALE
3l 1

SALIX PENTANDRA
3l 2

SCIRPUS SYLVATICUS
3l 3

STELLARIA NEMORUM
3l 4

ALCHEMILLA GLABRA
3m 1

BOTRYCHIUM LUNARIA
3m 2

VIOLA LUTEA
3m 3

CORYDALIS CLAVICULATA
3m 4

197

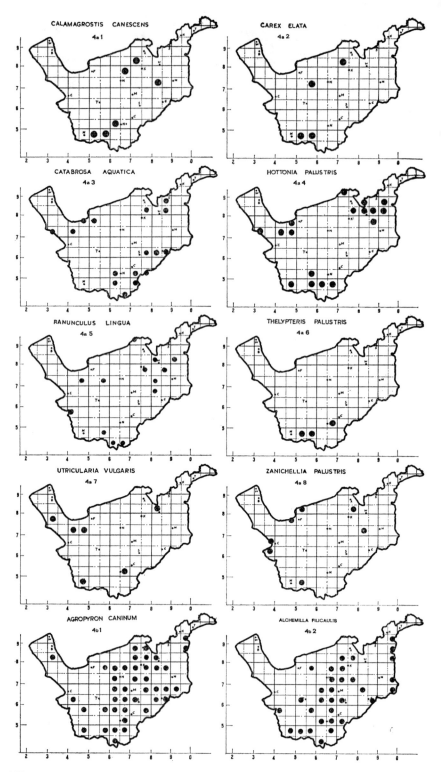

CALAMAGROSTIS CANESCENS
4a 1

CAREX ELATA
4a 2

CATABROSA AQUATICA
4a 3

HOTTONIA PALUSTRIS
4a 4

RANUNCULUS LINGUA
4a 5

THELYPTERIS PALUSTRIS
4a 6

UTRICULARIA VULGARIS
4a 7

ZANICHELLIA PALUSTRIS
4a 8

AGROPYRON CANINUM
4b 1

ALCHEMILLA FILICAULIS
4b 2

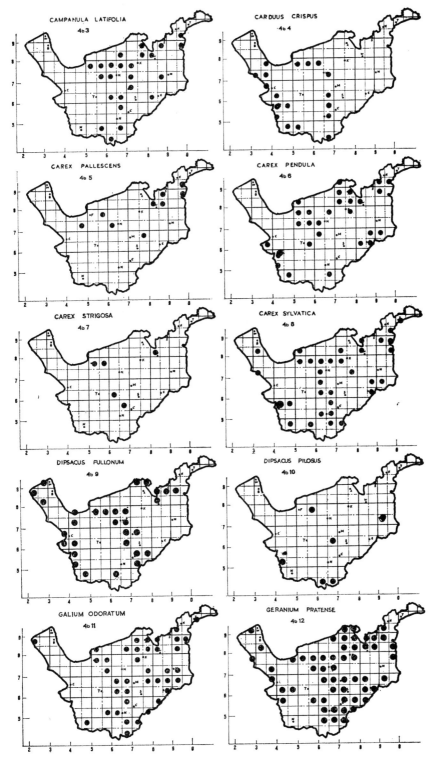

CAMPANULA LATIFOLIA
4b 3

CARDUUS CRISPUS
4b 4

CAREX PALLESCENS
4b 5

CAREX PENDULA
4b 6

CAREX STRIGOSA
4b 7

CAREX SYLVATICA
4b 8

DIPSACUS FULLONUM
4b 9

DIPSACUS PILOSUS
4b 10

GALIUM ODORATUM
4b 11

GERANIUM PRATENSE
4b 12

199

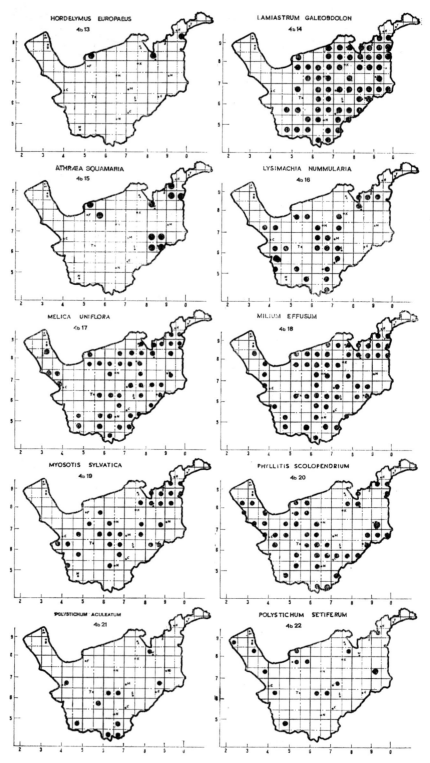

HORDELYMUS EUROPAEUS
4b 13

LAMIASTRUM GALEOBDOLON
4b 14

ATHRÆA SQUAMARIA
4b 15

LYSIMACHIA NUMMULARIA
4b 16

MELICA UNIFLORA
4b 17

MILIUM EFFUSUM
4b 18

MYOSOTIS SYLVATICA
4b 19

PHYLLITIS SCOLOPENDRIUM
4b 20

POLYSTICHUM ACULEATUM
4b 21

POLYSTICHUM SETIFERUM
4b 22

200

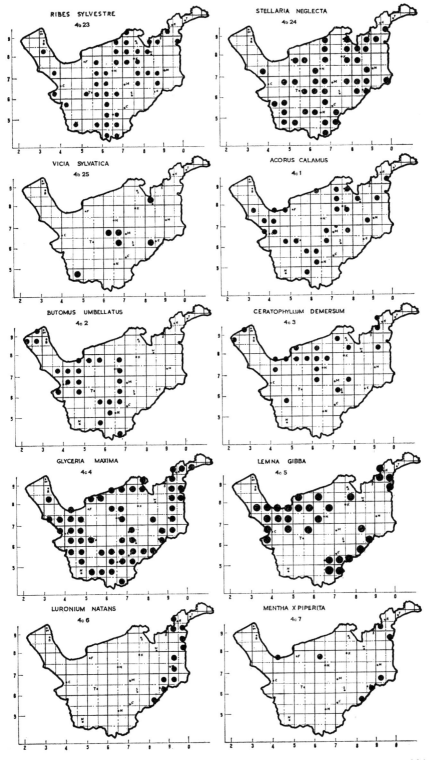

RIBES SYLVESTRE
4b 23

STELLARIA NEGLECTA
4b 24

VICIA SYLVATICA
4b 25

ACORUS CALAMUS
4c 1

BUTOMUS UMBELLATUS
4c 2

CERATOPHYLLUM DEMERSUM
4c 3

GLYCERIA MAXIMA
4c 4

LEMNA GIBBA
4c 5

LURONIUM NATANS
4c 6

MENTHA X PIPERITA
4c 7

201

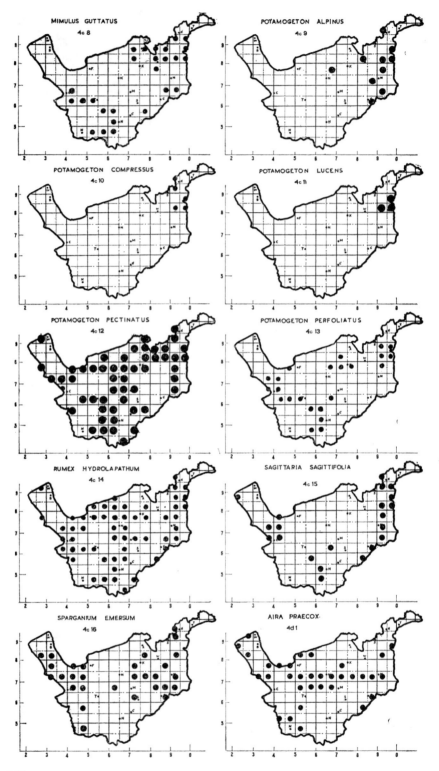

MIMULUS GUTTATUS
4c 8

POTAMOGETON ALPINUS
4c 9

POTAMOGETON COMPRESSUS
4c 10

POTAMOGETON LUCENS
4c 11

POTAMOGETON PECTINATUS
4c 12

POTAMOGETON PERFOLIATUS
4c 13

RUMEX HYDROLAPATHUM
4c 14

SAGITTARIA SAGITTIFOLIA
4c 15

SPARGANIUM EMERSUM
4c 16

AIRA PRAECOX
4d 1

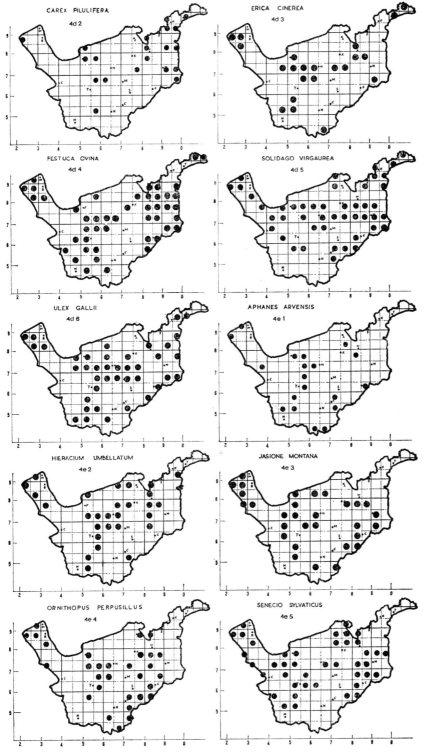

CAREX PILULIFERA
4d 2

ERICA CINEREA
4d 3

FESTUCA OVINA
4d 4

SOLIDAGO VIRGAUREA
4d 5

ULEX GALLII
4d 6

APHANES ARVENSIS
4e 1

HIERACIUM UMBELLATUM
4e 2

JASIONE MONTANA
4e 3

ORNITHOPUS PERPUSILLUS
4e 4

SENECIO SYLVATICUS
4e 5

203

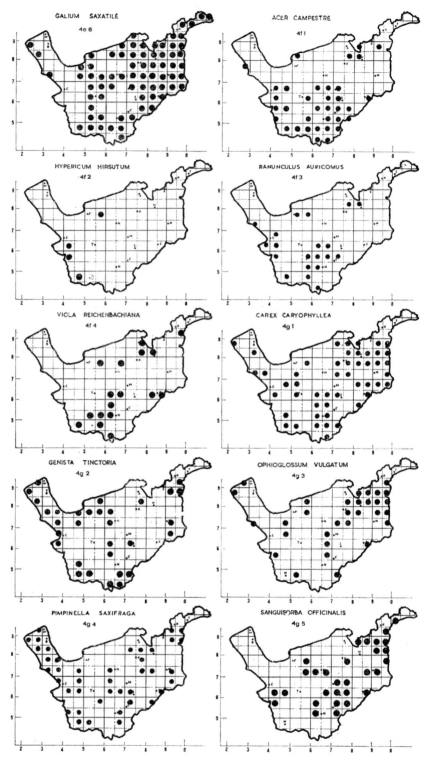

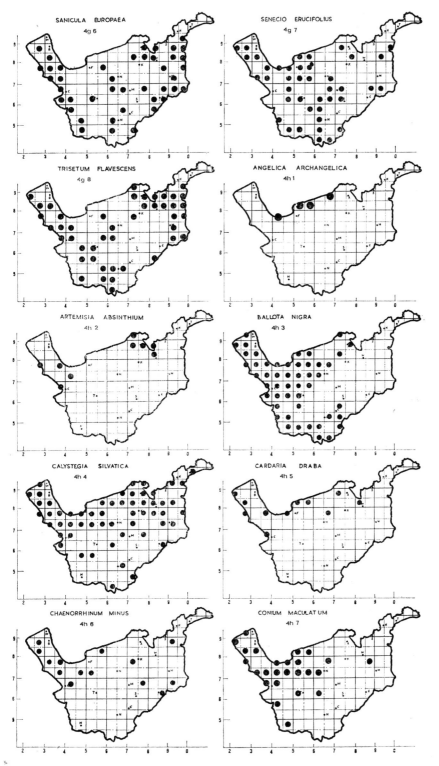

SANICULA EUROPAEA
4g 6

SENECIO ERUCIFOLIUS
4g 7

TRISETUM FLAVESCENS
4g 8

ANGELICA ARCHANGELICA
4h 1

ARTEMISIA ABSINTHIUM
4h 2

BALLOTA NIGRA
4h 3

CALYSTEGIA SILVATICA
4h 4

CARDARIA DRABA
4h 5

CHAENORRHINUM MINUS
4h 6

CONIUM MACULATUM
4h 7

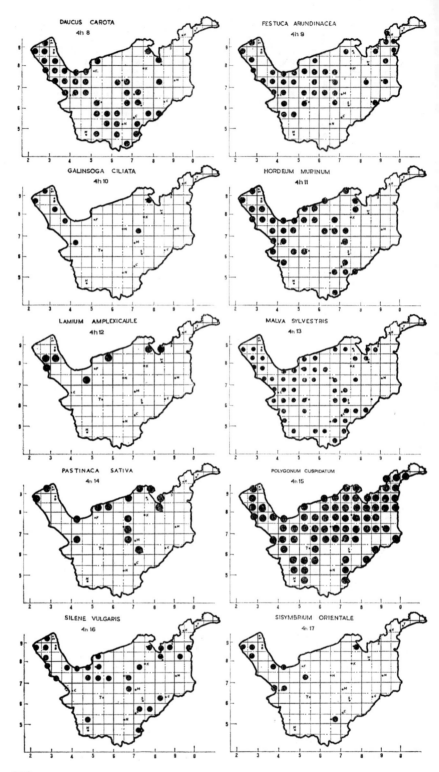

DAUCUS CAROTA
4h 8

FESTUCA ARUNDINACEA
4h 9

GALINSOGA CILIATA
4h 10

HORDEUM MURINUM
4h 11

LAMIUM AMPLEXICAULE
4h 12

MALVA SYLVESTRIS
4h 13

PASTINACA SATIVA
4h 14

POLYGONUM CUSPIDATUM
4h 15

SILENE VULGARIS
4h 16

SISYMBRIUM ORIENTALE
4h 17

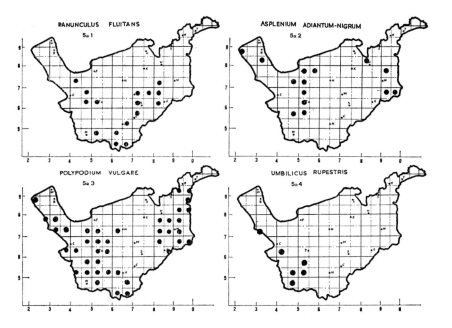

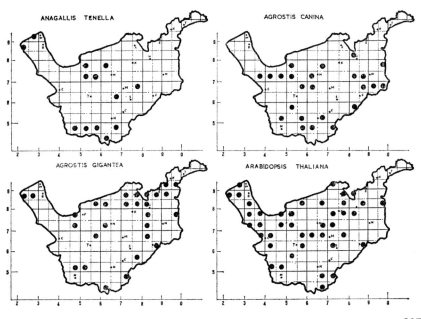

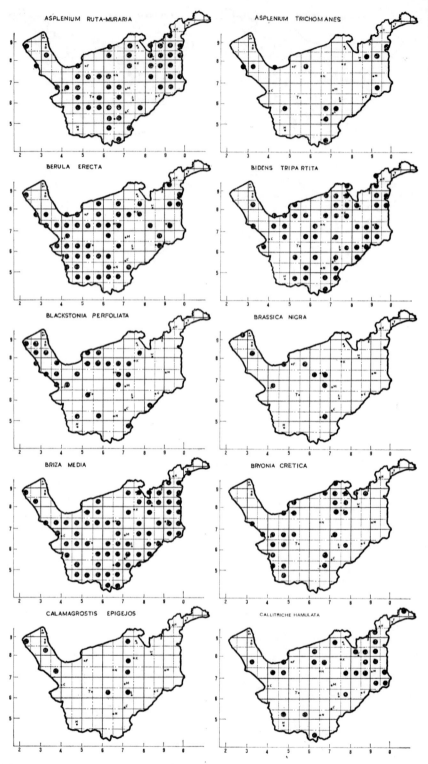

208

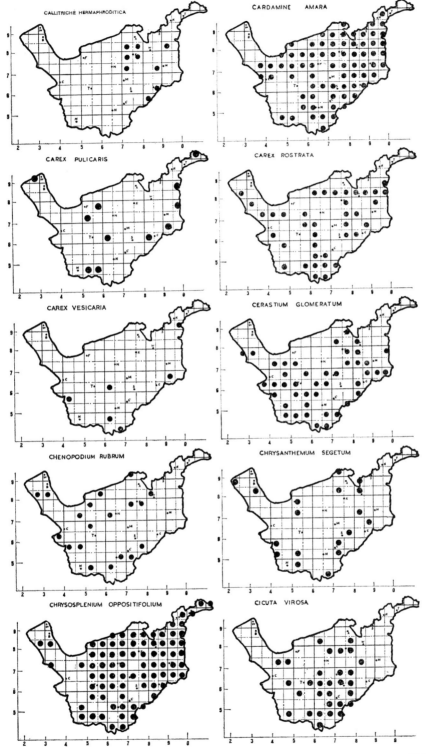

CALLITRICHE HERMAPHRODITICA

CARDAMINE AMARA

CAREX PULICARIS

CAREX ROSTRATA

CAREX VESICARIA

CERASTIUM GLOMERATUM

CHENOPODIUM RUBRUM

CHRYSANTHEMUM SEGETUM

CHRYSOSPLENIUM OPPOSITIFOLIUM

CICUTA VIROSA

209

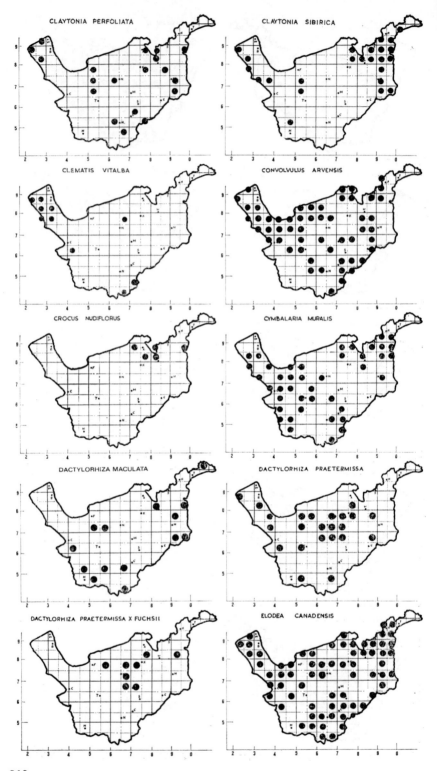

CLAYTONIA PERFOLIATA

CLAYTONIA SIBIRICA

CLEMATIS VITALBA

CONVOLVULUS ARVENSIS

CROCUS NUDIFLORUS

CYMBALARIA MURALIS

DACTYLORHIZA MACULATA

DACTYLORHIZA PRAETERMISSA

DACTYLORHIZA PRAETERMISSA X FUCHSII

ELODEA CANADENSIS

210

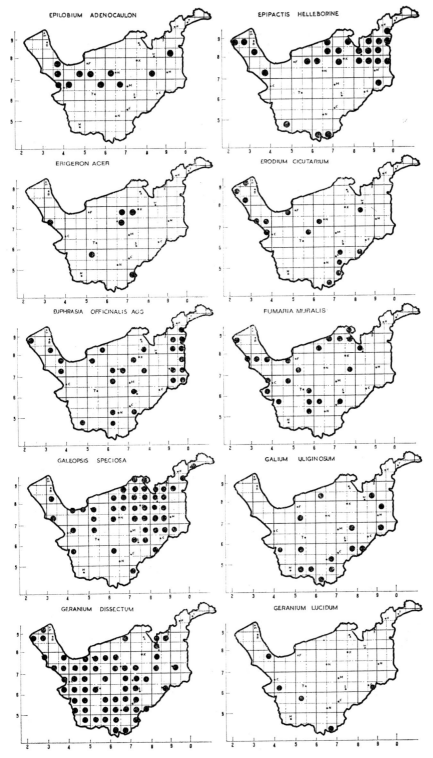

EPILOBIUM ADENOCAULON

EPIPACTIS HELLEBORINE

ERIGERON ACER

ERODIUM CICUTARIUM

EUPHRASIA OFFICINALIS AGG

FUMARIA MURALIS

GALEOPSIS SPECIOSA

GALIUM ULIGINOSUM

GERANIUM DISSECTUM

GERANIUM LUCIDUM

211

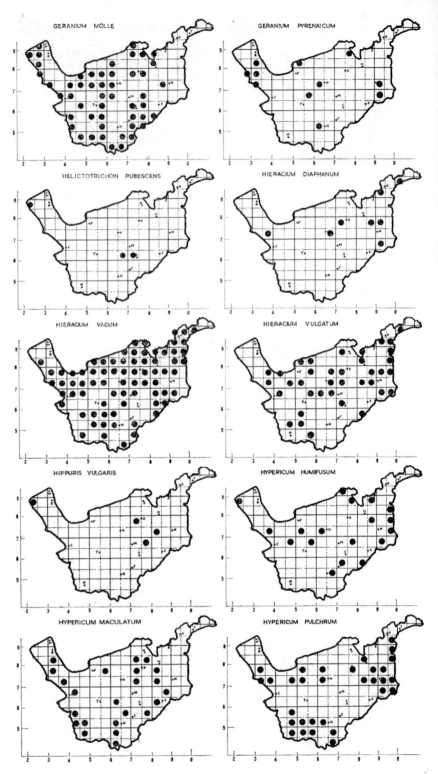

GERANIUM MOLLE

GERANIUM PYRENAICUM

HELICTOTRICHON PUBESCENS

HIERACIUM DIAPHANUM

HIERACIUM VAGUM

HIERACIUM VULGATUM

HIPPURIS VULGARIS

HYPERICUM HUMIFUSUM

HYPERICUM MACULATUM

HYPERICUM PULCHRUM

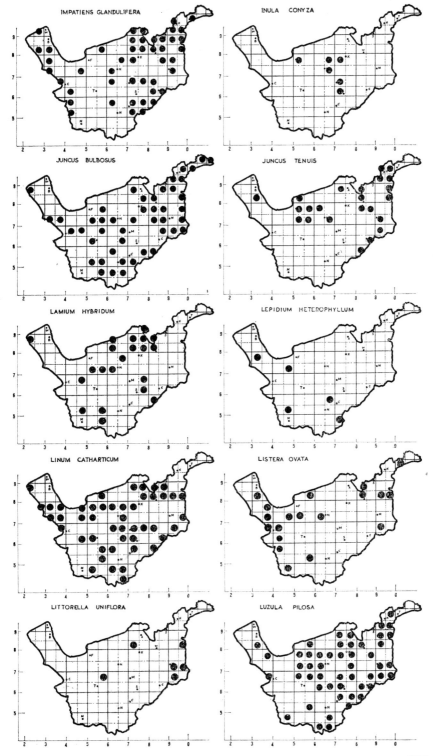

IMPATIENS GLANDULIFERA

INULA CONYZA

JUNCUS BULBOSUS

JUNCUS TENUIS

LAMIUM HYBRIDUM

LEPIDIUM HETEROPHYLLUM

LINUM CATHARTICUM

LISTERA OVATA

LITTORELLA UNIFLORA

LUZULA PILOSA

213

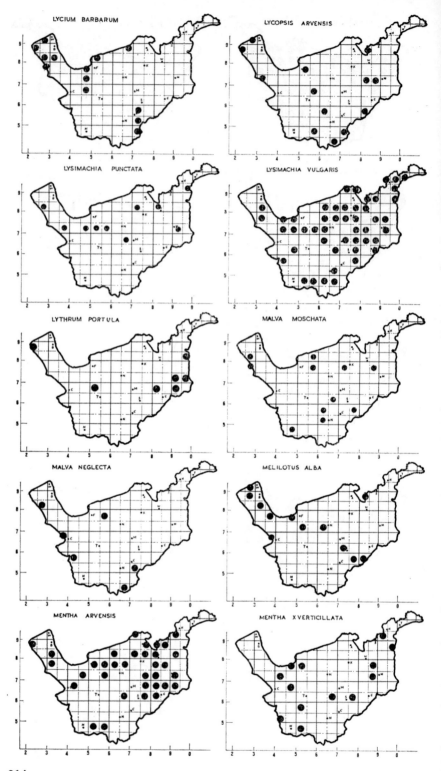

214

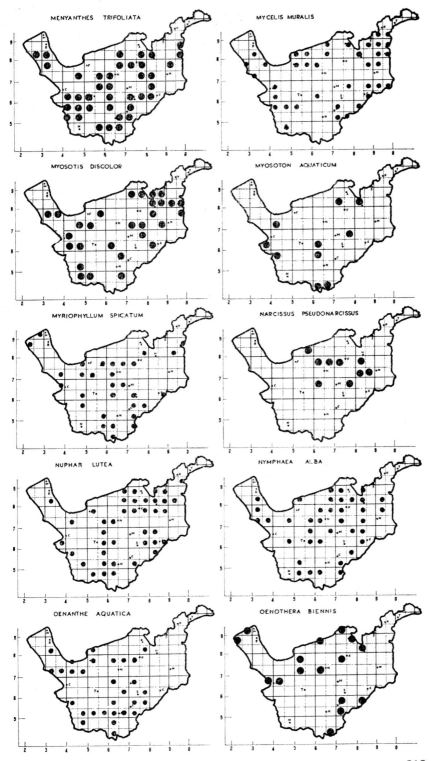

MENYANTHES TRIFOLIATA

MYCELIS MURALIS

MYOSOTIS DISCOLOR

MYOSOTON AQUATICUM

MYRIOPHYLLUM SPICATUM

NARCISSUS PSEUDONARCISSUS

NUPHAR LUTEA

NYMPHAEA ALBA

OENANTHE AQUATICA

OENOTHERA BIENNIS

215

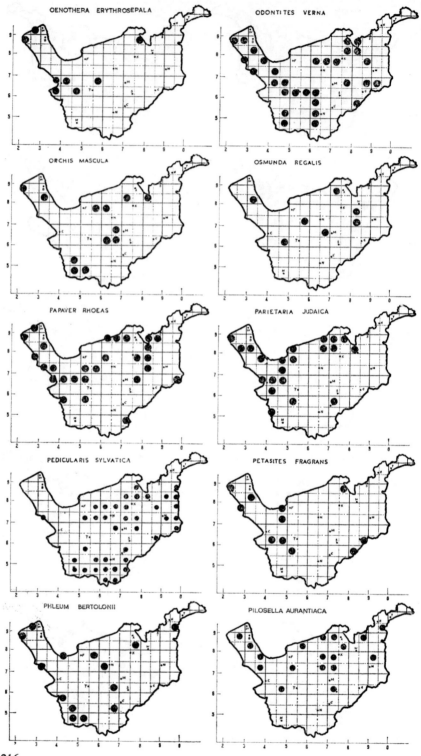

OENOTHERA ERYTHROSEPALA

ODONTITES VERNA

ORCHIS MASCULA

OSMUNDA REGALIS

PAPAVER RHOEAS

PARIETARIA JUDAICA

PEDICULARIS SYLVATICA

PETASITES FRAGRANS

PHLEUM BERTOLONII

PILOSELLA AURANTIACA

216

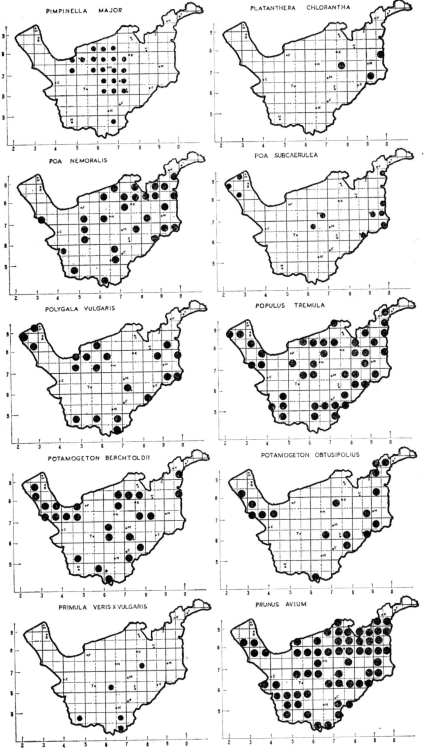

217

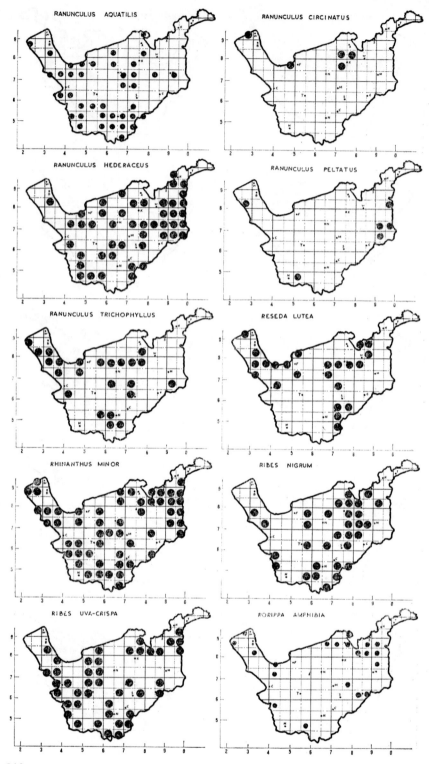

RANUNCULUS AQUATILIS

RANUNCULUS CIRCINATUS

RANUNCULUS HEDERACEUS

RANUNCULUS PELTATUS

RANUNCULUS TRICHOPHYLLUS

RESEDA LUTEA

RHINANTHUS MINOR

RIBES NIGRUM

RIBES UVA-CRISPA

RORIPPA AMPHIBIA

218

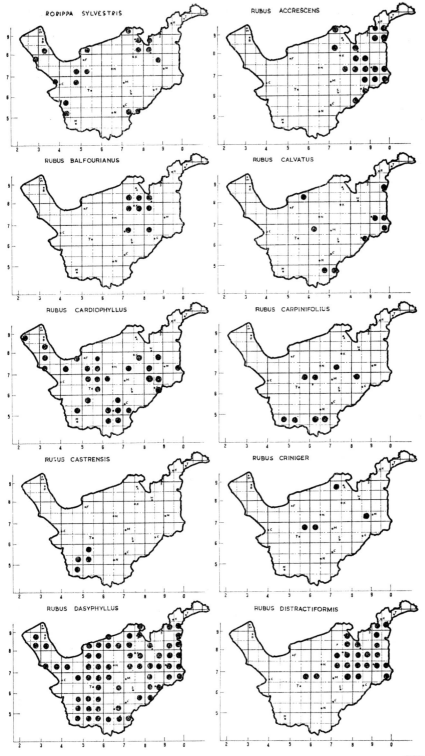

RORIPPA SYLVESTRIS

RUBUS ACCRESCENS

RUBUS BALFOURIANUS

RUBUS CALVATUS

RUBUS CARDIOPHYLLUS

RUBUS CARPINIFOLIUS

RUBUS CASTRENSIS

RUBUS CRINIGER

RUBUS DASYPHYLLUS

RUBUS DISTRACTIFORMIS

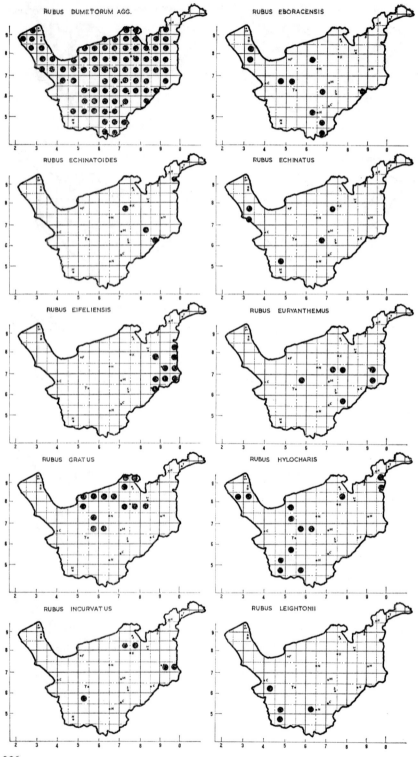

RUBUS DUMETORUM AGG.

RUBUS EBORACENSIS

RUBUS ECHINATOIDES

RUBUS ECHINATUS

RUBUS EIFELIENSIS

RUBUS EURYANTHEMUS

RUBUS GRATUS

RUBUS HYLOCHARIS

RUBUS INCURVATUS

RUBUS LEIGHTONII

220

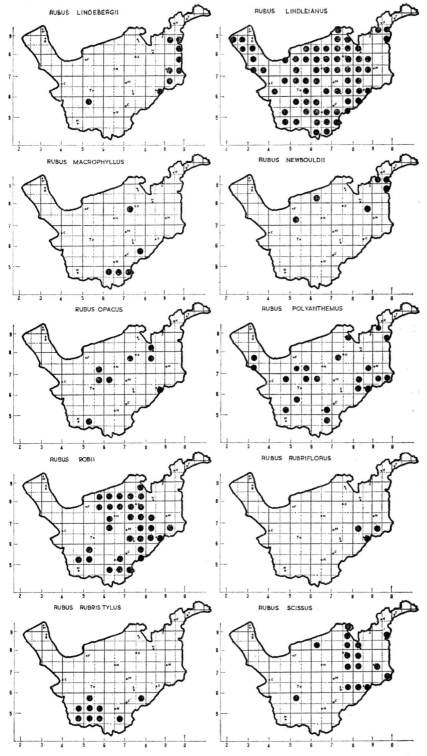

RUBUS LINDEBERGII

RUBUS LINDLEIANUS

RUBUS MACROPHYLLUS

RUBUS NEWBOULDII

RUBUS OPACUS

RUBUS POLYANTHEMUS

RUBUS ROBII

RUBUS RUBRIFLORUS

RUBUS RUBRISTYLUS

RUBUS SCISSUS

221

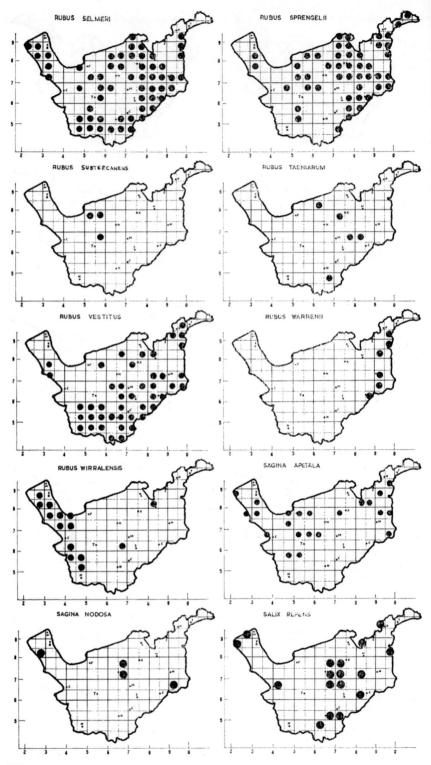

222

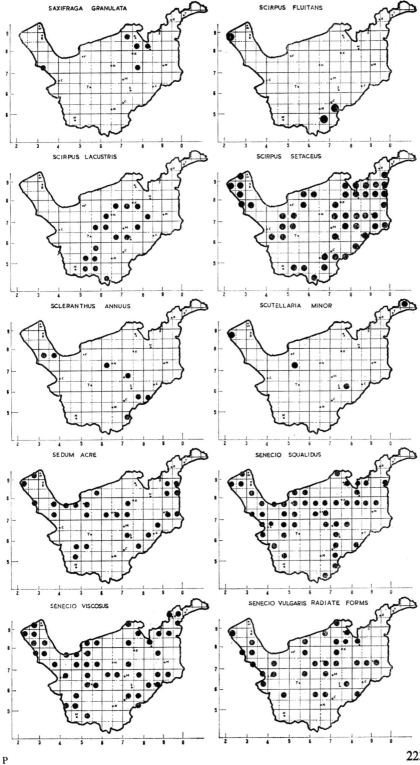

SAXIFRAGA GRANULATA

SCIRPUS FLUITANS

SCIRPUS LACUSTRIS

SCIRPUS SETACEUS

SCLERANTHUS ANNUUS

SCUTELLARIA MINOR

SEDUM ACRE

SENECIO SQUALIDUS

SENECIO VISCOSUS

SENECIO VULGARIS RADIATE FORMS

P

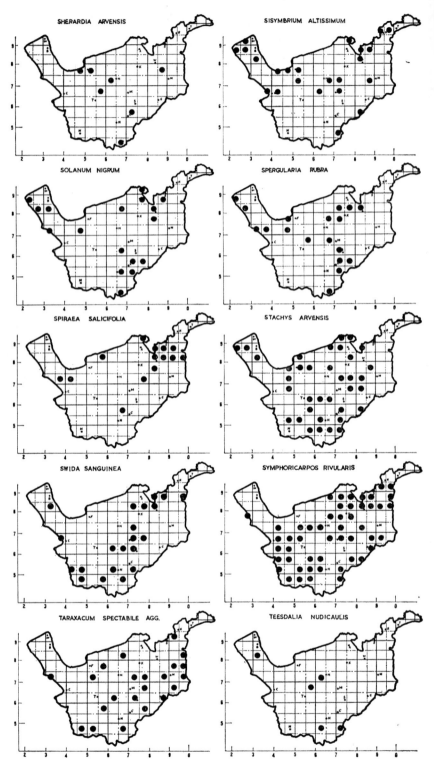

SHERARDIA ARVENSIS

SISYMBRIUM ALTISSIMUM

SOLANUM NIGRUM

SPERGULARIA RUBRA

SPIRAEA SALICIFOLIA

STACHYS ARVENSIS

SWIDA SANGUINEA

SYMPHORICARPOS RIVULARIS

TARAXACUM SPECTABILE AGG.

TEESDALIA NUDICAULIS

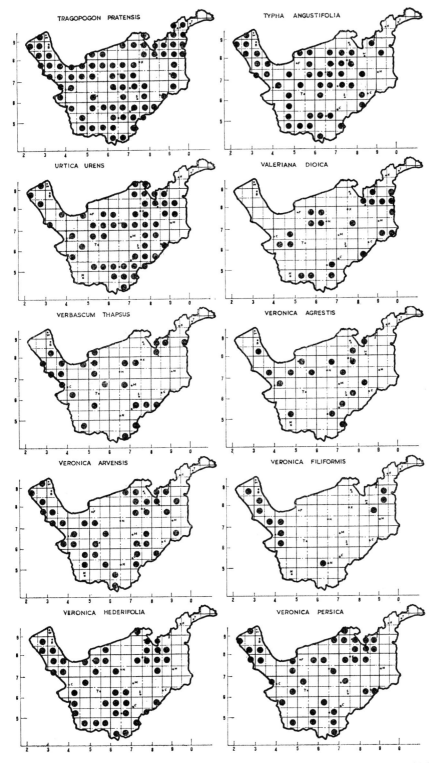

TRAGOPOGON PRATENSIS TYPHA ANGUSTIFOLIA

URTICA URENS VALERIANA DIOICA

VERBASCUM THAPSUS VERONICA AGRESTIS

VERONICA ARVENSIS VERONICA FILIFORMIS

VERONICA HEDERIFOLIA VERONICA PERSICA

225

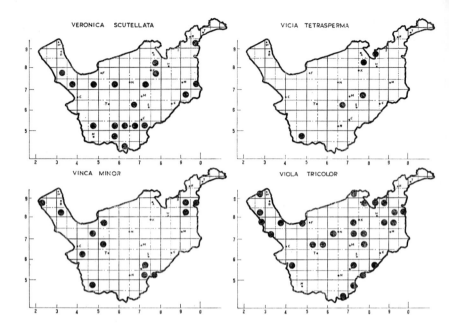

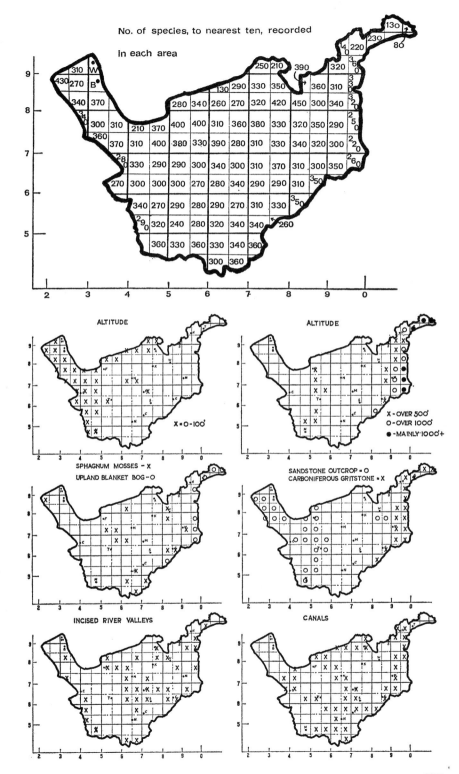

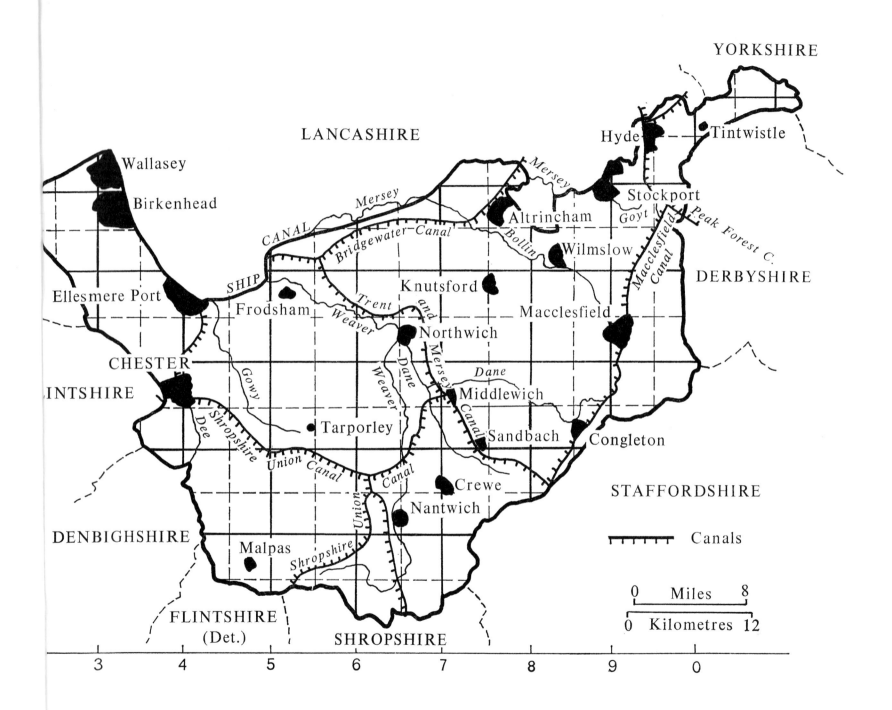

YORKSHIRE

LANCASHIRE

Hyde • Tintwistle

Wallasey

Birkenhead

Mersey

Mersey

Stockport

Bridgewater Canal

Altrincham

Goyt

Peak Forest C.

SHIP

Bollin

Wilmslow

DERBYSHIRE

CANAL

Macclesfield Canal

Ellesmere Port

Frodsham

Trent

Knutsford

Weaver

Macclesfield

CHESTER

Weaver

Northwich

Dane

and

Dane

LINTSHIRE

Gowy

Weaver

Mersey

Middlewich

Dee

Shropshire

Tarporley

Canal

Sandbach

Congleton

Union Canal

STAFFORDSHIRE

DENBIGHSHIRE

Crewe

Nantwich

Canals

Malpas

Shropshire Union

0   Miles   8

0   Kilometres 12

FLINTSHIRE
(Det.)

SHROPSHIRE

3   4   5   6   7   8   9   0

229

APPENDIX — THE GENUS *RUBUS* L.

In preparing this account of a notoriously difficult genus I am deeply indebted to Mr. E. S. Edees for his advice, encouragement and patient tuition over a period of several years.

The problems facing a beginner who wishes to study *Rubus* derive as much from the difficulty of deciphering the literature as from the plants themselves. Here we must chiefly rely on W. C. R. Watson's *Rubi of Great Britain and Ireland*, Cambridge University Press (1958), the most recent account of the subject, although W. Moyle-Rogers' *Handbook of British Rubi* (1900) is still useful. Unfortunately, while Watson was very well acquainted with the brambles of south-eastern and southern England, he was far less familiar with those of the midlands and north, and one cannot always be sure that, when he refers to a particular species as occurring in Cheshire (v.c. 58), this species is correctly named. Some of his distribution notes are based on Moyle-Rogers' evidence, and, once again, we cannot be sure that the species referred to in the *Handbook*, as e.g. *R. babingtonii*, occurring in Cheshire, is, in fact, the same as Watson's *R. phaeocarpus*.

The difficulty in using Watson's book is that one cannot know which parts are reliable and which are not. In addition, the keys are extremely difficult to use and, further, one cannot be sure that a particular species which appears to fall within, for instance, the *Discoloroides* Section of *Sylvatici*, has, in fact, been described or not. This may be a matter of luck, or whether a previous batologist has worked the area in question; if so, it is far more likely that the local species have been described than not. Otherwise it is likely that many previously undescribed species exist, some widely, or are concealed under some other name.

What profitable strategy can then be adopted? Firstly, localities given in previous Floras can be looked at (if they have not been destroyed), and herbarium specimens examined for interesting clues. Unfortunately there are serious limitations to both enquiries. If the last Flora was compiled a century ago, one must remember that the state of knowledge of *Rubus* was even more rudimentary than it now is, that there were fewer published names available, and that the habit of contemporary batologists was to say a specimen was "*X* going towards *Y*", or "*A* var. *B*". A classic determination of Lord de Tabley's exemplifies this dilemma—"*amplificatus macrophyllus umbrosus*, but not typical". The result is that the majority of records contained in de Tabley's Flora are but a loose indication of a group of similar plants which may now be more precisely named (or not). With all these disadvantages it is surprising how useful some of the statements still are and, incidentally, how long-lived are particular colonies of *Rubus*. To take two instances—F. M. Webb's record of *R. atrorubens* Wirt. (syn. *R. adornatus* P. J. Muell.), "copiously around College Fields Farm" turns out to be still plentiful, and to be a clearly identifiable species, *R. murrayi* Sudre, closely related to *R. adornatus* P. J. Muell., as presently recognised. Again, a specimen in Herb. Manchester Museum, from Flitto Gate Lane, Tabley, is mentioned as

231

" a distinct form of *R. koehleri*; I have seen it nowhere else hereabouts".
The plant is still there today in the identical place; unfortunately we are no
nearer to allocating a name unequivocally.

Many herbarium specimens consist of badly chosen parts of the plant,
and some have also suffered from long storage. Crucial characters are
sometimes obscured, even in the better-dried specimens, and it is impossible
to say with certainty which precise species is represented.

The first problem with *Rubus* in the field is to learn to recognise the basic
characters of each taxonomic division (*Suberecti, Triviales, Rubi* proper)
and then to learn the characters of the subdivisions of *Rubus* proper (*Sylvatici,
Discolores, Appendiculati, Hystrices*). This is rather similar to beginning
grasses or sedges; by looking at the prevalent species in a particular area it is
soon possible to distinguish the dozen most common, and to ascribe them to
the correct group. Having mastered this basic problem, and having become
accustomed to their aspect at different seasons and in different situations, it
would seem a relatively simple matter to recognise and collect specimens of
plants differing from the basic dozen, with the object of having them named
by a competent expert. In some cases he may be able to identify a plant from
a specimen, but in far more cases he needs to see the living bush. He may then
be able to name an isolated bush from his knowledge of the bramble flora
in the country as a whole and thus perform the valuable function of extending
knowledge of the distribution of a particular species and enabling it to be
written about. Often, however, brambles may be recognised and nameless, or
not recognised and nameless. The former state currently applies to ten clearly
marked species in Cheshire which all have a distribution abutting on to
adjoining vice-counties of South Lancashire, Shropshire, Staffordshire and
Derbyshire. The latter state applies mainly to isolated but healthy fruit-
producing bushes. Some of these may have names; it is likely that others ought
to have. It is the number of species which defeats us. A man may currently
be able to name 300 species with which he is familiar—there are probably
an equal number he cannot name. The writer of a county Flora must realise
that, for all his specimens to be named, detailed and encyclopaedic knowledge
of the complete bramble flora would be required, and a complete catalogue
of names.

He must also learn to recognise the signs of bushes of mixed parentage
typified by bad fruiting habits, or close similarity to the putative parents. Note
may be taken but names cannot be expected—not even in the case of Sect.
Triviales for the parents.

In order to present a coherent account of the brambles in a county, the
prospective author must first get to know his plants well. He must sharpen his
observation until he can separate the common from the uncommon, whether
nameable or not. He must become aware of the tell-tale signs of hybridity.
He must select good specimens if he is to stand any chance of them being
named. He must persuade a knowledgeable batologist to visit his plants and
give a professional opinion as to whether a name exists or not. Fortunately,
the constant recognisable species, clearly described and knowable, form the
bulk of the bramble flora and can therefore be recorded with confidence;

the equally recognisable but nameless, of wide occurrence, can be described if an authority can be persuaded to name them; and the isolated but well-marked bushes can be named or not, depending on the availability of a referee with extensive knowledge. The result, in the case of Cheshire, is a list of 51 *Rubus* species; a further list of a quarter of this number could be compiled of species which occur mostly as isolated but good, fruiting, healthy bushes or small colonies, but which at present lack names.

A paper describing six new species occurring in Cheshire appears in *Watsonia* vol. 8 part iv.

BIBLIOGRAPHY

De Tabley's *Flora of Cheshire* contains a comprehensive account of references in the literature to Cheshire plants up to 1875; the list below includes the most important references since then.

ADAMSON, R. S., Report of a meeting at Delamere Forest. *J. Ecol.* 2: 56 (1914).

ADAMSON, R. S., Notes on the flora of northern Cheshire. *J. Bot.* 57: 91-94 (1919).

BENNETT, A., Notes on the flora of Cheshire. *Naturalist* No. 535: 353-356 (1899); *ibid.*, No. 564: 22-23 (1904); *J. Bot.* 57: 129-130 (1919).

BICKHAM, S., Remarks on the flora of Cheshire. *Proc. Manch. Lit. & Phil. Soc.* 8: 165 (1870).

DALLMAN, A. A. & LEE, W., An old Cheshire herbarium. *L. & C. Nat.* 10: 166-168 (1917).

DRABBLE, E. & H., Notes of the flora of Cheshire. *J. Bot.* 48: 152-156 (1910).

DUNLOP, G. A., Field notes on plant associations of Hatchmere and Flaxmere. *Lancs. Nat.* 2: 315-319 (1910).

EGERTON, R., Botanising on Bidston marsh. *Lancs. Nat.* 6: 339-342 (1913).

FARMER, A. J., Additions to the Flora of Hilbre Island. *L.N.F.C. Proc. for* 1946: 19-24 (1947).

GEOLOGICAL SURVEY, Memoirs (H.M.S.O.).

GEOLOGICAL SURVEY, One-inch maps, sheets 96, 97, 98, 109, 110, 122.

HODGE, W., Interesting alien plants at Northwich. *Lancs. Nat.* 3: 223-224 (1910).

HODGE, W., Origin of meres in the Delamere country. *Lancs. Nat.* 5: 42-48 (1912).

LEE, A., Flora of Wirral [includes casual dock aliens]. *L. & C. Nat.* 16: 75, 141 & 197 (1923).

LEE, A., Old botanical haunts of Birkenhead (Gilbrook). *L .& C. Nat.* 16: 214, 243 (1923).

LINNAEAN SOCIETY OF ASHTON-UNDER-LYNE, *District Flora of Ashton-under-Lyne* (1888).

MARSHALL, E. S., Cheshire plants [Wybunbury Moss chiefly]. *J. Bot.* 34: 135-136 (1896).

MATTHEWS, J., Cheshire roses. *J. Bot.* 58: 137-141 (1920).

MCMILLAN, N. F., Botanical Notes. *L.N.F.C. Proc. for* 1952: 18 (1953).

McMILLAN, N. F. & HENDERSON, M., Wirral flowering plants. *N.W. Nat.* new ser. 2: 651 (1954).

MELVILLE, J. C., Wallasey sandhills, 1868-9. *L. & C. Nat.* 11: 21-24 (1918).

MOORE, S., Notes additional to the flora of Cheshire. *J. Bot.* 38: 74-76 (1900).

OWEN, G., *MS. Flora of Mid-Cheshire.* Brunner Central Library & Museum, Northwich.

PERRING, F. H. & SELL, P. D., *Critical Supplement to the Atlas of the British Flora* (1968).

SAVIDGE, J. P., Botanical notes and records. *L.N.F.C. Proc. for* 1953: 12-18 (1954); *ibid. for* 1954: 9-14 (1955); *ibid for* 1956: 15-21 (1957).

SAVIDGE, J. P., Flora of the Liverpool area, 1932-57. *L.N.F.C. Proc. for* 1957: 17-26 (1958).

SIMPSON, N. D., *A Bibliographical Index of the British Flora* (1962).

SYLVESTER, D. & NULTY, G., *The Historical Atlas of Cheshire* (1958).

THOMPSON, A. H., Flora of Delamere forest. *L. & C. Nat.* 16: 176 & 197 (1923).

WALTERS, S. M. & PERRING, F. H., *Atlas of the British Flora* (1962).

WARREN, J. L. (Lord de Tabley), On some doubtful species in the Cheshire flora. *J. Bot.* 13: 163-167 (1875).

WARREN, J. L. (Lord de Tabley), *Flora of Cheshire* (1899).

WATERFALL, C., *Plants from the county of Cheshire in his own collection,* 1910-1914 (privately printed).

WOODHEAD, N., Additions to the flora of Cheshire. *Naturalist* No. 831: 107-112 (1926).

WOLLEY-DOD, A. H., Flora of Cheshire (corrections). *J. Bot.* 37: 441 (1899).

The following periodicals also include passing references to Cheshire plants:

North Western Naturalist 1-23 (1926-51) and new series 1-3 (1953-55).

Journal of Botany 37-80 (1899-1945).

Lancashire Naturalist 1-6 (1907-13), continued as *Lancashire & Cheshire Naturalist* 7-17 (1914-25).

INDEX

Synonyms are set in italic type; the main page reference for each species is set in bold type, and page references to maps in italic type.

238

240

Q

254

255

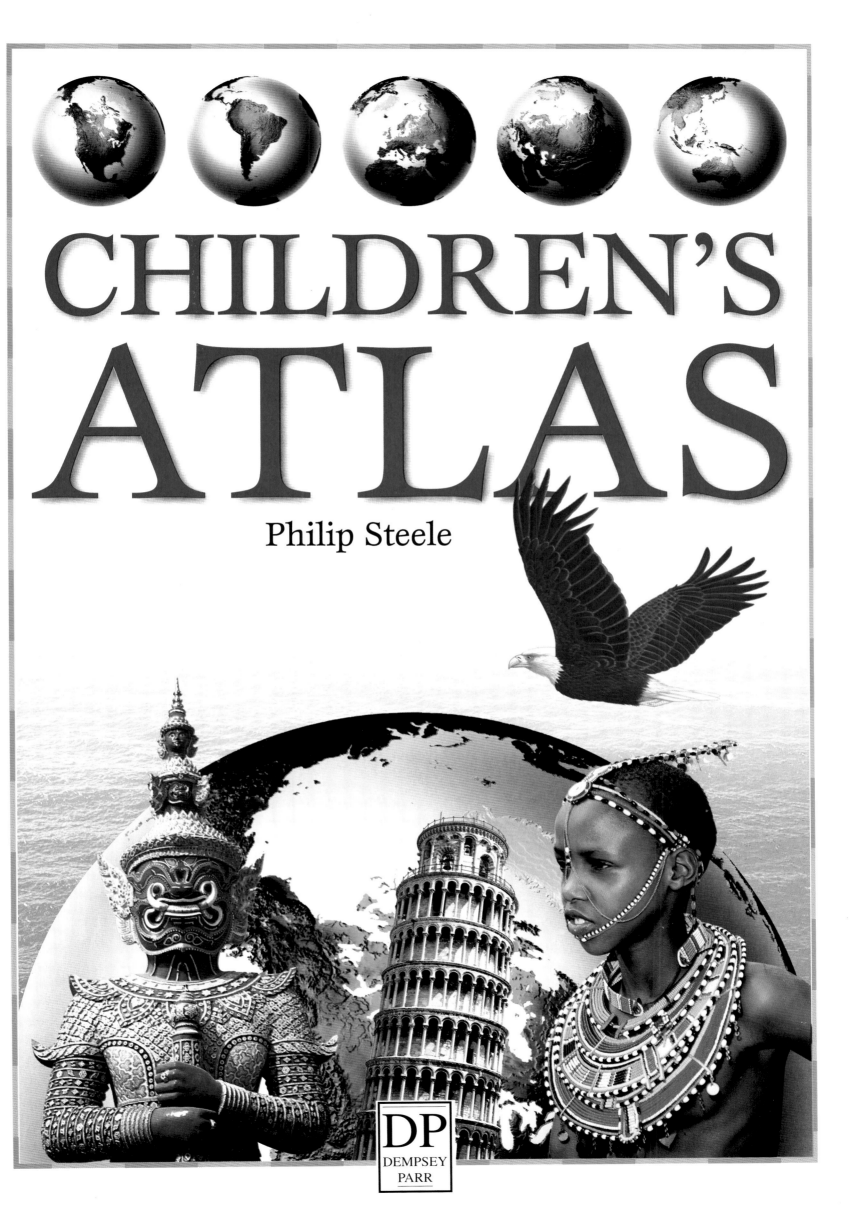

CHILDREN'S ATLAS

Philip Steele

DP

DEMPSEY
PARR

First published in 1998 by
Dempsey Parr,
13 Whiteladies Road, Clifton, Bristol, BS8 1PB

2 4 6 8 10 9 7 5 3 1

Produced by
Miles Kelly Publishing Ltd,
Unit 11, Bardfield Centre, Great Bardfield, Essex, CM7 4SL

© Copyright Dempsey Parr 1998

British Library Cataloguing-in-Publication Data
A catalogue record for this book is available from the British Library

Printed in Spain

ISBN 1 84084 040 4

Design: Full Steam Ahead
Cartographic Editor: Keith Lye
Cartography: Digital Wisdom
Artwork commissioning: Branka Surla
Project manager: Kate Miles
Additional help from Susanne Bull and Lynne French
Reprographics: DPI Colour Ltd

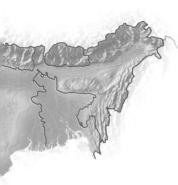

CONTENTS

CONTENTS

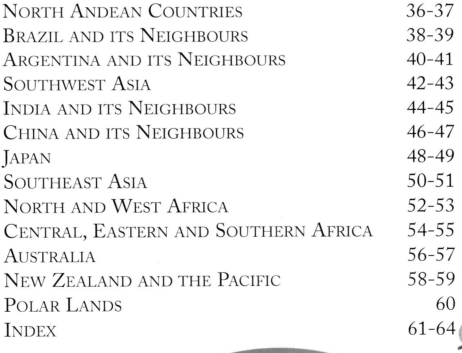

HOW TO USE THIS ATLAS

WELCOME TO THE PLANET EARTH! This atlas shows you the world we live in. An atlas is any large book of maps. Maps are plans which show the surface of a planet as if it was flat, instead of round. They show the lie of the land, the rivers and coastlines, mountains and seas.

Maps which just show the details of the landscape are called 'physical'. Maps which just show the borders of countries, states, counties or provinces are called 'political'. The maps in this book show the physical details of the land, but they show national borders and major cities as well. Maps use signs and symbols to give you more information. Look at the key to find out what they mean.

So how do you find the city or country you are looking for? First of all look up the name you want in the index on p.61. When you have found the right page, look for the name on the big map of the region. Next to each regional map, look for the little map which helps you to see at a glance which part of the world is being shown.

Next, read the words to find out more about the countries, the climate of the region, the peoples and how they live. Small boxes also give you key facts and figures about each of the countries. They tell you the area, the population size, the name of the capital city, the country's official language or languages and the currency, or type of money, used by the people there.

When you read about distant lands, it may help to compare them with where you live. Are they bigger or smaller, hotter or wetter, more crowded? You might use the maps to do a bit of detective work. Can you work out why most Australian cities are near the coast, or why most Canadian cities are in the south of the country?

Coastlines and borders

The borders of Japan are natural, because the country is made up of islands. Other countries may have land borders, marked by a line on the map.

Colours

On this map the different colours show you at a glance the physical features of the landscape. Each colour represents a type of geographic feature.

Spot the mountain

This symbol means 'mountain'. The mountain's name is printed next to it, along with the height of the summit above sea level. The height is given in metres.

N for north

This symbol represents a compass, with its magnetic needle pointing due north.

Capital cities

The most important town in any country is called the capital city. This is very often the biggest town and is normally where the government makes the laws. Some capitals, however, are quite small.

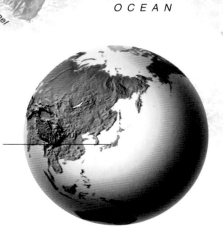

Where in the world

If you want to find out where the regional map fits into a map of the whole world, check these small circular maps. The areas coloured in red show the location.

Key to symbols

■ Capitals
● Towns
— Rivers
— Borders
Lakes
Mountains

EARTH FACTS

The world we live in is a huge ball of rock and metal spinning around, or rotating, in space. As the planet Earth rotates, it travels around the Sun, held on its path by a pulling force called gravity. The Earth is one of nine planets circling the Sun, and together they make up the Solar System.

When we see pictures of Earth taken from space, our planet appears blue, white and brown. The blue is the colour of the seas and oceans which cover over two-thirds of the Earth's surface. The swirling white patterns are the clouds – water vapour which hangs in the air, or atmosphere, surrounding the Earth's surface. The brown is the colour of the ground, which is divided into the Earth's landmasses or continents.

Photographs of the Earth's surface taken from space zoom in to show even more details – the world's great river systems, the high mountain ranges, the sprawling cities and the patchwork of crops that feed the hungry mouths of the world's population, which is expected to reach over 6,100 million by the year 2000.

PLANET EARTH
Circumference around the Equator: 40,075 kilometres
Circumference around the Poles: 40,008 kilometres
Diameter at the Equator: 12,756 kilometres
Surface area: About 510,000,000 square kilometres
Area covered by sea: 71 percent
Average distance from the Sun: 149,600,000 kilometres
Average distance from the Moon: 385,000 kilometres
Period of rotation: 23 hours 56 minutes
Speed of rotation: 1,660 kilometres per hour at the Equator
Period of revolution: 365 days 6 hours
Speed of revolution: 29.8 kilometres per second

The world's highest peak
Mount Everest or Qomolangma, between Nepal and China, is the highest point on the Earth's surface.

HIGHEST PEAKS

Mountain	Height	Location
Everest (Qomolangma)	8,848 m	China-Nepal
K2 (Qogir Feng)	8,611 m	India-Pakistan
Kanchenjunga	8,586 m	India-Nepal
Makalu 1	8,463 m	China-Nepal
Dhaulagiri 1	8,167 m	Nepal
Nanga Parbat	8,125 m	India
Annapurna 1	8,091 m	Nepal
Gosainthan (Xixabangma Feng)	8,012 m	China
Distaghil Sar	7,885 m	India
Nanda Devi	7,816 m	India

LONGEST RIVERS

River	Length	Location
Nile	6,670 km	North Africa
Amazon	6,448 km	South America
Chang Jiang (Yangtze)	6,300 km	Central China
Mississippi-Missouri-Red	6,020 km	North America
Yenisey-Angara-Selenga	5,540 km	Mongolia-Russia
Huang He	5,464 km	Northern China
Ob-Irtysh	5,409 km	Russia-Kazakhstan
Zaïre (Congo)	4,700 km	Central Africa
Lena-Kirenga	4,400 km	Russia
Mekong	4,350 km	Southeast Asia

LARGEST LAKES

Lake	Area	Location
Caspian Sea	371,800 sq km	Central Asia
Superior	82,103 sq km	USA-Canada
Victoria	69,484 sq km	East Africa
Aral Sea	65,500 sq km	Central Asia
Huron	59,569 sq km	USA-Canada
Michigan	57,757 sq km	USA-Canada
Tanganyika	32,893 sq km	East Africa
Baikal	31,449 sq km	Russia
Great Bear	31,328 sq km	Canada
Malawi	28,878 sq km	Southern Africa

LARGEST ISLANDS

Island	Area
Greenland	2,1830 sq km
New Guinea	821,000 sq km
Borneo	727,900 sq km
Madagascar	589,081 sq km
Baffin	509,214 sq km
Sumatra	431,982 sq km
Honshu	228,204 sq km
Great Britain	218,800 sq km
Victoria	212,200 sq km
Ellesmere	196,917 sq km

MAJOR WATERFALLS
Highest Waterfalls

	Height	Location
Angel Falls	979 m	Venezuela
Mardsalsfossen	774 m	Norway
Yosemite	739 m	United States

Greatest volume

Waterfall	Volume	Location
Boyoma	17,000 cu m per sec	Dem. Rep. Congo (Zaïre)

OCEANS

Name	Area
Pacific	166,242,000 sq km
Atlantic	106,000,000 sq km
Indian	73,500,000 sq km
Arctic	14,350,000 sq km

COUNTRIES OF THE WORLD

To the glory of God
Places of worship vary greatly around the world. This Christian cathedral, St Basil's, was built in the 1500s in Moscow, capital of today's Russian Federation.

There are 192 countries in the world that are recognized as 'independent' nations, which means that they govern themselves. Many other lands are colonies or 'dependencies', which means that they are governed by other nations. The numbers change very often, as one country joins up with another one, or another splits up into separate nations. For example Eritrea was part of Ethiopia until 1991, when it broke away to become an independent nation.

Some countries are huge, some are tiny. The Russian Federation is the largest, with an area of 17,078,005 square kilometres. The smallest is Vatican City, at just 0.4 square kilometres. Some countries are home to just one people, while others are made up of many different peoples or ethnic groups, each with their own way of life and customs. Some peoples have no national borders of their own. For example the traditional homeland of the Kurdish people is divided between Turkey, Iraq and Iran.

The peoples of the world live very different lives. They have different faiths and beliefs, eat different foods and speak over 5000 different languages. Some people are very poor while others are very rich. However, the people on our planet also have many things in common. The spread of radio, television and other communications links in recent years has made the world a smaller place. Once it took years to travel around the world, but today we can get on a plane or keep in touch with each other at the push of a button.

Most of the world's countries are linked by agreements or treaties. Many European countries belong to the European Union, while African nations belong to the Organization of African Unity. Nearly all countries belong to the United Nations, which tries to prevent conflict and to build links between the world's nations.

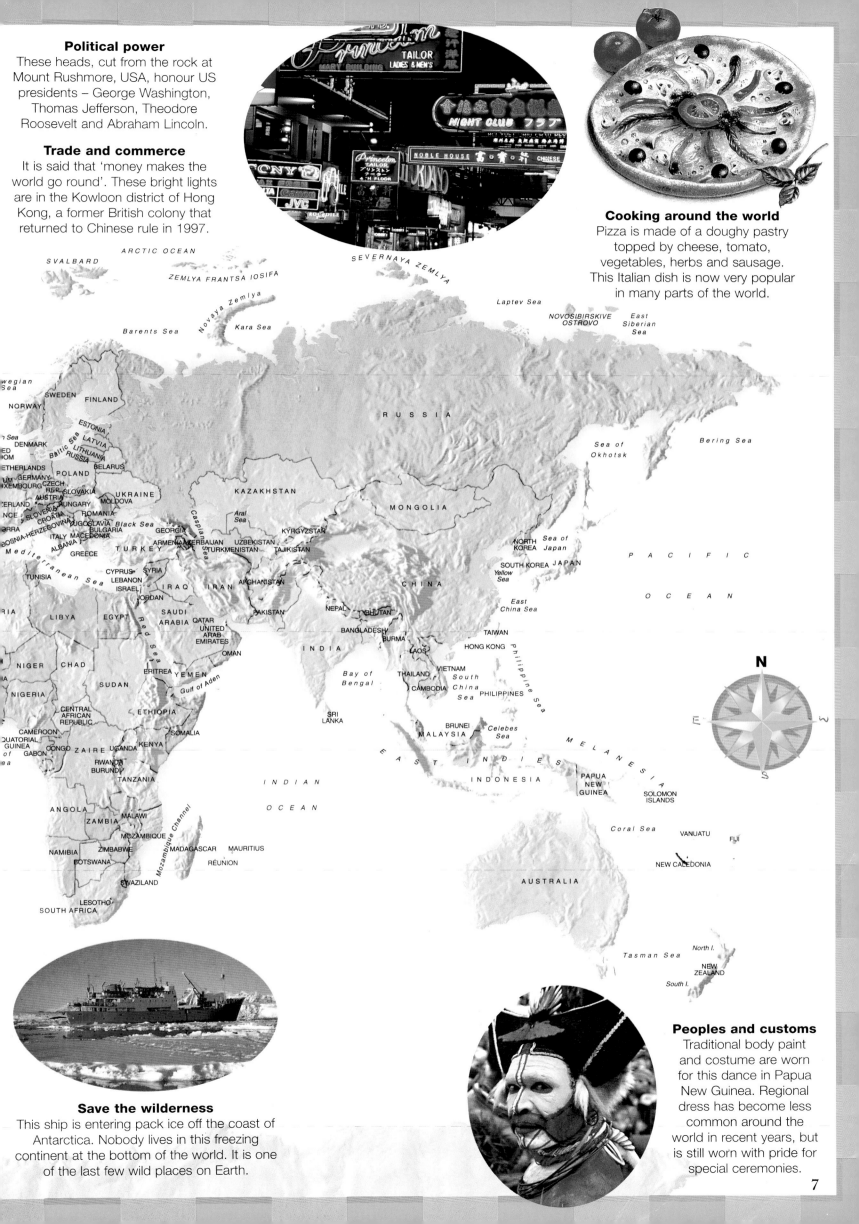

Political power
These heads, cut from the rock at Mount Rushmore, USA, honour US presidents – George Washington, Thomas Jefferson, Theodore Roosevelt and Abraham Lincoln.

Trade and commerce
It is said that 'money makes the world go round'. These bright lights are in the Kowloon district of Hong Kong, a former British colony that returned to Chinese rule in 1997.

Cooking around the world
Pizza is made of a doughy pastry topped by cheese, tomato, vegetables, herbs and sausage. This Italian dish is now very popular in many parts of the world.

Save the wilderness
This ship is entering pack ice off the coast of Antarctica. Nobody lives in this freezing continent at the bottom of the world. It is one of the last few wild places on Earth.

Peoples and customs
Traditional body paint and costume are worn for this dance in Papua New Guinea. Regional dress has become less common around the world in recent years, but is still worn with pride for special ceremonies.

ARCTIC OCEAN

SVALBARD

ZEMLYA FRANTSA IOSIFA

SEVERNAYA ZEMLYA

Novaya Zemlya

Barents Sea

Kara Sea

Laptev Sea

NOVOSIBIRSKIVE OSTROVO

East Siberian Sea

wegian Sea

SWEDEN

FINLAND

NORWAY

RUSSIA

Bering Sea

ESTONIA

n Sea

DENMARK

LATVIA

Baltic Sea

LITHUANIA

RUSSIA

BELARUS

Sea of Okhotsk

ETHERLANDS

GERMANY

POLAND

XEMBOURG

CZECH REP.

SLOVAKIA

UKRAINE

KAZAKHSTAN

MONGOLIA

 AUSTRIA

HUNGARY

MOLDOVA

NCE

SLOVENIA

CROATIA

ROMANIA

Aral Sea

RRA

YUGOSLAVIA

Black Sea

BULGARIA

GEORGIA

KYRGYZSTAN

NORTH KOREA

Sea of Japan

BOSNIA-HERZEGOVINA

ITALY

MACEDONIA

ARMENIA

AZERBAIJAN

UZBEKISTAN

ALBANIA

GREECE

TURKEY

Caspian Sea

TURKMENISTAN

TAJIKISTAN

SOUTH KOREA

JAPAN

Yellow Sea

PACIFIC

Mediterranean Sea

CYPRUS

SYRIA

CHINA

East China Sea

OCEAN

TUNISIA

LEBANON

ISRAEL

IRAQ

IRAN

AFGHANISTAN

JORDAN

NEPAL

BHUTAN

RIA

LIBYA

EGYPT

SAUDI ARABIA

QATAR

UNITED ARAB EMIRATES

PAKISTAN

BANGLADESH

TAIWAN

Red Sea

OMAN

BURMA

HONG KONG

Philippine Sea

NIGER

CHAD

ERITREA

YEMEN

INDIA

LAOS

NIGERIA

SUDAN

Gulf of Aden

Bay of Bengal

THAILAND

VIETNAM

South China Sea

PHILIPPINES

CENTRAL AFRICAN REPUBLIC

ETHIOPIA

CAMBODIA

CAMEROON

SOMALIA

SRI LANKA

QUATORIAL GUINEA

CONGO

ZAIRE

UGANDA

KENYA

BRUNEI

Celebes Sea

of GABON

RWANDA

MALAYSIA

MELANESIA

ea

BURUNDI

EAST INDIES

TANZANIA

INDIAN

INDONESIA

PAPUA NEW GUINEA

SOLOMON ISLANDS

ANGOLA

ZAMBIA

MALAWI

OCEAN

Mozambique Channel

MOZAMBIQUE

Coral Sea

VANUATU

FIJI

NAMIBIA

ZIMBABWE

MADAGASCAR

MAURITIUS

NEW CALEDONIA

BOTSWANA

RÉUNION

SWAZILAND

AUSTRALIA

LESOTHO

SOUTH AFRICA

N

Tasman Sea

North I.

NEW ZEALAND

South I.

7

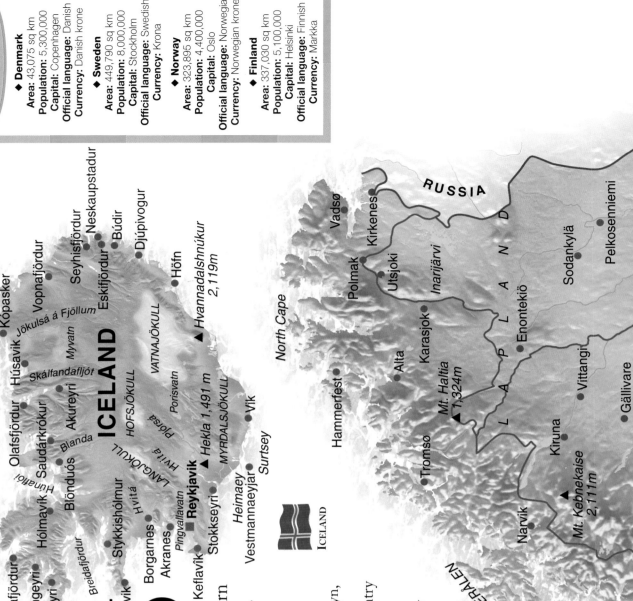

SCANDINAVIA AND FINLAND

TWO PENINSULAS extend from northwestern Europe, shaped rather like the claws of a crab. The southern peninsula, extending from Germany, is called Jutland.

Together with a chain of islands which includes Fyn, Sjælland, and Lolland, Jutland makes up the nation of **Denmark**. Most of Denmark is flat and low-lying, a country of green farmland. It exports bacon and dairy products.

Across the windy channels of Sgagerrak and Kattegat, between the North and Baltic Seas, lies the long northern peninsula occupied by **Sweden** and **Norway**. This is a land shaped by movements of ice in prehistoric times. Glaciers carved out the deep sea inlets called fjords along its ragged western coast. Ranges of mountains run down the peninsula like a backbone. They descend to a land of forests, bogs and thousands of lakes.

Summers can be warm, but winters are bitterly cold, with heavy snow. Norway lives by fishing and its North Sea rigs make it Western Europe's largest producer of oil and natural gas. Sweden is a major exporter of timber, paper, wooden furniture and motor vehicles.

The three nations of Denmark, Sweden and Norway form the region of Scandinavia. It was from here that the seafarers known as Vikings set out about 1,200 years ago. The Vikings raided and settled the coasts of Western Europe, traded in Russia and the Middle East, settled Iceland and Greenland and even reached North America. Today's Danes, Swedes and Norwegians are all closely related, as are the Germanic languages that they speak.

The Arctic lands of northern Scandinavia are home to the Saami (or Lapps), a people who traditionally lived by herding reindeer. Their neighbours are the Finns and the Russians.

Finland is a land of lakes, with coasts on the Gulfs of Bothnia and Finland. Its forests make it a leading producer of wood pulp and paper. Helsinki is the capital.

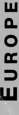

Stockholm, the heart of Sweden

The Swedish capital, Stockholm, is built between Lake Mälar and the Baltic Sea. The city covers several islands. It includes the mediaeval Old Town, merchants' houses from the 1900s and many modern factories and offices.

People of the Arctic

The Saami people live in Lapland, a region which extends right across the Scandinavian Arctic. Traditionally they are a nomadic people, who follow their herds of reindeer.

The Little Mermaid

This bronze statue in the Danish capital, Copenhagen, shows a character from one of the children's stories by Hans Christian Andersen (1805-75). Andersen created some of the world's best loved fairy tales.

LOW COUNTRIES

FACT BOX

◆ **Netherlands**
Area: 41,160 sq km
Population: 15,600,000
Capital: Amsterdam
Official language: Dutch
Currency: Guilder

◆ **Belgium**
Area: 30,520 sq km
Population: 10,200,000
Capital: Brussels
Official languages: Flemish, French
Currency: Belgian franc

◆ **Luxembourg**
Area: 2,585 sq km
Population: 400,000
Capital: Luxembourg
Official language: French, German, Letzebuergesch
Currency: Luxembourg franc

THE COUNTRY OF THE NETHERLANDS is sometimes called Holland, but that is really the name of just two of its provinces, North and South Holland. This is a very flat, low-lying part of northern Europe. Long barriers and sea walls have been built to protect the countryside from North Sea floods. Large areas of land called polders have been reclaimed from the sea over the ages.

After a period under Spanish rule, the **Netherlands** became wealthy in the 1600s by trading with Southeast Asia. Its capital city, Amsterdam, still has many beautiful old houses and canals dating back to this golden age. The Netherlands today remain a centre of commerce, exporting bulbs and cut flowers, vegetables and dairy products, especially cheese, and also electrical goods. Rotterdam is the world's busiest seaport. Peoples of the Netherlands include the Dutch and the Frisians, as well as people whose families came from former Dutch colonies in Indonesia and Surinam.

The Flemish people of **Belgium** are closely related to the Dutch and their two languages are very similar. Belgium is also home to a French-speaking people, the Walloons, who mostly live in the south of the country. Much of the countryside in Belgium is also low and flat, but the land rises to the wooded hills of the Ardennes in the south. The country is heavily industrialized, and is also known for its fine foods – chocolates, pâtés, hams and traditional beers.

Luxembourg is a tiny country, a survivor of the age when most of Europe was divided into little states, principalities and duchies. However, modern industry and banking have made Luxembourg wealthy and successful. The people of Luxembourg speak French, German and a local language called Letzebuergesch.

The three countries have close ties. In 1948, after the terrible years of World War II (1939–45), Belgium, the Netherlands and Luxembourg set up an economic union called 'Benelux'. In 1957 they went on to what is now the European Union (EU).

Bruges skyline

The brick gables of old merchants' houses make a pleasing skyline in many historical towns of the Lowlands. Bruges has been famous through the ages for its lacemaking. The city is linked by canal to the seaport of Zeebrugge.

Wetlands butterfly

The Large Copper butterfly is on the endangered species list in both Belgium and the Netherlands. The butterfly thrives in flooded fields. Its caterpillar can survive underwater for many weeks. However draining of wetlands by farmers and roadbuilders threatens its survival.

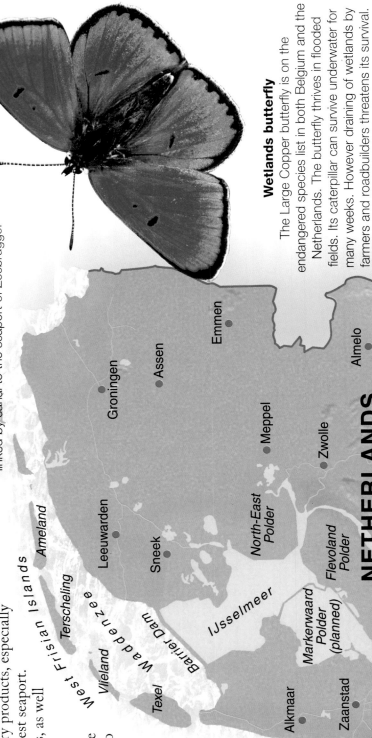

NETHERLANDS

Emmen
Assen
Groningen
Meppel
Zwolle
Almelo
Enschede
Leeuwarden
Sneek
North-East Polder
Flevoland Polder
Ameland
Terscheling
West Frisian Islands
Vlieland
Waddenzee
Barrier Dam
IJsselmeer
Markerwaard Polder (planned)
Texel
Alkmaar
Zaanstad
Amsterdam
Hilversum
Haarlem
IJsse

'When it's spring again...'
The classic Dutch landscape includes fields of brilliantly coloured tulips and old-fashioned windmills. Both attract the tourists and are seen here near the town of Haarlem.

Dutch cheese
Another popular attraction in the Netherlands is the cheese market at Alkmaar. The Netherlands exports mild cheeses such as Edam and Gouda around the world.

GERMANY

Arnhem
Nijmegen
s'Hertogenbosch
Venlo
Eindhoven
Heerlen
Maastricht
Vaalserberg 321m
Verviers
Botrange 694m
Spa

Maas
Waal
Lek

Delft
Rotterdam
Dordrecht
Breda
Tilburg
Genk
Hasselt
Liège
Meuse
Huy

Ostend
Zeebrugge
Bruges
Roeslare
Kortijk
Ghent
St. Niklaas
Antwerp
Mechelen
Aalst
Brussels
Waterloo
Leuven (Louvain)
Namur
Dinant
Sambre
Mons
La Louvière
Charleroi
Tournai

Schelde

BELGIUM

GERMANY

LUXEMBOURG

Buurgplatz 559m
Bastogne
Libramont
Luxembourg
Esch-sur-Alzette

ARDENNES MOUNTAINS

FRANCE

Oosterschelde
Vlissingen
Westerschelde

NETHERLANDS

LUXEMBOURG

BELGIUM

N

The future – 1958 style
This strange looking landmark is the Atomium. It was built for the World Fair held in Brussels in 1958 and was meant to be a symbol of a new age of atomic science and technology.

BRITISH ISLES

THE BRITISH ISLES lie off the northwestern coast of Europe, between the shallow waters of the North Sea and the stormy Atlantic Ocean. Their western shores are warmed by an ocean current called the North Atlantic Drift. The climate is mild, with a high rainfall in the west.

The largest island is called **Great Britain**, and its three countries (**England, Scotland** and **Wales**) are joined together within a United Kingdom. The second largest of the British Isles is called **Ireland**. Most of Ireland is an independent republic, but part of the north is governed as a province of the United Kingdom.

Great Britain has a landscape of rolling farmland. There are rugged highlands in Wales and Scotland, while England has rich farmland in the southeast, bleak moors in the north, flat fields in East Anglia and wild coasts in Cornwall. There are many beautiful old villages and towns, but also large cities and ports.

The Irish landscape is less crowded. It has green fields, misty hills and, in the west, steep cliffs pounded by Atlantic breakers. Its capital, Dublin, lies on the River Liffey.

English is spoken throughout the British Isles, but other languages may be heard too – Welsh, Irish and Scots Gaelic, and the various languages spoken by British people of Asian and African descent.

Both the UK and the **Republic of Ireland** are members of the

Wren

One of the most widespread birds of Britain, this short drab coloured bird with a cocked tail, has a loud warbling song. Wrens feed on caterpillars, beetles and bugs.

FACT BOX

◆ **United Kingdom:**
England, Scotland, Wales,
N. Ireland
Area: 242,480 sq km
Population: 58,000,000
Capital: London
Official language: English
Currency: Sterling pound

◆ **England**
Area: 130,420 sq km
Population: 48,675,119
Capital: London
Official language: English
Currency: Sterling pound

◆ **Scotland**
Area: 77,170 sq km
Population: 5,111,000
Capital: Edinburgh
Official language: English
Currency: Sterling pound

◆ **Wales**
Area: 20,770 sq km
Population: 2,899,000
Capital: Cardiff
Official language: Welsh,
English
Currency: Sterling pound

◆ **Northern Ireland**
Area: 74,120 sq km
Population: 1,610,000
Capital: Belfast
Official language: English
Currency: Sterling pound

◆ **Republic of Ireland**
Area: 70,283 sq km
Population: 3,552,000
Capital: Dublin
Official language: English, Irish
Currency: Irish pound (punt)

NORTH SEA

SHETLAND ISLANDS
Unst
Yell
Lerwick
Foula
Sumburgh Head
Fair Isle

ORKNEY ISLANDS
Westray
Kirkwall
Hoy
South Ronaldsay
John o'Groats
Thurso

SCOTLAND

Cape Wrath
North Minch
Butt of Lewis
Stornoway
Lewis
OUTER HEBRIDES
North Uist
South Uist
Barra

NORTH WEST HIGHLANDS
Moray Firth
Fraserburgh
Peterhead
Aberdeen
Dee
Don
Spey
Inverness
Loch Ness
GRAMPIAN MTS.
Mallaig
Ben Nevis ▲ 1,343 m
Oban
Skye
Rhum
Coll
Mull
Tiree
INNER HEBRIDES
Jura
Islay

Montrose
SIDLAW HILLS
Tay
Dundee
Perth
Firth of Forth
OCHIL HILLS
Loch Lomond
Forth
Edinburgh
St. Abbs Head
Berwick-upon-Tweed
Holy I.
Jedburgh
Tweed
Greenock
Glasgow
Clyde
Kilmarnock
Arran
Ayr
Kintyre pen.

SCOTLAND

NORTHERN IRELAND
Malin Head
Tory I.
Rathlin I.

Tower of London

Built in the eleventh century by William the Conqueror, this ancient fortress on the river Thames was once a royal home. It is now a museum and houses the crown jewels. It was here that Anne Boleyn, wife of Henry VIII, was beheaded. Yeomen of the Guard, or Beefeaters, still guard the Tower.

Ladies' View, Killarney, Eire

This famous beauty spot in southern Ireland enjoys wonderful views of Macgillycuddy's Reeks (a mountain range) and the lakes of Killarney. Of these lakes Lough Learne, or lower lake, is the largest with over 30 islands.

13

FRANCE AND MONACO

FRANCE IS A LARGE, beautiful country which lies at the heart of Western Europe. Its western regions include the massive peaks of the Pyrenees, vineyards and pine forests, peaceful rivers and Atlantic shores.

The north includes the stormy headlands of Brittany, the cliffs of Normandy and the Channel ports. Rolling fertile plains are drained by the winding river Seine, over whose banks and islands sprawls the French capital. Paris is one of the world's great cities, with broad avenues, historic palaces and churches.

The west of **France** is bordered by wooded hills which rise to the high forested slopes of the Jura mountains and finally the spectacular glaciers and ridges of the Alps. The rocks of the Massif Central, shaped by ancient volcanoes, rise in central southern France, to the west of the Rhône valley. The sun-baked hills of southern France border the warm seas of the Mediterranean Sea. This coast includes the wetlands of the Camargue, the great seaport of Marseilles and the fashionable yachting marinas of Cannes.

France has played a major part in history, and the French language is now spoken in many parts of the world. The French people are mostly descended from a Celtic people called the Gauls and Germanic peoples, such as the Franks and Vikings. Within France are several other peoples with their own languages and distinct cultures, such as Bretons, Basques, Catalans, Alsatians, Corsicans and Algerians.

France is a republic belonging to the European Union (EU) and is an important industrial power, producing cars, aerospace equipment, chemicals and textiles. The country is renowned for its wines, its cheeses, and its fine cooking.

Part of the Mediterranean coast is occupied by a very small principality called **Monaco**. It has close links with its large neighbour and shares the same currency. The state is famous for its casino.

Château de Charumont
France has many historical castles, palaces and stately homes, or châteaux. Some of the finest are in the Loire valley.

Cherbou
Carenta
Gulf of St-Malo Grar
Morlaix St.-Malo
Brest St-Brieuc Dinan
Foug
Douernenez Pontivy Rennes
Quimper
Lorient
Vannes
Belle-Ile Redon
St. Nazaire
Nante
La Roche-sur-
Isle d'Yeu
Les Sables-d'Olo
Ré I.
La Roch
Roch
Oléror.
Rc
Pa

Cape Corse
Bastia
Gulf of Sagone *CORSICA*
Ajaccio
Bonifacio
Strait of Bonifacio

Sacré-Coeur
The gleaming domes of this church soar above the Parisian district of Montmartre, once famed as the haunt of artists and writers.

Bayor
Biarritz
P
S P A

Shape of the future
The Futuroscope theme park and study centre, near Poitiers, is one example of France's many experimental modern buildings. This theatre looks like a huge crystal.

Vineyard harvest
Grapes are gathered at a vineyard in Alsace, on the slopes of the Vosges. Grapes, grown in many regions of France, are made into some of the world's finest wines.

Dunkerque
Calais
Boulogne
Lille
Montreuil
Arras
Douai
Valenciennes
Abbeville
Cambrai
Dieppe
St. Quentin
Fécamp
Amiens
Hirson
Bolbec
Montdidier
Charleville-Mézières

BELGIUM
LUXEMBOURG
GERMANY

FACT BOX

◆ **France**
Area: 543,965 sq km
Population: 58,600,000
Capital: Paris
Official language: French
Currency: French franc

◆ **Monaco**
Area: 1.9 sq km
Population: 28,000
Capital: Monaco
Official language: French
Currency: French franc

FRANCE

Bay of
the Seine
Le Havre
Caen
Louviers
Seine
Reims
Verdun
Metz
Lisieux
Meaux
Marne
Pont à Mousson
Evreux
Châlons-sur-Marne
Nancy
Strasbourg
Argentan
Paris
Versailles
St. Germain-en-Laye
St.Dizier
Toul
NORMANDY HILLS
Rambouillet
Seine
Moselle
Epinal
Colmar
Alençon
Fontainebleau
Chartres
VOSGES
Rhine
Mayenne
Nemours
Troyes
Saône
Mulhouse
Laval
Sens
Langres
LANGRES PLATEAU
Montbéliard
Loire
Orléans
Montargis
Le Mans
Gien
Auxerre
Dijon
Besançon
Doubs
Angers
Blois
Tours
Avallon
Dôle
JURA
Saumur
Vierzon
Autun
Pontarlier
Châtellerault
Loire
Bourges
Nevers
Le Creusot
Chalon-sur-Saône
Châteauroux
Cher
Montceau les Mines
St.Claude
SWITZERLAND
Poitiers
La Châtre
Saône
Niort
Moulins
Mâcon
Civray
Montluçon
Bourg-en-Bresse
Annecy
FRANCE
Vichy
Villefranches
Chamonix
Cognac
Limoges
Lyon
Villeurbanne
Mont Blanc
4,807m
Angoulême
Clermont-Ferrand
Villefranches
Chambéry
Rhône
Nontron
Puy de Sancy
1,886m
Vienne
Val d'Isère
Barbezieux
MASSIF
CENTRAL
St.-Étienne
ALPS
Périgueux
Annonay
Grenoble
Libourne
Souillac
Aurillac
Isère
Romans-sur-Isère
Bergerac
Cère
Valence
Drac
Bordeaux
Dordogne
Lot
Prives
Montélimar
Gap
Durance
Marmande
Lot
Mende
Rhône
LES
LANDES
Garonne
Cahors
Rodez
Aveyron
Millau
Alès
CÉVENNES
Carpentras
Verdon
Monte-de-Marsan
Montauban
Tarn
Avignon
Durance
Nice
MONACO
Gaillac
Albi
LANGUEDOC
Nîmes
Auch
Toulouse
Arles
Aix-en-Provence
Cannes
Garonne
Castres
Montpellier
St.Raphael
Ariège
Carcassonne
Sète
Brignoles
St.Tropez
Tarbes
Béziers
Marseille
Toulon
Côte d'Azur
Lourdes
St. Gaudens
Aude
Narbonne
PYRENEES
Foix
Perpignan

N
W
S

MONACO

ANDORRA

Quiche Lorraine
A speciality of north-eastern
France, this is a baked pastry
tart filled with eggs, cream,
cheese and bacon.

15

FACT BOX

◆ **Germany**
Area: 356,840sq km
Population: 82,000,000
Capital: Berlin
Official language: German
Currency: Deutsche mark

◆ **Switzerland**
Area: 41,285 sq km
Population: 7,100,000
Capital: Bern
Official languages: German,
French, Italian, Romansh
Currency: Swiss franc

◆ **Liechenstein**
Area: 160 sq km
Population: 30,000
Capital: Vaduz
Official language: German
Currency: Swiss franc

◆ **Austria**
Area: 83,855 sq km
Population: 8,100,000
Capital: Vienna
Official language: German
Currency: Schilling

Sylt
NORTH SEA
Flensburg
BALTIC SEA
Kiel Bay
Schleswig
Fehmarn
Rügen
Helgoland
Kiel
Mecklenburg Bay
Stralsund
Rendsburg
Neumünster
Rostock
Cuxhaven
Itzehoe
Lübeck
Wismar
Güstrow
Elmshorn
Norderstedt
Schwerin
Neubrandenburg
Wilhelmshaven
Bremerhaven
Emden
Hamburg
Buxtehude
Müritz Lake
Neustrelitz
Papenburg
Oldenburg
Bremen
Lüneburg
Delmenhorst
Uelzen
Wittenberge
Eberswalde-Finow
Ems
Weser
Vechta
Nienburg
Celle
Stendal
Berlin
POLAND
Nordhorn
Weser
Hannover
Aller
Wolfsburg
Brandenburg
Frankfurt (an der Oder)
Rheine
Osnabrück
Minden
Hildesheim
Brunswick (Braunschweig)
Magdeburg
Potsdam
Eisenhüttenstadt
Gronau
TEUTOBURG FOREST
Bielefeld
Hameln
Salzgitter
Oder
Neisse
Münster
Holzminden
Bad Harzburg
Halberstadt
Dessau
Cottbus
Bocholt
Hamm
Paderborn
Leine
Göttingen
HARZ MTS.
Halle
Hoyerswerda
Dinslaken
Dortmund
Arnsberg
Kassel
Münden
Nordhausen
Elbe
Leipzig
Meissen
Duisburg
Essen
G E R M A N Y
Görlitz
Krefeld
Wuppertal
Mühlhausen
Erfurt
Weimar
Freiberg
Dresden
Mönchen-Gladbach
Remscheid
Düsseldorf
Solingen
Bergisch-Gladbach
Jena
Gera
Chemnitz
Cologne (Köln)
Marburg
Zwickau
Aachen
Bonn
Siegen
Alsfeld
THURINGIAN FOREST
Plauen
Hof
Neuwied
Fulda
Fulda
Werra
Suhl
Koblenz
Giessen
Main
Coburg
Daun
Wiesbaden
Frankfurt am Main
Schweinfurt
Bayreuth
CZECH REPUBLIC
Rhine
Mainz
Offenbach
Würzburg
Bamberg
Trier
Mosel
Darmstadt
Main
STEIGERWALD
Worms
Kitzingen
Fürth
Nuremberg (Nürnberg)
HUNSRÜCK
Ludwigshafen
Mannheim
BOHEMIAN FOREST
Saar
Kaiserslautern
Heidelberg
Jagst
Saarbrücken
Karlsruhe
Heilbronn
Regensburg
LUXEMBOURG
Pforzheim
Stuttgart
Aalen
Ingolstadt
Passau
Baden-Baden
Neckar
Tübingen
SWABIAN JURA
Danube
Linz
BLACK FOREST
Reutlingen
Ulm
Augsburg
Braunau
Freiburg
Rhine
Memmingen
Munich (München)
Inn
Wels
Steyr
FRANCE
Lech
Rosenheim
Gmunden
Schaffhausen
Konstanz
Kempten
Salzburg
N
Basel
Winterthur
Lake Constance (Bodensee)
Kufstein
Hallein
AUSTRIA
Baden
St Gallen
Solothurn
Zurich
LIECHTENSTEIN
Zugspitze 2,963 m
Kitzbühel
Neuchâtel
Lucerne
Vaduz
Innsbruck
NIEDERE TAUERN
Bern
Zug
Brenner
HOHE TAUERN
Lake Neuchâtel
Inn
Mur
Fribourg
SWITZERLAND
Grossglockner 2,863 m
Wolfsbe
Lausanne
Thun
Interlaken
Chur
Davos
ITALY
Klagenfur
Lake Geneva
Andermatt
Villach
Montreux
Salzach
Drav
Thonon
BERNESE ALPS
LEPONTINE ALPS
St Moritz
SLOVENI
Geneva
Zermatt
Locarno
Bellinzona
Martigny
Matterhorn 4,478 m
Monte Rosa 4,634 m
Lugano

GERMANY

SWITZERLAND

LIECHTENSTEIN

AUSTRIA

GERMANY & THE ALPS

GERMANY LIES BETWEEN Western and Central Europe. In the south the high peaks of the Alps are flanked by belts of forest.

The rolling hills and heathland of the centre stretch to the North Sea, while in the west the rivers Rhine and Moselle wind through steep valleys planted with vines. In the northeast a vast plain is bordered by the Baltic Sea and by the rivers Oder and Neisse.

For most of its history Germany has been divided into different states. Today's united Germany dates from 1990. Germany is a federal republic, which means that its regions or Länder have considerable powers. The country is a leading member of the European Union and is a major world producer of cars, electrical and household goods, medicines, chemicals, wines and beers.

Switzerland is a small country set amongst the lakes and snowy peaks of the Alps and the Jura ranges. Its beautiful landscape and historical towns attract many tourists. Industries include dairy produce, precision instruments and finance. Zurich is a world centre of banking, while Geneva is the headquarters of many international agencies, such as the Red Cross and the World Health Organization.

To the east, the tiny country of **Liechtenstein** is closely linked with Switzerland and uses the same currency. The land of **Austria** descends from the soaring peaks of the Alps to the flat lands of the Danube river valley. Austria once ruled a large empire which stretched eastwards into Hungary and southwards into Italy. Today Austria still plays an important part in Europe, making its living from tourism, farming, forestry and manufacture.

German is spoken through most of the region, with a great variety of dialects. In parts of Switzerland there are people who speak French, Italian and Romansh.

Krems
Danube **Vienna**
t Pölten   **Bruck**
Baden
Neusiedler
Wiener Neustadt   See
apfenberg
en
Graz

HUNGARY

Edelweiss
This small herb, with its pretty white flower, grows in the European Alps. High mountain meadows are filled with wildflowers in spring and summer.

Brimming with beer
Munich, capital of Bavaria in southern Germany, hosts a famous beer festival every October. Regional dress is still common in the region.

River of ice
This impressive glacier grinds its way down the Alps near Zermatt. Many tourists and climbers visit Switzerland to enjoy the spectacular views.

Medieval revelry
Festival costumes recall the Middle Ages in Baden Württemberg. During that period Germany was made up of many small states.

IBERIAN PENINSULA

THE IBERIAN PENINSULA is in southwestern Europe, and juts out into the Atlantic Ocean. It is bordered to the north by the stormy Bay of Biscay and to the south by the Mediterranean Sea and the Balearic Islands. Across the Strait of Gibraltar, just 13 kilometres away, lies the continent of Africa.

The north coast, green from high rainfall, rises to the Cantabrian mountains, while the snowy Pyrenees form a high barrier along the Spanish-French frontier. Another range, the Sierra Nevada, runs parallel with the south coast. Inland, much of the Iberian peninsula is taken up by an extremely dry, rocky plateau, which swelters in the heat of summer. To the west are forested highlands and the fertile plains of Portugal, crossed by great rivers such as the Douro, Tagus and Guadiana.

The Iberian peninsula is occupied by four countries or territories. There is **Gibraltar**, a British colony since 1713, and the tiny independent state of **Andorra**, high in the Pyrenees. The two main countries of the region are **Spain** and **Portugal**. Both have a history of overseas settlement, and both Spanish and Portuguese have become the chief languages of Latin America. Many people speak other languages, including Basque and Catalan, and have their own traditions and history.

Both Spain and Portugal were ruled by dictators for much of the 20th century, but today both are democracies and members of the European Union. Spain produces olives, citrus fruits, wines and sherries, and has a large fishing fleet. Portugal also produces wine and port takes its name from the city of Oporto. Fishing villages line the coasts and cork, used for bottle stoppers and tiling, is cut from the thick bark of the cork oak tree.

PORTUGAL

Feria in Seville
At the Feria, held in the Spanish city of Seville every April, people ride into town dressed in traditional finery. The river is lined with tents and pavilions. The festival is celebrated with bullfights, flamenco music and dancing.

Map

N

Bay of Biscay
Cape Ortegal
Cape Peñas
La Coruña · El Ferrol · · Gijón · Llan
Carballo · Villalba · Oviedo ·
Cape Finisterre · CANTABRIA
Fonsagrada
Lugo · Sil
Santiago de Compostela · Sarria
Lalin · León ·
Monforte de Lemos · Astorga ·
Vigo · Miño · Orense · SIERRA CABRERA · Villada ·
Baltar · La Gudina · Esla
Braga · Bragança · Vallado
Tâmega · Tuela · Mogadouro · Zamora ·
Vila Real · Medina del Campo
Porto · Douro · Tormes
Lamego · Salamanca ·
PORTUGAL
Aviero · Viseu · Cuidad Rodrigo ·
Guarda · Béjar ·
Coimbra · Covilhã · SIERRA DE GREDO
Plasencia ·
Castelo Branco · Tajo
Leiria · Trujillo ·
Tomar · Cáceres ·
Caldas da Rainha
Tagus · Portalegre · Don Benito ·
Santarém · Badajoz
Lisbon · Almendralejo ·
Évora · Pozoblanc
Setúbal · Ardila · Azuaga ·
Beja · Guadiana · SIER
Constantina · Córdo
Chança · Nerva · Guadalquivir
Huelva · Seville · Puente Ge
Lagos · Faro · Costa de la Luz · Osuna ·
Cape Saint Vincent · Algarve · Las Marismas · Morón de la Fronte
Gulf of Cadiz · Ronda ·
Jerez de la Frontera · SIERRA DE RONDA · Marbe
Cádiz · Gibraltar (U.K
Algeciras ·
Strait of Gibraltar
Cueta (Spain

Fishing boats, Nazaré
Fishing boats line the beach at Nazaré, on the Portuguese coast. The fishermen brave the Atlantic waves daily in their search for the sardines and tuna that make up their catch.

FRANCE

▲ Pico de Aneto
3,404m

ANDORRA
Andorra la Vella

FACT BOX
◆ **Spain**
Area: 504,880 sq km
Population: 39,300,000
Capital: Madrid
Official language: Spanish
Currency: Peseta

◆ **Portugal**
Area: 91,630 sq km
Population: 9,900,000
Capital: Lisbon
Official language: Portuguese
Currency: Escudo

◆ **Andorra**
Area: 465 sq km
Population: 62,000
Capital: Andorra la Vella
Official language: Catalan
Currency: French franc,
Spanish peseta

Santander
Bilbao
San Sebastián
Reinosa
Vitoria
Pamplona
orno
Burgos
Logroño
PYRENEES
Arga
Gállego
Cinca
Figueras
Llobregat
Gerona
Costa Brava
Manresa
encia
Soria
Duero
Ebro
Saragossa
Jalón
Lérida
Tarrasa
Barcelona
SPAIN
Caspe
Reus
Tarragona
Costa Dorada
ANDORRA
govia
SIERRA DE GUADARRAMA
Tajuña
Tajo
Tortosa
Cape Tortosa
Guadalajara
Alcalá de Henares
Morella
Vinaroz
Costa del Azahar
Madrid
Teruel
Mijares
Menorca
Aranjuez
Cuenca
Castellón
de la Plana
Mallorca
Mahón
SPAIN
oledo
Turia
Sagunto
Palma
Manacor
ONTES
TOLEDO
Requena
Júcar
Valencia
BALEARIC
ISLANDS
Villarrobledo
Gulf of
Valencia
Daimiel
Alcira
Ibiza
Manzanares
Albacete
Ibiza
Ciudad Real
Cape
Formentera
adiana
Almansa
Neo
ertollano
Valdepeñas
Alcaraz
Yecla
Alcoy

Portuguese explorers
This monument is in Lisbon, the Portuguese capital. It honours the Portuguese seafarers who were among the first Europeans to explore the coasts of Africa, Asia and the Americas. Prince Henry (1394–1460) founded the first school of navigation.

RENA
La Carolina
Moratalla
SIERRA DE SEGURA
Alicante
Elche
Costa Blanca
Linares
Cehegín
Segura
Orihuela
Murcia
Jaén
Lorca
Cartagena
Cape Palos
Martos
Baza
Aguilas
Guadix
Huércal Overa
Costa Blanca
Genil
Granada
▲ Mulhacén 3,478m
equera
SIERRA NEVADA
Almería
álaga
Motril
Berja
Cape Gata
Costa del Sol
MEDITERRANEAN SEA

Spanish paella
Paella takes its name from the large pan in which it is cooked. It is made of rice with saffron and garlic, mixed with prawns and other seafoods, vegetables, chicken or ham.

Melilla (Spain)

ITALY AND ITS NEIGHBOURS

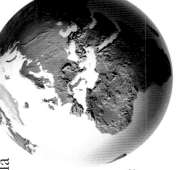

ITALY OCCUPIES a long, boot-shaped peninsula which stretches south from the snowy peaks and blue lakes of the Alps into the Mediterranean Sea. The country also takes in the large islands of Sardinia and Sicily. The northern regions of the mainland include the wide, fertile plains around the river Po and wealthy industrial cities.

A long chain of mountains, the Appennines, run down the spine of **Italy**. They descend to coastal farmland and the hot, dry plains of the south. Southern Italy and its islands are one of the world's volcanic danger zones. Olives and grapes grow well in its sunny climate and Italy is the largest wine producer in the world. Factories produce cars, textiles and leather goods.

Modern Italy has only been united since 1861, but in ancient times Rome was the capital of a vast empire which stretched across western Europe, southwest Asia and North Africa. Rome later became the centre of the Catholic Church and during the 1400s and 1500s cities such as Florence saw a great flowering of scholarship and the arts, known as the Renaissance. Many tourists visit Italy to see its ancient sites.

Italian, based on the ancient Latin language, is spoken throughout Italy, but in border regions you may hear other languages – French, German or Slovenian. The Ladin language is spoken in the Dolomite mountains and the people of Sardinia speak their own ancient dialect of Italian.

Two small independent states lie entirely surrounded by Italian territory. One is the world's smallest country, known as **Vatican City**. It is a district of Rome which serves as headquarters for the Pope and the Roman Catholic Church. The other is tiny **San Marino.**

South of Italy, towards the coast of North Africa is the chain of islands which make up **Malta**. The Maltese have their own language and live from building and repairing ships and from tourism.

Sun and sea

Portofino is a small town on the Gulf of Genoa, in Italy's Liguria region. Its pretty waterfront and fishing boats attract many tourists in the hot Mediterranean summer.

Spaghetti Bolognese

Spaghetti is a kind of pasta. Made from wheat and eggs, pasta is eaten in all kinds of shapes and sizes, each with its own name. Here it is served with a meat and tomato sauce, invented in the city of Bologna. Italians who have left their homeland have made their cooking popular around the world.

SLOVENIA

AUSTRIA

SWITZERLAND

FRANCE

MONACO

LIGURIAN SEA

VATICAN CITY

SAN MARINO

I T A L Y

Mont Blanc 4,807m
Monte Rosa 4,634m

Trieste
Udine
Portogruaro
Venice
Chioggia
Bolzano
Borgo
Treviso
Piave
Vicenza
Padua
Adria
Comacchio
Trento
Verona
L. Garda
Mantova
Po
Ferrara
Reno
Ravenna
Rimini
Panaro
Bologna
Forlì
San Marino
Pesaro
Ancona
Iesi
Macerata
San Benedetto
Bergamo
Brescia
Oglio
Carpi
Modena
Pistoia
Florence
Arezzo
Cortona
Perugia
Grosseto
Lecco
Monza
Lodi
Cremona
Piacenza
Parma
Reggio nell'Emilia
Lucca
Arno
Siena
L. Trasimeno
Piombino
Milan
Pavia
Massa
Carrara
Viareggio
Livorno
Pisa
Capraia
Elba
Novi Ligure
Alessandra
La Spezia
Savona
Genoa
Gulf of Genoa
Biella
Turin
Cuneo
Tanaro
Ticino
Como
L. Maggiore
Gubbio
Teramo

ITALY

20

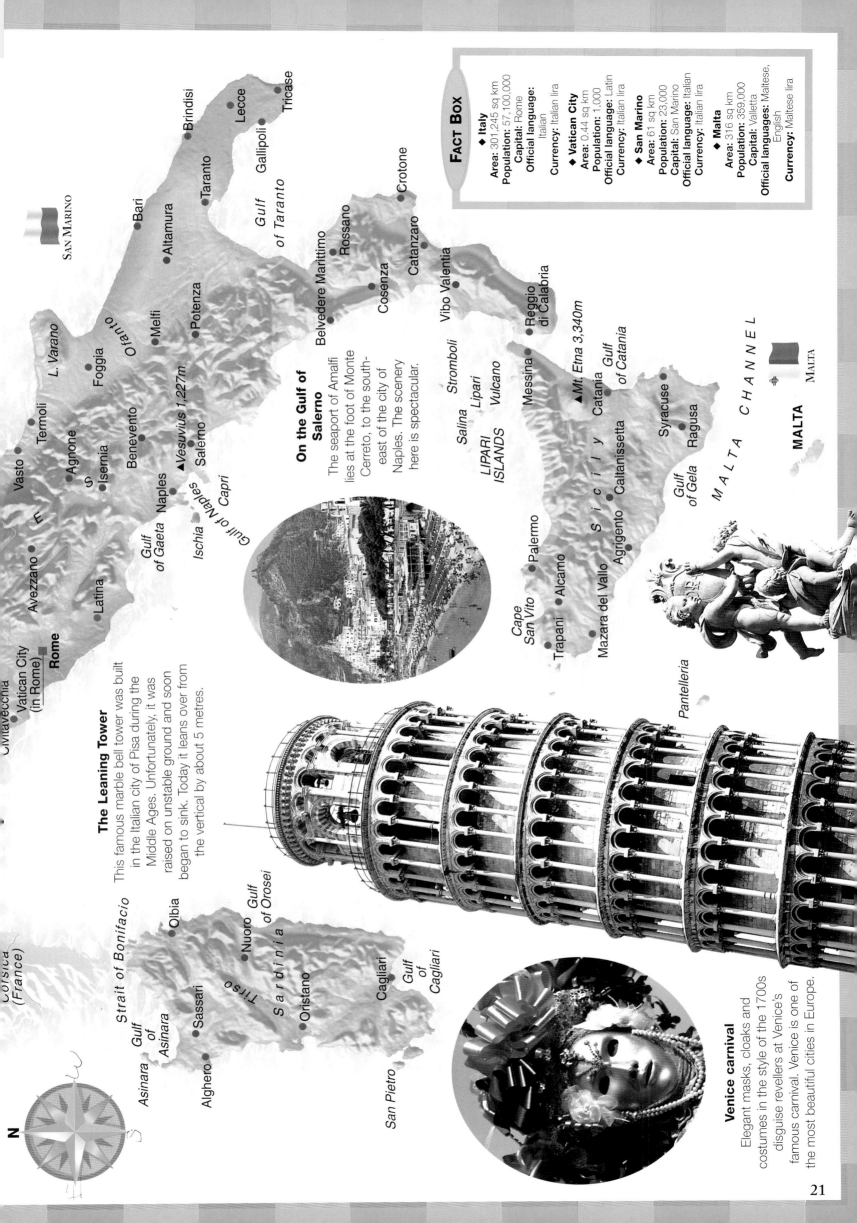

FACT BOX

◆ **Italy**
Area: 301,245 sq km
Population: 57,100,000
Capital: Rome
Official language: Italian
Currency: Italian lira

◆ **Vatican City**
Area: 0.44 sq km
Population: 1,000
Official language: Latin
Currency: Italian lira

◆ **San Marino**
Area: 61 sq km
Population: 23,000
Capital: San Marino
Official language: Italian
Currency: Italian lira

◆ **Malta**
Area: 316 sq km
Population: 359,000
Capital: Valletta
Official languages: Maltese, English
Currency: Maltese lira

SAN MARINO

MALTA

On the Gulf of Salerno

The seaport of Amalfi lies at the foot of Monte Cerreto, to the south-east of the city of Naples. The scenery here is spectacular.

The Leaning Tower

This famous marble bell tower was built in the Italian city of Pisa during the Middle Ages. Unfortunately, it was raised on unstable ground and soon began to sink. Today it leans over from the vertical by about 5 metres.

Venice carnival

Elegant masks, cloaks and costumes in the style of the 1700s disguise revellers at Venice's famous carnival. Venice is one of the most beautiful cities in Europe.

Map labels:

Corsica (France)
Civitavecchia
Vatican City (in Rome)
Rome
Latina
Avezzano
Vasto
Termoli
Agnone
Isernia
Benevento
▲Vesuvius 1,227m
Salerno
Naples
Gulf of Gaeta
Ischia
Gulf of Naples
Capri
Foggia
L. Varano
Melfi
Potenza
Ofanto
Altamura
Bari
Brindisi
Taranto
Lecce
Tricase
Gallipoli
Gulf of Taranto
Belvedere Marittimo
Rossano
Cosenza
Crotone
Catanzaro
Vibo Valentia
Reggio di Calabria
Messina
▲Mt Etna 3,340m
Catania
Gulf of Catania
Stromboli
Salina
Lipari
Vulcano
LIPARI ISLANDS
Palermo
Sicily
Caltanissetta
Agrigento
Gulf of Gela
Syracuse
Ragusa
Cape San Vito
Trapani
Alcamo
Mazara del Vallo
MALTA CHANNEL
Pantelleria
Strait of Bonifacio
Asinara
Gulf of Asinara
Alghero
Sassari
Olbia
Nuoro
Gulf of Orosei
Sardinia
Tirso
Oristano
Cagliari
Gulf of Cagliari
San Pietro

N

21

CENTRAL EUROPE

THREE SMALL COUNTRIES cluster around the eastern shores of the Baltic Sea. **Estonia**, **Latvia** and **Lithuania** were part of the Soviet Union (today's Russian Federation) from 1940 until 1991, when they became independent. Their lands include forests and lakes, farmland and industrial cities.

Poland, which has historic links with Lithuania, is a large country which has also known invasions and foreign rule through much of its history. Despite this, the Poles, a Slavic people, have kept a sense of independence and a pride in their traditions. The lands near Poland's Baltic coast are dotted with lakes. The north is a flat land of pine forests, part of the great plain which stretches from eastern Germany into Russia. It is cold and snowy in winter, but warm in summer. In southern Poland the land rises to highlands and the jagged peaks of the Tatra mountains, along the Slovakian border.

Slovakia and the **Czech Republic** were a single country until 1993. Slovakia is a land of high mountains dropping to fertile farmland around the River Danube, which forms its southeastern border. When the two countries divided, most industry lay on the Czech side of the border. The Czech Republic produces beer, glass, ceramics, steel and machinery. The country is bordered by mountains and, in the east, by the Bohemian centre of learning and the arts.

The Czechs and Slovaks are both Slavic peoples, but the Hungarians are Magyars, a people who invaded and settled in the region about 1200 years ago. **Hungary** is a country of wide open plains and low mountains. Its fertile farmland produces fruits, grains and grapes for making strong red wine. Its beautiful capital Budapest is on the River Danube.

Fact Box

◆ Poland
Area: 312,685 sq km
Population: 38,600,000
Capital: Warsaw
Official language: Polish
Currency: Zloty

◆ Czech Republic
Area: 78,864 sq km
Population: 10,330,000
Capital: Prague
Official language: Czech
Currency: Koruna

◆ Slovakia
Area: 49,035 sq km
Population: 5,400,000
Capital: Bratislava
Official language: Slovak
Currency: Koruna

◆ Hungary
Area: 93,034 sq km
Population: 10,294,000
Capital: Budapest
Official language: Hungarian
Currency: Forint

◆ Latvia
Area: 63,700 sq km
Population: 2,700,000
Capital: Riga
Official language: Latvian
Currency: Lats

◆ Lithuania
Area: 65,200 sq km
Population: 3,742,000
Capital: Kiev
Official language: Vilnius
Currency: Litas

◆ Estonia
Area: 45,100 sq km
Population: 1,517,000
Capital: Tallinn
Official language: Estonian
Currency: Kroon

Historical Prague

Prague, capital of the Czech Republic, is a fine old city on the River Vltava. Prague was the chief city of independent Bohemia in the Middle Ages.

ESTONIA

LATVIA

LITHUANIA

RUSSIA

Lake Peipus

Kohtla-Järve

Tartu

Munamagi 318 m ▲

ESTONIA

Pärnu

Hiumaa

Saaremaa

Gulf of Riga

Tallinn

▲ *Gaizina* 311 m

LATVIA

Daugavpils

Utena

Ukmerge

Vilnius

311 m ▲

LITHUANIA

Riga

Jelgava

Siauliai

Panevezys

Kaunas

Jurmala

Saldus

Ventspils

Liepāja

Klaipeda

Nemunas (Neman)

POLAND

Kaliningrad (RUSSIA)

Gulf of Gdansk

N

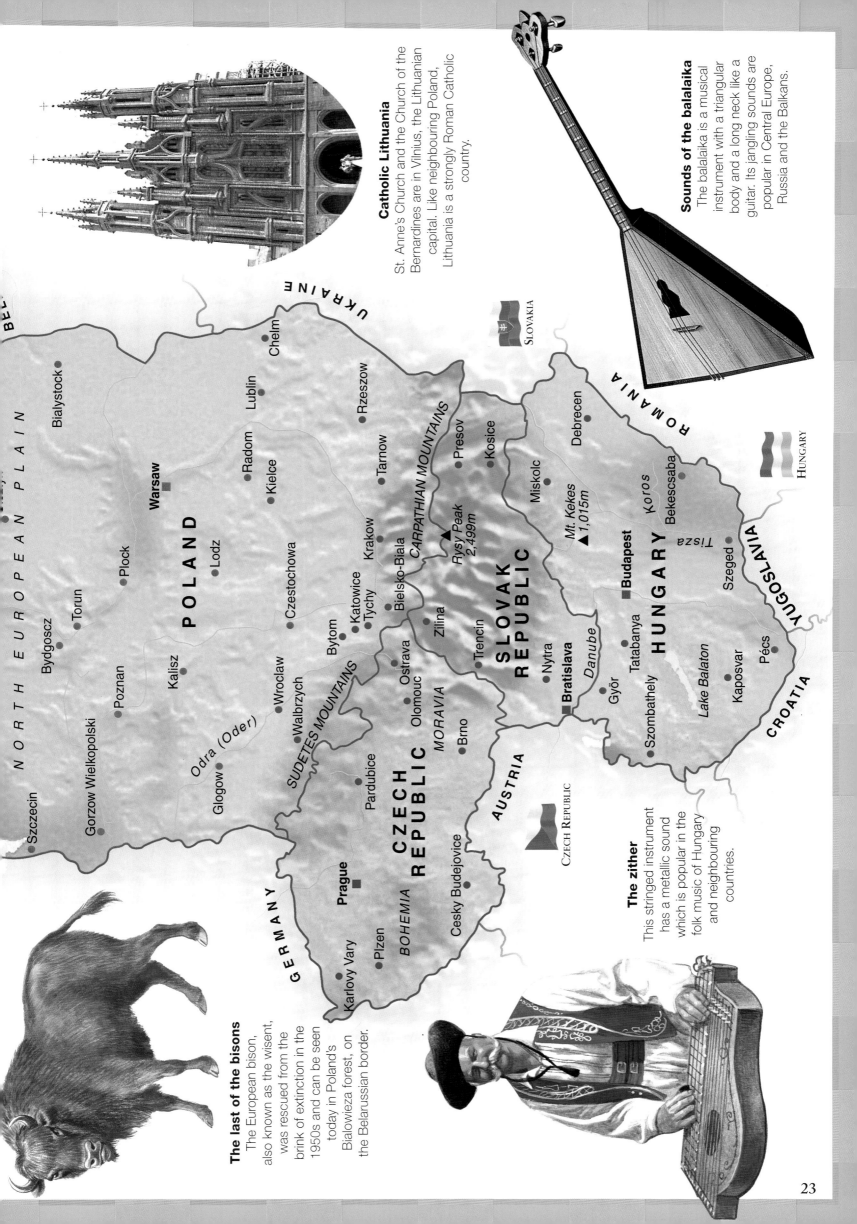

Catholic Lithuania
St. Anne's Church and the Church of the Bernardines are in Vilnius, the Lithuanian capital. Like neighbouring Poland, Lithuania is a strongly Roman Catholic country.

Sounds of the balalaika
The balalaika is a musical instrument with a triangular body and a long neck like a guitar. Its jangling sounds are popular in Central Europe, Russia and the Balkans.

UKRAINE

BEL

SLOVAKIA

ROMANIA

HUNGARY

Chelm

Bialystock

Lublin

Rzeszow

Radom

Tarnow

Presov

Kosice

Debrecen

Kielce

Miskolc

Warsaw

Koros

Bekescsaba

N O R T H   E U R O P E A N   P L A I N

CARPATHIAN MOUNTAINS

Lodz

Krakow

▲ *Rysy Peak*
2,499m

Mt. Kekes
▲ 1,015m

Tisza

P O L A N D

Plock

Czestochowa

Bielsko-Biala

Zilina

Budapest

Szeged

S L O V A K
R E P U B L I C

Torun

Kalisz

Katowice
Tychy

Trencin

H U N G A R Y

Bydgoscz

Bytom

Nytra

Lake Balaton

Pécs

Poznan

Wroclaw

Ostrava

Danube

Tatabanya

Kaposvar

Gorzow Wielkopolski

Walbrzych

Olomouc

Györ

Szombathely

SUDETES MOUNTAINS

Bratislava

Glogow

Odra (Oder)

Brno

MORAVIA

AUSTRIA

YUGOSLAVIA

Szczecin

Pardubice

C Z E C H
R E P U B L I C

CZECH REPUBLIC

CROATIA

BOHEMIA

Prague

G E R M A N Y

Cesky Budejovice

Plzen

Karlovy Vary

The last of the bisons
The European bison, also known as the wisent, was rescued from the brink of extinction in the 1950s and can be seen today in Poland's Bialowieza forest, on the Belarussian border.

The zither
This stringed instrument has a metallic sound which is popular in the folk music of Hungary and neighbouring countries.

23

BALKANS AND ROMANIA

THE STATES OF SOUTHERN Central Europe are known as the Balkans. They take their name from the Balkan peninsula, a great wedge of land which stretches south into the Mediterranean.

The warm, blue waters around the Balkan coast form the Adriatic, Aegean and Black Seas and are popular with tourists. The region is mountainous, with hot, dry summers. Winters are severe in the north of the region, but generally mild in the south. Earthquakes are common. The Balkan countries produce fruit, wines and spirits, dairy products such as yoghurt and cheese, olives, sunflowers and tobacco.

In the early 1990s the northwest of the region saw bitter fighting as the large nation of Yugoslavia broke up into separate independent states. These took the names of **Slovenia**, **Croatia**, **Bosnia-Herzegovina**, **Yugoslavia** (Serbia and Montenegro), and **Macedonia** (which is also the name of the northernmost province of Greece). The small and very poor country of **Albania** also suffered from political unrest and civil war in the 1990s.

The northeast of the Balkan peninsula is occupied by **Bulgaria**, a land of fertile farmland to the south of the river Danube, crossed by the Balkan and Rhodope mountain chains. Its northern neighbour is **Romania**, lying around the forested Carpathian mountain range and the Transylvanian Alps. On the Black Sea coast, the river Danube forms a marshy delta region.

The Balkan peninsula narrows to the south, breaking up into the headland of the Peloponnese and scattered island chains. **Greece** was the centre of Europe's first great civilizations, between 4,000 and 2,000 years ago. The rock of the Acropolis, with its temple, the Parthenon, still towers above the Greek capital, Athens.

Off to market
Romanian farmers gather for a cattle fair at Sugatag. The population as a whole is made up of Romanians, whose language is linked to the Latin language of the ancient Roman empire, as well as Magyars and Gypsies.

The sunflower crop
Sunflowers are grown in many parts of southern Europe. Their seeds may be roasted and eaten as snacks, turned into cooking oil or used to make margarine.

Old-fashioned style
Traditional Bulgarian costumes, with waistcoats, aprons and skirts may still be seen at many festivals or folk dances.

UKRAINE

ROMANIA

Satu Mare
Baia Mare
Somes
Oradea
Cluj-Napoca
Mures
MOLDAVIAN CARPATHIANS
Botosani
Iasi
MOLDOVA
Bacau
Siret

HUNGARY

Arad
Mures
Tîrgu Mures
Alba Iulia
ROMANIA
Galati
Braila

Subotica
Tisza
Timisoara
Deva
Sibiu
Moldoveanu
2,543 m
Brasov
TRANSYLVANIAN ALPS
DOBRUJA

VOJVODINA
Resita

Novi Sad
Belgrade
Jiu
Craiova
Pitesti
Ploiesti
Bucharest
Constanta

Sabac
Smederevo
Negotin
Vidin
Dunarea (Danube)
Ruse
Dobrich

Valjevo
Kragujevac
Cacak
Mikhaylovgrad
Iskur
Pleven
Shumen
Varna
Balchik

Krusevac
Nis
Vratsa
Lovech
Turgovishte
Kamchiya

Novi Pazar
SERBIA
Leskovac
BALKAN MOUNTAINS
Sofia
Kazanluk
Sliven
Burgas

YUGOSLAVIA
TENEGRO
Pristina
Pec
KOSOVO
Urosevac
Pernik
BULGARIA
Tundzha
Yambol
Stara Zagora

gorica
Lake Scutari
Pasardzhik
Maritsa
Musala Peak
2,925 m
Plovdiv
Khaskovo

Mt Korabit
2,751 m
Tetovo
Skopje
Struma
RHODOPE MOUNTAINS
Smolyan
Oresliás

rrës
Tiranë
MACEDONIA
Var dar
PIRIN MTS
Drama
Komotini
Xánthi
BULGARIA

Prilep
Palikaštron
Sérrai
Kaválla
Alexandroúpolis

Elbasan
Lake Ohrid
Bitola
Kilkís
Thásos
Samothrace

Lake Prespa
Edhessa
Thessaloníki
Límnos
MACEDONIA

ALBANIA
Náousa
Aliakmon

Vlore
Ptolemaïs
Mt Olympus
2,917 m
Mt Athos
2,033 m

Gjirokaster

GREECE

Joánnina
Trikkala
Lárisa
Mitilíni

Kérkira
Corfu
Párga
Arta
PINDUS MTS
Kardhítsa
Vólos
Skíathos
Lesbos

Lamia
Skópelos
Skíros

Pálairos
Leukas
Astakós
Agrínion
Akhelóös
Parnassus
2,547 m
Euboea
Kími
Khalkís
AEGEAN SEA
Chios

Cephalonia
Ithaca
Pátrai
Mégara
Marathon
Ándros
Sámos

IONIAN SEA
Amaliás
Lambia
Corinth
Piraeus
Athens
Tínos
Ikaría

Zante
Pírgos
Alfíos
Argos
Láyrion
Kéa
Míkonos
Pátmos

Tripolis
Návplion
Galatás
Kíthnos
Síros
Páros
Léros

Kalamáta
Sparta
PELOPONNESUS
Sérifos
Náxos
Kálimnos
Cos

Areópolis
Mílos
Íos
Astipálaia
Tílos
Rhodes

Neápolis
Thíra
Rhodes
Líndos

Cythera
SEA OF CRETE
Kárpathos

Khaniá
Réthimnon
Iráklion
Mt. Ida
2,456 m
Crete

Islands from volcanoes

The Greek island of Santorini (or Thira) is one of the islands that form the Cyclades in the Aegean Sea. Once a volcano, the island has steep cliffs and narrow, winding streets. It has become a popular destination for tourists.

Clear waters

A waterfall sparkles in the sunshine in Croatia. This is a small country of many landscapes.

FACT BOX

◆ **Slovenia**
Area: 20,250 sq km
Population: 1,990,000
Capital: Ljublana
Official language: Slovenian
Currency: Tolar

◆ **Croatia**
Area: 56,540 sq km
Population: 4,789,000
Capital: Zagreb
Official language: Serbo-Croat
Currency: Croatian dinar

◆ **Bosnia-Herzegovina**
Area: 51,130 sq km
Population: 4,366,000
Capital: Sarajevo
Official language: Serbo-Croat
Currency: Bosnian dinar

◆ **Yugoslavia (Serbia-Montenegro)**
Area: 102,170 sq km
Population: 10,600,000
Capital: Belgrade
Official language: Serbo-Croat
Currency: Dinar

◆ **Macedonian (former Yugoslav) Republic**
Area: 25,715 sq km
Population: 2,173,000
Capital: Skopje
Official language: Macedonian
Currency: Dinar

◆ **Albania**
Area: 28,750 sq km
Population: 3,363,000
Capital: Tiranë
Official language: Albanian
Currency: Lek

◆ **Romania**
Area: 237,500 sq km
Population: 22,767,000
Capital: Bucharest
Official language: Romanian
Currency: Leu

◆ **Bulgaria**
Area: 110,900 sq km
Population: 8,469,000
Capital: Sofia
Official language: Bulgarian
Currency: Lev

◆ **Greece**
Area: 131,985 sq km
Population: 10,500,000
Capital: Athens
Official language: Greek
Currency: Drachma

RUSSIA AND ITS NEIGHBOURS

FOR A LARGE PART OF THIS CENTURY all the countries on this map were part of one huge country, the Soviet Union. That nation was formed in the years after November 1917, when communists seized power from the czars. Communist rule ended in 1991 and many of the regions around the former Soviet borders then broke away to become independent countries.

St Basil's Cathedral, Russia
Moscow is famous for the onion-shaped domes of St Basil's Cathedral. It was built in 1555 by Czar Ivan IV to commemorate the defeat of invading Tartars.

The remaining part of the former Soviet Union was renamed the '**Russian Federation**'. It is still by far the largest country in the world, stretching across two continents, Europe and Asia. Eighty percent of the population are Russians, but the rest belong to one of the many other ethnic groups who live in this enormous region.

Northern Russia is a land of tundra, where deep-frozen soil borders the Arctic Ocean. To the south is the great belt of forest known as taiga, whose spruce trees are heavy with snow during the long, bitter winter. Southern Russia and the **Ukraine** have the fertile black earth of the rolling grasslands known as steppes. The lands to the south of Russia's new borders take in warm, fertile valleys, thin grasslands grazed by sheep and goats, deserts and high mountains.

Russia is rich in minerals, oil, natural gas and timber. Its industries were developed in a hurry during the Soviet years, but at great cost to its people and environment. Russia is still an economic giant, producing machinery, textiles, chemicals and vehicles.

Franz Josef Land

BELARUS

UKRAINE

MOLDOVA

GEORGIA

ARMENIA

AZERBAIJAN

UZBEKISTAN

TURKMENISTAN

KYRGYZSTAN

TAJIKSTAN

FINLAND

ESTONIA

LITHUANIA

RUSSIA

LATVIA

BELARUS
Minsk
Gomel
Chernobyl

UKRAINE Kiev
MOLDOVA
Chisinau

Khar'kov
Odessa
Donetsk
Sevastopol
Rostov-on-Don

BLACK SEA

Mt. Elbrus
5,642 m
Batumi
GEORGIA
Tbilisi
ARMENIA
Yerevan
AZERBAIJAN
AZER.
Baku

TURKEY

TURKMENISTAN
Ashgabat

IRAN

AFGHANISTAN

Murmansk BARENTS SEA

Novaya Zemlya

KARA SEA

Diks

L. Ladoga
St Petersburg
L. Onega
Archangel
Amderma

Salekhard

SIBERIAN LOWLAND

Smolensk
Yaroslavl'
Moscow
Kirov

N. Dvina

Pechora

Volga

Nizhniy Novgorod
Voronezh
Kazan
Perm

Kama

R U S S

Khanty-Mansiysk
Nizhniy Tagil
Ufa
Syzran
Saratov
Samara
Volgograd
Magnitogorsk
Astrakhan
Grozznyy

Don
Volga

URAL MOUNTAINS

Yekaterinburg
Chelyabinsk

Ural

Orsk

Ishim

Irtysh

Tobol'sk

Ob'

Omsk
Novosibirsk
Tor

Aqmola

KAZAKHSTAN

Karaganda
Semey

Caspian Sea

Aral Sea

Syr Dar'ya

TURANIAN PLATEAU

Nukus

Tashauz

UZBEKISTAN

Balkhash

Lake Balkhash

Almaty

CHINA

Bukhara
Tashkent

Amu Dar'ya

Dushanbe
TAJIKISTAN

Bishkek
KYRGYZSTAN

26

Coarse cotton
Cotton of a tough, coarse grade is grown in Uzbekistan. The country is a major world producer, but in this dry land the cotton crop needs a great deal of irrigation, and this has harmed the environment.

Happy Easter!
Many Russians are Christians belonging to the Eastern Orthodox Church. Traditionally, they exchanged beautifully decorated eggs as gifts at Easter.

Wrangel I.

EAST SIBERIAN SEA

RUSSIA

New Siberian Islands

vernaya emlya

LAPTEV SEA

Os. Lyakhovskiy

Delta of the Lena

Nordvik

Anadyr'

Kolyma

KOLYMA LOWLAND

KOLIMA MOUNTAINS

KAMCHATKA PENINSULA

Commander Is.

Indigirka

CHERSKIY RANGE

VERKHOYANSK RANGE

CENTRAL SIBERIAN PLATEAU

Lena

Yakutsk

Magadan

Petropavlovsk-Kamchatskiy

ver Tunguska

Olekminsk

ALDAN MOUNTAINS

DZUGDZHUR

A

Lensk

Lena

STANOVOY RANGE

SEA OF OKHOTSK

Sakhalin

Tatarskiy Proliv

SIKHOTE ALIN'

Yuzhno-Sakhalinsk

gara

YABLONOVVY MOUNTAINS

Amur

Khabarovsk

Bratsk

snoyarsk

Lake Baykal

CHINA

Irkutsk

Ulan-Ude

nisey

:

MONGOLIA

Vladivostok

KAZAKHSTAN

N

In the Caucasus
This woman wears a traditional costume of Dagostan, a part of the Russian Federation which lies between the Caucasus mountains and the Caspian Sea. About 30 different ethnic groups live in this region.

27

FACT BOX

◆ **Russia**
Area: 17,078,005 sq km
Population: 148,673,000
Capital: Moscow
Official language: Russian
Currency: Rouble

◆ **Belarus**
Area: 208,000 sq km
Population: 10,313,000
Capital: Minsk
Official language: Belarussian
Currency: Rouble

◆ **Ukraine**
Area: 603,700 sq km
Population: 52,194,000
Capital: Kiev
Official language:Ukrainian
Currency: Karbovanets

◆ **Moldova**
Area: 33,7000 sq km
Population: 4,356,000
Capital: Chisinau
Official language: Moldovan
Currency: Leu

◆ **Kazakhstan**
Area: 2,717,300 sq km
Population: 17,035,000
Capital: Almaty
Official language: Kazakh
Currency: Tenge

◆ **Armenia**
Area: 30,000 sq km
Population: 3,677,000
Capital: Yerevan
Official language: Armenian
Currencies: Dram, rouble

◆ **Georgia**
Area: 69,700 sq km
Population: 5,471,000
Capital: Tbilisi
Official language: Georgian
Currency: Lari

◆ **Azerbaijan**
Area: 87,000 sq km
Population: 7,398,000
Capital: Baku
Official language: Azeri
Currencies: Manat, rouble

◆ **Turkmenistan**
Area: 488,100 sq km
Population: 3,714,000
Capital: Ashkhabad
Official language: Turkmen
Currency: Manat

◆ **Uzbekistan**
Area: 447,400 sq km
Population: 21,207,000
Capital: Tashkent
Official language: Uzbek
Currencies: Som, rouble

◆ **Tajikistan**
Area: 143,100 sq km
Population: 5,514,000
Capital: Dushanbe
Official language: Tajik
Currency: Rouble

◆ **Kyrgyzstan**
Area: 198,500 sq km
Population: 4,528,000
Capital: Bishkek
Official language: Kyrgyz
Currency: Som

CANADA AND GREENLAND

FACT BOX

◆ **Canada**
Area: 9,922,385 sq km
Population: 30,000,000
Capital: Ottawa
Official languages: French, English

◆ **Greenland**
Area: 2,175,600 sq km
Population: 57,000
Capital: Nuuk (Godthåb)
Official languages: Danish, Inuktitut
Currency: Danish krone

CANADA is the second largest country in the world and yet it is home to only 30 million people. Most Canadians live in the big cities in the south, such as Toronto, Ottawa, Montréal and Vancouver.

The southern provinces take in the St Lawrence River and Seaway, the Great Lakes, the prairies along the United States border and the foggy coasts of the Atlantic and Pacific Oceans.

The severe climate makes it hard for people to live in the northern wilderness, which stretches into the **Arctic Circle**. Here, a broad belt of spruce forest gives way to bare, deep-frozen soil called tundra, and a maze of islands locked in ice.

Canada's wilderness includes rivers, lakes, coasts and forests. It is home to polar bears and seals, caribou, moose, beavers and loons. It also has valuable resources, providing timber, hydroelectric power and minerals, including oil. **Canada** is a wealthy country.

The first Canadians crossed into North America from Asia long ago, when the two continents were joined by land. They were the Native American peoples and they were followed by the Inuit people of the Arctic. Today these two groups make up only four percent of the population. About 40 percent of Canadians are descended from peoples of the British Isles, especially Scots. People of French descent make up 27 percent, and there are also many people of Eastern European and Asian descent.

Canada has two official languages, French and English. In recent years many people in the French-speaking province of Québec have campaigned to become separate from the rest of Canada.

Across the Davis Strait, **Greenland** (or Kallaalit Nunaat) is a self-governing territory of Denmark. Its peoples are descended from both Inuit and Scandinavians.

Map labels

ARCTIC OCEAN

Melville Island
Banks Island
Prince of Wales Island
Victoria Island

BEAUFORT SEA

ALASKA (U.S.A.)
Dawson
Norman Wells
Great Bear Lake
NORTHWEST TERRITORI
YUKON TERRITORY
MACKENZIE MOUNTAINS
Mackenzie
▲ Mt. Logan 5,951 m
Whitehorse
Liard
HORN MOUNTAINS
Yellowknife
Dubawnt Lake
Great Slave Lake
Fort Resolution
Fort Smith
CARIBOU MOUNTAINS
Lake Athabasca
BRITISH COLUMBIA
CANADA
Reindeer Lake
Prince Rupert
QUEEN CHARLOTTE ISLANDS
Peace
Peace River
Prince George
ALBERTA
MANITO
COAST MOUNTAINS
ROCKY MOUNTAINS
Fraser
Edmonton
N. Saskatchewan
Red Deer
Prince Albert
Lak
Vancouver Island
Kamloops
Lake Winn
Winnipegosis
Calgary
Saskatoon
Victoria
Vancouver
Medicine Hat
S. Saskatchewan
SASKATCHEWAN
Lake Manito
Regina
Winnip
UNITED STATES OF AMERICA

Wheat Harvest
Large combine harvesters cross the Canadian prairies. These are natural grasslands which are now largely given over to wheat and cattle production. They occupy parts of Manitoba, Saskatchewan and Alberta and stretch across the border into the northern United States.

Map Labels

LINCOLN SEA

GREENLAND

G R E E N L A N D

...mere ...and

...on Island

BAFFIN BAY

Baffin Island

D a v i s   S t r a i t

D e n m a r k   S t r a i t

FOXE BASIN

Southampton Island

LABRADOR SEA

Hudson Strait

...ats Island

Mansel Island

Ungava Peninsula

HUDSON BAY

...chill

CANADA

Belcher Islands

Feuilles

La Grande Rivière

● Goose Bay

NEWFOUNDLAND

Severn

JAMES BAY

Akimiski Island

OTISH MOUNTAINS

Péribonca

● Gander

Newfoundland   ● St John's

Anticosti Island

Gulf of St. Lawrence

Albany

ONTARIO

QUEBEC

St. Lawrence

PRINCE EDWARD ISLAND

NEW BRUNSWICK

● Charlottetown

NOVA SCOTIA

Lake Nipigon

Quebec ●

Fredericton ●

St John ●

● Halifax

Thunder Bay ●

Lake Superior

Montreal ●

Ottawa ■

ATLANTIC OCEAN

N

Georgian Bay

Lake Huron

Toronto ●

Lake Ontario

Hamilton ●   Niagara Falls ●

Windsor ●

Lake Erie

29

Toronto, Ontario view over city
The CN Tower soars 553 metres above Canada's largest city, Toronto. This is a centre of business and industry built on the shores of Lake Ontario. It is also the capital of the vast province of Ontario.

Arctic travel
In the ice and snow of the Canadian Arctic and Greenland, travelling can be difficult. Snowmobiles, rather like motorcycles with skis instead of wheels, have now mostly replaced the traditional dog sleds.

Ice hockey
Fast and hard, ice hockey is one of Canada's most popular spectator sports. The game was invented in Canada, its rules being drawn up in Montréal in 1879. There are two teams of six skaters. Both Canadian and US teams compete within two major leagues.

USA

THE UNITED STATES OF AMERICA

make up a huge country, which crosses no less than eight time zones. It extends from the Pacific to the Atlantic Oceans, from Canada south to Mexico.

The modern nation was formed by colonists from Europe, who from the 1500s onwards seized and settled the lands of the Native American peoples. In 1776 the British colonies in the east declared their independence, and the new country grew rapidly during the 1800s as it gained territory from France, Mexico and Russia. Today, in addition to the small Native American population, there are Americans whose ancestors originally came from Britain, Ireland, Italy, France, Germany, the Netherlands and Poland. There are African Americans, whose ancestors were brought to America to work as slaves. There are Armenians, Spanish, Chinese, Cubans, Vietnamese and Koreans. All are citizens of the United States.

The nation today is a federation of 50 states, which have the power to pass many of their own laws. The federal capital is at Washington, a large city on the Potomac River, in the District of Columbia (DC). Here is the Congress, made up of a Senate and a House of Representatives, and the White House, the home of the US presidents.

The American economy is the most powerful in the world. The country is rich in minerals, including oil, coal and iron ore. American companies produce computers and software, aircraft, cars and processed foods. There are also many large banks and finance companies. America leads in space exploration and technology. The films and television programmes produced in America are watched by people in many countries around the world.

FACT BOX

- **United States of America**
  Area: 9,363,130 sq km
  Population: 267,700,000
  Capital: Washington DC
  Official language: English
  Currency: US dollar

The woods of Vermont
Vermont is in New England and nicknamed the Green Mountain State. It is famous for its brilliant foliage in the autumn or fall.

Monument Valley, Arizona

This spectacular landscape is sculpted by nature and is formed of red sandstone. There are many Wild West legends rooted here.

The Bald Eagle

This is America's national bird. It has a white head, and a wingspan of up to 2 metres. Its natural habitat is by lakes and rivers, and for food it preys mainly on fish and rodents.

THE UNITED STATES OF AMERICA

N

Grand Forks
MINNESOTA
RTH
KOTA
mestown
Duluth
Lake Superior
Lake Huron
MAINE
Bangor
Augusta
Burlington
Montpelier
VERMONT
NEW HAMPSHIRE
Portland
Concord
arck
Fargo
Red
St. Cloud
Marquette
WISCONSIN
NEW YORK
MASSACHUSETTS
Cape Cod
Aberdeen
Minneapolis
St Paul
Green Bay
MICHIGAN
Rochester
Syracuse
Boston
Providence
James
Sioux Falls
La Crosse
Lake Michigan
Grand Rapids
Buffalo
Albany
Hartford
RHODE ISLAND
erre
OUTH
KOTA
IOWA
Milwaukee
Madison
Detroit
Lansing
Lake Erie
Erie
Windsor
Cleveland
Scranton
PENNSYLVANIA
CONNECTICUT
New York City
NEW JERSEY
Norfolk
Sioux City
Cedar Rapids
Rockford
Chicago
Gary
Toledo
Akron
Harrisburg
Philadelphia
Trenton
Dover
BRASKA
Omaha
Des Moines
Davenport
Peoria
INDIANA
OHIO
Columbus
Pittsburgh
Baltimore
DELAWARE
and Island
Platte
ILLINOIS
Indianapolis
Dayton
WASHINGTON D.C.
Annapolis
MARYLAND
Lincoln
Missouri
Springfield
Cincinnati
Ohio
WEST VIRGINIA
Chesapeake Bay
Kansas City
Jefferson City
Louisville
Frankfort
Charleston
Richmond
VIRGINIA
Abilene
Salina
Topeka
St. Louis
Evansville
Lexington
Roanoke
Norfolk
ANSAS
MISSOURI
Paducah
KENTUCKY
Greensboro
Raleigh
Cape Hatteras
Hutchinson
Joplin
Knoxville
Winston-Salem
NORTH CAROLINA
Wichita
Springfield
Nashville
APPALACHIAN MOUNTAINS
Charlotte
marron
Tulsa
ARKANSAS
TENNESSEE
Chattanooga
Greenville
Wilmington
OKLAHOMA
Fort Smith
Memphis
Alabama
SOUTH CAROLINA
Cape Fear
Oklahoma City
Arkansas
Tennessee
Birmingham
Atlanta
Columbia
Augusta
Charleston
Red River
Tupelo
Macon
Wichita Falls
Texarkana
Little Rock
Greenville
ALABAMA
Columbus
Savannah
ne
Brazos
Dallas
Fort Worth
Shreveport
Meridian
Montgomery
GEORGIA
EXAS
Waco
Alexandria
LOUISIANA
Jackson
MISSISSIPPI
Mississippi
Mobile
Albany
Jacksonville
ngelo
Austin
Beaumont
Baton Rouge
Biloxi
Pensacola
Tallahassee
St. Augustine
Daytona Beach
Houston
Port Arthur
New Orleans
Mississippi Delta
Cape Canaveral
Orlando
San Antonio
Galveston
Tampa
St. Petersburg
FLORIDA
West Palm Beach
Corpus Christi
GULF OF MEXICO
Fort Myers
Lake Okeechobee
Laredo
Miami
Brownsville
Key West
Florida Keys
Straits of Florida

31

The northeastern United States have a mild climate, although winter snowfall can be heavy and summers can be warm. Inland from the rocks and stormy shores of the Atlantic coast are the woodlands of the New England region, which turn to every shade of red and gold in the autumn. Here there are broad rivers and neat little towns dating back to the days of the early settlers, as well as the historic city of Boston, Massachusetts. In the far north the Great Lakes mark the border with Canada. On this border are the spectacular Niagara Falls, a major tourist attraction which also provides valuable hydroelectric power. The Appalachian mountain ranges run for 2,400 kilometres from north to south, through the eastern United States.

The northeastern United States include centres of industry and mining, and large cities with gleaming skyscrapers, sprawling suburbs, road and rail networks. New York City, centred around the island of Manhattan, is the business capital of the United States and also a lively centre of arts and entertainment. To many people, New York City is a symbol of America – fast-moving and energetic, a melting pot of different peoples and cultures. The northern city of Detroit is a centre of the motor industry, and Chicago, on the windy shores of Lake Michigan, is another bustling city of skyscrapers, and an important centre of business and manufacture.

Travelling south from the Delaware River and the great city of Philadelphia, you come to the federal District of Columbia, the site of Washington, capital city of the United States. Approaching the American South, you pass into warmer country where tobacco and cotton are grown in the red earth. The long peninsula of Florida extends southwards into the Caribbean Sea, fringed by sandy islands called keys. Along the Gulf coast the climate is hot and very humid, with creeks known as bayous and tangled swamps which are home to alligators.

Hurricanes are common in late summer and autumn. New Orleans, the home of jazz, has many picturesque old buildings with wrought-iron verandas. It lies 170 kilometres above the mouth of the Mississippi River, which together with the mighty Missouri drains the centre of the continent. Texas is a huge state which borders Mexico along the Rio Grande. Dry and dusty, it makes its living from cattle ranching and oil.

Prairies once covered the great plains of the Midwest, the home of vast herds of bison or buffalo. Today the grasslands are largely given over to farming vegetable crops and grain, or to cattle ranching. The wheat and maize produced on the Prairies have led to them being called the 'breadbasket of the world'.

Barren, stony 'badlands' rise towards the rugged Rocky Mountain ranges, which form the backbone of the United States as they stretch from the Canadian border south to Mexico. Southwards and westwards again there are large areas of burning desert, salt flats and canyons, where over the ages the rocks have been worn into fantastic shapes by wind and water. In places the Grand Canyon of Arizona is 24 kilometres wide and two kilometres deep, a spectacular gorge cut out by the waters of the Colorado River.

Jambalaya!

Rice, seafood, green peppers and hot spices make up this delicious dish from New Orleans, in Louisiana. The people of this city include many of French and African descent, and this shows in its cooking.

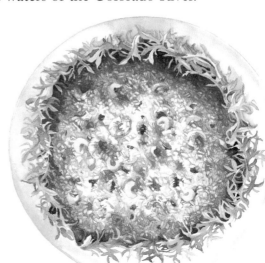

The Statue of Liberty

This huge monument, a gift from the people of France in 1886, was the first sight of America for many immigrants.

Badwater, in California's harsh Death Valley, is the lowest point in the United States, 86 metres below sea level.

The Sierra, Cascade and Coast ranges run parallel with the beautiful Pacific coast. The warm beaches, pines and gigantic redwood trees of California stretch northwards to the ferny forests of Oregon and Washington State, which is rainy and cool. Irrigation has made it possible to farm large areas of California, which produce citrus fruits and grape vines. Major cities of the west include Los Angeles, which takes in the world-famous film studios of Hollywood, beautiful San Francisco, set on a wide bay which can be warm and sparkling blue or shrouded in cool sea-fog, and the busy northern port of Seattle.

The United States has a northern outpost in oil-rich Alaska, its largest state. Alaska was purchased from Russia in 1867. Bordered by Canada, the Alaskan wilderness stretches into the remote Arctic, a deep frozen land of mountains and tundra.

Its islands are inhabited by large grizzly bears and its waters by schools of migrating whales.

Baseball
Baseball is the the big summer-season game in the USA. It is played with a bat and ball and there are two teams of nine players.

Mount McKinley, at 6,194 metres, is the highest point not just in the United States, but in all of North America.

Far to the west, in the Pacific Ocean, the Hawaiian Islands are also part of the United States. Tourists come here to enjoy the warm climate and the surf and to see the islands' spectacular volcanoes.

The United States also governs or has special links with various other territories, such as American Samoa, the Northern Marianas and the Midway Islands in the Pacific Ocean. Puerto Rico and the US Virgin Islands in the Caribbean are also governed by the United States.

The United States has close economic links with its neighbours, Canada and Mexico, through the North American Free Trade Agreement of 1994. It is also a member of many other international groupings, such as the the North Atlantic Treaty Organization (NATO), a military alliance which links it with Western and Central Europe.

As the world's most powerful country, the influence of the United States is to be seen in many other lands. Films and television programmes have made the American way of life influential around the world. Hamburgers and soft drinks are now bought in many other countries. American blues and jazz has influenced all kinds of popular music and American slang is used by people around the world.

Manhattan
The centre of New York City is built over the island of Manhattan. Unable to build outwards, architects have built upwards. The skyline includes many famous skyscrapers. These twin towers belong to the World Trade Centre.

Cops and crime
American policemen and detectives fight city crime. Their work has been made famous around the world by countless films and television series.

Heart of the nation
The impressive Capitol building is at the centre of Washington, District of Columbia. It is used by the United States Congress and was constructed between 1851 and 1863.

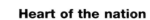

Blast-off!
The space shuttle leaves Earth on another mission. The United States has been a pioneer of space exploration since the 1960s.

MEXICO, CENTRAL AMERICA & THE CARIBBEAN

Ancient stones
Many great civilizations developed in ancient times in Mexico and Central America. Statues like this, called chacmools, were used during human sacrifices.

MEXICO is a large, mountainous country with a tropical climate. It stretches southwards from the Rio Grande on the United States border, and meets the Pacific Ocean in the west and the Gulf of Mexico in the east.

Mexico is a land of deserts, forests and volcanoes, dotted with the spectacular ruins of ancient Native American civilizations, such as the Maya, Toltec and Aztec. Mexico City, built on the site of an ancient Aztec city, is a vast, sprawling centre of population.

To the south, **Central America** narrows to a thin strip of land called the isthmus of Panama. Guatemala, Belize, Honduras, El Salvador, Nicaragua, Costa Rica and Panama are all small nations that live mostly by farming tropical crops such as bananas, coffee and sugar-cane. Many Mexicans and Central Americans are of Native American, Spanish or mixed descent.

Birds of a feather
The quetzal is a brilliantly coloured bird. It lives in rainforests from southern Mexico to Panama, where it feeds on berries and fruits.

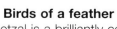

Many people in Mexico and Central America are poor and the region has a long history of political strife and civil war.

The **Caribbean Sea** is part of the Atlantic Ocean and is dotted with beautiful islands in warm, blue seas. These were once home to Native American peoples such as the Arawaks and the Caribs, after whom the region is named. Then came European invaders, including the Spanish, Dutch, French and British. Most of today's Caribbeans are descended from West Africans who were brought in as slaves by the early settlers. Caribbean islanders live by fishing, farming, manufacture and tourism. Favourite sports include baseball in Cuba and cricket in Jamaica and Barbados. The region is famous for its range of popular music, from calypso to salsa, from reggae to soca.

Coconut grove
Palms line sandy beaches in the Central American republic of Costa Rica. Coconuts are common around the tropical coasts of Central America and the Caribbean.

FACT BOX

◆ **Mexico**
Area: 1,972,545 sq km
Population: 95,700,000
Capital: Mexico City
Main language: Spanish
Currency: Mexican peso

◆ **Belize**
Area: 22,965 sq km
Population: 205,000
Capital: Belmopan
Main language: English
Currency: Belize dollar

◆ **Costa Rica**
Area: 50,900 sq km
Population: 3,500,000
Capital: San José
Main language: Spanish
Currency: Costa Rican colón

◆ **El Salvador**
Area: 21,395 sq km
Population: 5,900,000
Capital: San Salvador
Main language: Spanish
Currency: El Salvador colón

◆ **Guatemala**
Area: 108,890 sq km
Population: 11,200,000
Capital: Guatemala City
Main language: Spanish
Currency: Quetzal

◆ **Honduras**
Area: 112,085 sq km
Population: 5,800,000
Capital: Tegucigalpa
Main language: Spanish
Currency: Lempira

◆ **Nicaragua**
Area: 148,000 sq km
Population: 4,400,000
Capital: Managua
Main language: Spanish
Currency: Córdoba

◆ **Panama**
Area: 78,515 sq km
Population: 2,700,000
Capital: Panama City
Main language: Spanish
Currency: Balboa

◆ **Antigua and Barbuda**
Area: 442 sq km
Population: 100,000
Capital: St Johns
Main language: English
Currency: East Caribbean dollar

◆ **Bahamas**
Area: 13,865 sq km
Population: 300,000
Capital: Nassau
Main language: English
Currency: Bahamian dollar

◆ **Barbados**
Area: 430 sq km
Population: 300,000
Capital: Bridgetown
Main language: English
Currency: Barbados dollar

◆ **Cuba**
Area: 114,525 sq km
Population: 11,100,000
Capital: Havana
Main language: Spanish
Currency: Cuban peso

◆ **Dominica**
Area: 751 sq km
Population: 100,000
Capital: Roseau
Main language: English
Currency: East Caribbean dollar

◆ **Dominican Republic**
Area: 48,440 sq km
Population: 8,200,000
Capital: Santiago
Main language: Spanish
Currency: Peso

◆ **Grenada**
Area: 345 sq km
Population: 100,000
Capital: St George's
Main language: English
Currency: East Caribbean dollar

◆ **Haiti**
Area: 27,750 sq km
Population: 6,600,000
Capital: Port-au-Prince
Main language: French
Currency: Gourde

◆ **Jamaica**
Area: 11,425 sq km
Population: 2,600,000
Capital: Kingston
Main language: English
Currency: Jamaican dollar

◆ **St Christoper (St Kitts) – Nevis**
Area: 261 sq km
Population: 44,000
Capital: Basseterre
Main language: English
Currency: East Caribbean dollar

◆ **St Lucia**
Area: 616 sq km
Population: 139,000
Capital: Castries
Main language: English
Currency: East Caribbean dollar

◆ **St Vincent and the Grenadines**
Area: 389 sq km
Population: 111,000
Capital: Kingstown
Main language: English
Currency: East Caribbean dollar

◆ **Trinidad and Tobago**
Area: 5,130 sq km
Population: 1,300,000
Capital: Port of Spain
Main language: English
Currency: Trinidad & Tobago dollar

BAHAMAS
BAHAMAS

ANTIGUA AND BARBUDA

Turks & Caicos Islands (U.K.)
ros I.
ASSAU

PUERTO RICO

DOMINICA

Virgin Is. (U.K. & U.S.)

ANTIGUA & BARBUDA

magüey
DOMINICAN REPUBLIC
San Juan
Puerto Rico (U.S.)
ST. KITTS & NEVIS

Montserrat (U.K.)
Guadeloupe (FR.)
DOMINICA

ntiago
Cuba
HAITI
Santo Domingo

Port-au-Prince
R E A T E R   A N T I L L E S
Martinique (FR.)
ST. LUCIA
BARBADOS

Kingston
AMAICA   C A R I B B E A N   S E A
DOMINICAN REPUBLIC
ST. VINCENT & THE GRENADINES
GRENADA

L E S S E R   A N T I L L E S
TRINIDAD & TOBAGO

JAMAICA

HAITI

Netherlands Antilles

GRENADA

HONDURAS

PANAMA
NAMA
nama City
lf of ama

C O L O M B I A

ST VINCENT AND GRENADINES

TRINIDAD AND TOBAGO

ST LUCIA

BARBADOS

ST KITTS AND NEVIS

People of Panama
The Kuna are an indigenous people who live on the coasts and islands of Panama and Colombia. They mostly live by fishing and are well known for their craft work, which includes wood carving and the making of molas, the colourful blouses being worn here.

35

NORTHERN ANDEAN COUNTRIES

N

THE ANDES MOUNTAINS extend down the whole length of South America, from north to south. They rise in Colombia, the country which borders the narrow land link with Central America, the Isthmus of Panama.

Colombia is a beautiful country with three ranges of the Andes running through it. The mountains slope east to grasslands and then to rainforest. The chief cities are on the coast, which is warm and humid, or in the cooler mountain regions. The mountains are mined for gold, emeralds, salt and coal.

The Andes rise to 6,267 metres above sea level at Chimborazo in **Ecuador**. Bananas and sugar-cane are grown here. In the cooler foothills of the Andes coffee is an important crop. To the east of the mountains are rainforests, where oil is drilled. Ecuador is the second largest oil producer in South America after Venezuela.

In the 1400s, **Peru** was the centre of the mighty Inca empire, an advanced Native American civilization which produced beautiful textiles and jewellery in gold and precious stones. Ruined Inca cities such as Machu Picchu still perch high amongst the peaks of the Andes. Terraced hillsides allow crops such as potatoes to be grown in the mountains. Fishing is important along the foggy Pacific coast. In the far east, rivers flow through tropical forests into the river Amazon.

Lake Titicaca lies high in the Andes on the border between Peru and **Bolivia.** Bolivia is an inland country which lies across the high plateau of the Altiplano, where most Bolivians live, and stretches into hot, humid rainforest in the east. The city of La Paz is the world's highest capital city, at 3,660 metres above sea level. Bolivia produces tin, timber, rubber and potatoes.

The lands of the northern Andes are home to many Native Americans, such as the Quechua and Aymara peoples. The whole region was ruled by Spain from the 1500s to the early 1800s, and Spanish is spoken throughout the region as well as a number of Native

Inca crafts

This mask was made by Inca goldsmiths in Peru. The Incas came to power in the 1400s and were famous for their beautiful work with gold.

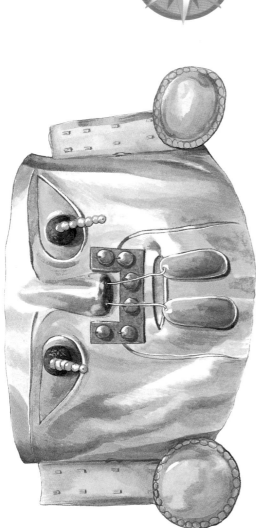

COLOMBIA

ECUADOR

PERU

Point. Gallinas

Barranquilla

Cartagena • — Cristobal Colón
5,775 m

Cape
Corrientes

Medellín
Manizales
Pereira •
Ibagué •

Buenaventura

Cali • Neiva
Nevado del Huila
5,750 m
Pasto •

Point
Galera   Quito

ECUADOR

Guayaquil • Chimborazo
6,267 m
Gulf of
Guayaquil

Piura

VENEZUELA

COLOMBIA
Bogotá

Meta

Guaviare

Magdalena
Cauca
S
N

Caquetá

Putumayo

Amazon

Iquitos

Marañón

ZIL

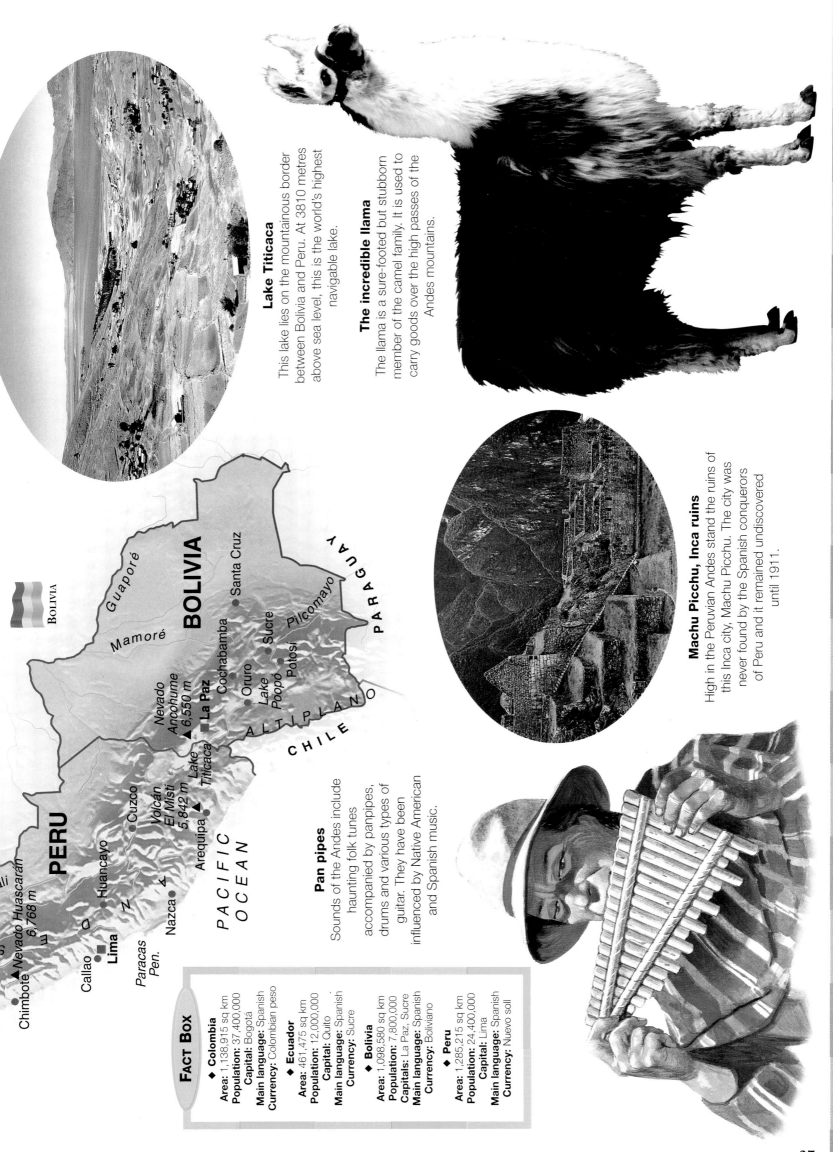

Lake Titicaca

This lake lies on the mountainous border between Bolivia and Peru. At 3810 metres above sea level, this is the world's highest navigable lake.

The incredible llama

The llama is a sure-footed but stubborn member of the camel family. It is used to carry goods over the high passes of the Andes mountains.

Machu Picchu, Inca ruins

High in the Peruvian Andes stand the ruins of this Inca city, Machu Picchu. The city was never found by the Spanish conquerors of Peru and it remained undiscovered until 1911.

Pan pipes

Sounds of the Andes include haunting folk tunes accompanied by panpipes, drums and various types of guitar. They have been influenced by Native American and Spanish music.

Fact Box

◆ Colombia
Area: 1,138,915 sq km
Population: 37,400,000
Capital: Bogotá
Main language: Spanish
Currency: Colombian peso

◆ Ecuador
Area: 461,475 sq km
Population: 12,000,000
Capital: Quito
Main language: Spanish
Currency: Sucre

◆ Bolivia
Area: 1,098,580 sq km
Population: 7,800,000
Capitals: La Paz, Sucre
Main language: Spanish
Currency: Boliviano

◆ Peru
Area: 1,285,215 sq km
Population: 24,400,000
Capital: Lima
Main language: Spanish
Currency: Nuevo soll

BOLIVIA

PERU
Chimbote
Nevado Huascarán 6,768 m
Huancayo
Cuzco
Volcán El Misti 5,842 m
Arequipa
Lake Titicaca
Callao
Lima
Nazca
Paracas Pen.

PACIFIC OCEAN

BOLIVIA
Guaporé
Mamoré
Nevado Ancohume 6,550 m
La Paz
Cochabamba
Santa Cruz
Oruro
Lake Poopó
Potosí
Sucre
Pilcomayo
ALTIPLANO
CHILE
PARAGUAY

Gulf of Venezuela
Netherlands Antilles
Port of Spain
TRINIDAD & TOBAGO
GUYANA

Maracaibo
Caracas
Barcelona
Lake Maracaibo
ANDES MTS.
LLANOS
Orinoco
Orinoco Delta

Pico Bolívar 5,002 m
VENEZUELA
Angel Falls
Georgetown
GUYANA
Paramaribo
SURINAM

COLOMBIA
G U I A N A
Branco
H I G H L A N D S
SURINAM
Cayenne
FRENCH GUIANA

Orinoco
Negro
VENEZUELA

Pico da Neblina 3014 m
Japurá
Macapá
Marajó Bay
Marajó I.
Belèm
São Marcos Bay
FRENCH GUIANA

Manaus
Amazon
Santarém
São Lu

S E L V A S
Madeira
Tapajós
Xingu
Tocantins
Teresina

Juruá
Purus
Aripuanã
Araguaia
Parnaiba

Rio Branco
Jiparaná
Arinos
BRAZIL
Sobradinho Reservoir

PERU
SERRA DOS PARECIS
Guaporé
BOLIVIA
MATO GROSSO PLATEAU
Brasília
BRAZILIAN HIGHLAND

Cuiabá
Goiânia
Uberlandia

Campo Grande
Belo Horizonte

Coffee beans
Brazil is the world's biggest producer of coffee. The crop is mostly grown in the south, on large estates and is exported worldwide.

PARAGUAY
Paraná
Campos

São Paulo
Rio de Janeiro
Cape Frio
Santos

Itaipu Res.
Itguaçu Falls
SERRA DO MAR
Curitiba
BRAZIL

ARGENTINA
Uruguay
Florianópolis

Santa Maria
Pôrto Alegre
Patos Lagoon
URUGUAY
Mirim Lake

N

Rio panorama
A huge statue of Christ stands high above the Brazilian port of Rio de Janeiro.

38

BRAZIL AND ITS NEIGHBOURS

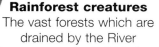

BRAZIL is South America's largest nation. It includes grasslands, fertile plateaus and dry areas of scrub.

About a third of the country is taken up by tropical rainforests. All kinds of rare plants, parrots, snakes and monkeys live in these dense, dripping forests, which are under threat from road-builders, farmers, miners and loggers. The forests are crossed by hundreds of rivers, which drain into the wide, muddy waters of the Amazon, one of the world's two longest rivers. The river basin of the Amazon is the world's largest, covering 7,045,000 square kilometres. Most Brazilians live in the big cities of the Atlantic coast, such as Rio de Janeiro and São Paolo. The country has rich resources, but many of the population are poor people who live in shacks built on the outskirts of the city. Brasília, with its broad avenues and high-rise buildings, was specially built as the country's new capital city in the 1960s.

To the northeast of Brazil, on the Caribbean coast, is **Venezuela**. This land, crossed by the Orinoco River, includes rainforests, high mountains and the tropical grassy plains of the Llanos. The beautiful Angel Falls (the world's highest at 979 metres) provide hydroelectric power, while Lake Maracaibo, in the northwest, is rich in oil.

The three other countries on the Caribbean coast are **Guyana**, **Surinam** and **French Guiana**. The first was once a British colony, the second was a Dutch colony and the third is still an overseas department governed by France. Most people live in the humid regions of the coast, while the rainforests and mountains of the remote south are more sparsely populated. Crops include sugar-cane, coffee, rice and bananas. An important mineral is bauxite, used in the making of aluminium.

Many different ethnic groups live in the region as a whole, including Native American peoples who have had to struggle to survive ever since Europeans invaded the region in the 1500s. The population of northern South America also includes many people of Asian, African, European and mixed descent, with ancestors from Spain, Portugal, Italy, Germany, France, Netherlands and Britain.

Map labels

taleza

Natal

SERTÃO

Recife

ão Francisco

Maceió

vador

FACT BOX

◆ **Brazil**
Area: 8,511,965 sq km
Population: 160,300,000
Capital: Brasília
Main language: Portuguese
Currency: Cruzeiro real

◆ **Venezuela**
Area: 912,045 sq km
Population: 22,600,000
Capital: Caracas
Main language: Spanish
Currency: Bolívar

◆ **Guyana**
Area: 214,970 sq km
Population: 800,000
Capital: Georgetown
Main language: English
Currency: Guyana dollar

◆ **Surinam**
Area: 163,820 sq km
Population: 446,000
Capital: Paramaribo
Official language: Dutch
Currency: Surinam guilder

◆ **French Guiana**
Area: 91,000 sq km
Population: 300,000
Capital: Cayenne
Main language: French
Currency: French franc

Rainforest creatures
The vast forests which are drained by the River Amazon, support all kinds of wildlife, such as this brightly coloured macaw. Sadly, many species are threatened by the clearance of the forests by farmers and illegal traders in wildlife.

Fishing for a living
A fishing crew check their tackle as children play on the beach. This scene is near Salvador, capital of the tropical Bahía region in northeastern Brazil.

Yanomami hunters
About 13,000 Yanomami people live in Venezuela and another 8000 in Brazil. They live by hunting, fishing and growing food in the rainforest.

ARGENTINA AND ITS NEIGHBOURS

THE SOUTHERN PART of South America stretches from the hot and humid Gran Chaco region to the cold and stormy waters of Tierra del Fuego and Cape Horn.

The largest country of this region is **Argentina**. Its highly populated capital is Buenos Aires on the river Plate. More than eight out of every ten Argentineans are city dwellers. However it was the country's cattle-farming regions – the Pampa grasslands and the northeast – that in the last 150 years brought wealth to the country and attracted large numbers of settlers from Europe. Argentina's western borders follow the high peak of the Andes range, which reach their highest point at Cerro Aconcagua (6,959 metres above sea level). To the south are the windswept plateaus of Patagonia, largely given over to sheep farming. The port of Ushuaia is the southernmost town in the world.

Northwards from Buenos Aires, across the river Plate, lies Montevideo, capital of **Uruguay**. This is another country which raises cattle and sheep, and whose rich grasslands and mild climate attracted European settlers. Neighbouring **Paraguay** is far from the coast. Most of its people farm the hills and plains of the east. Few live in the hot wilderness of the Gran Chaco.

To the west of the Andes is **Chile**, which covers a long and narrow area. Here is one of the driest regions on Earth, the Atacama desert. It also includes fertile orchards and productive vineyards, the big city of Santiago and the spectacular glaciers of the southern Andes. Spanish is spoken throughout the region, and some Native American languages such as Guaraní may also be heard.

Armadillo

The head and body of the armadillo is covered by an armour of plates made of horny and bony material. These usually nocturnal animals, feed mainly on insects and rest in a burrow by day.

Paraná River, Paraguay

Separating Paraguay and Argentina the Parana River flows some 4,500 km. The English explorer Sebastian Cabot was the first to sail up it in 1526.

BRAZIL

PARAGUAY

Cuidad del Este

Concepción

Verde

Pilcomayo

Asunción

Alto Paraná

Posadas

PARAGUAY

CHACO

Bermejo

Paraguay

Formosa

Resistencia

Corrientes

MESOPOTAMIA

Paraná

Uruguay

Salto

Concordia

Paysandú

Negro

URUGUAY

GRAN

Salado

Santiago del Estero

San Miguel de Tucumán

Mar Chiquito

Córdoba

Santa Fe

Paraná

Rosario

Río Cuarto

SIERRA DE CÓRDOBA

Salta

BOLIVIA

Catamarca

La Rioja

San Juan

Mendoza

Aconcagua 6,959 m

Santiago

CHILE

Arica

Iquique

Antofagasta

Calama

ATACAMA DESERT

Ojos del Salado 6,880 m

Copiapó

Coquimbo

Pta. Lengua de Vaca

Valparaíso

40

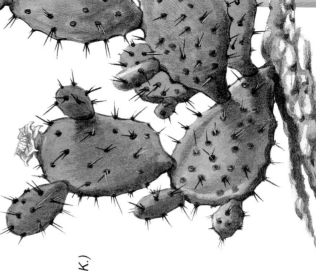

◆ **Argentina**
Area: 2,780,090 sq km
Population: 35,600,000
Capital: Buenos Aires
Official language: Spanish
Currency: Peso

◆ **Chile**
Area: 736,000 sq km
Population: 14,600,000
Capital: Santiago
Official language: Spanish
Currency: Peso

◆ **Paraguay**
Area: 406,750 sq km
Population: 5,100,000
Capital: Asunción
Official language: Spanish
Currency: Guarani

◆ **Uruguay**
Area: 176,210 sq km
Population: 3,200,000
Capital: Montevideo
Official language: Spanish
Currency: Peso

URUGUAY

Buenos Aires by night
The Monument of the Two Congresses stands in front of the domed Palace of Congress, built in 1906. The Argentinian capital is a large, lively city.

SOUTH GEORGIA (U.K.)

N

Prickly Pear
The flesh and seeds of the peeled fruit of the prickly pear have a pleasant taste. This cactus is low-growing and has flat oval stem joints and bright yellow flowers and occurs in Central and South America.

ARGENTINA

Cape San Antonio
Mar del Plata
Cape Corrientes
Bahía Blanca
Bahia Blanca
Colorado
Viedma
San Matias Gulf
Negro
Neuquén
Valdés Peninsula
Rawson
Limay
Chubut
Comodoro Rivadavia
San Jorge Gulf
C. Tres Puntas
Chico
Puerto Deseado
Deseado
Lake Buenos Aires
Chico
Santo Cruz
Puerto Santa Cruz
Bahía Grande
Río Gallegos
Strait of Magellan
Punta Arenas
Tierra del Fuego
C. San Diego
Ushuaia
Santa Inés I.
Cape Horn

ARGENTINA

FALKLAND/MALVINAS ISLANDS
West Falkland
East Falkland
Stanley

CHILE
Chillán
Concepción
Pta. Lavapié
Temuco
Valdivia
Pta. de la Galera
Osorno
Puerto Montt
Chiloé I.
C. Quilán
LOS CHONOS ARCHIPELAGO
Penas Gulf
Wellington I.
REINA ADELAIDA ARCHIPELAGO

PACIFIC OCEAN

ANDES
PATAGONIA

Mountains, Southern Chile
The long, narrow country of Chile has vast differences in climate. There is hot desert in the north, Mediterranean type in the centre and cool, humid conditions in the south. Some mountains are permanently snow-capped.

41

Turkish women
These women are from the port of Kas in southern Turkey. They are kneading dough and making pastry. Many Muslim women cover their heads with scarves or full veils.

ASIA

SOUTHWEST ASIA

SOUTHWEST ASIA IS SOMETIMES described as the Near East or the Middle East. Its peoples include Greek Cypriots, Turks, Jews, Arabs, Kurds and Iranians.

The region has seen many political disputes and wars in recent years – between Greeks and Turks on Cyprus, between Palestinian Arabs and Jews in Israel, between Iraqi and Iranians and between Iraqui and Kuwaiti Arabs. The Kurds, whose homeland is occupied by **Iraq**, **Iran** and **Turkey**, have also been at the centre of conflict.

It was in Southwest Asia that the world's first civilizations grew up, between the rivers Tigris and Euphrates, over 6,000 years ago. The region later gave birth to three world faiths – Judaism, Christianity and Islam. In the days of the Roman empire the Jews were scattered from their homeland, and over the centuries their culture spread to Spain, Central and Eastern Europe and the Americas. Arab armies and traders took the Islamic faith into Africa and Spain, and Arab scholars made great advances in mathematics and astronomy. From the 1500s the Turks established a great empire which stretched from Central Europe to the Indian Ocean.

Southwest Asia includes vast deserts, in the Arabian peninsula and in eastern Iran. It also takes in fertile plains, the marshes of southern Iraq and mountain ranges of Turkey and Iran. The north of the region borders the Black Sea and the Caspian Sea, grassy steppes and the Caucasus mountains. To the east lies Afghanistan, Pakistan and the Indian sub-continent.

The region's most valuable resource is oil, which brings wealth to the governments of the lands around the Persian Gulf. However many ordinary people of Southwest Asia remain poor, living by herding goats, sheep or camels. In Israel and some other regions irrigation has made it possible to grow crops in harsh, dry environments. Oranges, dates, grapes and many kinds of nuts are grown in the region.

A summons to prayer
Mosques, like this one in Kuwait, have tall towers called minarets. From here, faithful Muslims are called to prayer. This message is often broadcast from loudspeakers. Muslims are expected to pray five times a day.

Wealth from oil
These supertankers are taking oil on board, off the coast of Saudi Arabia. Wealth from oil has transformed the economy of the Middle East and given great power to the many small countries around the Persian Gulf.

IRAQ

Ararat 85 m

Aras

Tabriz

CASPIAN SEA

Rasht

Lake Urmia

Babol

ELBURZ MTS.

Mashhad

TURKMENISTAN

N

AFGHANISTAN

As Sulaymaniyah

Hamadan

Qom

▲ Mt. Damavand 5,604 m

Tehran

Dasht-e-Kavir

kuk

ghdad

Bakhtaran

Kashan

I R A N

KUWAIT

ZAGROS MOUNTAINS

Esfahan

Dasht-e-Lut

BAHRAIN

an Nasiriyah

Ahvaz

Yazd

Basra

Abadan

Kerman

IRAN

KUWAIT

Shiraz

Zahedan

■ **Kuwait**

Bushehr

The Gulf

Bandar Abbas

Ad Dahna

Ad Damman

Bandar e Lengeh

Jask

Al Manamah

Strait of Hormuz

Dubai

QUATAR

qra

BAHRAIN

QATAR

Gulf of Oman

Abu Dhabi

■ **Doha**

■ **Muscat**

Riyadh

UNITED ARAB EMIRATES

▲ *Jabal Ash Sham 3,035 m*

UNITED ARAB EMIRATES

A B I A

Sur

O M A N

Masirah I.

OMAN

(R u b ' a l K h a l i Empty Quarter)

On the move
In many parts of Southwest Asia people live as nomads, wandering with their herds from one pasture to another, or following ancient trade routes.

Salalah

Kuria Muria Is.

Tarim

Hadramaut

n'a

Y E M E N

YEMEN

Al Mukalla

Gulf of Aden

Socotra (YEMEN)

'Abd al kuri

INDIA AND ITS NEIGHBOURS

SOUTHERN ASIA stretches south into the Indian Ocean, forming a landmass so large that it sometimes called the 'sub-continent'. Its northern limits are marked by the Himalaya and Karakoram mountain ranges. These include many of the world's highest peaks and reach 8,848 metres above sea level at Everest, on Nepal's border with China.

The ranges pass through eastern Afghanistan, the Kashmir region on the border of India and Pakistan, India itself and the small mountain kingdoms of **Nepal** and **Bhutan**. Melting snows flow south from the mountains to form the five great rivers of the Punjab and also the mighty Ganges, which winds across the fertile plains of northern India before crossing Bangladesh into a maze of waterways around the Bay of Bengal. This area suffers from devastating floods.

Central and southern **India** form a triangular plateau called the Deccan, fringed on the east and west by the mountainous Ghats. These slopes are forested, catching the full force of the monsoon winds which bring rains from the Indian Ocean. For most of the year India is extremely hot and dry. Indian Ocean nations include the beautiful, tropical island of **Sri Lanka** and a chain of very low coral islands, the **Maldives.**

Advanced civilizations had developed around the river Indus by about 2500BC, and great religions grew up in India over the ages, including Hinduism, Buddhism and Sikhism. Invaders and traders brought Islam to the region. India today is a fascinating mixture of cultures, with over 800 different languages and dialects. There are many different customs, dress and foods. Spicy dishes from India are now popular everywhere.

The Indian sub-continent has a vast population, with many hungry mouths to feed. Many people make their living by farming, growing wheat, rice, millet, sugarcane, coconut and tea. Most industries are based in the highly populated cities of India and Pakistan.

Himalayan peaks

Breathtaking Mount Makalu, on the border between Nepal and China, rises to 8,470 metres above sea level. Eighty-eight percent of the world's mountains over 7,315 metres rise within the Himalaya-Karakoram ranges, many of them in the kingdom of Nepal.

AFGHANISTAN

PAKISTAN

TURKMENISTAN

TAJIKISTAN

AFGHANISTAN **Kabul**

HINDU

• Mazar-e-Sharif

• Herat

• Farah

• Qandahar

RIGESTAN DESERT

Khyber Pass Peshawar

Islamabad Rawalpindi

Quetta

BALUCHISTAN PLATEAU

PAKISTAN

Sukkur

Hyderabad

Karachi

Gulf of K

K2

KARAKORAM AREA 8,611m

DISPUTED

Srinagar

JAMMU & KASHMIR

Lahore

Faisalabad Amritsar

Multan PUNJAB

Bahawalpur Sutlej

Indus

SULAIMAN RANGE

GREAT INDIAN DESERT (THAR DESERT)

n p u l

Jodhpur

Udaipur

Ajmer

Jaipur

Delhi

New Delhi

Agra

Gwalior

Yamuna

Bareilly

Lucknow Kanpur

Nanda Devi 7,817m

Tibet (CHINA)

NEPAL

Annapurna 8,078m M Mt Everest 8,848m

Katmandu

Ghagara

NEPAL

BHUTAN

Thimphu Y

A

L

BHUTAN

Brahmaputra

A HILLS

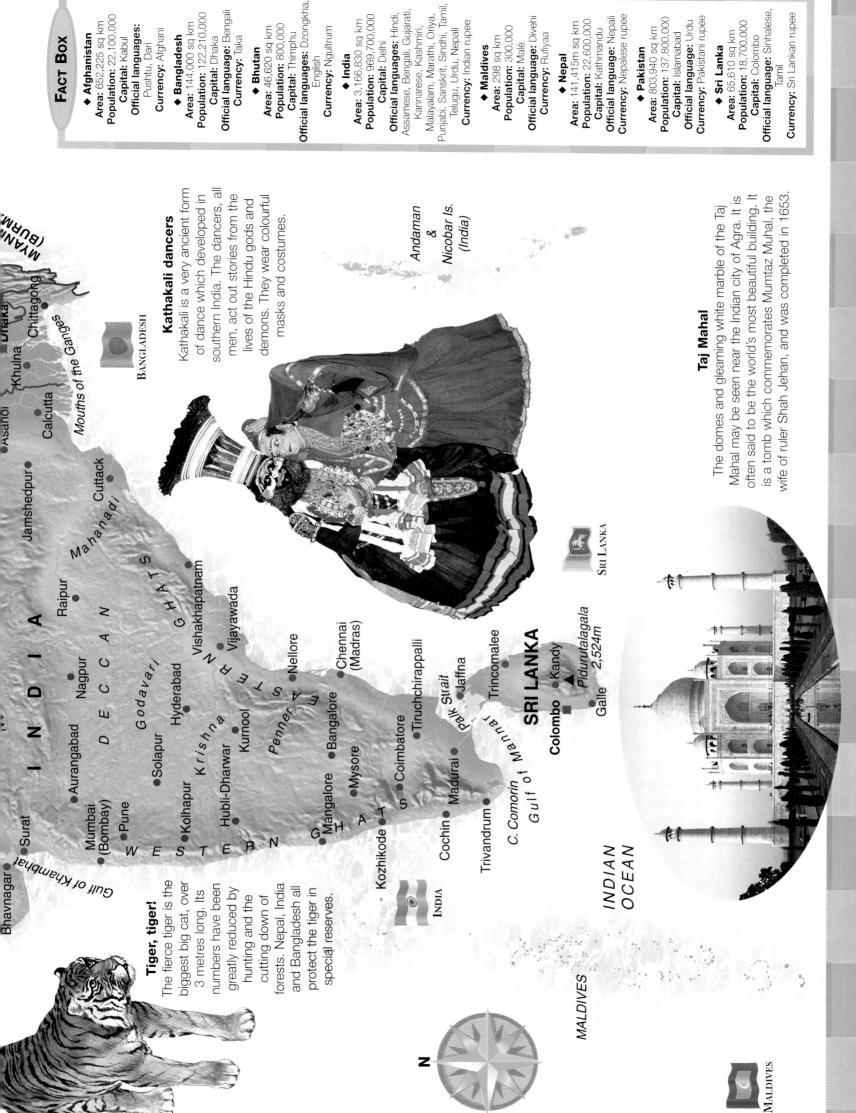

FACT BOX

◆ **Afghanistan**
Area: 652,225 sq km
Population: 22,100,000
Capital: Kabul
Official languages: Pushtu, Dari
Currency: Afghani

◆ **Bangladesh**
Area: 144,000 sq km
Population: 122,210,000
Capital: Dhaka
Official language: Bengali
Currency: Taka

◆ **Bhutan**
Area: 46,620 sq km
Population: 800,000
Capital: Thimphu
Official languages: Dzongkha, English
Currency: Ngultrum

◆ **India**
Area: 3,166,830 sq km
Population: 969,700,000
Capital: Delhi
Official languages: Hindi, Assamese, Bengali, Gujarati, Kannarese, Kashmiri, Malayalam, Marathi, Oriya, Punjabi, Sanskrit, Sindhi, Tamil, Telugu, Urdu, Nepali
Currency: Indian rupee

◆ **Maldives**
Area: 298 sq km
Population: 300,000
Capital: Malé
Official language: Divehi
Currency: Rufiyaa

◆ **Nepal**
Area: 141,415m sq km
Population: 22,600,000
Capital: Kathmandu
Official language: Nepali
Currency: Nepalese rupee

◆ **Pakistan**
Area: 803,940 sq km
Population: 137,800,000
Capital: Islamabad
Official language: Urdu
Currency: Pakistani rupee

◆ **Sri Lanka**
Area: 65,610 sq km
Population: 18,700,000
Capital: Colombo
Official language: Sinhalese, Tamil
Currency: Sri Lankan rupee

Kathakali dancers

Kathakali is a very ancient form of dance which developed in southern India. The dancers, all men, act out stories from the lives of the Hindu gods and demons. They wear colourful masks and costumes.

Taj Mahal

The domes and gleaming white marble of the Taj Mahal may be seen near the Indian city of Agra. It is often said to be the world's most beautiful building. It is a tomb which commemorates Mumtaz Muhal, the wife of ruler Shah Jehan, and was completed in 1653.

Tiger, tiger!

The fierce tiger is the biggest big cat, over 3 metres long. Its numbers have been greatly reduced by hunting and the cutting down of forests. Nepal, India and Bangladesh all protect the tiger in special reserves.

Andaman & Nicobar Is. (India)

MYANMAR (BURMA)

Chittagong
Dhaka
Khulna
Asanol
Calcutta
Mouths of the Ganges

BANGLADESH

Jamshedpur
Cuttack
Mahanadi

Raipur

I N D I A

D E C C A N

Nagpur
Aurangabad
Godavari
Hyderabad
Solapur
Krishna
Kolhapur
Hubli-Dharwar
Kurnool
Penner
Vijayawada
Vishakhapatnam

E A S T E R N   G H A T S

Nellore
Chennai (Madras)
Bangalore
Mysore
Tiruchirappalli
Mangalore
Coimbatore
Kozhikode
Palk Strait
Jaffna
Trincomalee
Cochin
Madurai
Gulf of Mannar
Trivandrum
C. Comorin

W E S T E R N   G H A T S

Mumbai (Bombay)
Pune
Surat
Bhavnagar
Gulf of Khambhat

INDIA

SRI LANKA
Colombo
Kandy
Pidurutalagala 2,524m
Galle

SRI LANKA

INDIAN OCEAN

MALDIVES

MALDIVES

N

CHINA AND ITS NEIGHBOURS

CHINA is the world's third largest country in area, and has a higher population than any other. It is bordered by the world's highest mountains, by deserts and by tropical seas.

Most people live in the big industrial cities of the south and east and on the fertile plains around two great rivers, the Huang He and the Chiang Jiang. Crops include wheat, maize, tea, sugar-cane and rice. Rice is eaten with almost every meal.

Chinese civilization dates back over thousands of years. Chinese inventions included paper and gunpowder and Chinese crafts included the making of fine porcelain and silk. Since 1949 China has been ruled by its Communist Party, but its politics are no longer really socialist. Its economy has become one of the most important in the Pacific region, and in 1997 it took back the territory of Hong Kong, an international centre of business which had been a British colony. China also claims the island of **Taiwan**, which is still governed independently by Chinese nationalists who lost power in 1949.

The **Korean peninsula** saw bitter fighting between 1950 and 1953, when Korea divided into two nations, North and South. These countries remain bitter enemies today. South Korea has become an important industrial power.

Far to the north the Mongol peoples live in the independent republic of **Mongolia**. This includes the barren Gobi desert and remote grasslands.

Map labels

KAZAKHSTAN

Ulaangom

Fuhai · Hovd

ALTAI MTS.

Ebinur Hu · Karamay

Yining · Kuytun · Dzungaria

KYRGYZSTAN

TIAN SHAN

Ürümqi

· Aksu · Bosten Lake · Turfan Depress

Kashi

TAKLIMAKAN DESERT

Hami

Yu

ALTUN SHAN

· Hotan

▲ Mt. K2

KARAKORAM

KUNLUN SHAN

INDIA

PLATEAU OF TIBET

Siling Lake · TANGGULA S.

Tangra Lake · Nam Lake

Lhasa

HIMALAYA

Mt. Everest ▲ 8,848 m · Xigaze

NEPAL

BHUTAN

The Great Wall
A defensive wall runs across the north of China for about 6,000 kilometres, with many extra twists and turns. It was started in about 246 BC and added to over hundreds of years.

Temple of Heaven
Tiantan, the Temple of Heaven in Beijing, is a beautiful group of buildings first raised in 1420. The Chinese emperors used to come here to pray for a good harvest.

Xinjiang herders

These herders are from Tangbula in Xinjiang, a remote region about the size of Alaska in China's far west. Xinjiang is home to several different peoples, including Uygurs, Kazakhs and Uzbekis.

FACT BOX

◆ **China**
Area: 9,597,000 sq km
Population: 1,236,700,000
Capital: Beijing
Main language: Standard Chinese
Currency: Yuan

◆ **Taiwan**
Area: 35,990 sq km
Population: 21,500,000
Capital: Taipei
Main language: Standard Chinese
Currency: New Taiwan dollar

◆ **North Korea**
Area: 122,310 sq km
Population: 24,400,000
Capital: Pyongyang
Main language: Korean
Currency: Won

◆ **South Korea**
Area: 98,445 sq km
Population: 45,900,000
Capital: Seoul
Main language: Korean
Currency: Won

◆ **Mongolia**
Area: 1,565,000 sq km
Population: 2,371,000
Capital: Ulan Bator
Official language: Mongolian
Currency: Tugrik

MONGOLIA

RUSSIA

HENTYN MTS.

Darhan
Choybalsan
Edernet
Tamsagbulag
Ulan Bator
GOBI DESERT
dzadgad
Baotou
Shizuishan
MU US DESERT
Yinchuan

GREATER HINGGAN
LESSER HINGGAN
Amur

Qiqihar
Harbin
Mudanjiang
Changchun
Jilin
Ch'ongjin
Tonghua
Fushun
Shenyang
Chifeng
Anshan
Hamhung
Jinzhou
P'yongyang
Wonsan

NORTH KOREA
NORTH KOREA

Dalian
Korea Bay
Kaesong
Seoul
SOUTH KOREA
SOUTH KOREA

Beijing
Tangshan
Bo Gulf
Weihai
Pusan
Tianjin
Yantai
YELLOW SEA
Kwangju
Shijiazhuang
Zibo
Qingdao
Jinan
Taiyuan

Cheju I.

EAST CHINA SEA

Xining
Huang He
Lanzhou
Xuzhou
Hongze Lake
Nantong
Zhengzhou
Xi'an
Nanjing
Shanghai
Chao Lake
Hangzhou
Macheng
Ningbo
Yichang
Wuhan
Linhai
Chang Jiang
Poyang Lake
Nanchang
Wenzhou
Dongting Lake
SICHUAN BASIN
Chengdu
Changsha
Chongqing
Leshan
Fuzhou
Luzhou
DALOU SHAN
Hengyang
Zhangzhou
Taiwan Strait
Taipei
TAIWAN
Guiyang
Xiamen
NAN LING MTS.
Shantou
Xiaguan
Kunming
Liuzhou
Xi Jiang
Gejiu
Nanning
Guangzhou
Hong Kong
MACAO
AILAO MTS.
Mekong
VIETNAM
Pingxiang
Zhanjiang
(urma)
LAOS
Haikou
CHINA
HONG KONG
Gulf of Tongkin
Hainan

CHINA

N HAR
AN

HUANG HE

N SHAN

gol

MONGOLIA

N

Panda country
The very rare giant panda lives in the misty bamboo forests of southwest China. It feeds mostly upon bamboo shoots, grasses and bulbs.

Rice bowl
The most important crop in China, and feeding a population of over a billion, rice is prepared in many exotic ways. Traditionally eaten with chopsticks Chinese food has become an international favourite.

TAIWAN

JAPAN

JAPAN is made up of over 3,000 islands, and these stretch for about 3,000 kilometres from north to south on the northwest rim of the Pacific Ocean.

The chief islands are called Hokkaido, Honshu, Shikoku and Kyushu. The islands extend from the tropical south to the chilly north, where winter snowfalls can be heavy. The region is a danger zone for earthquakes and Japan's highest mountain, Fuji, is a volcano.

The snow-covered slopes of Mount Fuji have been a favourite subject for Japanese artists over the years. Japan has a long history of excellence in art, theatre, poetry, architecture and pottery. Japanese civilization dates back over 2,000 years. The country has been ruled by emperors and, during the Middle Ages, it was fought over by powerful warlords and bands of knights called samurai. Faiths include Buddhism and Shinto, the country's traditional religion.

Japan is very mountainous and so land that is suitable for farming is very precious. Japanese farmers grow rice, tea and fruit and the country also has a large fishing fleet. Many meals are based on rice or fish. Japan has very few natural resources. Even so, over the last 50 years Japan has become a leading world producer of cars, televisions and other electrical goods.

The mountains also limit the spread of housing and so Japan's cities are mostly crowded on to the strip of flat land around the coast. Tokyo has spread out to join up with neighbouring cities, and now has a population of over 25 million.

The Japanese people make up 99 percent of the country's population. The remainder includes Koreans and the Ainu of the far north, who may be descended from the first people to inhabit Japan.

Mount Fuji

The beautiful peak of Mount Fuji, to the southwest of Tokyo, is a national symbol and, traditionally, a sacred mountain.

Sushi

Prawns, raw fish, seaweed, pickles and vegetables are used to make these tasty snacks. Like most Japanese dishes, they are served with rice. Japanese food is often beautifully arranged and thoughtfully served.

Tea time

Tea is harvested on the inland slopes. The Japanese are great tea-drinkers and have an ancient ceremony

Kuril Is. (Russia)

JAPAN

La Pérouse Strait

Rebun I.
Rishiri I.

Wakkanai

Teshio

H o k k a i d o

Asahigawa
▲ Asahi Mt.
2,290 m

Kushiro

Obihiro

Erimo Cape

Ishikari

Ishikari Bay

Otaru
Sapporo

Muroran

Uchiura Bay

Hakodate

Tsugaru Strait

Mutsa Bay

Aomori

Hachinohe

Hirosaki

Morioka

Kita

*S E A
O F
J A P A N*

Akita

Itsukushima, Japan

Japan has many ancient Shinto shrines and Buddhist temples and many of these are set in beautiful scenery or gardens. Japan has always produced very simple and beautiful architecture and design.

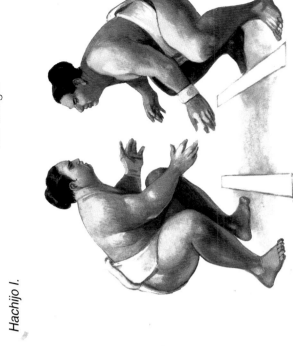

Sumo wrestlers

The ancient sport of sumo is still very popular in Japan. Super heavyweight wrestlers aim to ground their opponents or force them out of the ring. There are long ceremonies before each contest.

N

JAPAN

Sendai
Iwaki
Abukuma
Hitachi
Yamagata
Koriyama
Mito
Fukushima
Chiba
Niigata
Utsunomiya
Tokyo
Sado
Nagaoka
Takasaki
Kawasaki
Yokohama
Ueda
Kofu
Sagami Bay
Shinano
Mt. Fuji 3,776 m
Shizuoka
O-shima
Toyama
Matsumoto
Hamamatsu
Miyake I.
Kanazawa
Gifu
Toyota
JAPANESE ALPS
Takefu
Nagoya
Matsusaka
Fukui
Biwa Lake
Sakai
Kyoto
Osaka
Wakayama
Kobe
Honshu
Takamatsu
Okayama
Kii Channel
Tokushima
Shikoku
Oki Is.
Matsue
Inland Sea
Matsuyama
Kochi
Hiroshima
Suo Sea
Bungo Channel
Tsushima
Kitakyushu
Fukuoka
Kumamoto
Omuta
Kyushu
Sasebo
Sendai
Miyazaki
Nagasaki
Amakusa Is.
Yaku
Tanega
Koshiki Is.
Kagoshima

Hachijo I.

PACIFIC OCEAN

Ride the Bullet

Japan's Bullet Train offers one of the world's most famous passenger express services. It speeds across the country, linking the capital, Tokyo, with other large cities.

A Shinto wedding

Dressed in her beautiful silk robe, or kimono, a Japanese bride sits next to her new husband, who also wears traditional costume. The wedding has been a Shinto ceremony. Shinto is an ancient Japanese faith which honours ancestors and the spirits of nature.

SOUTHEAST ASIA

MYANMAR is a beautiful land lying between the hill country of India and China. It is crossed by the great Irrawaddy river, which flows south into the Indian Ocean. To the southeast is **Thailand**, a country green with rice fields and teak forests. To the west lie the lands once known as Indo-China – **Laos**, **Cambodia** and, on the long Mekong River, **Vietnam**.

Linked to the Asian mainland by a narrow isthmus, or strip of land, is **Malaysia**. This country also takes up the northern part of the island of **Borneo**, which it shares with the small oil-rich state of **Brunei**. Malaysia produces rubber, rice, tea and palm oil. Kuala Lumpur is a growing centre of international business with the 452 metre-high Petronas Towers, the world's highest building. **Singapore**, a small independent city state built on the islands across the Johor Strait, is another leader in the business world.

Indonesia makes up the world's largest island chain. It covers over 13,600 islands, which include Sumatra, Java, southern Borneo, Bali and Irian Jaya (the western half of New Guinea). Another large island chain, the **Philippines**, lie between the Pacific and the South China Sea.

All the islands bordering the Pacific Ocean lie in a danger zone for earthquakes and volcanoes. The region as a whole has a warm, often humid, climate, with monsoon winds bringing heavy rains. Southeast Asia's dwindling tropical forests are a last reserve for the region's rich wildlife, such as enormous butterflies and giant apes called orang-utans.

Many different peoples live in Southeast Asia, including Burmese, Thais, Vietnamese and Filippinos. There are also many people of Chinese and Indian descent. Buddhism is a major faith in the region. Most Indonesians are Muslims and the Philippines are largely Roman Catholic. During the last 50 years Southeast Asia has been torn apart by wars. The region now looks forward to a period of peace.

The face of a demon
This fierce-looking demon guards the gate of the Grand Palace in Bangkok, the capital of Thailand. Many tourists come to this kingdom, once known as Siam, to see its ancient temples and enjoy its beautiful scenery and beaches.

A dome of gold
The fantastic roofs of Shwe Dagon pagoda shimmer with gold. This holy site is in Yangon, capital city of Myanmar or Burma. The pagoda honours Gautama Buddha, the founder of the Buddhist faith.

Javanese carving

These beautiful figures, carved from stone, decorate Barobodur, on the island of Java. This 9th-century temple is the most splendid in Indonesia. Its carvings show scenes from the life of the Buddha.

PHILIPPINES

Laoag
Luzon
Mt. Pinatubo
■ **Manila**
Mindoro

PHILIPPINES

Panay
Iloilo
Tacloban
Palawan
Cebu City
Negros
Bohol

SULU SEA

Mindanao
Davao

BRUNEI

Mt. Kinabalu
4,094 m
Zamboanga
Mt. Apo
2,954 m
Sandakan
INDONESIA
SABAH
ndar
Seri
gawan

CELEBES SEA

RUNEI
AWAK
as
RNEO
Balikpapan
Manado

MOLUCCA SEA

Halmahera

Makassar Strait
Barito
Palu
Sulawesi
Moluccas
Sorong
Jayapura

I N D O N E S I A

anjarmasin
Ujung Pandang
Baubau

CERAM SEA

Buru
Seram
Ambon

IRIAN JAYA
Puncak Jaya
5,030m
NEW GUINEA

BANDA SEA

Aru Is.
Digul

PAPUA NEW GUINEA

FLORES SEA

Wetar
Tanimbar Islands

urabaya
Bali *Lombok*
Flores
ang
Sumbawa
Ende
Timor
Sumba
Kupang

Floating market

At a Thai market, fruit, vegetables or fish may be sold from small boats. These women traders wear broad-brimmed straw hats to protect them from the tropical sun and the heavy monsoon rains.

N

Kuala Lumpur

High-rise buildings are influenced by traditional styles in Kuala Lumpur, capital of Malaysia. 'KL' is one of the most important centres of industry, and business in Southeast Asia.

Komodo dragon

Meet the biggest lizard in the world, 3 metres long and weighing in at up to 136 kilograms. It is found on four small islands in Indonesia, called Rintja, Flores, Padar and Komodo.

NORTH AND WEST AFRICA

THE SAHARA IS THE WORLD'S LARGEST DESERT, made up of over 9 million square kilometres of baking hot sand, gravel and rock.

Its northern fringes, occupied by **Morocco**, **Algeria**, **Tunisia** and **Libya**, run into the milder, more fertile lands of the Mediterranean coast and the Atlas mountain ranges. They are home to Arabs and Berbers.

Deserts stretch from the Sahara eastwards to **Egypt** and the Red Sea. In ancient times one of the greatest civilizations the world has seen grew up in Egypt. Then as now, the country depended on water from the world's longest

Water for sale
A Berber water seller walks the streets of Marrakech, in Morocco, offering metal cups to passers-by.

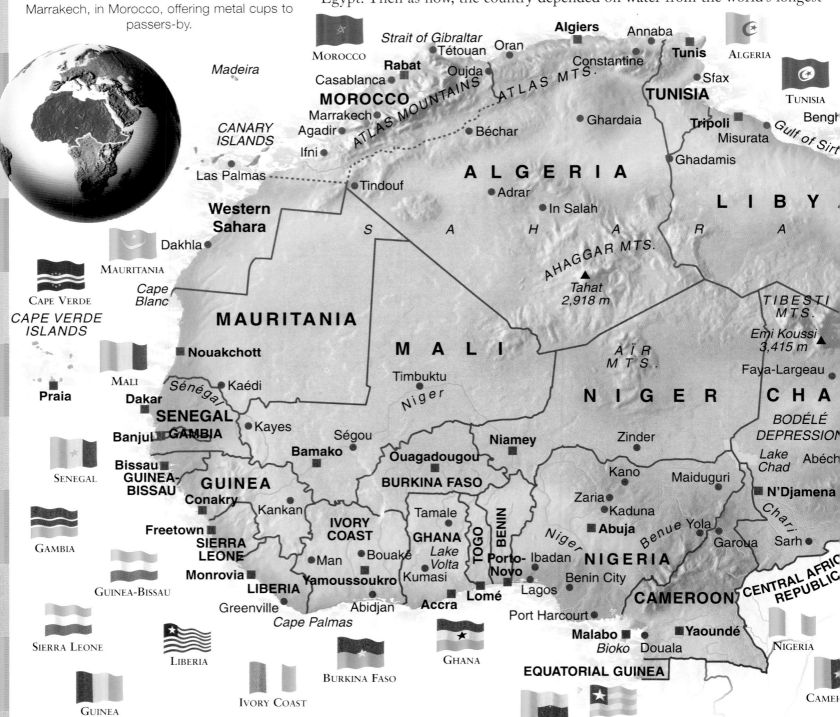

MOROCCO
Strait of Gibraltar
Tétouan · Oran
Rabat · Oujda
Casablanca
Madeira
CANARY ISLANDS
Marrakech
Agadir
Ifni
Las Palmas
Tindouf
Western Sahara
Dakhla
MAURITANIA
Cape Blanc
CAPE VERDE ISLANDS
Nouakchott
MAURITANIA
Kaédi
Sénégal
Dakar
SENEGAL
Banjul GAMBIA
Bissau
GUINEA-BISSAU
GUINEA
Conakry
Kankan
Freetown
SIERRA LEONE
Monrovia
LIBERIA
Greenville
Cape Palmas

Algiers · Annaba
Constantine
Tunis
Tétouan · Oran
ATLAS MTS.
ATLAS MOUNTAINS
Béchar
Ghardaia
ALGERIA
Adrar
In Salah
SAHARA
AHAGGAR MTS.
Tahat 2,918 m
MALI
Timbuktu
Niger
Kayes
Ségou
Bamako
Ouagadougou
BURKINA FASO
Tamale
IVORY COAST
GHANA
Bouaké
Man
Yamoussoukro
Kumasi
Abidjan
Accra
Lake Volta
Lomé

TUNIS
Sfax
TUNISIA
Tripoli
Misurata
Ghadamis
LIBYA
Gulf of Sirt
TIBESTI MTS.
Emi Koussi 3,415 m
Faya-Largeau
AÏR MTS.
NIGER
Niamey
Zinder
Kano
Zaria
Kaduna
Abuja
Benue Yola
Ibadan
NIGERIA
Benin City
Lagos
Port Harcourt
Malabo
Bioko Douala
EQUATORIAL GUINEA
Porto-Novo
BENIN
TOGO
CHAD
BODÉLÉ DEPRESSION
Lake Chad Abéché
N'Djamena
Chari
Garoua Sarh
CAMEROON
CENTRAL AFRICAN REPUBLIC
Yaoundé

MOROCCO
ALGERIA
TUNISIA
Bengh...
MAURITANIA
CAPE VERDE
MALI
SENEGAL
GAMBIA
GUINEA-BISSAU
SIERRA LEONE
LIBERIA
GUINEA
IVORY COAST
BURKINA FASO
GHANA
BENIN
TOGO
NIGERIA
CAMER...
Praia

52

river, the Nile. This flows north to the Mediterranean from the mountains of **Ethiopia** and the swamps of southern **Sudan**, Africa's largest country.

The region south of the Sahara is known as the Sahel. It includes **Senegal**, **Mauritania**, **Mali**, **Niger**, **Burkina Faso** and **Chad**. The people include the Fulani, Kanuri and Hausa. The thin grasslands of the Sahel allow cattle herding, but droughts are common and the desert is spreading. Many people are very poor.

Thirteen nations border the great bulge of the West African coast, around the Gulf of Guinea. The coastal strip is made up of lagoons and long sandy beaches fringed with palm trees. Inland there is a belt of forest, which rises to dry, sandy plateaus and semi-desert in the far north. West African history tells of African kingdoms and empires which grew up here long ago, but also of the cruel slave trade across the Atlantic, which lasted from the 1500s to the 1800s. In the 1800s, large areas of West Africa became colonies of Britain and France. Today these lands are independent. The region has rich resources, including oil and diamonds.

LIBYA

Abu Simbel
When the new Aswan dam was being built in the 1960s this great temple of the ancient Egyptian ruler Rameses II had to be moved stone-by-stone.

CENTRAL, EASTERN & SOUTHERN AFRICA

CENTRAL AFRICA is dominated by the river Congo, which flows through hot and humid rainforest to the Atlantic Ocean. The great river winds through the **Democratic Republic of the Congo**, and the network of waterways which drain into it provide useful transport routes for riverboats and canoes.

A long crack in the Earth's crust, the Great Rift Valley, runs all the way down **East Africa**. Its route is marked by volcanoes and lakes. Some East African mountains remain snow-capped all year round, even though they are on the Equator. The highest of these is Kilimanjaro, at 5,950 metres. It looks out over savanna, grasslands dotted with trees. Huge herds of wildlife roam these plains. Zebra, giraffe, elephants and lions are protected within national parks. The Indian Ocean coast includes white beaches and coral islands. Mombasa, Dar-es-Salaam and Maputo are major ports.

In southern Africa the Drakensberg mountains descend to grassland known as veld. There are harsh deserts too, the Kalahari and the Namib. The **Republic of South Africa** is one of the most powerful countries in Africa. It has ports at Durban and Capetown.

Central and southern Africa are rich in mineral resources, including gold, diamonds and copper. Eastern and southern Africa are important farming regions, raising cattle and producing coffee, vegetables, tropical fruits, tobacco, and grape vines.

African kingdoms flourished in the Congo region in the Middle Ages and the stone ruins of Great Zimbabwe recall gold traders of long ago. Today the region is home to hundreds of African peoples with many different languages and cultures.

Magnificent Masai
This young Masai girl wears her traditional beaded necklace and headdress. These noble, nomadic people herd cattle and live mainly in Kenya and Tanzania.

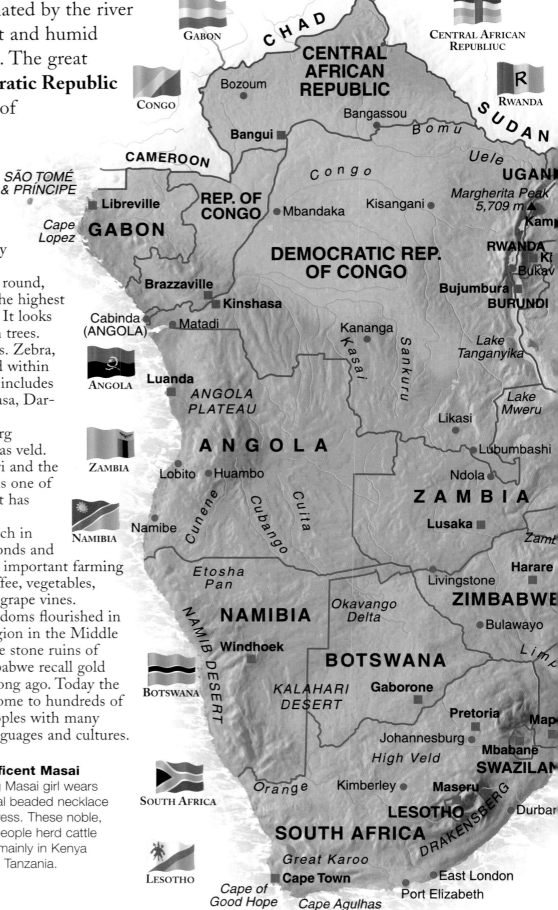

GABON

CHAD

CENTRAL AFRICAN REPUBLIUC

CONGO

R RWANDA

CENTRAL AFRICAN REPUBLIC

Bozoum

Bangassou

Bangui

CAMEROON

Bomu

Uele

SUDAN

UGANI

SÃO TOMÉ & PRÍNCIPE

Congo

REP. OF CONGO

Mbandaka

Kisangani

Margherita Peak 5,709 m ▲

Kam

Libreville

Cape Lopez

GABON

DEMOCRATIC REP. OF CONGO

RWANDA

KI

Bukav

Brazzaville

Kinshasa

Cabinda (ANGOLA)

Matadi

Kananga

Bujumbura

BURUNDI

ANGOLA

Luanda

ANGOLA PLATEAU

Kasai

Sankuru

Lake Tanganyika

Lake Mweru

Likasi

Lubumbashi

ZAMBIA

A N G O L A

Lobito

Huambo

Ndola

Z A M B I A

ZAMBIA

Namibe

Cunene

Cubango

Cuita

Lusaka

Zamt

NAMIBIA

Etosha Pan

Okavango Delta

Livingstone

Harare

ZIMBABWE

NAMIBIA

Windhoek

Bulawayo

Limp

BOTSWANA

NAMIB DESERT

KALAHARI DESERT

Gaborone

BOTSWANA

Pretoria

Map

Johannesburg

High Veld

Mbabane

SWAZILAN

SOUTH AFRICA

Orange

Kimberley

Maseru

DRAKENSBERG

LESOTHO

Durbar

SOUTH AFRICA

LESOTHO

Great Karoo

Cape Town

East London

Cape of Good Hope

Cape Agulhas

Port Elizabeth

La Digue, Seychelles
Over 100 islands make up the Seychelles. La Digue is only 15 square kilometres in area, but the third most populated.

Cape Caseyr

● Berbera

SOMALIA

KENYA

UGANDA

ETHIOPIA

N

Lake Turkana

KENYA

Kisumu Mt. Kenya ▲ 5,199 m

ria

Nairobi

Tana

● Kismayu

Juba

Mogadishu

INDIAN OCEAN

nza

▲ Kilimanjaro 5,895 m

● Mombasa

SOMALIA

BURUNDI

SEYCHELLES

doma

● Zanzibar

● Dar-es-Salaam

ufiji

NZANIA

MALAWI

SEYCHELLES

Aldabra Is.

Lake Nyasa

C. Delgado

COMOROS

C. d'Ambre

LAWI

ngwe

● Moçambique

Antisiranana

MADAGASCAR

Mozambique Channel

● Mahajanga

● Toamasina

MAURITIUS

Blantyre

MOZAMBIQUE

Antananarivo

MADAGASCAR

MAURITIUS

ra

MOZAMBIQUE

● Fianarantsoa

Réunion (France)

ZIMBABWE

C. Ste. Marie

Sting in the tail
Scorpions always look threatening. The curled-forward tail contains a sting which can be deadly. They eat insects and other animals which they catch with their claws. They are most common in desert areas.

AUSTRALIA

THIS COUNTRY is the size of a continent, a huge mass of land surrounded by ocean. The heart of **Australia** is a vast expanse of baking desert, salt pans, shimmering plains and dry scrubland. Ancient, rounded rocks glow in the morning and evening sun.

These barren lands are fringed by grasslands, tropical forests, creeks and fertile farmland. In the far east is the Great Dividing Range, which rises to the high peaks of the Australian Alps. The southeast is crossed by the Murray and Darling rivers. The Great Barrier Reef, the world's largest coral reef, stretches for over 2,000 kilometres off the eastern coast, while the island of Tasmania lies to the south across the Bass Strait.

Most Australians don't live in the 'outback', the dusty back country with its huge sheep and cattle stations and its mines. They live in big coastal cities such as Brisbane, Sydney, Adelaide and Perth. There they enjoy a high standard of living, an outdoor lifestyle, sunshine and surfing.

To the many people who in recent years have come from Europe and Asia to settle in Australia, this seems like a new country. However it is really a very ancient land, cut off from other parts of the world so long that it has many animals seen nowhere else on Earth, such as kangaroos, echidnas and platypuses.

Australia has probably been home to Aboriginal peoples for over 50,000 years. European settlement began in 1788, when the British founded a prison colony at Botany Bay, near today's city of Sydney. Many Australians still like to keep in touch with British relatives and traditions, but the modern country follows its own path as one of the great economic powers of the Pacific region.

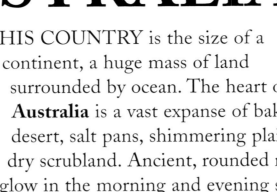

Opera on the harbour
Sydney's most famous landmark is its Opera House, built between 1959 and 1973. It rises from the blue waters of the harbour like a great sailing ship. Sydney, the capital of New South Wales, is Australia's biggest city with a population of about 3,700,000.

Map labels:
Bonapar[t] Archipe[lago]
Broome
Fitzroy
Eighty Mile Beach
Port Hedland
De Grey
Barrow I.
Fortescue
Ashburton
Mt. Bruce
GIBSON DESER[T]
Lake Macleod
Carnarvon
Murchison
Dirk Hartog I.
WESTERN AUSTRALI[A]
Geraldton
Laverton
Kalgoorlie-Boulder
Perth
Fremantle
Bunbury
C. Naturaliste
C. Leeuwin
Albany
Archipelago of th[e] Recherche

Christmas beetles
Australia and its surrounding islands are populated by many weird and wonderful insects and beetles. These beetles are from Christmas Island.

Aboriginal art
An Aboriginal artist from Groote Eylandt, an island in the Gulf of Carpentaria, completes a painting on bark. Paintings by Australia's Aborigines are admired around the world. They often recall the ancient myths and legends of their people, with bold, swirling patterns or pictures of animals.

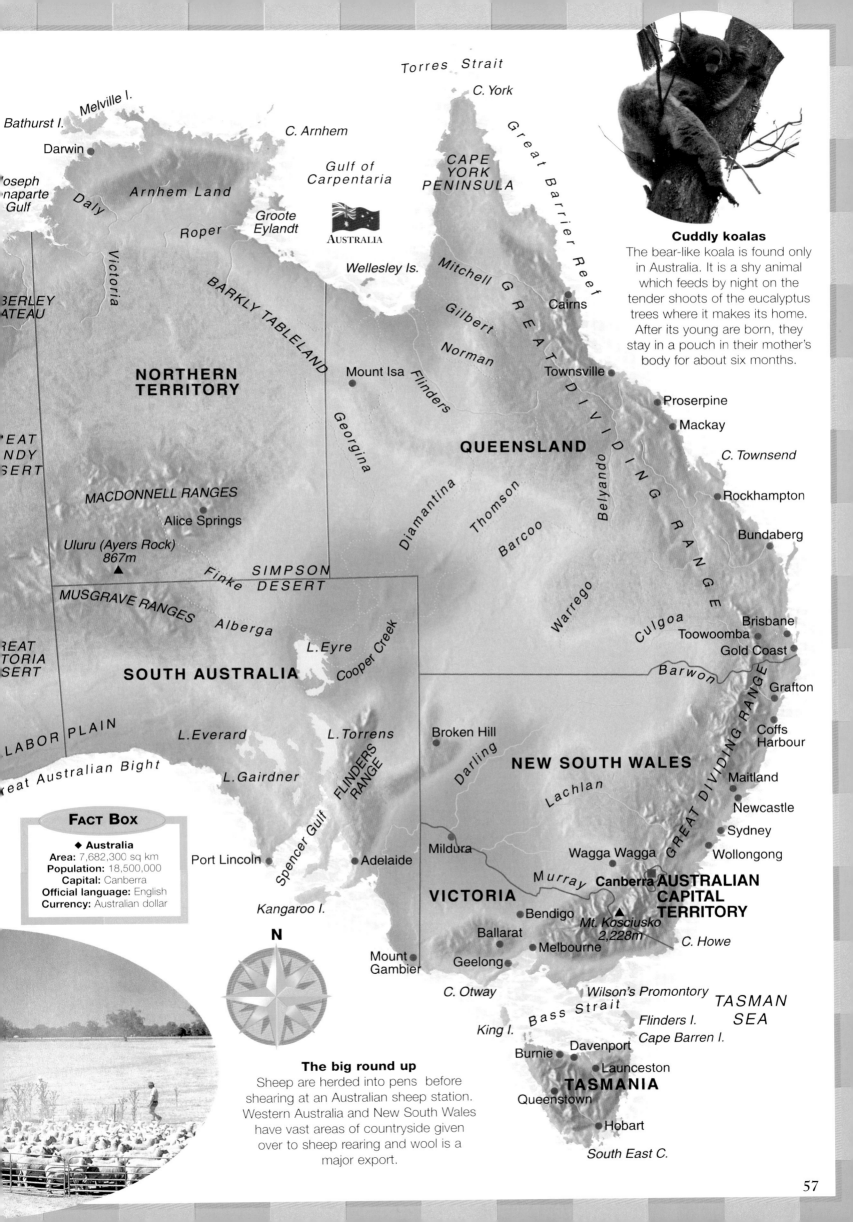

Torres Strait
C. York
Melville I.
Bathurst I.
Darwin
C. Arnhem
Gulf of Carpentaria
CAPE YORK PENINSULA
Great Barrier Reef
Joseph Bonaparte Gulf
Daly
Arnhem Land
Roper
Groote Eylandt
Wellesley Is.
Mitchell
Gilbert
Norman
Cairns
KIMBERLEY PLATEAU
Victoria
BARKLY TABLELAND
NORTHERN TERRITORY
Mount Isa
Flinders
Georgina
QUEENSLAND
Townsville
GREAT DIVIDING RANGE
Proserpine
Mackay
C. Townsend

Cuddly koalas
The bear-like koala is found only in Australia. It is a shy animal which feeds by night on the tender shoots of the eucalyptus trees where it makes its home. After its young are born, they stay in a pouch in their mother's body for about six months.

GREAT SANDY DESERT
MACDONNELL RANGES
Alice Springs
Uluru (Ayers Rock) 867m ▲
Finke
SIMPSON DESERT
Diamantina
Thomson
Barcoo
Belyando
Rockhampton
Bundaberg
MUSGRAVE RANGES
Alberga
GREAT VICTORIA DESERT
L. Eyre
Cooper Creek
SOUTH AUSTRALIA
Warrego
Culgoa
Brisbane
Toowoomba
Gold Coast
Barwon
Grafton
NULLARBOR PLAIN
L. Everard
L. Torrens
FLINDERS RANGE
Broken Hill
Darling
NEW SOUTH WALES
Coffs Harbour
Great Australian Bight
L. Gairdner
Lachlan
Maitland
GREAT DIVIDING RANGE
Newcastle
Sydney
Wollongong

Port Lincoln
Spencer Gulf
Adelaide
Mildura
Wagga Wagga
Murray
Canberra
AUSTRALIAN CAPITAL TERRITORY
Kangaroo I.
VICTORIA
Bendigo
Mt. Kosciusko 2,228m ▲
C. Howe
Ballarat
Mount Gambier
Geelong
Melbourne
C. Otway
Wilson's Promontory
TASMAN SEA
King I.
Bass Strait
Flinders I.
Cape Barren I.
Burnie
Davenport
Launceston
TASMANIA
Queenstown
Hobart
South East C.

N

The big round up
Sheep are herded into pens before shearing at an Australian sheep station. Western Australia and New South Wales have vast areas of countryside given over to sheep rearing and wool is a major export.

AUSTRALIA

57

NEW ZEALAND AND THE PACIFIC

NEW ZEALAND LIES in the Pacific Ocean, about 1,600 kilometres to the east of Australia. It has a moist, mild climate and many unusual plants, birds and animals may be found there.

Most of its people live on North Island and South Island. These beautiful islands, divided by the Cook Strait, are the largest of several which are included within the country. North Island has volcanoes, hot springs and gushing geysers. South Island is dominated by the peaks and glaciers of the Southern Alps. It also has deep sea inlets called fiords and rolling grassy plains. New Zealand, with its sheep, cattle and fruit farms, has one of the most important economies in the Pacific region.

Papua New Guinea is another island nation, bordering Indonesian territory on the island of New Guinea. It also includes several chains of smaller islands. Many of its mountain regions, blanketed in tropical forests, were only opened up to the outside world in the 20th century. The country is rich in mineral resources and its fertile soils produce coffee, tea and rubber.

Strung out eastwards across the lonely Pacific Ocean are many scattered island chains and reefs. Small coral islands surround peaceful blue lagoons ringed with palm trees. The islanders may make their living by fishing, growing coconuts, mining or tourism. Many of the island groups have banded together to form independent nation states.

Peoples of the Pacific are of varied descent. Some are the descendants of European settlers – for example the British in New Zealand, or the French on New Caledonia or Tahiti. Fiji has a large population of Indian descent. The original peoples of the Pacific fall into three main groups. Melanesians, such as the Solomon Islanders, live in the western Pacific, while Micronesians live in the Caroline and Marshall Islands. The Polynesian peoples, brilliant seafarers, colonized vast areas of the ocean, from New Zealand to the Hawaiian Islands. The Maoris, who make up nine percent of New Zealand's population, are a Polynesian people who have kept and valued many of their ancient traditions.

SEA OF JAPAN

MICRONESIA

SOLOMON ISLANDS

Yellow Sea

East China Sea

Northern Mariana Islands (USA)

Guam (USA)

Federated States of Micronesia

Palau

Philippine Sea

SOUTH CHINA SEA

Celebes Sea

Papua New Guinea

Irian Jaya (Indonesia)

Solomon Islands

Arafura Sea

Port Moresby

Coral Sea

AUSTRALIA

TASMAN SEA

New Guinea finery
Feathers and paint are worn by many young warriors at tribal gatherings and feasts in remote areas of Papua New Guinea. The country has a very rich culture with over 860 different languages.

Kiwi fruit
When farmers decided to grow this fruit in New Zealand, they decided to give it a local name to help sales. The kiwi is the national bird, and a nickname for a New Zealander.

BERING SEA

PAPUA NEW
GUINEA

PALAU

*NORTH
PACIFIC
OCEAN*

Midway Island
(USA)

ake Island
(USA)

VANUATU

MARSHALL
ISLANDS

Hawaii (USA)

arshall Island

KIRIBATI

uru   NAURU   **Kiribati**

Tuvalu

Samoa   American
Samoa

nuatu   **Fiji**

SAMOA

Galapagos
(Ecuador)

*SOUTH
PACIFIC
OCEAN*

TUVALU

Caledonia
(France)

Cook Islands
(New Zealand)

French
Polynesia

Pitcairn Island
(UK)

Tonga

Easter Island
(Chile)

NEW ZEALAND

FIJI

TONGA

**NEW
EALAND**

Easter Island
Hundreds of huge,
mysterious stone
heads tower above the
hills of Easter Island, in
the eastern Pacific.
They were erected by
Polynesians about
1,000 years ago. Today
Easter Island is
governed by Chile.

Gusher!
Steam bursts from volcanic
rocks near Rotorua on
North Island. New
Zealand's geysers and hot
springs are not just a
tourist attraction. They are
used to generate electricity.

NEW ZEALAND

North Cape

Whangerei

Auckland · Manukau

Gt. Barrier Island

Hamilton · Waikato

Bay of
Plenty   East Cape

*NORTH
ISLAND*

Rotorua

New Plymouth   L. Taupo   Gisborne

▲Ruapehu
2,797m

Wanganui

Napier
Hastings

Cape Farewell

Palmerston North

Nelson

Cook Strait

Westport   Blenheim

Wellington

Greymouth

SOUTHERN ALPS

Christchurch

*SOUTH
ISLAND*   Canterbury
Plains

Mt.Cook 3,764m▲

Timaru

Clutha

Dunedin

Foveaux Strait   Invercargill

Stewart Island

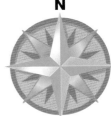

N

POLAR LANDS

THE NORTHERNMOST PART of our globe is called the Arctic. Within this bitterly cold region lie the northern borders of Alaska (part of the United States), Canada, Greenland (a self-governing territory of Denmark), Norway, Sweden, Finland and Russia.

However most of the area is covered by the Arctic Ocean, much of which is frozen solid all year round. At the centre of this great cap of ice is the North Pole. The **Arctic** supports a surprisingly wide selection of wildlife, including seals, walruses and polar bears. Peoples who have learned to live permanently in the far north include the Aleuts, the Inuit, the Saami, the Yakuts and the Chukchi. They have been joined in recent years by workers from the oil industry.

The only people to be found in **Antarctica**, at the other end of the globe, are scientists studying the weather and rocks of the coldest and windiest continent on Earth. The only other living things to survive here are the penguins which breed around the coast and the whales, birds and fishes of the Southern Ocean. The landmass is ringed by a shelf of ice, some of which breaks away to form massive icebergs in the spring. Inland there are mountain ranges and icy plains. The Antarctic winter takes place during the Arctic summer, and the Antarctic summer during the Arctic winter.

Various countries claim territory in Antarctica, and the continent is rich in minerals and fishing. However many scientists argue that this land should never be opened up to mining and industry, but left as the planet's last true wilderness.

Living in the Arctic
The Inuit peoples of northern Canada and Greenland have always lived by hunting and fishing and are experts at surviving in the harsh climate.

Antarctic melt
Each southern spring, the ice around Antarctica begins to melt, allowing ships to approach the ice shelves around this huge, frozen continent.

FACT BOX

◆ **Arctic Circle**
Area of ocean:
14,056,000 sq km

◆ **Antarctic Circle**
Area of land:
13,900,000 sq km

INDEX

The publishers wish
to thank the artists
who have contributed
to this book:
Julie Banyard; Martin
Camm; Mike Foster;
Josephine Martin;
Terry Riley; Guy
Smith; Roger Smith;
Michael
White/Temple
Rogers.

The publishers would
like to thank the
following for
supplying
photographs for the
Atlas

Page 5 (T/R) MKP; 5
(B) PhotoDisc; 6-7,
9, 10-11 all MKP; 12
(C/R) & (B/L)
Spectrum Colour
Library; 14 (T/R)
MKP; (B/L) & (B)
The Stock Market; 15
(B) MKP; 17 (C/R)
& B/R) The Stock
Market; (B) MKP; 18
(B) MKP; (T/R) &
(B/R) The Stock
Market; 20-21, 24-25
all MKP; 26 (T/C)
MKP; (B/C) The
Stock Market; 28
(B/C) The Stock
Market; 29 (T/R)
The Stock Market; 30
both MKP; 32-33 (C)
MKP; 33 (C) The
Stock Market; 33
(B/R); MKP; 34
(T/L) MKP; 34 (B)
The Stock Market; 35
(C) MKP; 37 (T/L)
The Stock Market;
(B/C) PhotoDisc; 38
(B/L) MKP; 39
(T/R) PhotoDisc; (C)
& (B/R) The Stock
Market; 40-41 all Sue
Cunningham
Photographic; 42-43
all MKP; 44 (T/L)
MKP; 45 (C/R) The
Stock Market; (B)
MKP; 46 (T/R) The
Stock Market; (B) &
(B/C) MKP; 47
(C/R) MKP; 48
(T/R) & (C) MKP;
49 (C/R) MKP;
(B/C) The Stock
Market; 50-51 all
MKP; 52-53 all
MKP; 54-55 all The
Stock Market; 56
(T/R) & (B/L) MKP;
(B/C) The Stock
Market; 58-59, 60-61
all MKP